U ntrepreneurship
r

This b
belr

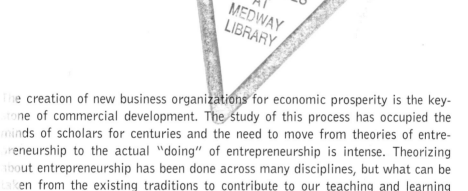

e creation of new business organizations for economic prosperity is the key-
one of commercial development. The study of this process has occupied the
minds of scholars for centuries and the need to move from theories of entrepreneurship to the actual "doing" of entrepreneurship is intense. Theorizing
about entrepreneurship has been done across many disciplines, but what can be
taken from the existing traditions to contribute to our teaching and learning
experiences?

Written for educators, researchers, and practitioners, *Entrepreneurship:
The Way Ahead* offers insight and perspective on entrepreneurship from the
foremost academic leaders in the field. Taking a contemporary approach to
entrepreneurial processes, the book considers how the convergence of individual, opportunity, and environment ultimately leads to success or failure,
while illuminating the true relationship between entrepreneurship and technological and social issues. It also explores innovations and developments in entrepreneurship education and training, while evaluating existing literature and
research.

Entrepreneurship: The Way Ahead represents some of the most advanced
thinking in the field of entrepreneurship, providing an essential grounding of
new theory for researchers and entrepreneurial managers alike.

Harold P. Welsch holds the Coleman Foundation Chair in Entrepreneurship at
DePaul University, U.S.A., and has been active in entrepreneurship for over
twenty years as an educator, consultant, researcher, author, and entrepreneur.

Entrepreneurship

The way ahead

Edited by

Harold P. Welsch

Routledge
Taylor & Francis Group

NEW YORK AND LONDON

First published 2004
by Routledge
29 West 35th Street, New York, NY 10001

Simultaneously published in the UK
by Routledge
11 New Fetter Lane, London EC4P 4EE

Routledge is an imprint of the Taylor & Francis Group

Typeset in Perpetua and Bell Gothic by
Wearset Ltd, Boldon, Tyne and Wear
Printed and bound in Great Britain by
TJ International Ltd, Padstow, Cornwall

Library of Congress Cataloging in Publication Data
Entrepreneurship: the way ahead/edited by Harold P. Welsch.
    p. cm.
Includes bibliographical references and index.
    1. Entrepreneurship 2. Electronic commerce. 3. New business enterprises. I. Welsch, Harold P.
HB615.563875 2003
338′.04–dc21

2003011928

British Library Cataloguing in Publication Data
A catalogue record for this book is available from the British Library

ISBN 0–415–32393–2 (hbk)
ISBN 0–415–32394–0 (pbk)

Contents

List of figures   viii
List of tables   ix
Notes on contributors   x
Foreword   xiv
Acknowledgments   xvi

PART ONE
Overview   1

1   Howard H. Stevenson
    INTELLECTUAL FOUNDATIONS OF ENTREPRENEURSHIP   3

2   Karl H. Vesper
    UNFINISHED BUSINESS (ENTREPRENEURSHIP) OF THE
    TWENTIETH CENTURY   15

3   Dianne Wyndham Wingham
    ENTREPRENEURSHIP THROUGH THE AGES   27

4   John Sibley Butler
    THE SCIENCE AND PRACTICE OF NEW BUSINESS VENTURES:
    WEALTH CREATION AND PROSPERITY THROUGH
    ENTREPRENEURSHIP GROWTH AND RENEWAL   43

5   Harold P. Welsch and Mark A. Maltarich
    EMERGING PATTERNS OF ENTREPRENEURSHIP:
    DISTINGUISHING ATTRIBUTES OF AN EVOLVING DISCIPLINE   55

PART TWO
Entrepreneurial processes

71

6 G.T. Lumpkin, Gerald E. Hills, and Rodney C. Shrader
OPPORTUNITY RECOGNITION

73

7 Michael H. Morris, Minet Schindehutte, and Raymond W. LaForge
THE EMERGENCE OF ENTREPRENEURIAL MARKETING: NATURE AND MEANING

91

8 Lynn Neeley
BOOTSTRAP FINANCE

105

9 Jianwen Liao
ENTREPRENEURIAL GROWTH: PREDICTORS AND INDICATORS

117

10 Jianwen Liao
ENTREPRENEURIAL FAILURES: KEY CHALLENGES AND FUTURE DIRECTIONS

133

PART THREE
Technology and entrepreneurship

151

11 Rodney C. Shrader, Gerald E. Hills, and G.T. Lumpkin
ELECTRONIC COMMERCE: CURRENT UNDERSTANDING AND UNANSWERED QUESTIONS

153

12 Michael Stoica
THE IMPACT OF MOBILE COMMERCE ON SMALL BUSINESS AND ENTREPRENEURSHIP

165

13 Lisa K. Gundry and Jill Kickul
E-COMMERCE ENTREPRENEURSHIP: EMERGING PRACTICES, KEY CHALLENGES, AND FUTURE DIRECTIONS

181

PART FOUR
Social entrepreneurship

193

14 Barbara A. Kuhns
DEVELOPING COMMUNITIES, PEOPLE, AND BUSINESSES: IN SEARCH OF A MODEL OF COMMUNITY-BASED ENTERPRISES

195

15 Gregory Fairchild and Patricia G. Greene
WEALTH CREATION IN DISTRESSED INNER CITIES: WHAT CAN BUSINESS SCHOOLS CONTRIBUTE?

211

PART FIVE
Entrepreneurship types   **225**

16   Lisa K. Gundry and Miriam Ben-Yoseph
WOMEN ENTREPRENEURS IN THE NEW MILLENNIUM: RECENT
PROGRESS AND FUTURE DIRECTIONS FOR RESEARCH,
ENTREPRENEURSHIP DEVELOPMENT, AND TEACHING   227

17   Steve Taplin
SERIAL ENTREPRENEURSHIP: AN IN-DEPTH LOOK AT THE
PHENOMENON OF HABITUAL ENTREPRENEURS   239

18   Eugene Fregetto
IMMIGRANT AND ETHNIC ENTREPRENEURSHIP: A U.S.
PERSPECTIVE   253

PART SIX
Entrepreneurship education   **269**

19   Patrick Sandercock
INNOVATIONS IN ENTREPRENEURSHIP EDUCATION: STRATEGY
AND TACTICS FOR JOINING THE RANKS OF INNOVATIVE
ENTREPRENEURSHIP PROGRAMS IN HIGHER EDUCATION   271

20   Gerald E. Hills
ENTREPRENEURSHIP EDUCATION: MARKET SEGMENTATION AND
LEARNER NEEDS   287

Index   301

Figures

5.1	Structure of the entrepreneurship field	57
5.2	Structure of entrepreneurial finance	57
5.3	Structure of entrepreneurship education	58
5.4	Structure of entrepreneurial practice	58
5.5	Taxonomy of emerging fields	60
5.6	Results of search for entrepreneurship journal articles	61
6.1	Creativity based model of entrepreneurial opportunity recognition	75
7.1	Five elements comprising the conceptualization of entrepreneurial marketing	98
10.1	Entrepreneurial failure: an integrative model	135
12.1	The mobile commerce value chain	169
15.1	Entrepreneurial Growth Resource Center, University of Missouri–Kansas City: EGRC organization chart	219
17.1	Overview of the types of entrepreneurs	240
17.2	Suggested model for framing serial entrepreneurial research	251
18.1	An illustration of the basic linear regression relationship	260
18.2	Interactive model of ethnic business development	261
18.3	Sources of ethnic strategies	262
20.1	Entrepreneurship education: a decision process model	289
20.2	Segmentation bases for entrepreneurship education market	293
20.3	Entrepreneurship learner/customer perception maps for entrepreneurship education programs	295

Tables

1.1	A process definition of entrepreneurship	6
3.1	Entrepreneurship to all people	35
5.1	Taxonomy of developing branches of entrepreneurship	61
6.1	Highlights of the opportunity recognition literature	76
6.2	Opportunity recognition behaviors: Hall of Fame Entrepreneurs (HFE) and Representative Entrepreneurs (RE)	82
6.3	Key opportunity recognition behavior findings	83
7.1	Six perspectives on the emerging nature of marketing	95
7.2	Contrasting conventional marketing and entrepreneurial marketing	102
8.1	Bootstrap finance categories and techniques	106
9.1	Frequency of growth predictors in 45 growth articles (1990–2002)	124
9.2	Top growth predictors in literature study by category	124
9.3	Frequency of growth indicators in 27 growth articles (1990–2002)	125
10.1	Entrepreneurial failure: a literature review	136
12.1	Characteristics of the wireless technology	168
12.2	Differences between technical components in e-commerce and m-commerce	171
14.1	Summary of community-based enterprise examples	205
17.1	Motivational factors	245
17.2	Search strategies	246
19.1	Summary of innovative entrepreneurship practices	273
20.1	Research opportunities at the entrepreneurship/segmentation interface	296

Contributors

Miriam Ben-Yoseph is a member of the Resident Faculty of the School for New Learning at DePaul University. She conducts research on women in management and women entrepreneurs across cultures, and more recently, on the future of work. Originally from Romania, she received her B.A. and M.A. from Hebrew University of Jerusalem and Ph.D. from Northwestern University.

John Sibley Butler is Professor of Sociology and Management at the University of Texas at Austin, and holds the Gale Chair in Entrepreneurship in the Graduate School of Business there. His research focuses on organizational behavior and entrepreneurship. Dr. Butler is the Sam Barshop Research Fellow at the IC2 Institute.

Gregory Fairchild is Assistant Professor of Business Administration at the Darden Graduate School of Business Administration at the University of Virginia. His research, which has received several awards, focuses on entrepreneurship and economic growth, managerial innovation, and management trends.

Eugene Fregetto is a member of the Department of Managerial Studies at the University of Illinois at Chicago. He provides consulting services regarding minority/women business participation and management assistance programs. Dr. Fregetto has nineteen years of experience teaching at the college level, conducting research, and writing about the latest management and marketing issues.

Patricia G. Greene is the Dean of the Undergraduate School at Babson College and holds the President's Endowed Chair in Entrepreneurship. She formerly held the Ewing Marion Kauffman/Missouri Chair in Entrepreneurial Leadership at the University of Missouri–Kansas City. Dr. Greene's research focuses on the identification, acquisition, and combination of entrepreneurial resources, particularly by women and minority entrepreneurs.

Lisa K. Gundry is Professor of Management in the Charles H. Kellstadt Graduate School of Business at DePaul University where she teaches courses in entrepreneurship and New Venture Management, Creativity in Business, and Entrepreneurship Strategy. Dr. Gundry is Director of the Leo V. Ryan Center for Creativity and Innovation at DePaul, which offers hands-on learning for creative discovery and business innovation.

Gerald E. Hills holds the Coleman/Denton Thorne Chair in Entrepreneurship, Executive Director of the Institute for Entrepreneurial Studies, Professor of Marketing, and former Associate Dean at the University of Illinois at Chicago. Dr. Hills has written and edited ten books and written more than 75 articles. He has served on the Editorial Boards of all of the leading entrepreneurship journals, including, currently, the *Journal of Business Venturing*.

Jill Kickul is the Elizabeth J. McCandless Professor in Entrepreneurship at the Simmons School of Management. Prior to joining Simmons, she served on the faculty in Entrepreneurship and Management of the Kellstadt Graduate School of Business at DePaul University. Her research interests include entrepreneurial intentions and behavior, strategic and innovation processes in start-up ventures, and, most recently, women in entrepreneurship.

Barbara A. Kuhns is Assistant Professor of Management at DePaul University. Dr. Kuhns' research interests include technology commercialization, new ventures in emerging markets, and entrepreneurial enterprises related to economic development. Her research has been presented at Academy of Management Annual Conferences and in *Simulation & Gaming*.

Raymond W. LaForge is the Brown–Forman Professor of Marketing at the University of Louisville. Dr. LaForge currently serves on the Direct Selling Education Foundation Board of Directors, DuPont Corporate Marketing Faculty Advisory Team for the Sales Enhancement Process, Family Business Center Advisory Board, Board of Trustees of the Sales and Marketing Executives International Accreditation Institute, and as Vice President of Marketing for the American Marketing Association Academic Council.

Jianwen Liao is on the faculty of Department of Management in School of Business and Management at Northeastern Illinois University. He has also been a visiting professor of DePaul University, Hong Kong University of Science and Technology and China European International Business School. Dr. Liao's research expertise and interests are in strategic formulation and implementation, management of technological innovation, venture creation process, and entrepreneurial growth.

G.T. Lumpkin is Associate Professor of Managerial Studies and Entrepreneurship at the University of Illinois at Chicago. His research interests include strategy-making processes, innovative forms of organizing work, and entrepreneurial orientation in a variety of organizations.

Mark A. Maltarich holds an MBA in Entrepreneurship from DePaul University and is currently pursuing doctoral education at the University of Wisconsin at Madison.

Michael H. Morris holds the Witting Chair in Entrepreneurship at Syracuse University. He previously served as the Noborikawa Distinguished Professor of Entrepreneurship at the University of Hawaii and the Cintas Chair in Entrepreneurship at Miami University. He has authored over one hundred articles in academic publications. His recent research interests have included small venture strategy, corporate entrepreneurship, the marketing and entrepreneurship interface, and entrepreneurship under adverse conditions.

Lynn Neeley is Professor of Management at Northern Illinois University at DeKalb. Her primary teaching and research interests are strategic management, entrepreneurial finance, bootstrapping, and efficient allocation of resources. She has served as President of the United States Association for Small Business and Entrepreneurship.

Patrick Sandercock received his MBA with a concentration in Entrepreneurship from DePaul University. He earned a Bachelor of Science degree from the U.S. Coast Guard Academy. Pat engaged in organizational development as both a U.S. Coast Guard (USCG) officer and a civilian. Pat has been an advisor and Director of Projects for OneBlueWorld, Inc. Currently, he is a small-business advisor with the Harris Bank in Chicago, where his responsibilities include cash management and identification of small business borrowing needs.

Minet Schindehutte is Assistant Professor in Entrepreneurship at Miami University and Director of the Foundation for Entrepreneurial Performance and Innovation. Her research and consulting interests include innovation processes in companies and entrepreneurial approaches to marketing.

Rodney C. Shrader received his Ph.D. in strategic management from Georgia State University and is Associate Professor of Managerial Studies at the University of Illinois at Chicago. His research examines the recognition of entrepreneurial opportunities, the accelerated internationalization of firms, and the internationalization of electronic commerce.

Howard H. Stevenson is Sarofim-Rock Professor of Business Administration at Harvard University's Graduate School of Business Administration. He has authored, edited, or co-authored six books and 41 articles, and has authored, co-authored, or supervised over 150 cases at Harvard Business School.

Michael Stoica is Professor at the School of Business, Washburn University. He holds Ph.D. degrees in business administration and engineering. Dr. Stoica has been involved in two entrepreneurial start-ups, and has done extensive teaching, research, and consulting in entrepreneurship in Romania, Canada, and the United States.

Steve Taplin received his MBA with a concentration in Entrepreneurship from DePaul University. He earned a Bachelor of Science degree in Management Information Systems from the School of Business at Northern Illinois University. Mr. Taplin was a highly successful Sales Executive for IBM from 1996–2003 selling Internet Outsourcing solutions to start up and Fortune 1000 companies. In 2003, Mr. Taplin embarked his entrepreneurial career and started Taplin Enterprises, LLC and AZ Investment Property Experts, LLC both of which are real estate investment companies.

Karl H. Vesper is Professor in the Department of Management of the School of Business Administration at the University of Washington. His primary research and teaching interests include venture development, entrepreneurship, and strategic management. Dr. Vesper is a recognized leading authority in the field of entrepreneurship and has published numerous books and innovative articles in the field.

Harold P. Welsch holds the Coleman Foundation Endowed Chair in Entrepreneurship at DePaul University and has been active in entrepreneurship development for over 20 years in his roles as educator, consultant, researcher, entrepreneur, author, and editor. In addition to his role as founder/director of the Entrepreneurship Program at DePaul University, Dr. Welsch has served as Chairman of the Academy of Management Entrepreneurship Division, President of the International Council for Small Business, and President of the United States Association for Small Business and Entrepreneurship.

Dianne Wyndham Wingham is Principal Researcher and Founding Entrepreneur of M.D. Wingham Consultants in Bicotn, Australia. Dr. Wingham is a Lecturer at Edith Cowan University in Western Australia and also at Rowan University.

Foreword

As in any dynamic field, entrepreneurship is evolving, reforming, and re-inventing itself as it passes through its stages of evolution. The most intriguing question is: "what will entrepreneurship look like in its next stage of development?" Thus the title: *Entrepreneurship: The Way Ahead*. As the world-class hockey player Wayne Gretzky suggested, one never skates to where the puck is or has been, but where it will be. In anticipation of where the field is going, some of the best minds in the field have been tapped to provide their prognostications and predictions of the future.

Howard Stevenson, Karl Vesper, Dianne Wingham, and John Sibley Butler provide the grounding foundations of the field and provide some innovative directions with which the field might experiment. Earlier, Howard Stevenson has suggested that "Entrepreneurship has won!," but later concludes that every entrepreneur, educator, and institution must refocus to take on the challenge of technology, globalization, and community development and their nuances within entrepreneurship. He is in close agreement with Karl Vesper who challenges us to recognize "Unfinished Entrepreneurship" as *the* opportunity of the twenty-first century. What battles are yet to be fought? What are the remaining or open issues in the field that will thrust us forward in our understanding?

Perhaps the most innovative and rapidly moving component in the field is entrepreneurship practice. Entrepreneurs themselves are expanding the boundaries with technology, network marketing, creative arts, serial, and social entrepreneurship. Academics are racing to keep up with theories to explain many of these new phenomena. Practitioners are often leading the way with innovations, inventions, new combinations, new markets, and new products and services. Opportunity recognition is becoming recognized as a burgeoning sub-specialty as well as a unique distinguishing characteristic of the field.

As leading thinkers in this field, Lumpkin, Hills, and Shrader view opportunity recognition as both a process involving iterations of creative thinking as well as the actual creation of a new venture. Following this functional approach, entrepreneurship can be viewed from a marketing, financing, or growth perspective. These chapters are constructed by some of the leading thinkers in their respective fields.

Despite the bursting of the technology bubble, this specialty continues to draw attention because it permeates entrepreneurship in a persistent manner. Do technology entrepreneurs do it differently? How is e-commerce and mobile commerce impacting the field? What are the emerging practices, key challenges, and future directions of this rapidly-paced industry? These are questions addressed by contemporary scholars such as Stoica, Kickul, and Gundry.

The evolution of entrepreneurship has also incorporated the not-for-profit sector of social entrepreneurship. Barbara Kuhns has recognized that entrepreneurial principles can also be effectively applied in community-based enterprises and assist in economic development of a region. Fairchild and Greene similarly suggest that wealth can be created in the inner-city through entrepreneurial endeavors.

Entrepreneurship can be sliced and analyzed in a myriad of ways — by gender (Gundry and Ben-Yoseph), by frequency (Taplin), or by ethnicity (Fregetto). Women entrepreneurs are one of the fastest growing segments of society as they become recognized as an equal partner or competitor in the economic system. The phenomenon of serial entrepreneurship has continued to intrigue scholars around the globe. What is it that drives individuals to commit to entrepreneurial endeavors over and over again? Is there a virus that infects these individuals? Is it the excitement of starting up that motivates repeat entrepreneurs? Are they fearful of daily management duties that drive them away from later-stage commitments?

Are immigrants more likely to become entrepreneurs because they are frozen out of the domestic/mainstream job market or do they simply value their freedom more than the corporate ladder climbers? Fregetto examines various ethnic groups in the U.S. and explains the displaced ethnic entrepreneur's role in the economy.

In the last section, we look forward to see what entrepreneurship education has in store for academia. Sandercock provides a review of the innovative, top-tier entrepreneurship programs and "puts a face" on the theory of entrepreneurship by introducing specific initiatives of higher education programs that characterize this evolving discipline.

Finally, Hills provides a provocative perspective on the new layers of entrepreneurship that have never been revealed. This blossoming flower of the field is made possible by the generation of new knowledge combined with conceptual and theoretical development represented by various schools of the thought within the context of market segmentation concepts.

All these perspectives, when combined into a total package, provide a guiding light to the road ahead in entrepreneurship.

Acknowledgments

Complex undertakings always require the contributions of a team including not only the authors, but individuals working in the background who help take the idea and move it into reality. The original idea emanated from a senior scholars' conference held in conjunction with an annual meeting of the U.S. Association for Small Business and Entrepreneurship (USASBE) sponsored by the Coleman Foundation. This roundtable discussion, spearheaded by the Council of Entrepreneurship Awareness and Education (CEAE) led to the identification of gaps in our field and forced us to look ahead to see where the field is going. Hence the title of the book. Through the foresight of the board of the Coleman Foundation, including John E. Hughes and Michael W. Hennessy, funds were allocated to the commissioning and writing of many significant white papers which formed the basis of this book. Internationally recognized scholars were selected to collect their best thoughts about where the field of entrepreneurship might be three to five years from now and commit these to paper so we can disseminate them to the community.

To the many editors at Routledge, we are grateful for their professional assistance as well as my staff, Lynne Wiora, Dajana Vucinic, Ilya Meiertal, Edward Papabathini, John Lanigan, and Dan Jarczyk who have spent many hours typing, tracking down references, editing, copying, and the dozens of tasks required to produce a quality product.

Dean Art Kraft, Alex Devience, Scott Young, and the Management Department of DePaul University allowed me the time to concentrate on completing the manuscript. Chairman John E. Hughes and President Michael W. Hennessy of the Coleman Foundation provided the guidance and focus on entrepreneurship development and had the courage to risk capital entrusted to their care into this project. For their moral and financial support we are forever grateful.

Harold P. Welsch, Ph.D.
Coleman Foundation Chair in Entrepreneurship
Professor of Management

August 18, 2003

PART ONE

Overview

Chapter 1

Howard H. Stevenson

Harvard Business School

INTELLECTUAL FOUNDATIONS
OF ENTREPRENEURSHIP

Introduction

THE FIELD OF ENTREPRENEURSHIP was described in 1983 as "an intellectual onion. You peel it back layer by layer and when you get to the center, there is nothing there, but you are crying." This description of the field by a senior faculty member at Harvard Business School was given to a young person being recruited into the field. This not-so-kind advice reflected a long-standing set of complaints (Cole 1968; Drucker 1985; Kirzner 1973). In spite of the lack of earlier academic attention, studies have shown the vital importance of new ventures and small businesses in job creation (Birch 1979, 1987). Silicon Valley, Silicon Alley, Route 128, Austin, and Research Triangle are the envy of the world. There has been a change in the sociology of entrepreneurship in many parts of the world (Thorton 1999). It is occurring at a higher rate (Gartner and Shane 1995) and with more capital behind it than at any time in the last century (Gompers and Lerner 1998).

Never before in history have so many individuals been able to identify and implement the definition that we use to guide our research and teaching at Harvard. That definition is: "Entrepreneurship is the pursuit of opportunity beyond the resources you currently control" (Stevenson 1983; Stevenson and Gumpert 1985; Stevenson and Jarillo-Mossi 1990). This definition takes into account both the individual and the society in which the individual is embedded. The individual identifies an opportunity to be pursued and then, as an entrepreneur, must seek the resources from the broader society. This approach follows on the work of early scholars such as Schumpeter (1934) who identified the interaction of the individual with the context in his early work. It corresponds to later admonitions, such as those of Aldrich (1992), who argued that individuals, organizations, and the context need to be studied to develop a theory of entrepreneurship.

This chapter will argue that progress in entrepreneurship has been enhanced by the societal environment in which it flourishes and by the strong development of theoretical underpinnings.

Societal change

The author would assert that the number of resources available for the pursuit of opportunity has never been greater, and has taken note of the availability of financial capital. This is perhaps the least unique resource required to pursue opportunity. Intellectual capital, human capital, and public capital in the form of infrastructure and social norms provide even more important resources to the entrepreneur. The embeddedness perspective (Granovetter 1985) addresses the descriptive and practical weaknesses of the dichotomous treatment of hierarchies and markets (Williamson 1985). When history and culture in more than forty countries over the last two decades are examined, some hypotheses emerge. They are:

1   entrepreneurship flourishes in communities where resources are mobile.
2   entrepreneurship is greater when successful members of a community reinvest excess capital in the projects of other community members.
3   entrepreneurship flourishes in communities in which the success of other community members is celebrated rather than derided.
4   entrepreneurship is greater in communities that see change as positive rather than negative.

It appears that the last two decades have seen major societal changes in all of these dimensions. Changes in the financial and labor markets have increased mobility substantially. Perhaps more important, improvement in logistics, cross-border flows of labor, capital, and ideas, weakening of intellectual property protection, and the growth in global communication have helped people, money, products, and ideas disperse throughout the world, flowing to the areas of greatest opportunity.

The entrepreneurial community's success has attracted capital on an unprecedented scale. The venture capital market and the market for initial public offerings have gone to unprecedented valuations. Perhaps most interesting, however, is the extent to which successful entrepreneurs have reinvested in venture funds and in angel networks. The entrepreneurial community is the basis of much of the monetary and managerial capital being invested in new companies (Darwall and Roberts 1998; Prasad and Linde 1999). Reinvestment in the entrepreneurial community by the entrepreneurial community continues and reinforces the tradition of entrepreneurial ethnic communities such as the offshore Chinese, the emigrant Koreans, and many others.

Out of the decade of greed of the 1980s emerged the celebration of the entrepreneur. Gates, Walton, and countless others are honored by schools, nominated to prestigious charities, extolled in the popular press, and studied by the new generation of potential entrepreneurs. More remarkable, perhaps, than these mega successes are the many "entrepreneurs" who have achieved great visibility and wealth in record time. Amazon's Jeff Bezos was *Time Magazine*'s man of the year in 1999. Meg Whitman of eBay and countless others are providing role models for the impatient entrepreneurs. Their success is celebrated without regard to the potential of failure.

The value of change is highlighted in the current environment of the Internet. Unlike biotechnology, which caused many people to see both risk and reward, the Internet brings information that is fast and free. Connectedness is seen as an unmitigated positive value, and studies that show the positive effect of the number of network nodes (Hagel and Armstrong 1997) are cited in both the academic and the popular press. Perhaps the speed and magnitude of the creation of wealth has been important in society's recognition of the value of change. Weakness in the protectionist power of unions in the face of new technology has accompanied envy and frequent emulations of the capitalist system. These factors have given people comfort about change.

Changes in society have many roots. Scholars have written about the psychological change that has occurred (Mills 1987). There have been a number of explanations, starting perhaps in 1911 with Schumpeter (1934). Collins and Moore (1964) put a lot of attention on the individual. Both early and later authors have focused on the cultural setting (Weber 1904), ethnicity (Aldrich and Waldinger 1990), and the individual experience (Cooper and Dunkelberg 1986). Some authors have written extensively about an ecological perspective on entrepreneurship (Aldrich and Wiedenmayer 1993; Aldrich 1999).

The author has, in other settings, criticized these approaches as lacking in operational import (Stevenson and Jarillo 1991). There is little that the individual can do to change his or her basic psychological make-up or even the cultural setting. The individual can become embedded in a context that facilitates the recognition of opportunity and the pursuit of it.

A research perspective

Perhaps the greatest change in the academic field of entrepreneurship has been new vigor in the development of deep intellectual roots. The Babson Research Conference on Entrepreneurship began in 1983 with thirty-seven papers. The entrepreneurial research community now has its own division in the Academy of Management. Following on the development of the field, most schools have courses in entrepreneurship, and there are, at the last count, more than 150 chairs in the field. Studies of business education have argued for even more (Porter and McKibben 1988).

Harvard Business School has taken a slightly different approach to research in the field by announcing that entrepreneurship should not be what scholars study but rather the entrepreneurial firm should be where people study. The issues and problems in entrepreneurial firms have proved to be central to the research domain of many respected academics.

Harvard Business School changed to a focus on research by scholars from many fields following the symposium on entrepreneurship held in 1983. At that time, practitioners and scholars were brought together to set an agenda for the school. As part of that program, the author published a paper entitled "Perspectives on Entrepreneurship" (Stevenson 1983). That paper and subsequent works emphasize the "how" of entrepreneurship rather than the "who" or "what."

The paper identified six dimensions on which entrepreneurial organizations differed from administratively driven organizations. These dimensions are shown in Table 1.1.

Perhaps success in overcoming the reputation as an intellectual onion was achieved because of the emergence of traditional academics interested in the characteristics of the entrepreneurial firm. Over the last seventeen years, a great deal of serious academic attention has been paid to entrepreneurial behaviors.

Opportunity analysis has always been part of the strategic literature (Ansoff 1956; Learned *et al.* 1965). Serious analysis of the sources of opportunity (the first dimension) first appeared in the field of economics and in early work by business scholars such as Rumelt (1974) but migrated to the mainstream business literature with Porter's seminal work (1980, 1981, 1985). That work was followed by national analysis (Porter 1990) that emphasized the role of context for successful competitive behavior. At the same time as there was positive movement toward the opportunity driven side of the spectrum, there were serious critiques of the traditional resource-based approaches. The inertial impact of social contracts (Walton 1985) and the weaknesses of performance measurement systems based upon resources (Johnson and Kaplan 1987) set the stage for scholars to re-examine the assumptions regarding continuity of opportunity and the value of controlled resources for pursuing opportunity.

Table 1.1 A process definition of entrepreneurship

Entrepreneur	Key business dimension	Administrator
Driven by perception of opportunity	Strategic orientation	Driven by resources currently controlled
Quick commitment	Commitment to opportunity	Evolutionary with long duration
Multi-stage with minimal exposure at each stage	Commitment process	Single-stage with complete commitment upon decision
Episodic use or rent of required resources	Control of resources	Ownership or employment of required resources
Flat with multiple informal networks	Management structure	Formalized hierarchy
Value-based and team-based	Compensation and reward system	Resource-based, individual and promotion oriented

The second dimension, which identifies a difference in the process of commitment to opportunity, has also been affected by both positive reinforcement in academic research and stern warnings regarding the viability of the opposing approach based upon systematic planning. Porter (1981) among others first described mover advantage. Later work on time-based competition (Stalk 1996) has reinforced the power of speed as a competitive weapon. The innovation literature (Abernathy and Clark 1985; Wheelwright and Clark 1992) has all pointed to the benefits of quick response to change and the need to create organizations that can move. More recent work, such as Christensen's (1997), has shown how larger firms can be overwhelmed with inertia in spite of advanced technology and superb market intelligence. This shows the practical problems created by the scholarly work urging managers to recognize multiple constituencies (Lodge 1980, 1984) and the complexity of the processes for internally negotiating strategies (Dyer *et al.* 1987).

The third dimension, identified in 1983, came as a surprise to many scholars of entrepreneurship. Since the late 1700s, many observers in both the academic community and the world of practice have identified the entrepreneur with risk-taking. This is based on Ricard Cantillion's observations that the entrepreneur buys at certain prices and sells at uncertain prices and thereby bears the risk of the transaction.

The author has written or co-written over 170 case studies at Harvard, half of these specifically on entrepreneurs. Very few of these entrepreneurs would be identified as risk seekers. They tend to be risk-takers who seek to manage the risk by sequential commitment to the opportunity. This method of commitment contrasts strongly with the planning approach advocated by many authors (Lorange *et al.* 1986; Bower 1986). A multi-staged commitment process corresponds to the needs of many resource providers (Sahlman 1988), who expect demonstrated results before adding to the meager resource base provided initially. Subsequent studies of the venture capital process have built on this model (Gompers and Lerner 1999).

The traditional disciplines have also recognized the practice with the title of real options theory. The notion that delay of a decision provides a valuable option builds on the Nobel-Prize-winning work of Fisher Black, Myron Scholes, and Robert Merton, and the earlier insights of Howard Raiffa and Robert Schlaifer. A stream of literature is building in this field (Ghemawat 1991).

The fourth dimension differentiates forms of control over resources. Chandler (1977) illustrated how firms grew large to exploit economies of scale. Under the communication conditions of the early twentieth century, this often required vertical integration. Early students of entrepreneurship observed other forms of organization (Larson 1988) that avoided "hierarchies" with their attendant agency costs (Pratt and Zeckhauser 1985). Those forms of organization shortened both the innovation cycle and the product cycle (Hayes and Wheelwright 1984). Jensen (1993) warns of the impact of hierarchical control over resources and the creation of barriers to exit. Increasingly, the economics literature is addressing the question of optimal scale and optimal diversification (Grossman and Hart 1986). The network structure of the Internet world has provided an object lesson regarding the new forms of organizational control.

"Alliances," "partnerships," "market teams" are the new lexicon as entrepreneurs struggle to match resources with unpredictable needs. Big companies such as Cisco Systems are forming alliances as well as acquiring companies to keep their options open. There is a strong recognition of the fact that, in a world of knowledge-based competition, the assets are never acquired because they can go home at night (Bhidé 2000).

The fifth dimension focuses on management through networks rather than hierarchy. Understanding the network form of management is now a hot topic (Eccles and Nohria 1992; Nohria 1992). The impossibility of achieving the theoretical limits of formal organization had already been well documented (Gulick and Urwick 1937; Lawrence and Lorsch 1967; Williamson 1975), but the success of the entrepreneurial firm propelled deeper study of the alternatives. The relationship between the entrepreneur and the key human resources that determine success is often far more complex than the theoretical structure observed from the outside. Because the key resources are often external, trust, persuasion, and salesmanship are not well represented on a formal organizational chart (Bhidé and Stevenson 1990).

The sixth dimension has also emerged as an area of serious academic pursuit. Sharing the value created is an issue for the start-up business because often, until value is created, there is nothing to share. At the same time, Jensen, Murphy, and others have focused considerable attention on the lack of sharing within large organizations and the consequences. Jensen and Meckling (1976) began a whole stream of serious inquiries into the role of ownership in the allocation of rewards and decision rights. The entrepreneurial setting provides a clear illustration for the value-added concepts (Brandenburger and Nalebuff 1995). This setting also illustrates the importance of the process of commitment. Studies in the venture business of the sharing economics illustrate some of the challenges in devising appropriate sharing arrangements (Gompers and Lerner 1996). Bhidé (1993) pointed out the hidden costs associated with capital that is not tied to ventures but is perpetually seeking liquidity.

A retrospective look

No claim is being made that the author's 1983 paper drove the academic agenda. Rather, the observation is that the arena of entrepreneurship involves many fascinating and important problems that have come to the attention of mainstream scholars. Entrepreneurship, properly conceived, is an intellectual domain of hard and important problems that can be attacked with the best possible scholarship. The progress of the field has been substantially enhanced as it attaches its problems to discipline-tested tools.

The caveat must be given, however, that entrepreneurship is more than the sum of its parts. Successful entrepreneurship is a study of the dynamic fit between a set of individuals, an opportunity derived from a particular context, and the deal that unites them. The nature of the fit requires constant vigilance. There is no such thing as an everlasting opportunity. Context changes, and the opportunity becomes a trap. Deals need to be robust, but the best deals are subject to strategic behavior when their consequences are fully understood. Individuals change too. The assumption that rational, evaluating, maximizing individuals start businesses cannot begin to account fully for the instances of creative genius, self-sacrificing loyalty, and charismatic leadership.

The last two decades have shown the importance and the relevance of the field of entrepreneurship. It is not important in isolation. Its importance is part of the global change that is affecting the way we live and work.

The future

The changes occurring in the world require every educator and educational institution to refocus. Entrepreneurship at Harvard has benefited by being chosen as one of the initiatives of Dean Kim Clark. We believe that if we are successful in rising to the challenge, the school can have the same degree of impact in this century as it has had in the last. The challenge is exacerbated by the requirement to understand technology, globalization, and community development as well as the nuances of entrepreneurship.

Technology is changing the way we live and work. Educators must be at the leading edge in order to model, by their behavior and their institutions' behavior, the world in which the educational participants will live. Faxes, e-mails, instant access to enormous amounts of information on the Internet, high-speed data transmission, CAD/CAM, cell phones, and ubiquitous linkages define our New World. When communications, computation, and storage are almost free, there are profound changes that must occur in the way people manage people and produce and distribute goods and services. The increasing role of technology implies that entrepreneurial teachers must focus themselves and their students on the management of technology and of technological development. The fast-paced, high-stakes world of technology yields different exciting problems for research.

The changes in technology coupled with changes in the political and economic scene are leading to the second challenge of globalization. Federal Express and others provide fast, cheap air freight. Modern logistical control, the communication revolution, and the emergence of energetic market-based economies are opening the world to truly becoming one market. Companies tend to ignore traditional geographic boundaries when identifying the boundaries of the arena in which they will develop their play. Some say that if a start-up does not have a global perspective, it cannot survive in the long term. Political barriers have been reduced, but the volatility of politics and economics seem to be increasing. To be an effective business person in this New World requires an understanding of how to work on a global scale. Competitors, customers, suppliers, and employees may spring from other cultures and other systems. Understanding how to work across cultural divides and learning from that experience is a critical new challenge.

In the face of the need to work in and through other cultures, entrepreneurship becomes a critical dimension. Since 1947, Harvard Business School has taught a course in starting new ventures. After 1983, when the school began using the working definition of entrepreneurship as "the pursuit of opportunity beyond the resources that you currently control," new ties were formed, and much new research continues to be spawned. Globalization and the immediate access to huge amounts of information have reinforced the trend toward entrepreneurial behavior. Few organizations can own or employ all of the resources that are critical to them in their pursuit of opportunity. The behavioral characteristics of entrepreneurial organizations identified in 1983 were noted previously: pursuit of opportunity, rapid commitment, willingness to change, multi-staged commitment processes, use of others' resources, managing through networked relationships, and rewards based upon value created. These characteristics are the ones needed to pursue global opportunity in the face of rapid change.

With global enterprises and entrepreneurial behavior, hierarchy does not and cannot suffice. Being part of a supportive community becomes the basis for repeated, mutually beneficial transactions. Contracts are incomplete and often only marginally enforceable through judicial processes. Legal systems and ethical systems are often in conflict. Therefore, to interact effectively and efficiently, individuals must sense that they are part of a community that cares, protects, and ensures legitimate behavior on the part of others. Trust, caring, agreed-upon standards for performance, and agreed-upon sanctions are the oil that lubricates the friction inherent in free exchange. Building a sense of community is a leadership task. Learning to live as part of a community that is dispersed, asynchronous, and diverse is one of the initiatives that shapes character as well as knowledge. Such a community is created and linked by the technology that is evolving.

These four challenges for the future are mutually reinforcing. Scholars and practitioners who attempt to deal with one of the challenges without understanding the others do so at their own peril. Entrepreneurship creates the technology and is enabled by it. Communities that form across traditional boundaries enable globalization and enable growth through entrepreneurship. Entrepreneurs build community by managing networks rather than hierarchies and by reinforcing the community through celebration and reinvestment in other community members' new ideas. They share the rewards of innovation with customers, suppliers, and other partners in the enterprise in order to assure cooperation.

Schools and educators, like successful businesses, must be engaged in renewal. The four initiatives aimed at improving our technology, educating for global perspective, building entrepreneurship, and supporting a strong sense of community are at once new and deeply rooted traditions in history and practice. Emphasis upon these initiatives is required to prepare our students for the world of tomorrow. The community of entrepreneurial scholars should note that entrepreneurship is an important part of the future but is not the only critical future arena in which progress is required.

The risks

With the benefit of hindsight, the opportunity of the last twenty years is evident. An entrepreneurial revolution has occurred. Some of the early volunteers have had a most exciting time. The danger lies in presuming that the future is without challenge.

Surely there will be massive, public, and costly failures among the current "entrepreneurs," just as there have been when many have seen other exciting market-based opportunities (Sahlman and Stevenson 1985).

Our colleagues see massive funds pouring in to support research and teaching. The Batten Center for Entrepreneurship at the Darden School was recently given $60 million. Much will be expected from such a resource commitment. Entrepreneurial educators must be more than cheerleaders. We can no longer simply say "entrepreneurship is different." Entrepreneurship is now a part of the mainstream.

Perhaps the greatest danger of all is that the hardy band of entrepreneurial scholars will become like many successful businesses. Businesses and scholars fail by not valuing change. Guarding the past, espousing orthodoxy, and refusing to see the wisdom inherent in the challenges of the young and inexperienced will lead to the same problems in education as in business.

Seeing entrepreneurship as part of a systemic response to change and as an initiator of the changes should help us avoid "the innovator's dilemma." In the meantime, let us celebrate the victory and thank our colleagues for their profound help.

References

Abernathy, W.J. and Clark, K.B. (1985) "Innovation: mapping the winds of creative destruction," *Research Policy*, 14: 3–22.

Aldrich, H. (1992) "Methods in our madness? trends in entrepreneurship research," in Sexton, D.L. and Kasarda, J.D. (eds) *The State of the Art in Entrepreneurship*, Boston, MA: PWS-Kent, pp. 191–213.

Aldrich, H. (1999) *Organizations Evolving*, London: Sage.

Aldrich, H. and Waldinger, R. (1990) "Ethnicity and entrepreneurship," *Annual Review of Sociology*, 16: 111–135.

Aldrich, H.E. and Wiedenmayer, G. (1993) "From traits to rates: an ecological perspective on organizational foundings," in Katz, J.A. and Brockhaus, R.H. (eds) *Advances in Entrepreneurship, Firm Emergence, Growth, Volume 1*, Greenwich, CT: JAI Press, pp. 145–195.

Ansoff, H.I. (1956) *Corporate Strategy*, New York, NY: McGraw-Hill Book Co.

Bhidé, A. (1993) "The hidden costs of stock market liquidity," *Journal of Financial Economics*, 34: 31–51.

Bhidé, A. (2000) *The Origins and Evolution of New Businesses*, New York, NY: Oxford University Press.

Bhidé, A. and Stevenson, H.H. (1990) "Why be honest if honesty doesn't pay?," *Harvard Business Review*, 74(6): 120–130.

Birch, D. (1979) *The Job Generating Process*, Cambridge, MA: MIT Press.

Birch, D. (1987) *Job Creation in America: How Our Smallest Companies Put the Most People to Work*, New York, NY: The Free Press.

Bower, J. (1986) *The Resource Allocation Process*, Boston, MA: Harvard Business School Press.

Brandenburger, A. and Nalebuff, B.J. (1995) "The right game: use game theory to shape strategy," *Harvard Business Review*, 73(4): 57–71.

Chandler, A.D., Jr. (1977) *The Visible Hand*, Cambridge, MA: Harvard University Press.

Christensen, C. (1997) *The Innovator's Dilemma: When New Technologies Cause Great Firms To Fail*, Boston, MA: Harvard Business School Press.

Cole, A. (1968) "The entrepreneur: introductory remarks," *American Review of Economics*, May: 60–63.

Collins, O. and Moore, D. (1964) *The Enterprising Man*, East Lansing, MI: Michigan State University.

Cooper, A. and Dunkelberg, W. (1986) "Entrepreneurship and paths to business ownership," *Strategic Management Journal*, 7: 53–68.

Darwall, C. and Roberts, M.J. (1998) "The band of angels," Case No. 898–188. Boston, MA: Harvard Business School Publishing.

Drucker, P. (1985) *Innovation and Entrepreneurship, Practice and Principles*, New York, NY: Harper & Row.

Dyer, D., Salter, M., and Webber, A. (1987) *Changing Alliances*, Boston, MA: Harvard Business School Press.

Eccles, R. and Nohria, N. (1992) *Beyond The Hype: Rediscovering the Essence of Management*, Boston, MA: Harvard Business School Press.

Gartner, W.B. and Shane, S.A. (1995) "Measuring entrepreneurship over time," *Journal of Business Venturing*, 10: 238–301.

Ghemawat, P. (1991) *Commitment: The Dynamic of Strategy*, New York, NY: Free Press.

Gompers, P. and Lerner, J. (1996) "The use of covenants: an empirical analysis of venture partnership agreements," *Journal of Law and Economics*, 39: 463–498.

Gompers, P. and Lerner, J. (1998) "Capital formation and investment in venture markets: an assessment of market imperfections," in U.S. Department of Commerce (ed.) (2001) *Papers and Proceedings of the Advanced Technology Program's International Conference on the Economic Evaluation of Technological Change, June 15–16, 1998*, Washington, DC: U.S. Department of Commerce.

Gompers, P. and Lerner, J. (1999) *The Venture Capital Cycle*, Cambridge, MA: MIT Press.

Granovetter, M. (1985) "Economic action and social structure," *American Journal of Sociology*, 5(1): 53–81.

Grossman, S.J. and Hart, O.D. (1986) "The costs and benefits of ownership: a theory of lateral and vertical integration," *Journal of Political Economy* 94(14): 691–719.

Gulick, L. and Urwick, L. (eds) (1937) *Papers on the Science of Administration*, New York, NY: Institute of Public Administration.

Hagel, J., III and Armstrong, A. (1997) *Net Gain: Expanding Markets Through Virtual Communities*, Boston, MA: Harvard Business School Press.

Hayes, R.H. and Wheelwright, S.C. (1984) *Restoring our Competitive Edge: Competing through Manufacturing*, New York, NY: John Wiley and Sons.

Jensen, M. (1993) "The modern industrial revolution, exit, and the failure of the internal control systems," *Journal of Finance*, 47(3): 831–881.

Jensen, M. and Meckling, W. (1976) "Theory of the firm: managerial behavior, agency costs and ownership structure," *Journal of Financial Economics*, 3: 305–360.

Johnson, H.T. and Kaplan, R. (1987) *Relevance Lost: The Rise & Fall of Management Accounting*, New York, NY: Harper & Row.

Kirzner, I. (1973) *Competition and Entrepreneurship*, Chicago, IL: University of Chicago Press.

Larson, A. (1988) "Networks as social systems," unpublished Ph.D. dissertation, Harvard University Graduate School of Business.

Lawrence, P. and Lorsch, J. (1967) *Organizations and Environment*, Boston, MA: Harvard Business School Press.

Learned, E., Christensen, C.R., Andrews, K., and Guth, W. (1965) *Business Policy Text & Cases*, Homewood, IL: Irwin.

Lodge, G. (1980) *The New American Ideology*, New York, NY: Alfred A. Knopf.

Lodge, G. (1984) *The American Disease*, New York, NY: Alfred A. Knopf.

Lorange, P.M., Scott-Morton, M.S., and Ghoshal, S. (1986) *Strategic Control Systems*, St. Paul, MN: West Publishing.

Mills, D. (1987) *Not Like Our Parents*, New York, NY: William Morrow.

Nohria, N. (1992) "Is a network perspective a useful way of studying organizations," in Nohria, N. and Eccles, R.G. (eds) *Networks and Organizations*, Boston, MA: Harvard Business School Press.

Porter, L. and McKibben, L. (1988) *Management Education and Development*, New York, NY: McGraw-Hill Book Co.

Porter, M.E. (1980) *Competitive Strategy: Techniques for Analyzing Industries and Competitors*, New York, NY: Free Press.

Porter, M.E. (1981) "The contributions of industrial organization to strategic management," *Academy of Management Review*, 6(4): 609–620.

Porter, M.E. (1985) *Competitive Advantage: Creating and Sustaining Superior Performance*, New York, NY: The Free Press.

Porter, M.E. (1990) *The Competitive Advantage of Nations*, New York, NY: Free Press.

Prasad, A. and Linde, L. (1999) "Harvard Business School and Massachusetts Institute of Technology venture support system project: angel investing analysis," unpublished paper, M.I.T. Entrepreneurship Center and Genesis Technology Partners.

Pratt, J. and Zeckhauser, R. (eds) (1985) *Principals and Agents: The Structure of Business*, Boston, MA: Harvard Business School Press.

Rumelt, R. (1974) *Strategy, Structure and Economic Performance*, Cambridge, MA: Harvard University Press.

Sahlman, W. (1988) "Aspects of financial contracting in venture capital," *The Continental Bank Journal of Applied Corporate Finance*, 1(2): 23–26.

Sahlman, W. and Stevenson, H.H. (1985) "Capital market myopia," *Journal of Business Venturing*, 1(1): 7–30.

Schumpeter, J. (1934) *The Theory of Economic Development*, translated by Redvers Opie, Cambridge, MA: Harvard University Press.

Stalk, G. (1996) "Fast-cycle capability for competitive advantage," in *Time Based Competition Collection*, *Harvard Business Review Collection*, Boston, MA: Harvard Business School Press.

Stevenson, H.H. (1983) "A perspective on entrepreneurship," Harvard Business School Working Paper no. 9–384–131.

Stevenson, H.H. and Gumpert, D.E. (1985) "The heart of entrepreneurship," *Harvard Business Review*, 63(2): 85–94.

Stevenson, H.H. and Jarillo, J.C. (1990) "A paradigm of entrepreneurship: entrepreneurial management," *Strategic Management Journal*, 11: 17–27.

Stevenson, H.H. and Jarillo, J.C. (1991) "A new entrepreneurial paradigm," in Etzioni,

A. and Lawrence, P. (eds) *Socioeconomics: Toward a New Synthesis*, New York, NY: M.E. Sharpe, Inc.

Thorton, P. (1999) "The sociology of entrepreneurship," *Annual Review of Sociology*, 25: 19–46.

Walton, R.E. (1985) "Toward a strategy of eliciting employee commitment based on policies of mutuality," in Walton, R.E. and Lawrence, P.R. (eds) *Human Resources Management: Trends and Challenges*, Boston, MA: Harvard Business School Press.

Weber, M. (1904) *The Protestant Ethic and the Spirit of Capitalism*, New York, NY: Routledge.

Wheelwright, S.C. and Clark, K.B. (1992) *Revolutionizing Product Development: Quantum Leaps in Speed, Efficiency and Quality*, New York, NY: Free Press.

Williamson, O. (1975) *Markets and Hierarchies: Analysis and Antitrust Implications*, New York, NY: Free Press.

Williamson, O. (1985) *The Economic Institutions of Capitalism: Firms, Markets, Relational Contracting*, New York, NY: Free Press.

Chapter 2

Karl H. Vesper

University of Washington

UNFINISHED BUSINESS (ENTREPRENEURSHIP) OF THE TWENTIETH CENTURY

Introduction

A TRADITION BEGAN IN 1997 with the first of the United States Association of Small Business and Entrepreneurship (USASBE) keynote lectures. It was given by Arnold Cooper of Purdue University and carried the title: "Entrepreneurship: The Past, The Present, The Future." Now there is a challenge for this chapter. What else is there to talk about?

Actually quite a bit, because his topic does not treat "Entrepreneurship: the Wasn't, the Isn't and the Won't be." That leaves unfinished business to work on. But which of it is worth working on? This chapter will discuss that, as unfinished business, or better yet Unfinished Entrepreneurship as the opportunity of the twenty-first century.

Seven categories might help classify this unfinished business, as follows.

Legitimacy

Although entrepreneurship has certainly become fashionable, there are signs that it has not yet attained full citizenship in the academic world. There are now an estimated 200 endowed chairs in entrepreneurship, broadly defined. Many, however, have been appointed to individuals whose major dedication has been to a field other than entrepreneurship, which suggests that for many faculty members who vote on those appointments entrepreneurship is not a validated faculty source. Moreover, at some schools, such as University of Washington and, I understand, a number of others, entrepreneurship chairs remain unfilled years after the donors gave them. Washington managed to find candidates internally who were "good enough" for 95 percent of its two dozen chairs in other business subjects but could not recruit anybody, even from a nationwide advertised search, considered qualified for its entrepreneurship chair.

There are over a hundred university entrepreneurship programs worldwide, and the number is growing. Top U.S. universities, such as Carnegie-Mellon, Chicago, Columbia, Harvard, Northwestern, Stanford, Wharton, the University of California at Los Angeles, Berkeley, and the University of Southern California, now have programs in entrepreneurship. But so far every university degree entrepreneurship program, whether at those universities or others, is subordinate to a business school, with the exception of one that is under an engineering school. No U.S. university has a school of entrepreneurship, to the best of my knowledge. So entrepreneurship, as an academic subject area, seems not yet to have arrived as other fields have.

Most university entrepreneurship programs are heavily staffed with adjunct faculty. It is a good way to operate, because adjunct faculty are typically real-world entrepreneurs who have been successful and therefore bring to class a kind of magic that non-entrepreneur academics cannot. They are low in cost to the school, which is an advantage in gaining support from administrators who must balance budgets. And they are untenured, which administrators also like because it allows flexibility to add and subtract people from the faculty at will.

But adjuncts are not full citizens of the university. They cannot vote, and they do not have tenure, which renders them politically weak. That leaves the non-entrepreneurship faculty politically strong, which in turn handicaps entrepreneurship faculty members who want to take initiatives and blaze trails. With greater political strength, for instance, entrepreneurship faculty might be able to supplant conventional core courses by incorporating basic training in core subjects like marketing, finance, and accounting into entrepreneurship courses and teaching only those parts of such subjects as entrepreneurs find most useful. Entrepreneurship faculty might even shrug aside concern about conventional business accreditation or introduce their own accreditation.

At present it is the other way around. Entrepreneurship faculty can do only what non-entrepreneurship faculty let them do and within accreditation constraints.

Targeting, market-wise

It is obvious that we have some very different categories of customers in entrepreneurship classes. But there is still much to be done in sorting them out and fine-tuning courses to serve them. We need clearer ideas about what the categories are, which of them we should recruit to which classes, and how those classes should be tailored to them.

Here and there are data points. But how do they fit together? In 1997 some of us followed up a commercial program sponsored by US West called NX Level, a clone of the Fast Track program. I heard participants say that, because they had taken the course, they had been able to start successful enterprises that they would otherwise not have started. So the course impact seemed to be very real and positive.

In contrast, at one school when we were discussing entrepreneurship curricula designed to serve the entire campus, a computer science professor who was part of the program asked what the point of the MBA entrepreneurship course was. It was not necessary, he said, for his computer science department. The real core of their start-ups, after all, was new software. They could easily pick up information and expert help on topics like business planning, venture capital, and selling from other sources without participation of the business school. So an MBA entrepreneurship course, for his department at least, was a redundancy. (Coincidentally, the December 28, 1998, cover story in *Forbes* uses government data to question, very logically, the necessity of even a university education for business, let alone for successful entrepreneurship.)

More encouraging seem to be reports on the Scottish Enterprise Program presented at the Babson conference in 1997. The program aimed to have an impact on entrepreneurship on a national basis through education from elementary school through university, plus public relations and financing initiatives. Moreover, the program collected tracking data on the effects of those efforts. The results indicated that the program really worked on a national basis, both to develop in the public a more favorable attitude toward entrepreneurship and to increase the number of start-ups.

But where does that leave us in the universities? We have a mix of students with varying backgrounds and objectives. How do we aim? Is it better for us to offer survey courses in entrepreneurship that hit a spread of topics shallowly or specialized courses in topics like intellectual property and IPOs that treat some in depth? Should we have courses that specialize by industry, like software, Web technology application, biotechnology, and restaurant creation? Should universities themselves specialize differently?

Our finding in the US West study offered some relief from the need to target too finely because it appeared that participants drew upon the various course elements, such as instructor, book, exercises, other class members, and assignments selectively according to their needs. It was as if the course were a buffet table from which students individually selected meals. That is not to say, however, that tuning could not improve the courses further. The choice of what to put on the table is important.

How should a given university focus its entrepreneurship education efforts on the spectrum that runs from nuts and bolts of start-up at one end to cultivation of general mental abilities at the other end? Graduates of top law schools are notorious for their inability to pass bar examinations without supplementary trade school preparatory courses. But the schools are highly regarded for teaching students to think like lawyers, whatever that is taken to mean. Does it follow that the best university entrepreneurship programs will be those that teach students to think like entrepreneurs? If so, how is it that entrepreneurs think, anyway? Or does it depend on the particular entrepreneur, the particular industry, or the particular venture, and, if so, how?

I hope and suppose we are groping our way toward answers to questions like these. But I have not noticed systematic reporting of the results, except here and there, as I mentioned earlier. The Int Ent conferences of the European Business School at Frankfurt are a useful forum for exchange, and some sharing of information occurs at the Babson and Academy of Management research conferences. However, a better coordinated data-sharing system could, I think, help further. I see real optimism for progress on this frontier as we move into the twenty-first century.

Paradigms

We should also have more and better paradigms for grasping the field of entrepreneurship to transmit its growing body of knowledge to others. One of Arnold Cooper's predictions was that there would be no great entrepreneurial paradigm for the field (perhaps just like the great American novel). That may be true, but we do need more paradigms, at least smaller ones if not "the big one."

One reason we need them is to deal with what might be called the "snippets problem." A letter I received from a dean in the Midwest illustrated this difficulty. He said that he liked the idea of introducing entrepreneurship as a field of concentration in his school but he could not figure out how its content should be defined. He had looked at various textbooks with the word "entrepreneurship" on the cover and had come away with the impression that they were mostly just books for survey courses in business. The topics included a little bit of accounting, a little bit of law, and some marketing, production, and human resource management – snippets duplicating parts of other courses across his business school's curriculum.

Are we stuck with that? After all, entrepreneurs on occasion can find useful the tools of law, marketing, production, human resource management, and even finance. Does that mean the subject of entrepreneurship is inescapably redundant?

Maybe not. For one thing, it hooks information from these traditional subjects together somewhat differently. Because of the way new companies develop and the fact that not everything can be done at once by the entrepreneur, it may make sense to treat the topics as linked sequentially in ventures. If this paradigm is used, the field may be considered as a series of linkages among specialties, rather than just snippets of information.

For entrepreneurship, there is a different starting point, and consequently it is possible that topics like marketing and finance might be taught as parts of venture development processes, rather than as separate courses in separate departments. That would be a different way of looking at those topics, which is not to say it is a great new paradigm. But it is different from what we now use, and, for teaching about venturing as a distinct field, it may be worth trying.

Content

Although paradigms may be part of knowledge content, the content goes beyond them. Entrepreneurship as an academic field is criticized by some for having insufficient content. Part of our job is to figure out what is useful for entrepreneurs to know and then to decide what part of that knowledge can be taught in school.

The following is one simple way to classify knowledge useful to entrepreneurs, as I have described elsewhere (Vesper 1996: 20–24). Business schools that have entrepreneurship courses normally offer the first two categories of knowledge. The second two are typically not offered.

Business-general knowledge

This is knowledge that applies to businesses in general, both new and established firms. It includes such subjects as basics of accounting, marketing, business law, finance, operations, and human resources, plus subdivisions of those subjects. In short, it includes the curricular core. It also includes some of the electives that branch off from the core, but not all of them. There may be specialized courses for auditors, in insurance or real estate, and in research methods that apply to particular groups of students.

Venture-general knowledge

This is the content in entrepreneurship courses that is distinct from business-general knowledge but fairly general to ventures. It includes information such as:

- what is venture capital and how does it work?
- how do entrepreneurs find opportunities and ideas for new firms?
- what is a venture plan, who finds it useful and how, where does information for it come from and what is the difference been a mediocre and a good one?
- how is developing initial customers for a start-up different from developing customers for an established business, and how do founders cope with the problem more rather than less effectively?
- how should founders best find partners and recruit talent?
- how may defense of intellectual property be special for entrepreneurs, and how should they decide what to do about it?
- how do the headwaters of great success get built into a new company and in what stage of its development?

Opportunity-specific knowledge

This is knowledge about the existence of an unserved market and where physical resources to serve it might be obtained. With that type of knowledge, Jim Bezos was able to start Amazon.com through recruitment of individuals who possessed the fourth type, venture-specific knowledge.

Venture-specific knowledge

This is the knowledge of how to produce a particular product or service. In the case of the Apple entrepreneurs, it was how to make a good microcomputer; in the case of Gates and Allen, it was how to write computer code. Starting with these abilities, the entrepreneurs found their way to unserved markets by acquiring opportunity-specific knowledge. Business-general and venture-general knowledge they acquired through seeking advice and recruiting other individuals.

Neither of these last two types of knowledge applies to ventures in general. They are specific to a particular start-up. Moreover, as soon as others become aware that potentially profitable ventures exist, those ventures quickly become obsolete discoveries. For both of these reasons, schools cannot deliver the two types of specific knowledge, except in rare and, typically, anomalous situations.

Sadly for us, the last two are generally the most important of the four types of knowledge for start-up success. They are like maps to unclaimed gold veins, rarely available and then only at extremely high cost. The general business and general venture types of knowledge are, to continue the analogy, like how to shovel and transport ore. They are necessary but relatively easy to learn or cheap to buy.

So is there something of real value to entrepreneurs for scholars of entrepreneurship to study and teach?

I think so, and it is part of our job to add more. To continue the mining analogy, there are such things as shoveling better, transporting better, smelting better, getting a better price, and parlaying the mine into something valuable rather than losing the venture, as many entrepreneurs do. Adam Osborne and others spotted and pursued wonderful opportunities in the early days of the microcomputer industry with great technical sophistication but went broke anyway.

Another helpful analogy can be an automobile race, the Indy 500. Typically, each year the speeds get higher in this race owing to the discovery of ever better techniques, despite the refinements made over many decades. The speeds creep up to a point where the race becomes too dangerous. Then the officials inject some new handicap, such as smaller engine size, restricted fuel composition, or reduced intake area, to lower the speed to a safe range. Consequently, speeds drop. Then speeds start to creep up again, even with the handicap, until again they become unsafe, at which point another new handicap is added.

What produces the increase in speed? Sometimes big breakthroughs, like the introduction of two-way radio for the drivers or controllable spoiler wings, and always many small things, like better tire material, tiny aerodynamic refinements, and improved coordination patterns for pit crews.

We have seen both types of improvements also for the practice of entrepreneurship. There have been big breakthroughs like microcomputers for many business functions and the Web as an electronic vending machine.

There have also been lots of smaller things (LOST is the acronym) like annual improvements in tax software, more telephone feature options, and revelation of new tricks available through specialized consultants. For instance, a recent restaurant start-up in the Seattle area used special consultants not only for architecture and law but also for recipe design, menu design, interior design, focus group utilization, and staff training. The venture took two years to design and set up and then was opened with no advertising. Within two weeks, the waiting line for dinner was two hours, and it still is. No doubt much of what the consultants provided was venture-specific. But when and how to use the consultants may have been venture-general techniques that a school can help with.

Inevitably, it is the people in industry who will originate most of the improved methods for venturing. They, by the millions, are tinkering and trying approaches that will let individuals enter business more profitably. This represents a massive experimentation effort, with industry as the laboratory. Academics certainly cannot match the effort but can assist. Our job must include noticing the improvements that arise from these experiments and helping diffuse them to other application sites. "Just do it" may have been good enough for the twentieth century, but in the twenty-first century it should not. Instead, the slogan should be: "Do it better than last time."

Magazines and other media also have this mission of tracking and reporting about best entrepreneurship practices, in parallel with us. But for them there is higher priority on discovery of the occurrences, whereas we are called upon more to codify and cumulate the information about improved methods so that useful knowledge will go forward and not be forgotten, only to need rediscovery.

This adds to the content we offer, so it can reach beyond snippets and also beyond paradigms for looking at or connecting snippets. It builds a unique content for the field of entrepreneurship. A likely result will be that other fields will tear off pieces of it to claim as their own.

Balance, research-wise

In the search for new knowledge that research represents, we have much to work on, not just in quantity but in direction, balance, and even underlying philosophy. Top priority, it seems to me, should be to work on two types of balance that need to be improved in entrepreneurship research.

The first is topical balance. Too little attention is being given to some topical areas in relation to others. From reviewing the distribution of articles by topic of 1,679 articles from three academic periodical series – *Journal of Business Venturing (JBV)*, *Marketing at the Entrepreneurship Interface (MEI)*, and *Frontiers of Entrepreneurship Research (FER)* plus *Inc. Magazine* – I found a wild imbalance of treatment among topics without a discernible rationale, except perhaps for the convenience of data available.

For instance, there were numerous articles about the make-up and distribution of entrepreneurs according to various economic and social categories but almost none about how they perform their tasks, let alone what connections there might be between how they perform their tasks and what results they achieve. There were numerous studies of venture capital and venture capitalists, from whom only a tiny fraction of entrepreneurs ever get funding. But there are almost no studies of how entrepreneurs interact with bankers, which virtually all of them do, many with major consequences. A large proportion of studies focuses on management processes of ventures downstream from start-up, which of course is where most businesses are, rather than on processes of inception, where entrepreneurs begin.

More important appeared to be the almost complete lack of attention to subjects such as how to find viable venture ideas, how to check them out, how to protect ideas in a new venture, and how to deal with acquisitions as a way of marshalling resources. Certainly, these are important subjects to entrepreneurs and areas where undoubtedly things can be done better. So it is regrettable that they appear to be so under-treated.

By far the most treated are topics that have to do with overall occurrence of entrepreneurship in various economies, plus the psychological make-up of entrepreneurs. How study of those topics is likely to give insights into better techniques for entrepreneurs is not so easy to see, which makes it hard to defend the unbalanced attention the topics appear to receive.

Emphasis also seems inordinately high on topics directed toward the study of generating and coping with growth in existing companies. Those topics are of high interest and importance to managers in ongoing companies. But theirs is not the role of the entrepreneur, according to Webster's definition. Management of ongoing companies is a subject with an abundance of literature, research and otherwise. Entrepreneurship lacks such abundance and is, therefore, where the research is needed more.

Reasons for the apparent misdirection probably include inertia and resistance owing to the traditional emphasis of management schools and of researchers on following the money. Start-up businesses generally cannot pay for high consulting fees or expensive management programs, whereas many fast-rising companies can and do. It is always easier to study companies that are established, because most of the time they are easy to find and they stay put. Moreover, there is usually information about them in print from any number of sources. To study established companies rather than entrepreneurs in action is like photographing a cow rather than a grasshopper on the move.

This extension of the term entrepreneur into the realm of management also adds confusion. Two persons talking about entrepreneurship may have very different subjects in mind. One may be thinking about individuals or teams who start companies, while the other may be thinking of executives like the CEO of Chrysler. Perhaps we should develop a lexicon for the entrepreneurship field, which includes different types of entrepreneurs having different appellations.

Concentrating research on individuals and teams who enter independent businesses, and in particular on what actions they take to establish those businesses, would shift focus more away from the economics and psychology of venture populations and thereby help add balance.

Another major driver of imbalance is created by academic fashion in research methodology. Using statistics is the proper way to establish representativeness. But in entrepreneurship representativeness, typicality, normality, the mode, median, or mean is not all we should be interested in. Entrepreneurship is based upon exceptionality. Entrepreneurs prosper by finding and exploiting anomalies, which is what they and their ventures often turn out to be, at least until they are up, running, and successful. At that point management, hopefully still creative and resourceful, succeeds in entrepreneurship.

So we should be looking in our research not just for the typical in populations but also for the outliers and the range. We should seek to identify and map the arrays of venturing methods that are effective and the causes of those arrays. That can help change the injunction for would-be company starters from "just do it," to "do it better."

Maybe USASBE should each year impanel two teams of scholars and have each team answer two questions. First, in what ways, maybe for selected industries, is new venture creation performed better today than it was five years ago? Second, how might best practices in entrepreneurship be better five years hence than they are today? After five years, the answers should be graded, and one team should be given an award for guiding vision. This could be continued on a rolling basis year after year to keep our eyes directed on the course.

Endowment

All the tasks mentioned so far require time, money, and persistence. It is not enough to have an effort begin and then be blown away. But that is what has happened repeatedly over the years. Consider the start-up studies by pioneers in the field like Hoad and Rosko at the University of Michigan and Collins and Moore at Michigan State University. They put the two schools at the forefront then, but that leadership has not been continued at either one. Had there been endowments behind those early and significant research activities, instead of only temporary government contracts, and had those endowments been written with tight contracts binding them permanently to entrepreneurship, those schools would almost certainly still be prominent in the field, and we would have more good research results from the continuation of their efforts.

What the money is for also seems to make a difference. A good thing about the two studies mentioned above was that their aim was to produce published results. Consequently, their output lasted.

A contrast to that publication emphasis would be previous programs that concentrated on activity to the exclusion of collection and dissemination of findings about entrepreneurship. For instance, in the 1970s the National Science Foundation spent millions on "innovation centers" at several major U.S. universities. Unfortunately, nobody was contracted to monitor the results independently, so the only reporting of the experiments consisted of what amounted to applications for renewal of the contracts. Later, years after the projects had begun and finally ended, an investigation to report the results in hindsight was mounted, but since it was commissioned by the same agency that had spent the money, it was not very penetrating. It seems likely that a considerable amount of learning about what worked well and what did not work was lost. This invites repetition of mistakes and consequently financial waste.

During the 1980s, the Canadian national government mounted several dozen entrepreneurship stimulation projects at universities around the country.

Again, nobody was given a contract to monitor the results as a third party, and again we have no results, that I am aware of, to show for the projects.

Without sustained effort, all those programs vanished. Very recently, the same thing has happened at two other universities. At the University of Dortmund in Germany, an outstanding program in entrepreneurship was going on, including development of new software, new outreach courses, and a major international conference on entrepreneurship education. The university, however, was less than fully supportive of all this. When the prime mover received a better offer and moved to the European Business School near Frankfurt, the Dortmund program completely dried up.

What should be done? One remedy would be to develop longer-range plans for financial support, including creation of endowments for entrepreneurship program development and research. The second is to make sure that when money is given it goes to entrepreneurship, not to some sort of undesignated purpose beyond simply memorializing the donor's name. Universities always prefer unrestricted funds. But when they get such funds, universities rarely make entrepreneurship the beneficiary.

Flagship

Even with endowed financial support, however, entrepreneurship in universities still must deal with barriers and constraints that we should keep finding ways to penetrate. Entrepreneurship in universities has so far been developed as an add-on to business education, first as an elective course, then more courses, and finally as a concentration, major, or program. So far entrepreneurship has largely been tucked in around the existing core. Its teachers presently must be approved by established faculty in other fields. Its courses currently must fit into the existing curriculum, grading system, and calendar. It serves the students who, for the most part, apply for a conventional business education.

But what might be different if we had started first with a school of entrepreneurship and then added a few courses for a concentration or major in middle management? Would it be a school of art, science, or profession? Would it be aimed at imparting knowledge content, tools, and skills or ways of thinking? If ways of thinking, what would they be and how would the school seek to impart them? What would graduate students carry with them in the way of not only course content but also venture memories, mentor memories and perhaps portfolios of their creations, such as product designs and prototypes, business plans, parts of plans, contacts from field studies, and ideas about potential future opportunities, as well as plans for continuation of their personal development and contact networks to enable them more effectively, with time, to become successful as venturers and helpers of other venturers?

Is there some reason, other than lack of progress, that there should not be a graduate school of entrepreneurship in the United States? Why should it not be first class? And why shouldn't that new school be, like this meeting, in San Diego?

The San Diego business community, although not as large as the business communities of other major cities on the West Coast, has a rapidly advancing growth frontier that includes both high technology and a very active adjacent international border with Mexico that also links it with other countries in both Europe and Asia. Many entrepreneurs work here, and many more within commuting distance just up the coast. Hundreds of venture capital firms from elsewhere show up in San Diego annually for the technology showcase hosted by the University of California at San Diego (UCSD).

San Diego State University has a world-class venture plan contest and an active entrepreneurship program that is well supported by the community faculty. But it has no doctoral program and, by the nature of the California State University system, has a mission that is oriented primarily toward teaching, not research. Both those functions are assigned by the state mainly to the University of California system. But if a new graduate school of entrepreneurship were created nearby, and if adequate financial support could be raised, then faculty from San Diego State could participate as members of the new school's faculty on either a joint or a summer basis. They could also belong to or supervise committees for doctoral students doing relevant research.

The University of California at San Diego, like Berkeley, UCLA, and the other members of the University of California system, has the mission to pioneer and develop new knowledge. It has strong schools in engineering, medicine, and the sciences. It also has an exemplary extension program that is strongly oriented toward new business ventures. But it is headed toward creating another management school, the emphasis, therefore, is likely to be on serving established companies.

There is also a business school at the University of San Diego, a small school with two active faculty members in entrepreneurship who might collaborate with a graduate school of entrepreneurship on doctoral or other research if conditions were right.

Each of these schools provides important parts to the picture of entrepreneurship education in San Diego. But their combination still leaves, as opportunities, some gaps. The existing business schools here either have or are seeking American Assembly of Collegiate Schools of Business (AACSB) accreditation, which imposes some restrictions that an entrepreneurship school might be better off without. A new school free from accreditation could make unrestricted use of adjunct faculty. It could offer a one-year master's degree in entrepreneurship without the inertia of traditional business core courses. It could design its own doctoral program around the special research needs of entrepreneurship. That doctoral program, by its wide-open nature, might be able to draw participation of distinguished doctoral mentors in entrepreneurship at universities elsewhere in the nation in addition to faculty of nearby schools, and it could include scholastically-inclined members of the entrepreneurship community outside the academic world as well. The array of programs that would then be available, including those of a new graduate school of entrepreneurship, should be complementary and not duplicative.

In the longer term such a school, if organized with sufficient freshness, imagination, and quality, might even be eligible for adoption by UCSD, which would thereby become the only top-quality university in the world with a graduate school of entrepreneurship separate from its management school.

That, it seems to me, would make an interesting page in the twenty-first century history of the United States and one that everyone concerned could be proud of. It could also pave the way for the emergence of other such schools in the United States and elsewhere.

A graduate school of entrepreneurship in America could have happened in the twentieth century, but did not. To give it a good start, money would clearly be required, dozens of millions to do it right, and such amounts usually take time to get. So maybe such a school should begin in the twenty-first century, and the sooner the better, if not in San Diego, then still somewhere in the United States.

To be done

In summary, Arnold Cooper is right. The field is young, has come a long way in a short time, and is likely to keep on building, because its driving forces are continuing, for the foreseeable future. But there is also a tremendous potential for doing more than is likely to happen automatically. We have to drive it if we are going to maximize the win from it.

Many opportunities are bound to be exploited sooner or later, if not by one person or group or institution, then by another. But there are also opportunities that will never be exploited within our experience even though they could be. Maybe skateboards, snowboards, and windsurfers were inevitable, but they certainly could have been developed earlier. The same is true of the Internet, Fed Ex, and jet airliners, not to mention products like *Trivial Pursuit*, *Pictionary*, and the *Happy Massager*. All of these could have been developed sooner or not at all. Initiative made the difference.

Our initiatives should recognize that, although the entrepreneurship field is growing, it is still short of both legitimacy and permanence. Further clarification of student market segments and finer tuning of curricula for them can help, as can more creative thinking about fresh paradigms for understanding the subject. Research efforts should be guided more toward areas that are thinly treated and with an eye toward discerning and disseminating the small improvements industry invents for performing entrepreneurial processes better. Emphasis on study of central tendencies, means, and modes should be reduced in favor of more study about ranges and exceptions to be found in the tails of sample curves. We should develop a better science of our own for raising money and making sure it gets applied to entrepreneurship, not for just doing it but for learning how to do it better. And somewhere in the United States the twenty-first century should see a full-blown American graduate school of entrepreneurship.

Reference

Vesper, K.H. (1996) *New Venture Mechanics*, Seattle, WA: Vector Books.

Chapter 3

Dianne Wyndham Wingham

College of Business, Rowan University

ENTREPRENEURSHIP THROUGH THE AGES

Introduction

ENTREPRENEURSHIP AS WE KNOW it in the twenty-first century developed from the economic outreach of the early Phoenician socio-political entrepreneurship of the eleventh century BC. The Phoenician culture created broadly based trading relationships that enhanced the quality of life in much of the Mediterranean region. In 539 BC, the Persian Empire took control, and Phoenicia ceased to exist as an entity. By 64 BC, Phoenicia had been absorbed into Syria (Kjeilen 2000). The decline of the Phoenicians as a trading power coincided with the evaporation of obvious entrepreneurial activity in the region. However, their entrepreneurial philosophy lives on, as it did through a number of waves of powerful forces from Asia minor, Africa, and Europe that swept the world.

The entrepreneurial state

Phoenicia (approximately 1100 BC–500 BC) was a nation of independent city-states, populated by merchants and traders, with skills and trading practices that enabled them to develop colonies as far away as modern-day Spain, Syria, Cyprus, Libya, Tunisia, Italy, Malta, Algeria, and Morocco. However, colonization was a by-product of trade based on efficient use of the sea routes enabling the Phoenicians to trade in a broad spectrum of products and from a number of diverse countries, many of which are represented by modern territorial boundaries. "...silver, iron, tin and lead from Tarshish (modern-day Spain), ivory and ebony from Africa and India, cloth, wool, wine, and precious stones from Syria, perfumes from Dor, Are, and Joppa (modern-day Israel) and Judah; and garments, embroidery, and cord from the Mediterranean sea ports, Carthage and Ugarit (today's Tunisia)" (Kjeilen 2000). True entrepreneurs took risks, explored the unknown, facing the resultant chaos on a daily basis. They sought and recognized difference in trade, returning profit to merchants and themselves, and investors (generally, in the earlier eras, a wealthy landowner, and nowadays, more likely, a corporate giant).

The impact of the Phoenician trading and entrepreneurial culture outlasted their empire, largely because of the trade-based non-aggressive philosophy of the Phoenician traders, and because they were instrumental in disseminating communication and shared elements of language throughout their colonies. The Greek language owes much to the twenty-two letter alphabet used in the Phoenician language. This influence on language has persisted in a variety of forms globally into modern languages (Kjeilen 2000). The Phoenician era was doomed to pass into history, and with it the degree to which entrepreneurial practice contributed directly and so significantly to sustainable regional economies. Adventurers, armies, and entrepreneurs sailed from global ports based on economic and military might, fleets swept the world looking for "difference," the "exotic," "new," and "rare." These adventures to the other side of the globe established trade through uncertain environments that presented personal and financial risk. Armies brought back spoils and traded for profits for the entrepreneurs who undertook the journeys and to the early venture capitalists who financed imports of tobacco, tomatoes, and rice and other "new" products into the economies of Europe from the New World.

The entrepreneurial Dark Ages

Emergence from the Dark Ages for entrepreneurial activity for trade and not territory, saw a renewed interest in the synergistic trade activity, that had sustained the Phoenicians. Trade and colonization were however combined, as countries sought to impose trading relationships that gave them sovereignty over the trade routes and the source of the product, to ensure continued access to produce and trade that was brought from distant lands to the European mainland. The increasing demand for luxury items was largely due to the reduction of isolationism that had prevailed throughout the middle ages. During this era, the term "entrepreneur" meant the organizing role applied to an agent of the government with responsibility for administering fixed-price contracts and reaping any profit that could be extracted through parsimonious management. Increasingly the term came to mean, generally, someone who took advantage of an opportunity (or created it) to achieve out-of-the-ordinary results. Efficient and effective management enhanced the entrepreneur's profit. In the early stages of the sixteenth century, there was a change in which the application of the term reflected traders and innovators. Although travel to distant lands was not part of the definition applied in the sixteenth century, there was a need for the entrepreneur to be innovative and a risk-embracing individual.

The seventeenth century also saw a redefinition of entrepreneurship and that reflected both the type of person who was risk tolerant, and the economic impact of the outcomes of entrepreneurial activity. Entrepreneurial impact on the economy that was causing some concern to the economic purists was studied by Richard Cantillon (1680–1734), an Irish-born, Austrian economic analyst, turned French banker and entrepreneur – the founding father of modern economics. He determined that entrepreneurs were able to see the alternative uses for resources, and were certainly risk-takers. Also, that they had a tolerance of risk at several levels, and undertook ventures based on uncertainty of both achievement and profitability. One example of early entrepreneurship was found in the activities of John Law (1671–1729), who moved his banking interests to the New World based on a franchise agreement to trade with France.

One economic contention was that entrepreneurial behavior impacts on the production and flow of new money. Any large increase in money will give a new turn to consumption, thus changing relative prices, velocity, and the distribution of income. New money is also seen as affecting the ongoing cost of money. The eighteenth century inventors were capital users who were largely dependent upon the vagaries of the venture capital marketplace. Thomas Edison was an inventor of a substantial number of innovative advances in modern living – his entrepreneurship needed capital equity to reach the marketplace. Alexander Graham Bell (1847–1922), a Scottish-born inventor and educator, launched his innovative advancement of the telephone technology through third-party capital intervention.

Physical invention was not the only means to be entrepreneurial, as innovative adaptation of existing skills and changes in the manner of their use prevailed. Capital user entrepreneurs such as John D. Rockefeller (1839–1937), and Andrew Carnegie (1835–1919), the father of the American steel industry, were considered entrepreneurial, although not for any inventions. Carnegie developed and maintained an entrepreneurial approach to corporate governance that was both innovative and risk-taking. It supported the growing understanding that re-creation and revolutionizing existing patterns and activities were skills attributable to the entrepreneur creating a "new" commodity through innovative re-engineering or a "new" outlet through innovative thinking, or reorganizing an industry to take full advantage of the facilities and market needs (Pavlov 2000).

The need to understand the process of entrepreneurship led to a number of linguistic definitions being formalized. Vérin (1982) determined that the current connotations were applied to entrepreneurship in the seventeenth century. British economists such as Adam Smith (1776), David Ricardo (1772–1823), and John Stuart Mill (1806–1873) wrote of the activities of business management that had the characteristics of entrepreneurship, but for which they lacked an appropriate defining term other than the French term entrepreneur (Schumpeter 1951). Arnold (1996) claims that economists envisage entrepreneurship as the fourth factor that coordinates the other three factors of production (land, labor, capital, and organization) underpinning economic thinking. This determination makes the role of entrepreneurship overarching, and is not universally accepted. Long (1983) proposed that greater progress of its study would be possible through the adoption of a common definition of the term. To that end, he provides an historical account of the development and uses of the term, indicating that the root of the word can be traced as far back as 800 years, to the French verb "entrepren-dre," or "to do something." Over time, the assigned meanings of entrepreneur have been almost as diverse. Three hundred years later, "entrepreneur" appeared in language, and soon thereafter, both verb and noun entered the English language (Bygrave and Hofer 1991).

From economics and philosophy

In 1730, "entrepreneur" was used by Richard Cantillon to mean a "self-employed person with a tolerance for the risk he believed was inherent in providing for one's own economic well being." This term was applied in the context of entre-preneurial activities until these were broadened, with the onset of the Industrial Revolution (1830), by Jean-Baptiste Say, recognizing possession of managerial skills as an essential element for the definition of a "successful" entrepreneur to include. John Bates Clark's (1899) doctrine of specific productivity shed a flood of light on this relationship and the recesses of economic life, and was the starting point of much modern entrepreneurship discussion. Entrepreneurial terms and their accepted meanings changed, describing entrepreneurial culture, philosophy, characteristics, and behavior as the twentieth century advanced. The endeavor to define twentieth-century entrepreneurship from an economic and a behavioral perspective was receiving a great deal of attention from researchers. Prior to the twentieth century, the neoclassical economic model had too long ignored the impact of entrepreneurship on the mechanism of wealth distribution. It was timely, that with the turn of the century, against a background of the rumblings of economic change, classical economists began to question the validity of ignoring the impact of entrepreneurship in an attempt to achieve predictability through logical and mathematical rigor.

Francis Walker (1876) distinguished between fund user and funding provider. However, there was a gap in major contribution to entrepreneurial discourse of almost eighty years. In his 1912 *Theorie der wirtschaftlichen Entwicklung* (or *The Theory of Economic Development*). From the insightful contribution to entrepreneur-ial definition mode by Say, Joseph Schumpeter, the Austrian economist, argued that entrepreneurship was a vital element of economic capitalism. He published his ideas as a theoretical treatise on the dynamics of economic development, in which his now frequently discussed definition of entrepreneurship as the primary engine of economic development was first mooted. According to Schumpeter, both entrepreneurship and innovation – the use of an invention to create a new commercial product or service – were essential elements of national economies. Furthermore, Schumpeter saw entrepreneurs themselves as forces of creative destruction. "Without innovations, no entrepreneurs; without entrepreneurial achievement, no capitalist returns and no capitalist propulsion" (as cited in McGraw 1991: 380). Although Schumpeter does not provide a great deal of detail on the characteristics of successful entrepreneurs, he did state that entrepreneurs must expend great energy and possess a strong will to be successful.

Schumpeter also observed that, in general, the concept of a free market environment was erroneous. He observed that markets were driven by a few sellers, and that buyers were constrained with regard to product and price. However, through the introduction of new products and services into the market, entrepreneurs increased the size of the basket of available goods and services. Schumpeter maintained that the entrepreneur would, through increasing the value and type of goods, thereby challenge the established dominant sellers and destroy the market structure. The resulting redistribution of wealth from tensions of market chaos directly contrasts to the neoclassical systemic theories of passive, reactive buyers and responsive suppliers, using price fluctuations to maintain market equilibrium, reflecting Schumpeter's idea of a clear association with innovation.

> The essence of entrepreneurship lies in the perception and exploitation of new opportunities in the realm of business ... it always has to do with bringing about a different use of national resources in that they are withdrawn from their traditional employ and subjected to new combinations.
>
> (Schumpeter 1928)

Not only did Schumpeter associate entrepreneurs with innovation, his imposing work shows the importance of entrepreneurs in explaining economic development. He also provided a canvas for the rich tapestry of economic and behavioral argument about entrepreneurship and its social and economic impact. It would be some time, however, until David Birch (1979) would introduce economists to the extent of the economic impact of entrepreneurship and small business on the national economy. Writing contemporaneously with Schumpeter, Knight (1921) and later, economists Mill (1848), Higgins (1959), Baumol (1968), Schloss (1968), and Leibenstein (1978, 1979) reflect the long history of seeking to understand and to explain the role played by the entrepreneur as the motor of the economic system (Filion 1998). Through discovery over time, Israel Kirzner (1973) isolated an entrepreneurial element – individuals spontaneously discovering means of satisfying their wants. In individual decision-making and entrepreneurship in the market interaction, the serendipity that underlies accidental satisfaction of want causes the entrepreneur to develop alertness to hitherto undiscovered opportunities. Copying learned habits was seen as reinforcing the benefits through the repetition of the action, along with the entrepreneur assuming the right of personal decision-making, providing the environment for entrepreneurship in the market economy arbitrage (Kirzner 1973).

Economists were daily faced with the published and physical evidence of their theories. Bureaucratic, industrial monoliths could be seen as the visible drivers of industry in the early twentieth century. These businesses, and industries to which they belonged, contributed openly to pollution, were given consideration in government decision-making, and were influential in helping to maintain, if not in establishing, social norms of the era. Entrepreneurs were largely "second-tier" economic participants, detecting business opportunities, sometimes in direct opposition to existing big business, sometimes in a support role creating peripheral enterprises (Ely and Hess 1893; Oxenfeldt 1943; Schloss 1968), and generally, as risk-takers (Buchanan and Di Pierro 1980;

Kihlstrom and Laffont 1979; Leibenstein 1978), with entrepreneurial activities, identifying and informing the marketplace of new opportunities and innovations (Higgins 1959; Kirzner 1976; Penrose 1959). Leibenstein (1979) applied his model of entrepreneurial efficiency and inefficiency measurement. In 1982, Casson undertook significant studies to develop a theory linking entrepreneurs with economic development. Although based on economic cant and ideology, his conclusions were perceived as too qualitative, and were limited in econometric/economic acceptance due to the lack of mathematical rigor.

Behaviorist intervention

Economists were concerned about understanding the impact on the marketplace, while behaviorists, through parallel exploration, sought to understand the entrepreneur and the drivers of the "man behind the condition," the body of behavioral studies of entrepreneurship becoming too large to ignore, presenting interesting counterfoils to the economic canons. Attributes of the entrepreneur became areas of extensive research. Hoselitz (1952) was particularly impressed by the reported higher levels of tolerance of ambiguity, uncertainty, and risk, as discerned by Cantillon in the 1730s. Long (1983) also explored the trait theories of organizational behavior concluding that three traits have, to varying degrees, been included in the definition of entrepreneurship: "uncertainty and risk," "complementary managerial competence," and "creative opportunism." Baumol (1993) also addressed the individual dimensions, proposing two categories of entrepreneurs, entrepreneur–business organizer, addressed by Say (1815), Knight (1921), and Kirzner (1983). Also, the entrepreneur–innovator is described progressively by Cantillon (circa 1730), Schumpeter (1934), and Bygrave and Hofer (1991).

National entrepreneurial propensity

There is a long history of entrepreneurial behavior in the U.S.A. existing throughout history. However, the prevailing view of society in the nineteenth and early twentieth centuries, until the late 1970s, was dominated by industry barons and corporate giants, with corporatism seen as a necessary economic model to reflect the appropriate balance, taking advantage of the economies of scale provided. By inhibiting cost of production accompanied by economies of scale, neoclassical economics was seen as the foundation of a secure economy in the United States. William Whyte, in *The Organization Man* (1956), postulated that World War II, accompanied by unemployment and the resulting increase in poverty levels resulting from the depression, reinforced the reliance on the bureaucratic and multi-level organizations. Those that had survived the economic downturn were seen as the blueprint for productivity and profitability. This was supported by J.K. Galbraith's proposal in his *The New Industrial State* (1967), which stated that a coordinated big business and big government with big unions would be the formula for economic growth and stability. This corporatist view of job creation was sustained for a considerable time.

However, the ground-breaking work of David Birch in 1979 provided overwhelming evidence that those small firms which had 100 or fewer employees created 81 percent of the new jobs in the United States. Birch had presented a challenge to the accepted wisdom of the day that "big business is the way forward." Small businesses were creating a significantly larger proportion of the economic growth. The Schumpeterian theory of creative destruction was revisited, and found to give substantial support to the new understanding of economic growth. There was vigorous economic foundation to this claim, and, after all, new job creation had long been established as a reliable measure of economic growth. While economists insisted on mathematical formulae to determine entrepreneurship, behaviorist Max Weber (1930) gave psychological credence to understanding entrepreneurs and their activities from an entrepreneurial value system. David C. McClelland, in 1961, redefined the entrepreneur as energetic, moderate risk-taker:

> An entrepreneur is someone who exercises control over production that is not for his own personal consumption. According to my definition, for example, an executive in a steel-producing unit in the USSR is an entrepreneur.
>
> (McClelland 1971)

McClelland's interpretation of the entrepreneur per se is evidenced within the intrapreneurial definition. Peter Drucker (1964) contends that entrepreneurs maximize opportunities. This has also been found to be an intrapreneurial activity. However, there was some dissent in relation to broadening the definition. The *Webster's Dictionary* (1999) definition identifies entrepreneurial as a term characterizing individuals who undertake risk for the sake of profit. This definition is continually being stretched (Vesper 1999) to accommodate managers and owners of small companies. Vesper also suggests that individuals who inherit businesses from their parents – who were the real entrepreneurs who created the business – are increasingly being themselves erroneously represented as entrepreneurs. Over the next twenty years, following McClelland's 1961 pronouncements, researchers explored the behavioral dimensions in their search for the definition and the constructs of the entrepreneur. Much of this research was limited in scope and a significant amount of it was contradictory. Strongly evident in findings is a proposition of a number of authors that the entrepreneur is a "product of an era," reflecting the characteristics of the surrounding society (Ellis 1983; Gibb and Richie 1981; Julien and Marchesnay 1996; McGuire 1976; Newman 1981; Toulouse 1979). Overall, the study of entrepreneurship embraces both the trading propensity (economic) facility of the individual (nation) with the overlaying propensities identified in organizational (behavioral) theories. Long (1983) identified twenty-seven dominant themes of current research into entrepreneurship. They are seen, in part at least, to be an outcome of the disciplines of the researchers, and reflection of the broad impact that entrepreneurship has on academic study among these disciplines. However, these disciplines have failed to agree as to the particularities of entrepreneurial activity. Kilby (1971) described this dilemma as "hunting Heffalumps" (a reference to a character in the children's book, *Winnie-the-Pooh*). Supporting the "Heffalump" relationship, he maintains that almost all economists are familiar with entrepreneurs, and in many cases have studied their work. However, despite this, there is little agreement as to what an entrepreneur really looks like (Wilken 1979). There is, nonetheless, general agreement that entrepreneurs are "an integral ingredient for economic growth" (Gillis 1996). This approach is not new, and revisits Schumpeterian definitions, which can best be seen in the context of the discipline-based approaches taken over time.

Despite divergent views, a "theory of entrepreneurship" should be formulated based on accumulated "common knowledge" (Kirchhoff 1992). What is known of entrepreneurs is that they are at the heart of job growth and economic dynamics; they are the creators of wealth through their association with innovation; they provide the mechanisms for wealth creation and distribution-based innovation, hard work, and risk-taking, often based on "undeliberate learning" (Kirzner 1985), replacing or supplementing innovation per se, relying on the alertness of the entrepreneur, the proclivity toward opportunity recognition resulting in changing outputs and "creative imitation" (Leibenstein 1995), forming a future service or good from a need or an opportunity (Drucker 1985).

Raymond W. Smilor (1997) uses the Socratic approach to develop a picture of the twenty-first century, which he claims to be the century of the entrepreneur. Significant among the recommendations made by Smilor is the identification of four critical abilities of successful entrepreneurship, elements of skills for inclusion and reflection:

* the ability to create meaning,
* the skills in the orchestration of talent,
* sufficient confidence and capacity to embrace chaos, and
* the ability to accelerate personal and team learning.

Smilor (1997) also recognizes the variety of groups in the body of innovators – young entrepreneurs (Colleran and Ginsberg 2002), female entrepreneurs (Duffy *et al.* 2002), minority entrepreneurship (Fairlie and Robb 2002), community entrepreneurship (Welsch and Kuhns 2002), team entrepreneurship (Reich 1987), and technology-based entrepreneurship (Brazeal and Azriel 2002) are currently impacting on traditional entrepreneurial literature, growing faster as individual classifications than the traditional entrepreneurs.

Sandberg (1992) reports on the levels of influence of managerial competencies on entrepreneurship. Reich (1987) asserts that team-oriented entrepreneurship will be crucial for maintaining U.S. economic competitiveness in the new global marketplace.

The twenty-first century: entrepreneurial diversity

The Global Entrepreneurship Monitor (GEM) estimates more than 460 million adults globally are engaged in entrepreneurial activity (Reynolds *et al.* 2002). With a proactive approach to maximizing entrepreneurial activity, policy-

Table 3.1 Entrepreneurship to all people

Discipline	Knowledge users	Studied	Disciplines impacted	Approach	Discipline-based definition
Behaviorists	Researchers, practitioners	Entrepreneurial characteristics and environment	Behaviorists, sociologists, anthropologists	Quantitative	Entrepreneurs have characteristics of creativity, persistence, locus of control, and leadership
Engineers and operations management	Entrepreneurs, nascent entrepreneurs, educators	Entrepreneurial characteristics and environment	Economists, sociologists	Quantitative and qualitative	Entrepreneurs are good distributors and coordinators of resources
Finance specialists, economists	Political system	Financing, government policies, regional	Economists, financiers	Quantitative and qualitative	Entrepreneurs are people able to measure risk
Management specialists	Entrepreneurs, nascent entrepreneurs, educators, consultants	Business practice, management activities, leadership, strategic thinking	Management	Quantitative and qualitative	Entrepreneurs are resourceful and good organizers
Marketing specialists	Big business, educators, consultants	Entrepreneurial characteristics and environment	Marketing	Quantitative and qualitative	Entrepreneurs identify opportunities, differentiate themselves, and adopt customer-oriented thinking

Source: Adapted from Filion (1998), Table of Entrepreneurial Research.

makers need to determine the drivers for entrepreneurship participation. Fundamental to this understanding are the two elements of opportunity and willingness to become an entrepreneur (Praag and Van Ophen 1995). Also important to entrepreneurial involvement levels are regional variations and a positive correlation between "cultural and economic–structural determinants of a new firm formation rate" (Davidsson and Wiklund 1995).

The entrepreneur

Given the supply and demand nature of market forces, entrepreneurs are the gap-fillers who, through their skills, perceive and take steps to correct market deficiencies (Leibenstein 1978). To encourage entrepreneurs to transform the market, they not only provide new goods and services, they also create more and newer jobs (Praag and Van Ophen 1995). The jobs increased not only in number but also in diversity – supermarkets have created the job of trolley collector; technology support desks are a by-product of computer technology; medical innovations have resulted in increased layers of new job classifications and descriptions. One hundred years ago, there was no perceived need for these services, nor was there any basis for exploring such a need.

As elements of its simplest form, entrepreneurship is seen as involving determination, drive, motivation, and perseverance. The entrepreneur must be willing to take the individual responsibility to set goals, to solve problems, and to reach goals by their striving (Klees 1995). Where are these elusive qualities to be found in the twenty-first century? Despite some setbacks, the following entrepreneurs have demonstrated that they have these attributes in abundance. They are also representative of the entrepreneurs who have made a difference to the working and social environment. Dr. Wallace C. Abbott (Abbott Laboratories) refined measured drug dispensing (1888); Elias Howe and Isaac Singer – the sewing machine; Rowl and Hussey Macy – N.Y. retailers; George Eastman – Eastman Kodak (1888) – cameras and photography in their earlier years, and on to office copiers and industrial photography, etc.; Joseph Engelberger – the father of robotics is changing the face of heavy and dangerous industrial activities, and military tasks to this day. Perhaps the greatest impact has been made by Microsoft – Paul Allen and Bill Gates (1975). Innovative entrepreneurial entities are at the base of many of the current global giants. Entrepreneurship has not, however, stopped evolving, and the future directions of innovation are as elusive to the common man as science fiction. Studies of twenty-first century entrepreneurship are seeking information about the impact of such influences as technology, evidenced in the Silicon Valley era and, more recently, in the rise and fall of the dot.com industry. However, this is only one part of the new innovative environment that is developing to accommodate the number and variety of entrepreneurial ventures that are beginning. Innovation and invention have long been part of the definition of entrepreneurship; however, changes in the way business is done, and a transformation of the uses of products, make adaptation a viable alternative to invention. Ninety-three percent of entrepreneurally active adults consider their business to be a replication of an existing business activity (Reynolds et al. 2002).

Further, the GEM study indicates that a small minority (7 percent) expected their firms to create a significant new market niche or economic sector. A very small proportion of these expected to create new market niches, to provide twenty or more new jobs in the next five years, and also to impact on the economy through earned income from exports outside their own country. Most of these "high potential" new ventures reflected the pursuit of opportunity, though many "necessity" entrepreneurs also expect that their firms would have a high impact.

The future of entrepreneurial history

Evidence continues to accumulate that the national level of entrepreneurial activity has a statistically significant association with subsequent levels of economic growth. Economic downturns and market slumps are often indicators among regular businesses that it is time to withdraw, downsize, retrench, etc. It would appear, based on the GEM 2002 survey, that this trend is reflected in entrepreneurial businesses. However, contra-indications are also found. Tenacity is perceived as an entrepreneurial strength (Muoio 1997), with entrepreneurs having the tenacity to plow through creative blocks. Literature cites that innovation is a critical driver of economic growth, and a means to develop and maintain prosperity.

Necessity and/or opportunity have been behind all innovation over time, without regard for the accepted definition or discipline under which it has been addressed. However, innovative ideas are not sufficient of themselves to establish an entrepreneurial business. Additionally, the driving forces for actualizing outcomes of innovative ideas and concepts are:

- education and skills-based applied research capabilities,
- a critical mass of industries and capabilities,
- tools for commercialization – venture and family capital,
- robust sustainable market access.

In addition to the emphasis on the economic contribution and outcomes of entrepreneurial endeavor that have occupied large segments of research over time, a further significant issue is the source of financial support for entrepreneurial ventures. The aggregate amount of venture capital allocated for start-up activities in 2001 was US$59 billion for the thirty-seven countries included in the GEM (2002) data. This study also reported, based on the most comprehensive database currently available on the global impact of entrepreneurship, that informal funding provided to new firms was significant. Recent studies have shown a marked increase in the number of women entrepreneurs and that this group has a greater level of family-sponsored ventures reported globally (GEM 2002). Banks are reportedly easing restrictions on women entrepreneurs' borrowing to start or grow a business. However, the same cannot be said for minority borrowers, for whom, along with female entrepreneurs already discussed, family resources remain a dominant source of entrepreneurship funding.

Families appear to remain the best source of funding micro start-ups. Reynolds *et al.* (2002) reports that informal funding was provided by 1 percent–7 percent of the adult population to literally tens of millions of individuals involved in the start-up process. However, this money was in amounts between US$100 and US$30,000. The report states that the majority of new firms seemed to begin with substantial support from the immediate family. The U.S.A. was reported by Reynolds *et al.* (2002) to have greater than 10 percent entrepreneurial participation (larger than the 8 percent country average for the combined thirty-seven nations studied). Reynolds *et al.* (2002) also indicates that only China, with 17.9 percent of the adult working population involved in entrepreneurial activities, and India, with 12.3 percent, have a higher percentage of entrepreneurial representation than the U.S.A. With differing types and levels of venture capital, entrepreneurship is manifested in a number of ways. This begs the question for researchers of the next entrepreneurial wave. Who are the entrepreneurs in the twenty-first century?

Three discrete entrepreneurial topics for review have developed recently. The first of these is the emergence of women entrepreneurs who have entered the market in the past three decades (Swartz 2002). Much of the earlier research on women entrepreneurs looked for differences. Studies identified traits and approaches that were "female" and the special needs that women addressed. A significant effect of this has been the failure to relate to mentors, who could assist in the realignment to compensate for lack of life-plans, which has resulted in women who did enter the entrepreneurial environment having a narrow choice of jobs based on high-school career decisions. Reynolds *et al.* (2002) indicated that age and gender have a very stable relationship with entrepreneurial activity, with men twice as likely to be involved as women, and those twenty-five to forty-four years of age were more likely than any other category to do so. Still, the female entrepreneur is making her mark on economic growth and, in some cases, forcing acceptance and access. In a study of nascent entrepreneurs in the U.S.A. (Reynolds *et al.* 2002), entrepreneurship was identified as a pervasive social and economic activity. Further, entrepreneurs are found among all ethnic groups and among both men and women from all ethnic classifications. This is not to imply an equal representation of a level playing-field for entry. In fact, some of the entries develop from recognized opportunity whilst the majority from all sectors enter from the basis of necessity (Reynolds *et al.* 2000).

The future of world economic growth is to be found through stimulated entrepreneurial activity. This perception underlies the imperative to understand the needs of minority entrepreneurs, and to encourage entrepreneurship diversity. A major benefit of undertaking a study of entry and success trends among the diverse classifications of entrepreneurs is that, in recognizing the substantial contribution to economic growth of these firms, this provides a precursor to productive intervention.

Proactivity is not necessarily reflected in the current sociopolitical environment, despite historical recognition that businesses likely to drive the U.S. economy twenty-five years from now will come not from large established companies but from today's start-up firms (Reynolds *et al.* 2000). The diverse minority group of entrepreneurs has been identified variously. Women entrepreneurs, for example, have been identified (Lavoie 1985; Moore and Buttner 1997), defined as "the head of a business, who has initiated the business, owns at least 50% of the business, is actively involved in managing it and therefore accepts some risk exposure associated with being in business" (Swartz 2002). Women from minority groups enter entrepreneurships at a rate significantly higher than white women. Black men and women are about 50 percent more likely to try to start a business than white men and women (Reynolds *et al.* 2000). Collaborative research by Duffy *et al.* (2002) shows how the gap between knowledge and industry skills, and the current level of women's education, are being closed proactively.

Growing levels of multiculturalism will clearly impact on the twenty-first century entrepreneurship. However, Hileman *et al.* (2002) maintain that it is increasingly essential that studies reflect differences between minority entrepreneurs and tribal or community entrepreneurism. Literature suggests that there are shared elements among tribal and community entrepreneurship.

The U.S.A., India, and China appear to have addressed entrepreneurship and to be seemingly aware of the extent of its potential. Larry Cox, director of research at the Kauffman Foundation, has stated, in relation to the current entrepreneurial position in the U.S.A., "It appears that the U.S. has stabilized at a level of entrepreneurial activity that will allow us to begin rebuilding or at least maintaining our current position for some time."

Conclusions

Historically, there are economic and social "actors" who have made important contributions to the individual era or activity. It is also interesting to note that there are more than 12,000 publications appearing annually in the field of entrepreneurship, across the divergent disciplines, with journals and conferences adding significantly to the avenues for entrepreneurial discourse. Clearly, these papers will not all agree. However, from the collated knowledge, its goal has been to describe and discuss the core elements of current knowledge of entrepreneurs based on their historical beginnings. This has been done, and there remain suggested trends that are developing that will shape the way in which business in the twenty-first century will be conducted. Always for the entrepreneur, this will be innovative, potentially risky, and pushing knowledge to the limits.

References

Arnold, R. (1996) *Economics*, Minneapolis, MN: West Publishing Company, 18.

Baumol, W. (1968) "Entrepreneurship in economic theory," *American Economic Review*, 58: 64–71.

Baumol, W. (1993) *Entrepreneurship, Management and the Structure of Payoffs*, Cambridge, MA: MIT Press.

Birch, D.L. (1979) *The Job Creation Process*, Cambridge, MA: MIT Program on Neighborhood and Regional Change 8.

Brazeal, D.V. and Azriel, J.A. (2002) "Learning to cruise on 'Internet time': making the connection between strategic entrepreneurial archetypes and environmental scanning activities," *An Entrepreneurial Bonanza*, proceedings of the 16th Annual USASBE National Conference, January 17–20.

Buchanan, J.M. and Di Pierro, A. (1980) "Cognition, choice and entrepreneurship," *Southern Economic Journal*, 46(3): 693–701.

Burnett, D. (2000) *Hunting for Heffalumps: The Supply of Entrepreneurship and Economic*

Development. Online, available at: http://www.technoproneurial.com/articles/history.asp (accessed June 3, 2003).

Bygrave, W.D. and Hofer, C.W. (1991) "Theorizing about entrepreneurship," *Entrepreneurship Theory and Practice*, Winter 16(2): 13–22.

Cantillon, R. (2003) *Essai sur la Nature du Commerce en General (Essay on the Nature of Trade in General)*, Frank Cass and Company, 1959. Trans. Henry Higgs, Library of Economics and Liberty.

Carree, M., van Stel, A., Thurik, R., and Wennekers, S. (2000) *Business Ownership and Economic Growth in 23 OECD Countries*. Online, available at: http://www.fee.uva.nl/bieb/edocs/TI/2000/TI00001.pdf.

Casson, M. (1982) *The Entrepreneur: an Economic Theory*, Oxford: Blackwell.

Colleran, K. and Ginsberg, S. (2002) Students as entrepreneurs. Proceedings USASBE Conference, Hilton Head, U.S.

Davidsson, P. and Wiklund, J. (1995) *Cultural Values and Regional Variations in New Firm Foundation*. Online, available at: http://www.babson.edu/entrep/fer/papers95/per.htm.

Drucker, P.F. (1964) *Managing for Results*, New York, NY: Harper & Row.

Drucker, P.F. (1985) *Innovation and Entrepreneurship: Practices and Principles*, New York, NY: Harper & Row, 220–225.

Duffy, S.G., Nixdorff, J.L., Ezzedeen, S., Filtzer, D., Millman, A., and Winslow, E.K. (2002) "Designing undergraduate women's entrepreneurship education: encouraging entrepreneurial success through knowledge, skills, and experience," *An Entrepreneurial Bonanza*, proceedings of the 16th Annual USASBE National Conference, January 17–20.

Ellis, W.H. (1983) *Canadian Entrepreneurs: Innovators or Manipulators*, paper presented at the 2nd international conference of the International Council for Small Business, Halifax, Nova Scotia, Canada, June 26 to 29. Also in Vesper, K.H. (1982) *Frontiers of Entrepreneurship Research*, Wellesley, MA: Babson Center for Entrepreneurial Studies, pp. 16–24.

Ely, R.T. and Hess, R.H. (1893) *Outline of Economics*, New York, NY: Macmillan.

Fairlie, R. and Robb, A. (2002) "Minority business and public policy," *An Entrepreneurial Bonanza*, proceedings of the 16th Annual USASBE National Conference, January 17–20.

Filion, L.J. (1998) "From entrepreneurship to entreprenology: the emergence of a new discipline," *Journal of Enterprising Culture*, 6(1): 1–23.

Galbraith, J.K. (1967) *The New Industrial State*, Harmondsworth: Penguin.

Gibb, A. and Ritchie, J. (1981) "Influence on entrepreneurship: a study over time," in *Bolton Ten Years On*, Proceedings of the U.K. Small Business Research Conference held November 20 and 21 at the Polytechnic of Central London.

Gillis, M., Perkins, D.H., Roemer, M., and Snodgrass, D.R. (1996) *Economics of Development*, New York, NY: W.W. Norton & Company.

Higgins, B.H. (1959) *Economic Development: Principles, Problems, and Policies*, New York, NY: Norton.

Hileman, A.E., Altman, J., Edminster, P. *et al.* (2002) "Issues in entrepreneurship: identifying best practices by American Indian tribes," *An Entrepreneurial Bonanza*, proceedings of the 16th Annual USASBE National Conference, January 17–20.

Hoselitz, B.F. (1952) "Entrepreneurship and economic growth," *American Journal of Economic Sociology*, 97–106.

Julien, P.A. and Marchesnay, M. (1996) *L'entrepreneuriat*, Paris: Economica.

Kautz, J. (2003) "Social entrepreneurism," *History of Entrepreneurism*. Online, available at: www.smallbusinessnotes.com/history/histent.html (accessed June 3, 2003).

Kihlstrom, R.E. and Laffont, J.-J. (1979) "A general equilibrium entrepreneurial theory of firm based on risk aversion," *Journal of Political Economy*, 87(4): 719–748.

Kilby, P. (1971) *Entrepreneurship and Economic Development*, New York, NY: Free Press.

Kilby, P. (1983) "An entrepreneurial problem," *The American Economic Review*, 73: 107–111.

Kirchhoff, B.A. (1992) "Entrepreneurship's contribution to economics," *Entrepreneurship Theory and Practice*, Winter: 93–111.

Kirzner, I. (1973) *Competition and Entrepreneurship*, Chicago, IL: The University of Chicago Press.

Kirzner, I. (1976) "Discussion," in *The Economic System, in an Age of Discontinuity: Long Range Planning or Market Reliance?* New York, NY: New York University Press.

Kirzner, I. (1983) "Entrepreneur and the entrepreneurial function: a commentary," in Ronen, J. (ed.) *Entrepreneurship: Where Did It Come From, and Where Is It Going?* Lexington, MA: Lexington Books.

Kirzner, I.M. (1985) *Discovery and the Capitalist Process*, Chicago, IL: The University of Chicago Press.

Kjeilen, T. (2000) *Safety in Morocco*. Online, available at: www.lexicorient.com/morocco/z_safety.htm (accessed December 6, 2000).

Klees, E. (1995) *Entrepreneurs In History: Success vs. Failure*, Rochester, NY: Cameo Press.

Knight, F.H. (1921) *Risk, Uncertainty, and Profit*, New York, NY: Century Press.

Lavoie, D. (1985) "A new era for female entrepreneurship in the 80's," *Journal of Small Business, Canada*, Winter: 34–43.

Leibenstein, H. (1978) "On the basic proposition of X-efficiency theory," *American Economic Review*, 68(2): 328–332.

Leibenstein, H. (1995) "The supply of entrepreneurship," *Leading Issues in Economic Development*, New York, NY: Oxford University Press, pp. 273–275.

Long, W. (1983) "The meaning of entrepreneurship," *American Journal of Small Business*, 8(2): 47–59.

Marshall, A. (1994) *Principles of Economics*, Philadelphia: Porcupine Press, 248–250. In Doen, M.L., Cees, G., Nijkamp, P., and Rietveld, P. (eds) *Ethnic Entrepreneurship and Migration: A Survey from Developing Countries*. Online, available at: http://www.fee.uva.nl/bieb/edocs/TI/1998/ TI98081.pdf, 1998 (accessed June 3, 2003).

McClelland, D.C. (1961) *The Achieving Society*, Princeton, NJ: Van Nostrand.

McClelland, D.C. (1971) "Entrepreneurship and achievement motivation: approaches to the science of socioeconomic development," in Lengyel, P. (ed.) Paris: U.N.E.S.C.O.

McGraw, T.K. (1991) "Schumpeter ascending: re-emerging intellectual interest in entrepreneurship, innovation, and economic development," *The American Scholar*, 60: 371–392.

McGuire, J.W. (1976) "The small enterprise in economics and organization theory," *Journal of Contemporary Business*, 5(2): 115–138.

Mill, J.S. (1848) "The principles of political economy with some of their applications to social philosophy," London: John W. Parker.

Moore, D.P. and Buttner, E.H. (1997) *Women Entrepreneurs: Moving Beyond the Glass Ceiling*, Thousand Oaks, CA: Sage.

Muoio, A. (1997) "Unit of one: they have a better idea . . . do you?," *Fast Company*, August.

Newman, P.C. (1981) *The Acquisitors*, Toronto: McClelland and Stewart.

Oxenfeldt, A.R. (1943) *New Firms and Free Enterprise: Pre-War and Post-War Aspects*, Washington, DC: American Council of Public Affairs.

Pavlov, V. (2000) *The Fundamentals of Entrepreneurship*, Moscow: The Moscow Institute of Business Administration.

Penrose, E.T. (1959) *The Theory of the Growth of the Finn*, Oxford: Basil Blackwell, New York, NY: Wiley.

Praag, C.M. and Van Ophem, H. (1995) "Determinants of willingness and opportunity to start as an entrepreneur," *Kyklos*, 48(4): 513–540.

Reich, R.B. (1987) "Entrepreneurship reconsidered: the team as hero," *Harvard Business Review*, May/June.

Reynolds, P.D., Hay, M., Bygrave, W.D., Camp, S.M., and Autio, E. (2000) *Global Entrepreneurship Monitor: 2000 Executive Report*, Babson College, Kauffman Center for Entrepreneurial Leadership and the Marion Kauffman Foundation, London Business School.

Reynolds, P.D., Bygrave, W.D., Hay, M.G., Autio, E., and Cox, L.W. (2002) *Global Entrepreneurship Monitor: 2002 Executive Report*, Babson College, London Business School and Ewing Marion Kauffman Foundation.

Sandberg, W.R. (1992) "Strategic management's potential contributions to a theory of entrepreneurship," *Entrepreneurship Theory and Practice*, 16(3): 73–90.

Say, J.B. (1815) *Catechisme d'economie politique*: translated (1821) by John Richter, *Catechism of Political Economy*, London: Sherwood.

Schloss, H.H. (1968) "The concept of entrepreneurship in economic development," *Journal of Economic Issues*, June: 228–232.

Schumpeter, J.A. (1928) "The Instability of Capitalism," *Economic Journal*, XXXVIII, September: 361–368.

Schumpeter, J.A. (1934) *The Theory of Economic Development*, Cambridge, MA: Harvard Business School Press.

Schumpeter, J.A. (1951) *Essays of J.A. Schumpeter*, Cambridge, MA: Addison Wesley Press, Inc.

Smilor, R.W. (1997) "Entrepreneurship in the next century: where will venture capitalists find their next pearl?," *Journal of Private Equity*, 1(2).

Swartz, E. (2002) *"Ultra-modern": The Emergence of a New Breed of Female Entrepreneur in the United States of America*, Female Entrepreneurs Networking Group (FENG), Rothman Institute of Entrepreneurial Studies, Center for Women's Business Research, Fairleigh Dickinson University.

Toulouse, J.M. (1979) *L'entrepreneurship au Québec*, Montreal: Les Presses HEC et Fides.

Vérin, H. (1982) *Entrepreneurs, enterprises, histoire d'une idée*, Paris: Presses universitaires de France.

Vesper, K. (1999) *Maintaining Focus: Entrepreneurship Education, Research and Service*. Fairleigh Dickinson University Rothman Institute of Entrepreneurial Studies. Online, available at: http://www.fdu.edu/academic.rothman/vesperessay.htm (accessed June 3, 2003).

Weber, M. (1930) *The Protestant Ethic and the Spirit of Capitalism*, translated by Talcott Parsons, London: Allen & Unwin.

Welsch, H.P. and Kuhns, B.A. (2002) "Community-based enterprises: propositions and cases," *An Entrepreneurial Bonanza*, proceedings of the 16th Annual USASBE National Conference, January 17–20.

Whyte, W.H. (1956) *The Organization Man*, New York, NY: Simon & Schuster.

Wilken, P.H. (1979) *Entrepreneurship: A Comparative and Historical Study*, Norwood, NJ: Ablex Publishing Corporation.

Chapter 4

John Sibley Butler

The University of Texas at Austin

THE SCIENCE AND PRACTICE OF NEW BUSINESS VENTURES: WEALTH CREATION AND PROSPERITY THROUGH ENTREPRENEURSHIP GROWTH AND RENEWAL

THE CREATION OF NEW BUSINESS organizations for economic prosperity is one of the oldest activities of people throughout history. The study of this process, which has been called entrepreneurship, has occupied the minds of scholars for centuries. The economic arrangement that enhances entrepreneurship, capitalism, has had to fight its way through competitive types of economic structures throughout history. The decline of the Soviet Union, and the intense interest in market economies, has made the demand for knowledge about the entrepreneurial process great. Although there are different kinds of market economies, new venture creation must stand at the center of it all. Given this reality, it is not surprising that the demand to move from theories of entrepreneurship to the "doing" of entrepreneurship is intense world-wide, as well as in the U.S.A.

Historically, theorizing about entrepreneurship has been done across many different disciplines, including history, engineering, anthropology, economics, sociology, and psychology. In the last three decades or so, business schools have taken center stage in the academy for the study of entrepreneurship. Chaired professors and entrepreneurial centers are indicators of the commitment of business schools around the U.S.A. and the world. The same thing is happening in the disciplines that make up colleges of engineering and natural sciences.

Despite all of the historical scholarship developed by scholars, we do not have a "science of entrepreneurship." The question is whether or not what we call the *study* of entrepreneurship across all disciplines can be carved into the *science* of entrepreneurship. The purpose of this chapter is to share with you my ideas on the science of new ventures; ideas that I hope will further advance the academic study of this discipline as well as the "do" or practice part of entrepreneurial education.

In order to achieve our purpose, the first section of the chapter concentrates on the historical and theoretical knowledge that has been generated around the field of new venture development. We also pay attention to the nature of science and disciplines that have been engaged in creating measurable, theoretical models of entrepreneurship. The second section concentrates on how the entrepreneurial process, or what I call the "do" or practice of entrepreneurship, is integrated with the theoretical model that disciplines have created. We do this by concentrating on what the research literature calls "the Austin Model."

Science has been defined as a systematic procedure for explaining phenomena that is empirical in nature. Of course empirical simply means things that one can observe and measure. Phenomena are events, occurrences that appear in patterns in nature, processes, events, and groups of people, behaviors, beliefs, opinions, emotions, feelings, and thoughts. The purpose of the science of something is to explain the something; this explanation is based on a set of interrelated statements that produce a theory. A theory sets out to provide an understanding about a phenomenon, paying special attention to the conditions under which it occurs and, when this is done, prediction is possible.

To be sure, the academic literature has developed a strong tradition of scholarship observing the phenomenon of "entrepreneurship" and creating testable propositions. Can we pull from this massive literature information that can contribute to the development of a science of entrepreneurship, with practical implications for professional schools? It is important to note that this early literature does not have a "do" component for entrepreneurship. This literature can be divided into two parts. The first is from the ancient world, and comes to us as a result of the hard work of business history and anthropology; next is the literature that is concerned with the development of the ideas that had an influence on the development of "modern" market societies that depend on entrepreneurship, including the contributions of "economic theory," which was more concerned with developing a theory of economics than about accounting for entrepreneurship. Although these traditions overlap, they stand as separate contributions to the literature. Understanding these traditions moves us toward what I call the science of new ventures.

Data from anthropology inform us that wealth creation through entrepreneurship has existed for centuries and that the region is the unit of analysis; or that the region stands at the center of new venture development. As they excavate business tablets of ancient civilizations, the theoretical paradigms of how regions create enterprises through innovation and entrepreneurship come to life (Moore and Davis 1999). For example, in order for enterprises to work on first a regional and then a "global" scale (or "old-world" scale), the ancient Assyrians created structures that involved transfer of innovations, the creation of knowledge workers, and the development of a standard form of communication (Luckenbill 1926).

Students of the ancient world recognize that pottery was invented in the ancient East no later than the early sixth millennium BC. From a theoretical point of view, one can say that the ancient Assyrians, who inherited a system of private enterprise from Sumer and Babylon, were largely responsible for its commercialization throughout the ancient world. It was made of skillfully fired clay and painted in attractive patterns and became highly valued. The Assyrians also wove textiles with newly-invented spindle whorls, used knives made of obsidian and chert, and used ax-shaped implements made of stone (Albright 1985). Also around this time it was discovered that, when soft red-brown copper ore was mixed with tin in a very hot furnace, bronze could be produced. This made it possible for the production of sturdy plows, tools for construction, kitchen utensils, and a host of other items that were commercialized around the ancient world (Moore and Lewis 1999).

Business history asks questions such as: how did spin-off civilizations such as Babylon and Assyria develop a region with a competitive advantage so superior to other civilizations? As asked by Moore and Lewis (1999: 44), "Why did Mesopotamian Iraq come to excel in world politics and trade while richer lands like Egypt, India and China played more peripheral roles?"

The answer given by ancient regional advantage scholars revolves around the introduction and commercialization of technologies. In this case, the record clearly shows that between 3100 BC and 2900 BC the Bronze Age started and gained momentum. As a result, an urban revolution started as dense clusters of cities such as Kish, Ur, Lagash, Hamazi, and Shurppak started to take shape. Certainly the same phenomenon would take place in other parts of the ancient world. Regions such as Anatolia, the Indus Valley, Syria, and northern Mesopotamia would experience growth. But it was the Sumerians who saw people crowding into cities searching for new economic opportunities as they took the lead in capital formation, technology transfer, and urban development (Moore and Lewis 1999).

Just as the discovery of knowledge for other disciplines started in the ancient world (e.g. mathematics, engineering), a science of entrepreneurship should include patterns of new venture start-ups during this time period. Thus business history becomes a strong component as we think about constructing a science of new venture development.

Early scholarship within the Western tradition tried to account for social structures which produced people who started new ventures. Writing in the late 1800s, the German scholar and sociologist Georg Simmel (Wolf 1950) was fascinated by the introduction of entrepreneurial behavior into hunting and gathering societies. What fascinated him was the fact that the entrepreneurs, or those who introduced market economies to these societies and developed innovations in marketing, product development, and what we now call technology transfer, were never from the local communities they found themselves in. Simmel did not refer to these early people as entrepreneurs but, rather, simply called them strangers. Scholars who write in the tradition of Simmel argue that these "strangers" came at a time when subsistence agriculture and home crafts were in decline and represented the city, cosmopolitan values, customs that were strange and a different way of life (Butler and Green 1997). In the tradition of early scholarship in Europe, Simmel identified strangers as distinctive ethnic groups who occupied the position as business people because they were new to communities and could not find work in established jobs of the state. In addition, entrepreneurship, money lending, and commerce were not considered prestigious, and indeed were looked down upon. It was the strangers, therefore, who were forced into this activity for economic stability. Simmel's work produced scholarship on all continents that examined strangers and business activities in the "old world" (Butler and Greene 1997).

From a theoretical point of view, this literature from the experiences of old-world merchants makes a structural contribution to the study of entrepreneurship, in the sense that it is socially embedded and emerges from the experiences of individuals and their group. As such the approach is strictly sociological. This is opposite of the psychological literature, which would emerge and concentrate on traits of individuals (Hornaday and Abound 1971; McClelland 1961). We can also add that this early research provided the theoretical reasoning for the strong tradition of studies on immigrant entrepreneurship in America (Butler 1991; Butler and Greene 1997; Light 1972). I also believe that the stranger concept can account for individuals who do not complete formal education and become "strangers" to the process of creating a strong educational resume. Being outside of the qualification system of education, they pursue their dreams as strangers and thus become entrepreneurs.

Max Weber, a scholar of society and economics, acknowledges the importance of the stranger in the development of business activity, but argued that, after the Reformation, there was a change in the value structure of society and entrepreneurship was embraced. In *The Protestant Ethic and the Spirit of Capitalism* (1930), he argued that the ideas developed by Protestants legitimated the process of business development and innovation. Put differently, he argued that capitalism in Europe received a critical stimulus from thinkers such as Calvin and Luther that allowed a break from guild traditionalism and the negative attitude toward strangers (Butler and Greene 1997). Weber also introduced ideas of the boundedness and the maintenance of enforceable trust within social networks (Butler and Greene 1997; Spencer 1995). He argued that the first people to develop this new economic approach were merchants who belonged to the Protestant sects. Their methods of hard work, or what is called the "protestant work ethic," soon lost its original religious tone and became thoroughly secular (Swedberg 2000). In his later work, Weber turns from arguments about the origin of the spirit of entrepreneurship to how individuals respond to opportunities within the economy and questions of innovation and business creation (Swedberg 2000). Werner Sombart, in *The Jews and Modern Capitalism* (1951), challenged Weber's Protestant assumptions, and traced the contributions of Judaism's contribution to the philosophical and practical side of market economies. This debate happened at a time when the study of religion stood at the center of behavioral explanations.

One of the most interesting things about the historical data on the study of entrepreneurship is what the discipline of economics, or mainstream economics, has not done. Indeed, the economist William Baumol wrote an article in 1968 which noted that the entrepreneur had almost disappeared from the study of economics, and the whole thing was something like a performance of

Hamlet with the Danish prince missing (Baumol 1968; Swedberg 2000). Bruck Kirchhoff's article, "Entrepreneurship's Contribution to Economics," urges economists to desert their major guiding idea, equilibrium theory, and search for a new macro-theory that incorporates entrepreneurship (1991).

The theoretical shelf of Joseph Schumpeter shows the importance of entrepreneurship within a general theory of our capitalism economy. Like a voice in the wilderness, he set out to show that a theory of economics has to include the entrepreneur. Set against the theoretical background of equilibrium theory, which can be seen in the writings of the "classical economists" from Ricardo, to Mill, Marx, and Keynes, he finds a place for not only entrepreneurs, but also entrepreneurial profit. Perhaps Peter Drucker gives the best interpretation:

> Schumpeter's *Economic Development* does what neither the classical economists nor Marx nor Keynes was able to do: it makes profit fulfill an economic function. In the economy of change and innovation, profit, in contrast to Marx and his theory, is not a *Mehrwert*, a "surplus value" stolen from the workers. On the contrary, it is the only source of jobs for workers and of labor income. The theory of economic development shows that no one except the innovator makes a genuine "profit"; and the innovator's profit is always quite short-lived. But innovation in Schumpeter's famous phrase is also "creative destruction." It makes obsolete yesterday's capital equipment and capital investment. The more an economy progresses, the more capital formation will it therefore need. Thus what the classical economist – or the accountant or the stock exchange – considers "profit" is a genuine cost, the cost of staying in business, the cost of a future in which nothing is predictable except that today's profitable business will become tomorrow's white elephant. Thus, capital formation and productivity are needed to maintain the wealth-producing capacity of the economy and, above all, to maintain today's jobs and to create tomorrow's jobs.
>
> (Drucker 1986: 109–110)

Schumpeter argued that innovation should be included within analysis of the economic system, rather than something that is foreign or outside of the system.

No other economic scholar has been showcased as much as Schumpeter in what we called entrepreneurial studies. Because his ideas are about a theory of economics, he augured that capitalism would destroy itself. But the destruction of capitalism, even if he were correct, does not mean the destruction of the entrepreneur. Understanding this point brings us closer to understanding the science of innovation and entrepreneurship.

Business schools and the entrepreneurial phenomenon

The last two decades saw a boom in interest in entrepreneurship because of structural changes that occurred world-wide. International competition in key industries, and the movement of manufacturing away from mainland America, created hard economic times. Large enterprises that traditionally provided the core of jobs were struggling, and the future did not look pleasant. David Birch, in 1979, took notice of the developing "entrepreneurial economy" and published a work that concluded that "small enterprises" created about 66 percent of all new jobs in America, whereas "middle sized and large firms provided relatively few new jobs when all things are considered" (Birch 1979). In that same year, *Inc.* magazine occupied the newsstand and along with publications like *Business Week* and *Fortune*, enjoyed tremendous success. America was in the process of rediscovering its entrepreneurial roots and would create wealth in certain regions that created new jobs, opportunities, and hope.

The tremendous growth of interest in entrepreneurship in the larger society saw a parallel interest in business schools. Unlike early theorizing on entrepreneurship that developed in social sciences, business schools became serious about the teaching of entrepreneurial process and growth. The big question was how to integrate this practice into research traditions of management, accounting, finance, and management science and information systems. Another related question was, and is, could business schools integrate the ideas on entrepreneurship that developed in the sciences since the 1700s? Put another way, can the theory of entrepreneurship be combined with the practice of entrepreneurship as we design courses for students in business schools as well as those in the overall academy?

These questions have become a matter of standard debate, and an interesting literature has evolved which tries to shed light on these issues. Perhaps the most systematic scholarly treatment appears in a work edited by Richard Swedberg entitled *Entrepreneurship: The Social Science View* (2000). As noted by Swedberg, the social sciences have played a minor role during the renewal period of entrepreneurship in America and the approach taken by business schools emphasized the practice rather than the theory.

Over the last two decades or so, business professors certainly have made their contributions to the theory and practice of entrepreneurship. Karl Vesper's (1997) review divided research into the psychology of entrepreneurship, the sociology of entrepreneurship, venture finance, and economic development through entrepreneurship. The Babson Research Conference has produced an impressive literature; works that bring research together (Sexton and Smilor 1986, 2000) serve to add continuity to the rapidly growing research area. This research is different from early efforts discussed earlier in this chapter because of the emphasis on "doing." As noted by Amar Bhidé (2000), the distinctive feature of most of the research and classroom teaching emphases in business schools is on entrepreneurial functions. There is a concentration on new product development, process, forms of organizations, the management of risk, and on the coordination of functions and inputs.

Despite the success of entrepreneurship within business schools, there is still the critical strain that faculty can bring to the table. A number of years ago a faculty member informed me that if students are interested in entrepreneurship, they should leave the business school and go do it, for there was nothing to teach them in the academy. As noted by Bhidé, some have argued that there is a sort of Heisenberg principle related to entrepreneurial acts; when reported in detail, the described act is no longer entrepreneurial. He further notes that literature has pointed out that the performance of new enterprises depends on things that cannot be studied and taught, and business scholars have argued that education in business administration was, at best, a minor factor in successful start-up enterprises. He drills further in the literature and notes that an experienced teacher of entrepreneurship argued, based on his data, that people who engage in entrepreneurship see no relationship between business education and their success. Instead, success was related to guts, timing, luck, and determination (Bhidé 2000).

Despite the critical strain, over the last two decades or so, business scholars have developed outstanding teaching programs in entrepreneurship throughout the U.S.A. Ideas from core business disciplines have been integrated into the teaching literature of entrepreneurship. We also have to concentrate on practice; to take knowledge and know-how from the academy to the region.

The Austin Model and the science of entrepreneurship

I remember the call from George Kozmetsky, former Dean of the Business School at The University of Texas at Austin, and founder of the IC^2 Institute, inviting me for a luncheon date to talk about the importance of combining the practice of entrepreneurship with the theory from "core" disciplines. I remember the excitement at the University of Texas at Austin when a laboratory at IC^2 Institute, the Austin Technology Incubator, was put in place to see if it could generate companies that could produce about 200 jobs. I also remember all of the people who could not see the vision, and what I have seen in Austin can only be described as a miracle in wealth creation and job creation, a process that must be constantly regenerated in the Schumpeter-type economy. More importantly, the model, which is based on the old agricultural model of county agents taking agricultural research from the academy and labs to the farmer in order to improve efficiency and yields, brings together the theory and best practices of new ventures and the overall entrepreneurial process.

Going beyond research and teaching entrepreneurship, and carrying innovations to the community, demands that we understand the timelessness of our task. What we call the Austin Model is based on the ancient science city. When we connect theory to practice, and past knowledge, we understand that cities which concentrated on creating wealth through entrepreneurship are not new. Thus Moore and Lewis note the following:

> Long before their armies marched up and down the Tigris and Euphrates to terrorize the ancient world, groups of talented Assyrian traders peacefully took up residence in foreign countries hundreds of kilometers away from home, being welcomed by the prince of Babylon, Aram and even distant Anatolia as a blessing and not a scourge. As they formed their numerous commercial colonies in foreign lands, these old Assyrian merchants of the second millennium BC perfected

a thousand-year-old system of private enterprise inherited from
Sumer and Babylon. Living and trading near the dawn of civil-
ization, these corporate traders, moreover, were innovative to a
startling degree, for the commercial structures they created may
rightly be described as one of the first attempts at the "entrepreneurial government" being celebrated in the 1990s. Even more
importantly, the business operated by the ancient Assyrian colonists
constituted the first genuine multinational enterprises in recorded
history.

(Moore and Lewis 1999: 27)

The major contribution of Moore and Lewis's work, and others in this tradition (for example Rostow 1978; Lewis 1998) is that it connects the past to the
present, and provides the patterns for a science of entrepreneurship. This scholarship notes that all of the characteristics associated with the modern literature
on successful business communities and enterprises were found in the ancient
world. Branding and advertising, global economies, virtual corporations, the
rise of nations, foreign investment attraction, industry clusters, knowledge-
based economy and knowledge workers, being mean and lean, could be found
in the ancient world. More importantly, the practice of entrepreneurship is
ingrained into the history of the world. Given all of the historical data, one
would think that we would have a science of entrepreneurship, with metrics
coming from the rich historical data from the ancient world to the present.

Annalee Saxenian, in *Regional Advantage: Culture and Competition in Silicon
Valley and Route 128* (1996) documented an interesting comparison between the
latter two communities. From a theoretical point of view, these communities
are the most recent permutations of forms that we have seen since the ancient
Assyrians.

Thirty years ago, Austin was a solid town with job opportunities dominated
by state government and education. As the Texas state capital, government provided some of the best jobs. The University of Texas at Austin also provided a
job market. Within both domains there were primary jobs that provided for
great mobility and had great benefits, and secondary jobs that did not have these
advantages. There were the usual "mom" and "pop" stores and insurance companies that provided service to the community. But, for the most part, Austin
was viewed as a place to go for an education at one of its many universities and
colleges, and then find a great job in a major metropolis of the state or somewhere further afield.

George Kozmetsky founded the IC^2 Institute in the School of Business and
the transformation was put in practice (Cooper *et al.* 1997). The concept of
technopolis was introduced to Austin as a model, *ca.* 1989, at a conference
hosted by the IC^2 Institute. As noted by David Gibson, an IC^2 Fellow who has
chronicled the emergence of Austin as a technopolis:

the roots of technopolis – a utopian, radiant city based on science
and technology – sprang from the humanistic mind of the Renaissance. The first example was T. Campanella's 17th-century vision of

a "City of the Sun." This was a culturally diverse, polytechnical city –
a showcase of science and continuing education. There, science was
not just for an aristocratic elite. Philosophers, political planners and
social prophets were intrigued by the idea of creating a "city of light,"
designed and ruled by wise scientists, where research and innovation
were a way of life and invention and creativity were venerated. The
ideal cities were to be the poles around which the economy of
nations would grow and society would progress.

(Gibson 1999: 50–52)

Gibson further notes that the modern technopolis – *techno* for technology
and *polis* being Greek for city-state – combines research and invention with the
practical applications of technology through innovation.

The technopolis is an innovative approach to economic development and
links technology commercialization with effective public and private sector initiatives to create new infrastructures for wealth and job development and global
competition. The emphasis is on providing both strategic and tactical know-how
into developing infrastructures for the twenty-first century (Gibson *et al.* 1992;
Porter 2001).

The emphasis on the technopolis, or the theory and practice of entrepreneurship, is on researching and creating structures so that entrepreneurs can
flourish. It means creating landing zones for ideas so that high-growth start-up
companies can create wealth and jobs – and the entrepreneurial spirit can multiply within a community. The unit of analysis is moved from nations, as was
done in Adam Smith's *Wealth of Nations*, to the city or region. The literature on
entrepreneurship has certainly captured the importance of regions. Indeed, any
analysis of wealth creation from the ancient world shows that the concentration
was on structures within regions that produced wealth and jobs.

What are these structures that are important for the development of new
ventures, as we make a concentrated effort to combine practice with theory?
Or, as David Gibson (1999) has asked, how do we anoint a city or region with
light and wisdom? Research shows that there should be a high quality of education at all levels, from kindergarten to the graduate student and beyond, vision-
aries and implementers at the regional level who come from academia, business,
and government – and an entrepreneurial culture. A technopolis is energized by
start-ups and mid-size firms, not just large ones. The best technology research
leads to new industries and home-grown tech companies, and a globally
competitive infrastructure, both "physical," as in roads, airports, the Internet,
and city services, and "smart," as in talent, capital, and know-how (Gibson
1999). It also helps if the area is a great place to live.

The first thing that one recognizes here is that when you anoint a city with
light and wisdom, there are many partnerships that must be developed. More
specifically, it is a partnership between universities, the public sector, and the
political sector. Within the partnership the university provides know-how networks to individuals who are engaged in the start-up process. Innovations and
technologies are transferred from public laboratories and university laboratories. In the case of Austin, an experimental laboratory, which everyone now

knows as the Austin Technology Incubator, served as the place where new ideas were tested and developed. This laboratory has been very successful over the years, and was the only institution in the city devoted to start-ups until the process became commonplace to many institutions and enterprises. In a sense, it was the catalyst, along with the broader university and city and county government, that created the entrepreneurial revolution in Austin.

The Austin Technology Incubator was founded by IC^2 in 1989 to create wealth, generate jobs, diversify Austin's economy, and to act as a learning laboratory for UT faculty, students, and staff. It incubated incubators in Silicon Valley, Houston, Texas, and Charleston, South Carolina, and developed an international reputation by recruiting start-ups from Brazil, Israel, Canada, Austria, and Japan. The companies it created also generated $280 million revenues in the year 2000 and 1.2 billion since 1989. Three companies are public on NASdaq (DTM, Concero, and Encore Orthopedics) and a dozen graduate companies from Austin Technology Incubator have been purchased, including Metrewerks by Motorola for $95 million, EXTI by BMC for $100 million, Exterprise by CommerceOne for $75 million, DTM Corporation by 3D Systems Cooperation for $45 million. Companies have raised more than $300 million in funding the last two years (www.ic2.org).

The major point in presenting the Austin example, which certainly has taken places in other parts of the world on different scales, is to stress the importance of theory and practice: entrepreneurship within the academy is most effective when it has a "do" component. Like all organizations, the Austin Technology Incubator is in the process of reinventing itself so that it can be positioned for its next contribution.

The start-up process, or the renewal and growth process, will certainly benefit from the know-how network within the disciplines of accounting finance, management, MSIS, and marketing. One has to understand when to inject this knowledge into the entrepreneurial process. Like the Agricultural Agent, who takes results from the laboratory to the farmer, the future of the professor of entrepreneurship is to become an entrepreneurial agent for wealth and job creation within cities and regions. Simply presenting case studies in class is a necessary but not a sufficient condition for the science and practice of entrepreneurship. Understanding historical data and historical clusters of wealth creation encourages the study of entrepreneurship to draw from disciplines such as sociology, business history, engineering, bio-technical sciences, and others.

As we concentrate on practice, it is also important to understand that new innovations within the academy are coming from disciplines as diverse as the bio-technical sciences, engineering, music, pharmacy, and other content-producing disciplines within the liberal arts. Partnership is the key word. At The University of Texas at Austin, one of the most popular courses is entitled "From Lab to Market," a management course cross-listed with the Colleges of Natural Sciences and Engineering. It is also drawing students from the Law School. They are interacting with venture capitalists, business angels, and the know-how networks within the Austin region.

A science of entrepreneurship draws together data from the history of people and seeks to explain the dynamics of wealth creation through innovation transfer and market economies. I think that this can be done, and requires the bringing together of broad theoretical frameworks that produce this dynamic science, which is forever changing with new ideas, new products, and the commercialization of those products.

References

Albright, W.F. (1985) "Assyria," *Encyclopedia Americana*, Danbury, CT: Grolier: 534–540.

Baumol, W. (1968) "Entrepreneurship in economic theory," *American Economic Review*, 58: 64–71.

Bhidé, A. (2000) *The Origin and Evolution of New Business*, Oxford: Oxford University Press.

Birch, D.L. (1979) *The Job Creation Process*, Cambridge, MA: MIT Program on Neighborhood and Regional Change.

Butler, J.S. (1991) *Entrepreneurship and Self-Help Among Black Americans: A Reconsideration of Race and Economics*, New York, NY: SUNY Press.

Butler, J.S. and Greene, P. (1997) "Ethnic entrepreneurship: the continuous rebirth of American enterprise," in Sexton, D.L. and Smilor, R.W. (eds) *Entrepreneurship 200*, Chicago, IL: Upstart Publishing Company.

Cooper, W.W., Thore, S., Gibson, D., and Phillips, F. (1997) *How IC² Institute Research Affects Public Policy and Business Practices*, London: Quorum Books.

Drucker, P.F. (1986) *The Frontiers of Management*, New York, NY: Truman Talley Books.

Gibson, D. (1999) "Anointing a city of light and wisdom," *Austin American Statesman*, Austin, TX: Technopolis section.

Gibson, D., Kozmetsky, G., and Smilor, R. (1992) *The Technopolis Phenomenon: Smart Cities, Fast Systems, Global Networks*, Savage, MD: Rowman & Littlefield.

Hornaday, J.A. and Aboud, J. (1971) "Characteristics of successful entrepreneurs," *Personnel Psychology*, 24: 141–153.

Kirchhoff, B.A. (1991) "Entrepreneurship's contribution to economics," *Entrepreneurship Theory and Practice*, 16(2): 93–111.

Lewis, D. (1998) "The return of Charlemagne: the Middle Ages, the European and the European Right," *Florileium*, The University of Western Ontario.

Light, I. (1972) *Ethnic Enterprise in America: Welfare Among Chinese, Japanese and Blacks*, Berkeley, CA: University of California Press.

Luckenbill, D. (1926) *Ancient Records of Assyria and Babylonia: Historical Records of Assyria*, Chicago, IL: University of Chicago Press.

McClelland, D.C. (1961) *The Achieving Society*, Princeton, NJ: Van Nostrand.

Moore, K. and Lewis, D. (1999) *Birth of the Multinational: 2000 Years of Ancient Business History*, Copenhagen: Copenhagen Business School Press.

Porter, W.A. (2001) *The Knowledge Seekers: How to Turn your Community into an Engine for Economic Success*. Austin, TX: The IC² Institute: London Road Design.

Rinder, N.B. (1958) "Stranger in the land: social relations in the status gap," *Social Problems*, 6: 253–260.

Rostow, W. (1978) *The World Economy: History and Prospect*, Austin, TX: The University of Texas Press.

Saxenian, A. (1994) *Regional Advantage*, Cambridge, MA: Harvard University Press.

Saxenian, A. (1996) *Regional Advantage: Culture and Competition in Silicon Valley and Route 128*, Cambridge, MA: Harvard University Press.

Sexton, D.L. and Smilor, R. (1986) *The Art and Science of Entrepreneurship*, Cambridge, MA: Ballinger Publishing Company.

Sexton, D.L. and Smilor, R. (1997) *Entrepreneurship 2000*, Chicago, IL: Upstart Publishing Company.

Simmel, G. (1950) "The stranger," in Wolf, K. (ed.) *The Sociology of Georg Simmel*, Glencoe, IL: The Free Press.

Simon, G. (1993) "Immigrant entrepreneurs in France," in DeJong, G. and Gardner, R.W. (eds) *Immigrants and Entrepreneurship: Culture, Capital and Ethnic Networks*, New Brunswick, NJ: Transaction Publishers.

Sombart, W. (1951) *The Jews and Modern Capitalism*, New Brunswick, NJ: Transaction Press.

Spencer, R. (1995) "Progress and success in the development of Black-owned franchise units," *Review of Black Political Economy*, 22(2): 73–88.

Swedberg, R. (ed.) (2000) *Entrepreneurship: The Social Science View*, Oxford: Oxford University Press.

Vesper, K.H. (1997) "Subfields of entrepreneurial research," *Proceedings of the 37th Annual Meetings of the Academy of Management*, Orlando, FL: Academy of Management.

Weber, M. (1930) *The Protestant Ethic and the Spirit of Capitalism*, New York, NY: Charles Scribner and Sons.

Wolf, K (ed.) (1950) *The Sociology of Georg Simmel*, Glencoe, IL: Free Press.

Zenner, W. (1991) *Minorities in the Middle: A Cross-Cultural Analysis*, Albany, NY: State University of New York Press.

Chapter 5

Harold P. Welsch

DePaul University

Mark A. Maltarich

University of Wisconsin at Madison

EMERGING PATTERNS OF ENTREPRENEURSHIP: DISTINGUISHING ATTRIBUTES OF AN EVOLVING DISCIPLINE

Overview

A SIGNIFICANT AMOUNT of academic attention has been directed at the academic discipline of entrepreneurship. In Chapter 2, Howard Stevenson traces the journey of the field of entrepreneurship within the academic community. The now-respected field found its starting point as an academic curiosity not to be taken seriously. As it moved forward, editors published newspaper accounts of the virtues and success of entrepreneurs, and research articles investigated the nature of entrepreneurship. Gradually, the strength of the field and the extent of its impact on society led it to gather momentum, attract investigators who added infrastructure and theory. Universities offered courses, then programs, and finally degrees in the field. Foundations established endowed chairs in entrepreneurship. In the 50 years since the first entrepreneurship course, enrollment has increased from 188 to an estimated 180,000. The number of entrepreneurship classes has skyrocketed to over 2,200 at over 1,600 institutions, and more than 44 academic journals have been founded (Katz 2003).

Individual branches of entrepreneurship can be seen as following a parallel path. As innovators devise new methods of exploiting opportunity, they may spread and develop, or they may fade away. If one survives, its practitioners will organize, it will be defined and quantified, and eventually organized theories that explain it will develop and be tested.

Using as a basis the historical work done in parallel investigations, this chapter presents:

1   a taxonomy for branches of practice in various stages of development, that will classify them according to their level of development as clusters, classes, or categories;
2   a set of criteria to identify the progress a branch of practice has made along this trajectory – their numbers, the existence of associations, the conduct of empirical research and availability of descriptive statistics, and the development and testing of systematic theories around it; and
3   some implications for further investigation and the field of entrepreneur-ship as a whole.

Introduction

In order to build and assess a taxonomy of emerging branches of entrepreneur-ship, one must begin with an examination of the branches themselves – their origin and context.

Adaptation

Entrepreneurship has been characterized by its adaptability, which is comprised of flexibility, a realistic view, a global perspective, and an ability to deal with technology among key factors for success (Thomas 2003). Each of these factors is predicated on the ability to change quickly, nimbly adapt to a changing environment, and grow as a consequence.

Certainly, the successful entrepreneur is adaptive. Similarly, the innovative nature of the entrepreneurship field has resulted in a chaotic mass of constantly appearing branches of entrepreneurship. Some of these emerging branches will develop into full fields, and others may diffuse, merge or fold into other sectors.

Incongruities in adaptation

Figure 5.1 shows that those interested in entrepreneurship generally specialize according to their relation to the entrepreneurial process: they either practice it, study and teach it, or finance it. This classification of specializations surrounding the field of entrepreneurship is quite well established.

Though the practitioner's side of entrepreneurship is ever-changing, the financial and educational support functions around entrepreneurship have evolved with relatively well-defined boundaries within established frameworks. The specialization of entrepreneurial finance is extraordinarily structured. The

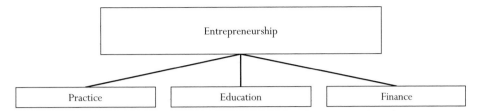

Figure 5.1 Structure of the entrepreneurship field

very reason the area is not discussed here is that it consists of very well-defined boundaries and has developed its own growth pattern and subspecialties. Small-business financiers generally fit neatly into the framework shown in Figure 5.2.

Entrepreneurship education is also quite well defined and can be visualized as fitting within the framework presented in Figure 5.3. The E-University is an example of the efforts of educators to expand the scope of their educational efforts. However, although it is less structured than the finance area, education has established a solid framework in which to hold its constituents.

The practice of entrepreneurship, however, is seen as a seething cauldron of bubbling activity and new developments – full of innovations and evolving concepts, constantly changing, and in many cases eluding classification. The ephemeral nature of many of these budding activities means that any framework built to hold them must allow for constant change. Figure 5.4 illustrates the loose structure of these sectors.

The incongruity between the loose structure and rapid change of the practice of entrepreneurship, and the relatively rigid structure and slower rate of change for the academic treatment of entrepreneurship, suggests a need to identify emerging trends quickly and focus academic efforts on those emerging branches that are likely to develop and increase in relevance. This chapter builds a foundation for distinguishing developing branches and evaluating their progress.

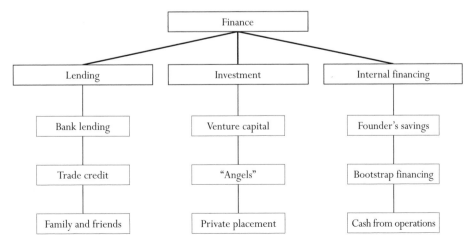

Figure 5.2 Structure of entrepreneurial finance

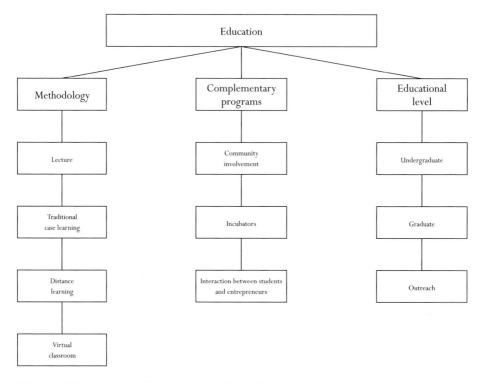

Figure 5.3 Structure of entrepreneurship education

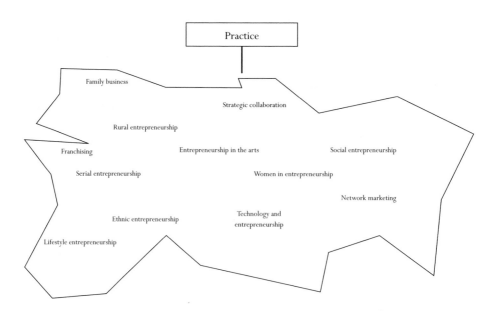

Figure 5.4 Structure of entrepreneurial practice

Taxonomy and criteria

Trajectory of entrepreneurial branches

Like political movements, marketing fads, and scientific beliefs, emerging branches of entrepreneurial practice come and go in a predictable fashion. Many different styles and types of entrepreneurship arise. Some are found to be unsuccessful and are abandoned, while others, because of necessities in the marketplace, efficiencies of the branch, or competitive advantage, are blessed with acceptance. These may spread and become common, widespread, or even standard practices. The ascension of entrepreneurship branches exhibits many similarities to the biological evolution described by Charles Darwin – and characterized as – survival of the fittest (Aldrich and Martinez 2000).

As emerging branches of entrepreneurship develop and become structured, the practitioners begin to find each other. They communicate by organizing themselves through professional associations and other groups. These associations begin to hone definitions of their common practice and generate research and statistical data. As their group profile rises, they begin to draw attention from researchers and educators, who analyze the newly available data and solidify clear definitions. Eventually, the academic community constructs theories to explain and predict behaviors and events associated with the specific branch of entrepreneurial practice.

Taxonomies in other fields

Investigators in many fields have studied proliferation – from religion to marketing – and applied classifications to developing groups. Epidemiologists classify diseases according to their incidence, geographic, and temporal spread as secular, sporadic, endemic, epidemic, or pandemic (Bittle 2003). Theologians have classified emerging religious bodies as sects, denominations, and churches (Niebuhr 1929). In the science of ecology, conglomerations of individuals are labeled as groups, organizations, populations, and communities. In each case, collections of individual instances compile, combine, or coordinate until they form a distinctly different level of organization.

For this chapter, the classification methodologies of most interest are those that have arisen from the study of business-related fields or have been applied to business models. Among taxonomies describing business practices, a progression based on implementation of marketing tactics has been identified as: action, program, system, and policy (Bonoma 1984; Go *et al.* 1992).

In the field of entrepreneurship, the labels developed for population ecology (group, organization, population, community) have been applied to increasingly complex human organizations within and among firms and used to examine environmental forces on entrepreneurial endeavors (Aldrich and Martinez 2000, 2003). A summary of taxonomies in various fields is presented in Figure 5.5.

	Increasing level of development →				
Disease	Secular	Sporadic	Endemic	Epidemic	Pandemic
Religion	Sect		Denomination		Church
Ecology	Group	Organization		Population	Community
Kuhnian "normal science"	Pre-paradigmatic			Paradigmatic	
Marketing	Action	Program		System	Policy
Emerging branches of entrepreneurship	Cluster		Class		Category

Figure 5.5 Taxonomy of emerging fields

Taxonomy for branches of entrepreneurship

These analogies suggest a model for treating the proliferation of branches of entrepreneurship as they move from isolated instances to standard practices. A tripartite taxonomy is used here to classify branches of entrepreneurship according to their development stage. A branch in the early stage can be named a cluster. Clusters are characterized by being few in number, disorganized, ill-defined, and without significant academic theory. A branch that has developed in some or all of these areas – that has ways of facilitating communication among its practitioners, that is somewhat defined, or which has captured the attention of the academic world will be named a class. The most developed and structured type of branch will be named a category. Categories of entrepreneurship are widespread, well defined, and quantified, enjoy many associations, and have been investigated by academics who have developed and tested theories around the branch. This classification system is presented in Table 5.1.

Evaluation of parallel paths

To begin an exploration of these questions, an examination of several distinct and identifiable branches of entrepreneurship will be undertaken. Each will be classified according to its maturity – its progress along the path from cluster to trend to category. In order to classify each branch according to its progress, a set of preliminary criteria must be developed that can be used to approximate the developmental stage of each area.

In order to track the parallel path of the field of entrepreneurship as an academic discipline, theorists have proposed several methods of evaluation. A review of the number of journal articles resulting from database searches gives a preliminary indication of the exponential growth of the discipline (see

Table 5.1 Taxonomy of developing branches of entrepreneurship

	Cluster	*Class*	*Category*
Number of firms engaged	Isolated/sporadic	Some/increasing	Many/numbers available from several sources
Definitional clarity	Vague	Forming/competing	Accepted
Existence of associations	None/few	Some/no established leaders	Established associations/subspecialties
Availability of statistics	None/few	Available from associations	Readily available with analysis from academics
Existence of theories	None	Application of theories from other areas	Well-developed tested theories unique to the branch

Figure 5.6). Some have sought to evaluate the field based on Kuhnian definitions of normal or unified science (Kuhn 1970). They have made distinctions based on classifying:

1   research as exploratory or causal;
2   samples as large or small, and
3   samples as framed or samples of convenience, as well as classifying the content of research studies.

(Aldrich 1992)

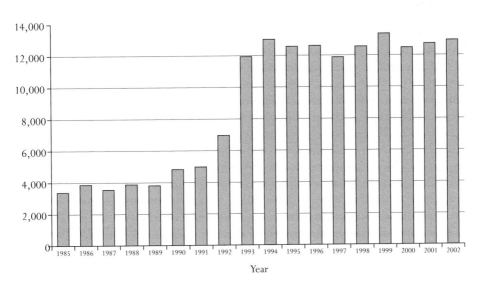

Figure 5.6 Results of search for entrepreneurship journal articles

Others have expanded the criteria to address practical as well as research issues. These researchers tracked entrepreneurship according to:

1   systematic theories exclusive to the domain in question;
2   the existence of associations;
3   the development of a professional culture; and
4   the potential for the field to lead to an occupational career.
(Plaschka and Welsch 1990)

In exploration of the family business branch of entrepreneurship, Bird *et al.* (2002) have focused on the unified science approach to analyze and assess progress in the types of quantitative research that have been done in that field.

Evaluation of branches of entrepreneurship

The methods used to evaluate fields of academic study are a useful reference. However, evaluation of a branch of entrepreneurship must place more emphasis on its practical component, since that is the portion evolving most rapidly. Using efforts in other areas as a guide, four criteria will be examined here to investigate the development of branches of entrepreneurial practice:

1   the number of firms engaged;
2   the existence of organized associations;
3   the conduct of empirical research and availability of statistical information;
4   the development and testing of systematic theories.

Application of evaluative criteria

The set of criteria can be applied to various emerging branches of entrepreneurship to classify them within a taxonomy that distinguishes branches based on their level of development. Several representative branches of entrepreneurship have been chosen to demonstrate the application of the criteria and framework proposed: family business, franchising, corporate entrepreneurship, entrepreneurship in the arts, social entrepreneurship, strategic collaboration, and network marketing.

Family business

We know that under a broad definition where family businesses are liberally defined – without regard to operational involvement but retain ownership intention, while maintaining operational control and strategic direction – 20.3 million firms represent 92 percent of all businesses, contributing $3.3 trillion (49 percent) of GDP, employing 59 percent of the workforce and have created 78 percent of the new jobs in the U.S.A. (Lucaccini and Muscat 2001).

Associations consisting of and benefiting family businesses are plentiful and well established. The Family Firm Institute has been formally connecting family business practitioners, educators, consultants, and others for over 15 years. Statistics are readily available from associations of family firms as well as from results of academic investigation.

Theories of family business have been developed and are being tested. For example, complications that arise as a younger-generation person enters the family business have been examined. Managing growth is another challenging aspect of a family firm and experts are emerging who are versed not only in business consulting but also in psychology. Competitive advantages of family businesses have been identified (Habbershon 2003). A comprehensive review of journal articles around family businesses showed a definitive shift over time from exploratory research to causal research (Bird *et al.* 2002).

Based on the proposed criteria, this area can be considered among the most developed emerging branches of practice, and seems to have earned the status of a category within entrepreneurship.

Franchising

In the United States, franchises account for 38 percent of all retail sales (Dicke 1992). The trillion dollars in sales this represents makes up over one-fifth of the GDP of the country (Trutko *et al.* 2001). Franchises employ over 8.5 million Americans.

From the aspect of the existence of associations, franchising is quite advanced. Since Howard Johnson created the concept in 1935, the entire field has been predicated on – in fact created by – the existence of associations. The Encyclopedia of Associations (Hunt 2002) lists 13 large national or international organizations supporting franchisers, and the American Franchisee Association (2003) claims 30,000 members.

Because of its large contribution to the economy, and the fact that many franchise owners are individuals without formal business training, the sector has begun attracting increasing attention from researchers, consultants, and educators. Statistics regarding participation in larger franchises are readily available through franchiser organizations.

Some excellent quantitative research has started investigating the application of general theories such as first-mover advantage (Michael 2003) to franchises, but highly developed theories that apply specifically to franchises are yet to develop.

Franchising exhibits significant organization among its practitioners, and has received increasing attention from the academic community. Overall, this branch would appear to belong under the rubric of class.

Corporate entrepreneurship

Largely because of the lack of practitioner associations, the number of companies involved in this branch of entrepreneurship is not known. Possibly because of concerns about confidentiality and competitive practices, companies have apparently been reluctant to share information about their implementation of entrepreneurial processes in the corporate environment. Basic descriptive statistics are unavailable and even the definition of corporate entrepreneurship is continuing to develop.

Associations of firms engaged in corporate entrepreneurship are only now beginning to develop. The International Association of Institutional Venturing and Intrapreneurship held its introductory meeting as recently as July 2002 (IAIVI 2003). Many individual corporations are thought to be involved in this branch of entrepreneurship but their affiliation is loose at best.

Although practitioners of corporate entrepreneurship are just now beginning to organize, the academic community has already formed several units to exchange ideas and theories about corporate entrepreneurship. USASBE, one of the largest and most prestigious academic associations in entrepreneurship, have a division devoted to this topic. It would seem that researchers are ahead of practitioners, presenting a case of theories leading, rather than following, the field.

However, research in this area has so far failed to develop beyond the descriptive phase, focusing its efforts on describing and categorizing the ventures of corporations. Schindehutte *et al.* (2000) have made some progress placing corporate ventures on such continua as internal–external, opportunity driven–threat driven, technology push–market pull, top down–bottom up and deliberate search–opportunistic.

Oddly, academics have attempted to organize theories around corporate entrepreneurship even with a dearth of data. This is a departure from what is appearing as a typical sequence – practitioner organization, statistical data collection, academic exploration, theory building. Corporate entrepreneurship presents a special case from the standpoint of the relation between academic treatment and practitioner development. Viewed strictly from the standpoint of practitioner, it would appear to be undeveloped and would be classified in the most undeveloped category of branches of practice – a cluster. Viewed from the aspect of the academia-related criteria, the branch is more developed and would qualify as a class.

Entrepreneurship in the arts

Entrepreneurial mega-enterprises in the arts industry have raised the profile of arts business. The creation of DreamWorks SKG by Steven Spielberg, Jeffrey Katzenberg, and David Geffen, was announced in October of 1994. By 1996, revenues reached $89 million, and a billion dollars in 1998. After eight years of business, *Forbes* magazine estimates DreamWorks' worth at $3 billion, and the combined personal net worth of any two of the founders can match that number (Kafka and Newcomb 2003).

Associations of artists are well established and have an extensive history. However, they differ from associations in other branches of entrepreneurial practice in that they largely ignore business considerations. Many firms have been founded to manage the business affairs of artists. Currently, more than 3000 arts agencies exist to aid them in preparing and presenting their performances to their target audiences (Welsch and Kickul 1997). But the development of organizations of artists by artists to aid in the entrepreneurial endeavors of the artists themselves is just beginning.

The recent surge of interest in the entrepreneurship of artists has led to significant availability of statistical data. Since 1965, the number of non-profit theaters and dance companies has each grown by four times, opera companies and orchestras have each tripled in number (Welsch and Kickul 1997). Empirical research in this area is starting to accelerate, and academic treatment of entrepreneurship in the arts is now starting to develop.

Much of the academic focus in this area revolves around integrating entrepreneurship training into arts education, and the development of theories around the individual aspects of arts entrepreneurship that separate it from other areas has not begun in earnest.

This branch exhibits many of the characteristics of a class. Whether the practice of entrepreneurship in the arts is significantly different from other forms of entrepreneurship remains to be investigated.

Social entrepreneurship

Not-for-profit organizations have long represented a large sector of the economy whose commercial aspects have been neither emphasized by the sector nor examined by outsiders. The sector represents more than $500 billion and employs 8.6 million people (Sokolowski and Salamon 1999). As the U.S. economy has slowed, social service organizations have suffered from reduced corporate and personal giving, as well as reduced government funding. The U.S. federal government has increased the proportion of social service expenditures to be borne by states, and states have responded by cutting budgets. In an effort to avoid their demise, many social service organizations have taken steps to run their organizations more professionally and in ways that create funds internally. A Yale University study found that, by 2002, 42 percent of the non-profits surveyed were involved in some money-making venture (Massarsky and Beinhacker 2002). The overriding principle is to better apply the practices of the private sector to social service enterprises.

Associations of social services organizations have existed for some time, and are gradually beginning to address the issues of sound business practices directly. There is no real clear information on the extent to which these organizations treat such matters.

As in most endeavors, academic investigation has started with definitional work. Investigators have identified two types of social entrepreneurship endeavors – the affirmative business and the direct service business (Boschee 1995). Only since 2002 has detailed quantitative work been undertaken (Massarsky and Beinhacker 2002). Theories that are differentiated for this specific type of entrepreneurship have not emerged.

Participants in social entrepreneurship are numerous. The definitions, associations, and academic treatment of the branch, however, remain in the early stages. Social entrepreneurship appears to best fit within the classification of cluster.

Strategic collaboration

One of the least defined emerging areas of entrepreneurship is loosely named strategic collaboration. Strategic collaboration involves the sharing of information or integration of business systems among separate entities to benefit both. In order to qualify as collaboration, a joint effort must meet several criteria (Hartl *et al.* 2003):

● the involved parties maintain legal and economic independence;
● the effort is voluntary and can be terminated unilaterally by either party at any time;
● the agreement is explicit, and involves some kind of oral or written agreement about rights and duties of the parties.

The very definition of strategic collaboration, however, is still in question. The broad definition of collaboration leaves room for much creativity and innovation in its execution, but indicates a lack of sufficient definition and distinction among those who investigate and report on it. Collaboration can include something as simple as allowing engineers working on similar products to share a common workspace (Karlenzig and Patrick 2002) or as complex as a full legal combination of entities. Currently, the most common advanced form of strategic collaboration is the integration of business systems for inventory, order, and order fulfillment between a supplier and its customer.

Associations that connect firms specifically around collaboration are not known to exist. Statistics describing the extent of collaboration rely on definitions that have not been solidified. Empirical research faces the same barrier, and academic work so far has focused on descriptive and definitional aspects of the branch of practice. Theory building has been restricted to sporadic initiatives.

The branch of practice of strategic collaboration is a cluster. Its very definition is only now being clarified, and it has yet to be quantified in any organized way. The ways in which it may be differentiated from other forms of entrepreneurship or categories of business have yet to be fully determined.

Network marketing

Like franchising, the very existence of network marketing relies on association building. Communication and interaction among participants in network marketing is well structured and a prominent feature of the industry. This criterion alone would point toward a high level of development. Within the practitioner group, associations are well structured and efficient. Every network marketer is, by definition, part of a larger organization. Additional associations like the Direct Selling Association have developed to extend the structure between network marketing organizations.

In the same way, the associations have made statistics deceptively plentiful. The Direct Selling Association conducts surveys of the industry that provide detailed information about the prevalence, geography, income patterns, product mix, and strategies of its membership. However, these statistics come from an association, not from independent or academic research, which is scarce.

While network marketing presents a real opportunity to make money, the industry has been tarnished by so-called "pyramid schemes." Also known as Ponzi schemes, these opportunities rely only on recruiting to earn profits and have no products or nominal products. Partly because of the stigma of associated scams, network marketing has received less attention from academics than many smaller sectors of the small-business world.

Developed theoretical treatment of network marketing is lacking. Much of the existing literature comes from practitioner magazines, and the topic has received minimal attention in academic journals. Academics have largely ignored this branch of entrepreneurship, though efforts to recognize and examine it are underway.

Network marketing affects a significant portion of the economy, and its members freely associate and exchange information. The definition is broadly accepted. Academic attention is gathering momentum, but is still in the beginning stage. Network marketing can most likely be categorized as a class.

Conclusions

Conclusions from evidence

The exploration presented here has suggested that evolving branches of entrepreneurship make a journey from inception to acceptance that mimics better-understood paths found in natural and social sciences. Using studies of these parallel paths as a guide, this chapter has designed a taxonomy of branches of entrepreneurship, established criteria to assess the categorization of individual branches, and demonstrated how those criteria may be applied.

Implications for further investigation

The criteria presented here have been based on analogs from other fields, and have been designed as a logical starting point. Additional attention is needed to operationalize these variables and find ways to evaluate them in a more rigorous fashion. As suitable operationalizations are found, quantitative research can be undertaken to refine this set of criteria. Other criteria may be tested – for instance, the number and types of publications specific to an emerging branch may be a valuable proxy for the organization and interaction among practitioners.

Critical mass

Perhaps the most important issue raised by the results of this study revolves around the issue of critical mass. The gap that exists between practitioners and academics can be seen as natural and valuable in some cases – a method of practice that is idiosyncratic and short in number fails to qualify as a branch of entrepreneurship and probably does not warrant a use of academic resources. On the other hand, a widespread practice that represents a large portion of the small-business community or exerts significant impact on the economy cannot be ignored. If a dividing line can be identified here – a point of critical mass where an emerging branch can be expected to survive and grow – it can be very important prescriptively for academics establishing qualifying criteria for whether a branch of entrepreneurship should receive significant academic attention.

Corporate entrepreneurship

The special case of corporate entrepreneurship warrants further investigation. In most branches, it was found that academic treatment lags behind the spread of a certain practice, and a fairly regular pattern was observed. In the case of corporate entrepreneurship, however, the exact opposite case was found – academics have lavished the branch with attention, formed organizations around the study of the branch, and developed significantly complex theories around the field, yet the practitioners have organized and communicated among themselves minimally. It would appear that a gap exists, but in the opposite direction of that predicted.

Competition among ideas

The evidence presented identifies the path of maturation of an emerging branch of entrepreneurship. Some branches of entrepreneurship grow and expand, and others die in a Darwinian process of ideological evolution. The healthy competition represented by this process is seen as a positive sign that the field is continuing to develop and improve. Because every idea that falls by the wayside is replaced by a superior one, strategies and methods of undertaking entrepreneurial endeavors strengthen over time.

Academic consequences

Academics studying entrepreneurial practice via emerging branches of entrepreneurship play a vital role in facilitating the evolutionary process and growth of the field. The rigorous definition, quantification, and evaluation of emerging branches advances the field in several ways: identifying emerging branches, discovering best practices, disseminating information about innovations, recommending new combinations, and promoting progress through professional associations.

If the practice of entrepreneurship remains in a phase of rapid growth and expansion, if the practice still presents a strong healthy marketplace of competing novel ideas, if the practice shows all indication of increasing strength, then the study of entrepreneurship has a bright future.

The vigorous nature of emerging branches of entrepreneurship – that is the rate at which novel modes of undertaking entrepreneurial endeavors come about – would indicate that the field is still in a state of rapid growth and development. The expanding base and evolution of branches demonstrate that the practice of entrepreneurship is still on an upswing and has not yet found its plateau.

References

Aldrich, H. (1992) "Methods in our madness? Trends in entrepreneurship research," in Sexton, D. and Kasarda, J. (eds) *The State of the Art of Entrepreneurship*, Boston, MA: PWS-Kent Publishing.

Aldrich, H. and Martinez, M. (2000) "Many are called but few are chosen: an evolutionary perspective for the study of entrepreneurship," *Entrepreneurship Theory and Practice*, 25(4): 41–56.

Aldrich, H. and Martinez, M. (2003) "Entrepreneurship as social construction: a multi-level evolutionary approach," in Acs, Z. and Audretsch, D. (eds) *Handbook of Entrepreneurship Research*, Hingham, MA: Kluwer Academic Publishers.

American Franchisee Association (2003) Online, available at: http://www.franchisee.org (accessed March 21, 2003).

Bird, B., Welsch, H., Astrachan, J., and Pistrui, D. (2002) "Family business research: the evolution of an academic field," *Family Business Review*, 15 (4): 337–351.

Bittle, M. (2003) "Epidemiology." Online, available at: http://www.uta.edu/nursing/bsn/3421–epidemiology.pdf (accessed April 23, 2003).

Bonoma, T. (1984) *Managing Marketing: Text, Cases and Readings (Teacher's Manual)*, New York, NY: Free Press.

Boschee, J. (1995) "Social entrepreneurship," *Across the Board*, 32(3): 20–25.

Cooper, A. (1998) "Entrepreneurship: the past, the present, the future," presented as the plenary speech, USASBE Conference 1998, Clearwater, FL.

Dicke, T.S. (1992) *Franchising in America*, Chapel Hill, NC: University of North Carolina Press.

Direct Selling Association (2003) *2002 Growth and Outlook Survey*. Portions online, available at: http://www.dsa.org/research/numbers.htm (accessed March 3, 2003).

Go, F., Milne, D., and Lorne, J. (1992) "Communities as destinations: a marketing taxonomy for the effective implementation of the tourism action plan," *Journal of Travel Research*, 30(4): 31–37.

Habbershon, T. (2003) "Improving the long-run survival of family firms," Wharton School of Business Working Paper. Online, available at: http://knowledge.wharton.upenn.edu/PDFs/982.pdf (accessed March 3, 2003).

Hartl, R., Pleitner, H., Schermerhorn, J., and Welsch, H. (2003) "Collaboration initiatives among SMES," presented at the International Council for Small Business Conference, Belfast, Ireland.

Hunt, K.N. (ed.) (2002) *Encyclopedia of Associations*, 1(3), Farmington Hills, MI: The Gale Group.

International Association of Institutional Venturing and Intrapreneurship (2003) *Welcome to the IAIVI Web Site*. Online, available at: http://www.progenyvc.com/iaivi/default.htm (acccessed April 25, 2003).

Kafka, P. and Newcomb, P. (2003) "Cash me out if you can," *Forbes*, 171(5): 78.

Karkofsky, P. (2001) "Growth drives family firms crazy," *Time.com*. Online, available at: http://www.time.com (accessed March 21, 2003).

Karlenzig, W. and Patrick, J. (2002) "Tap into the power of knowledge collaboration," *Customer Inter@ctionSolutions*, 20(11): 22–26.

Katz, J. (2003) "The chronology and intellectual trajectory of American entrepreneurship education 1876–1999," *Journal of Business Venturing*, 18: 283–300.

Kuhn, T. (1970) *The Structure of Scientific Revolutions*, second edn, Chicago, IL: University of Chicago Press.

Lucaccini, L. and Muscat, E. (2001) *Family business and careers: classic and contemporary issues.* Online, available at: http://www.usfca.edu/sobam/faculty/family%20business%20and%20careers.doc (accessed March 21, 2003).

Massarsky, C. and Beinhacker, S. (2002) *Enterprising nonprofits: revenue generation in the nonprofit sector*, Yale School of Management – The Goldman Sachs Foundation Partnership on Nonprofit Ventures. Online, available at: http://www.ventures.yale.edu/factsfigures.asp (accessed March 20, 2003).

Michael, S.C. (2003) "First mover advantage through franchising," *Journal of Business Venturing*, 18(1): 61–80.

Niebuhr, H.R. (1929) *The Social Sources of Denominations*, New York, NY: H. Halt.

Plaschka, G. and Welsch, H. (1990) "Emerging structures in entrepreneurship education: curricular designs and strategies," *Entrepreneurship Theory and Practice*, 14(3): 55–71.

Schinderhutte, M., Morris, M., and Kuratko, D. (2000) "Triggering events, corporate entrepreneurship and the marketing function," *Journal of Marketing Theory & Practice*, 8(2): 18–30.

Sokolowski, S.W. and Salamon, L. (1999) "The United States," in Salamon, L., Anheier, H., List, R. *et al.* (eds) *Global Civil Society: Dimensions of the Nonprofit Sector*, Baltimore, MD: The Johns Hopkins Center for Civil Society Studies.

Thomas, P. (2003) "Entrepreneurs' biggest problems – and how they solve them," *The Wall Street Journal*, 241(52): R1, R3.

Trutko, J., Trutko, I., and Kostecka, A. (2001) *Franchises Growing Role in the U.S. Economy, 1975–2000*, Springfield, VA: U.S. Department of Commerce.

Welsch, H. and Kickul, J. (1997) "Successful entrepreneurship careers in the creative arts," paper presented at IntEnt 1997 Conference, Monterey, CA.

PART TWO

Entrepreneurial processes

Chapter 6

G.T. Lumpkin

University of Illinois at Chicago

Gerald E. Hills

University of Illinois at Chicago

Rodney C. Shrader

University of Illinois at Chicago

OPPORTUNITY RECOGNITION

Introduction

OPPORTUNITY RECOGNITION (OpR) is a vitally important area of entrepreneurship research. This is evidenced by a frequently cited definition of an entrepreneur as someone "who perceives an opportunity and creates an organization to pursue it" (Bygrave and Hofer 1991: 14). A recent *Academy of Management Review* article also confirmed this when it stated, "We define the field of entrepreneurship as the scholarly examination of how, by whom, and with what effects opportunities to create future goods and services are discovered, evaluated, and exploited" (Shane and Venkataraman 2000: 218).

Until recently, remarkably little research has been done on the topic of opportunity recognition. Fortunately, significant contributions have been made in conceptualizing the phenomenon, and empirical studies have begun to generate new knowledge. This chapter endeavors to review several recent contributions to the opportunity literature and present a model of OpR, then to report on two studies of OpR, and, finally, to discuss implications of OpR for entrepreneurs and entrepreneurship education.

Literature review

Numerous scholars view opportunity recognition as a multi-staged and often complex process. The process perspective of OpR has proved to be a fruitful area of research because it acknowledges that OpR is a multifaceted phenomenon influenced by numerous factors. Long and McMullan (1984), for example, proposed a model of the opportunity recognition process with four stages: pre-vision, point of vision, opportunity elaboration, and the decision to proceed. Pre-vision is affected by both uncontrollable and controllable factors, such as environmental and job forces, as well as venture alertness cultivation, moonlight venturing, and job selection. Ardichvili *et al.* (2003) suggest that the opportunity identification process begins when alert entrepreneurs notice factors in their domain of expertise that result in the recognition and evaluation of potential business opportunities.

Christensen *et al.* (1989) proposed a definition of opportunity recognition that captures the essence of this concept. They suggested that opportunity recognition consists of either perceiving a possibility to create new businesses, or significantly improving the position of an existing business, in both cases resulting in new profit potential (Christensen *et al.* 1989: 3). (The concept of perceiving profitable new business possibilities is the definition used in the empirical analysis reported below.)

Bhave (1994), as part of his process model of venture creation, found two types of opportunity recognition. The first was externally stimulated opportunity recognition, in which the decision to start a venture preceded opportunity recognition. The entrepreneurs in this study engaged in a search for opportunities by filtering through them, massaging ideas, and elaboration. The second was internally stimulated opportunity recognition. Here, entrepreneurs discovered problems to solve or needs to fulfill and only later decided to create a new venture.

Other scholarly research has also contributed to developing a process approach to opportunity recognition. Kaish and Gilad (1991) found that entrepreneurs are opportunistic learners that pay special attention to risk cues about new opportunities. Cooper (1981) suggested that entrepreneurs perceive opportunities on the basis of an intuitive and informal feel for the market. Stevenson *et al.* (1985) suggested that entrepreneurship is driven to a greater extent by perception of opportunity than by resources controlled. Similarly, Stevenson and Jarillo-Mossi (1986) view entrepreneurship as the process of creating value by combining resources to exploit an opportunity. These studies suggest that opportunity recognition is a critically important aspect of the new venture formation process.

A comprehensive model of opportunity recognition

Recently, a model of opportunity recognition was introduced that addresses the OpR process (Hills *et al.* 1999). This approach suggests an OpR model based on theory from the creativity and psychology literature. The proposed model assumes that OpR is inherently a creative process. This is consistent with numerous studies that have emphasized the essential role of creativity in entrepreneur-ship. In his seminal work, Schumpeter (1942) described entrepreneurship in terms of creative destruction, whereby an innovation disrupts the equilibrium or status quo in the marketplace, allowing the entrepreneur to earn a profit. Long and McMullan (1984) described OpR as a process involving iterations of creative thinking. Christensen *et al.* (1994) discussed opportunity identification as the cre-ative stage of the entrepreneurial process. Others have described OpR as includ-ing the actual creation of a new venture (Bhave 1994; Hills 1995) when the opportunity continues to be formalized on the basis of market feedback.

The elements of the creative process have been identified in several recent scholarly studies of creativity. In his book, *Creativity*, Csikszentmihalyi (1996) identified five basic elements – preparation, incubation, insight, evaluation, and elaboration – that have emerged over years of research into creativity. Drawing on this framework, we have identified five steps that can be divided into two phases. The two phases correspond roughly to the discovery and evaluation aspects of opportunity recognition identified by Shane and Venkataraman (2000). Discovery consists of preparation, incubation, and insight; formation involves evaluation and elaboration. The theoretical framework is illustrated in Figure 6.1. In the sections that follow, existing OpR and new venture research is reviewed briefly to inform the discussion of each of the five dimensions. Table 6.1 summarizes key scholarly contributions to the OpR literature using the creativity-based opportunity recognition framework.

Preparation

Preparation refers to the experience and knowledge that begins the OpR process. Such preparation is typically viewed as a conscious effort based on one's interest and curiosity about a given domain (Csikszentmihalyi 1996). In the context of OpR, preparation refers to the experience and prior knowledge (Shane 2000) that an entrepreneur brings to the process. This is consistent with research that indicates that more than 50 percent of start-up ideas emerge from

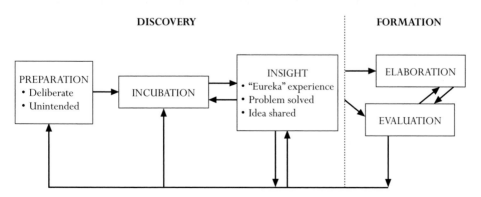

Figure 6.1 Creativity based model of entrepreneurial opportunity recognition
Source: Based on Hills, Shrader, and Lumpkin (1999).

Table 6.1 Highlights of the opportunity recognition literature

	Preparation	Incubation	Insight	Evaluation	Elaboration
Csikszentmihalyi (1996)	Conscious or subconscious immersion in problem(s)	Subconsciously mulling things over	"Aha!" experiences usually with a cognitive shift	Consciously deciding whether insight is valuable and worth pursuing	The process of actualizing the creative insight
Kirzner (1979)			OR depends on "entrepreneurial alertness," defined as the ability to notice opportunities without search		
Long and McMullan (1984)	Ad hoc or focused search influenced by controllable and uncontrollable factors		Point of vision is the sudden recognition of a new possibility; an "Aha!" experience	Amplification of vision to overcome major objections; may involve iterations of creative thinking and additional preparation	Decision to proceed
Koller (1988)	Work experience and/or desire to be an entrepreneur precede conscious search or passive discovery		Ideas recognized as opportunities because they use prior experience		
Teach et al. (1989)	Prior experience, technology, and market need precede deliberate search or accidental discovery			Some entrepreneurs use formal evaluation, while others eschew it	

Study				
Kaish and Gilad (1991)	Entrepreneurs are more alert, rely on non-traditional information sources	Preparedness allows entrepreneurs to recognize opportunities spontaneously	Entrepreneurs rely more on subjective impression than conventional economic analysis	
Gaglio and Taub (1992)	Pre-recognition stew of environmental, technological, social, economic, cultural, and personal forces simmers over time	"Eureka!" experience at moment of recognition	Idea developed by examining its value, market potential, and resource requirements	Decision to go, modify, or quit
Bhave (1994)	External circumstances and/or desire to start business motivate conscious search	Opportunities recognized and filtered; one selected	Opportunity refined; business concept identified that aligns skills and resources with market need	Organization created and gradually formalized on the basis of customer feedback
Christensen et al. (1994)	Profound technological and market knowledge required at creative stage		Formal strategic planning based on feasibility and desirability helps evaluate opportunities, set priorities, and in implementation	
Hills (1995); Hills and Shrader (1998)	Alertness and making time to think; specific needs and market knowledge mattered more than work experience		Business concepts refined through informal intuitive procedures	Once in the market, firm must quickly adjust to market requirements

Table 6.1 continued

	Preparation	Incubation	Insight	Evaluation	Elaboration
Singh et al. (1999)	Entrepreneurial alertness and social network affect number of ideas and opportunities recognized			Evaluation determines which ideas are opportunities; more evaluation needed before decision to proceed	
De Koning (1999)	Ongoing information scanning without a specific objective produces initial ideas		Sudden convergence of ideas happens more than once during process	Thinking through, talking, information seeking, and resource assessment are used to develop concept	Commitment to create
Gaglio and Katz (2001)	Alertness to external change, which can be ignored, discounted, or further examined		Breaks existing means–ends framework		

a person's prior work experience (e.g. Bygrave 1997; Ronstadt 1988). However, since potential entrepreneurs may be unaware that they will someday launch a new venture, the preparation is often neither systematic nor deliberate but may simply be part of an individual's life experience.

Numerous factors may contribute to preparation for OpR, including work experience, technological and market knowledge, hobbies, and one's social networks.

Incubation

Incubation is the part of the process that occurs when a person is thinking about a problem or considering an idea. Discussions of the incubation phase often make reference to a specific problem that someone is trying to solve. Csikszentmihalyi (1996: 79) states that during incubation, "ideas churn around below the threshold of consciousness." It does not, however, refer to conscious problem-solving or systematic analysis. Instead, it is typically an intuitive, non-intentional style of considering possibilities or options. Incubation, because it involves the intermingling of ideas in an unstructured fashion, is the stage of the process in which the "new combinations" that Schumpeter (1942) emphasized might emerge. Gaglio and Taub (1992) aptly described incubation as "simmering" of the pre-recognition stew over time.

Insight

Insight refers to the point at which an entrepreneur consciously realizes that an idea may indeed represent an entrepreneurial opportunity. Gaglio and Taub (1992) referred to this as the "Eureka!" experience at the moment of recognition. Long and McMullan (1984) referred to it as an "Aha!" experience or "point of vision." Gaglio and Katz (2001) described this cognitive shift as one that breaks existing mean–ends frameworks. Prior research suggests that entrepreneurs sometimes have the experience of being immediately confident that an idea will work (Hills 1995). In other cases, a person gets an idea that solves the problem he or she has been considering or incubating. Such creative insights are common in studies of innovation (e.g. Amabile 1988). In some cases, potential entrepreneurs become consciously aware of opportunities through their social networks. Research indicates that entrepreneurs with wider networks of social contacts identify more ideas and recognize more opportunities than entrepreneurs with fewer contacts (Singh 1998).

Evaluation

Formation is the phase in the process when insights are formed into viable businesses. In the context of launching new ventures, evaluation often involves feasibility analysis. De Koning (1999) described a formation process whereby potential entrepreneurs tested and refined their ideas by talking through them with other people in their networks. In this phase of the process, ideas are also put to the test via various forms of investigation, such as preliminary market testing and financial viability analysis (Bhave 1994; Gaglio and Taub 1992). Long and McMullan (1984) suggest that entrepreneurs amplify a vision to overcome major objections through iterations of creative thinking and preparation. The basic question is: "Is the business concept sufficiently valuable and worthwhile to pursue?" Neglecting this type of analysis is one of the frequently cited reasons for new venture start-up failures (Vesper 1996).

Elaboration

Elaboration is the stage in which the creative insight is actualized. Csikszentmihalyi (1996) argues that elaboration is generally the most difficult and time-consuming part of the process. Elaboration represents a continuation of the process of business planning and may even extend into actual venture start-up. When a business idea has survived the formation stage, this is the stage when problems are resolved and many details are worked out through feedback and testing. Bhave (1994) described how organizations are created and gradually formalized on the basis of customer feedback. Furthermore, even after a venture has been launched, the opportunity is often refined or changed on the basis of the additional learning gained through actual trial and error. Hills (1995) and Hills and Shrader (1998) found that, once they enter the market, new ventures must quickly adjust to market requirements.

In summary, it should be noted that opportunity recognition is a recursive process. Although the components of the model can be called "stages" of the OpR process, it is important to note that they are not necessarily linear and may not follow any predetermined sequence. This allows for numerous approaches to OpR, which better reflects the equifinality of the OpR process demonstrated in the literature. Thus, the model of opportunity recognition presented here is comprehensive enough to provide a robust framework for studying this complex phenomenon, while at the same time its five components are simple and parsimonious.

Opportunity recognition behaviors

To address the issue of how entrepreneurs think about the OpR process, we investigated how entrepreneurs perceive opportunity recognition. Our overall research objective was to ask: how do the entrepreneurs' perceptions of the nature and importance of opportunity recognition inform us about how to teach this topic to entrepreneurship students and improve the practices of entrepreneurs? The 218 entrepreneurs in our sample included highly successful entrepreneurs, that is, those who have qualified to be included in the Chicago Area Entrepreneurship Hall of Fame, and a group of representative entrepreneurs, that is, a randomly selected group of business owners with substantial track records. Although the findings from these two groups are very similar, we will also point out differences in the two groups and how those differences might provide clues for understanding the opportunity recognition aspects of entrepreneurship.

Methodology

Sample and procedures

Two groups of entrepreneurs were surveyed for this research project. In one segment, a group of exceptionally successful entrepreneurs in the seven-county Chicago area was identified. Over a three-year period, more than 100 entrepreneurs were searched for and identified, both for this study and to be inducted into the Chicago Area Entrepreneurship Hall of Fame. Several steps were used to qualify an entrepreneur for inclusion into the Hall of Fame. Leading criteria for selection into the Hall of Fame included innovativeness, sales growth, and performance. The final selection was made by a panel of highly professional judges. The individuals selected are stellar entrepreneurs by any measure.

A total of 53 participated in this study and are referred to as "HFE" in Tables 6.2 and 6.3. Although the HFE companies ranged in size from $1.45 million to $448 million in annual revenues and employed between nine and 5,118 people, it should be noted that 39 percent had revenues between $5 million and $20 million and another 15 percent had sales between $21 million and $50 million. The mean values for this entrepreneurial sample were $42 million in annual revenues and 371 employees.

Data for the second segment of the study were collected by mail survey of business owners/entrepreneurs in the seven-county Chicago area, yielding a comparative representative sample. The sampling frame for this portion of the study was obtained from Dun and Bradstreet. The list included a randomly selected set of 1,500 organizations (from a total of 18,000) with revenues between $5 million and $100 million. A cover letter and questionnaire were mailed to 1,419 entrepreneurs. Eighty-one were eliminated either because their business entity was a non-profit organization or because the contact individual was not the owner, president, or CEO. Following the first mailing, another 128 of the 1,419 in the sample were eliminated because:

1   the firm had either moved or gone out of business,
2   the individual surveyed was no longer with the firm,
3   the business entity was a non-profit organization.

This left a total potential sample of 1,291 businesses. Following the mail survey and one postcard follow up, 187 useable surveys were returned for a response rate of 14.5 percent. Six franchisees and respondents who were not founders or co-founders were deleted, leaving 165 respondents who were entrepreneurs. Then, respondents were compared with non-respondents; this revealed that there was little difference between the two groups. In Tables 6.2 and 6.3, the sample of representative entrepreneurs is referred to as "RE." The

Table 6.2 Opportunity recognition behaviors: Hall of Fame Entrepreneurs (HFE) and Representative Entrepreneurs (RE)

Item	HFE					RE				
	(0%)	(1–2%)	(3–4%)	(5–10%)	(>10%)	(0%)	(1–2%)	(3–4%)	(5–10%)	(>10%)
How many new, major business opportunities have you pursued (invested time and money) in the last five years?	2	29	33	24	12	1	30	29	27	13
How many of these new business opportunities can be said to be successes?	4	40	40	12	4	7	51	23	15	3
How many of these new business opportunities were unrelated to the existing business at the time?	28	42	21	9	0	56	30	10	2	2

Note
$n = 53$ HFEs, 165 REs.

Table 6.3 Key opportunity recognition behavior findings

Item	HFE						REI					
	(SA %)	(PA %)	(N %)	(PD %)	(SD %)	Mean	(SA %)	(PA %)	(N %)	(PD %)	(SD %)	Mean
1 New business opportunities often arise in connection with a solution to a specific problem.	53	41	2	2	2	1.60	56	39	3	2	0	1.51
2 I listen extremely well to what customers say they want and don't want as a way of identifying opportunities.	61	23	10	6	0	1.61	67	24	6	3	0	1.44
3 Being creative is very important to identifying business opportunities.	50	40	8	2	0	1.63	58	30	6	4	1	1.60
4 I am not a very creative person.	2	13	11	17	57	4.15	3	9	15	25	48	4.05
5 Identifying opportunities is really several learning steps over time, rather than a one-time occurrence.	44	42	10	0	4	1.78	61	31	5	2	1	1.50
6 Our company experiments with new venture ideas which result in both failures and successes.	40	42	8	4	6	1.92	35	42	13	9	1	1.99
7 Other people bring new venture business ideas to me.	25	35	23	13	4	2.35	14	44	26	11	5	2.49

Notes
SA = strongly agree = 1; PA = partly agree = 2; N = neutral = 3; PD = partly disagree = 4; SD = strongly disagree = 5.
n = 53 HFEs, 165 REs.

RE executives' companies ranged in size from $3 million to $100 million in annual revenues and employed between 2 and 1,100 people. The mean values for this entrepreneurial sample were $16.7 million in annual revenues and 121 employees.

Research instrument and analysis

Five focus groups were conducted, yielding a rich discussion of opportunity recognition and related issues used in the questionnaire design. In addition to numerous new survey items, the questionnaire replicated and modified selected items from previous studies by Teach *et al.* (1989), Christensen and Peterson (1990), and Kaish and Gilad (1991). The questionnaire was extensively pre-tested in the focus groups as well as in a convenience sample of 47 business owners (not reported here). Frequency analysis was used to explore character-istics and differences between the two sets of entrepreneurs studied. T-tests were used to compare the means of responses.

Findings

Table 6.2 indicates that both groups of entrepreneurs have considerable experience with opportunities. Nearly all of them have pursued major, new business opportunities in the past five years, with approximately one-third of both groups having pursued three to four opportunities and another quarter having pursued five to ten opportunities. Note that 12 percent and 13 percent, respectively, pursued more than ten major, new business opportunities in the last five years.

Although the success rates are by definition lower than the sheer pursuit of opportunities, 16–18 percent of the HFE and RE samples had five or more suc-cesses and 74–80 percent had one to four successes. Forty percent of the HFEs had three to four successes as compared with 23 percent of the REs. But this is the only notable difference concerning successes. It is striking that so many of the opportunities pursued were unrelated to their existing businesses: this is more often the case for the HFEs than for the REs. Tables 6.2 and 6.3 reveal several important insights for entrepreneurs. Practical implications and implica-tions for entrepreneurship education are discussed further in the next sections.

Practical implications

Implication 1: opportunity recognition is inherently a creative process

Opportunity recognition involves a high degree of creativity. Table 6.3 indicates how strongly successful entrepreneurs associate creativity with opportunity recognition. Many scholars have acknowledged that creativity is essential to entrepreneurship and strong creativity skills are often associated with effective problem-solving (e.g. Senge 1990). Along with attributes such as imagination and spontaneity that are typically associated with creativity, other traits that are usually considered good for business also indicate high levels of creativity – self-confidence, resourcefulness, enthusiasm, and independence (Barron and Harrington 1981).

The importance of creativity has several implications for entrepreneurs. First, they must take steps to create an environment that is open and receptive to creative thought. This applies to entrepreneurs themselves as well as the people who work for them. An environment that is free of criticism and conducive to "out of the box" thinking may stimulate creative problem-solving. Second, if entrepreneurs do not consider themselves to be creative, they need to surround themselves with creative people who can enhance their opportunity recognition process.

Implication 2: opportunity recognition involves experimentation

All new ventures and innovative activity involves trying novel ideas that are unproven. This is a normal part of opportunity recognition as well. In fact, Vesper (1996) suggests that one way to test the viability of a business concept is to launch the business and see what happens. He recommends this in the context of ventures that have few start-up costs and low downside risks. The cost of launching such a business may actually be less than the cost of extensive market research and/or product testing that may be required to get some small businesses started.

Table 6.3 shows that more than 80 percent of the entrepreneurs experimented with new ideas, some of which were failures. This has important implications – entrepreneurs must not be afraid to make mistakes. Failures and false starts are a normal part of the OpR process, and the knowledge gained from such experiences often leads to future gains that are more solid. As Ronstadt (1988) has found, entering into a new business – even if it is not initially successful – opens doors and generates possibilities that may not have been apparent before.

Implication 3: high levels of domain knowledge enhance opportunity recognition

Most models of OpR emphasize the importance of preparation in opportunity recognition. Entrepreneurs with prior knowledge of a given domain are alert to opportunities in that business environment. Venture capitalists, when asked about the reasons for the rash of dot.com failures, stated that most of the new Internet-based businesses had been founded by entrepreneurs with a high degree of technical skill but insufficient domain knowledge – they were not prepared to run the businesses they had started because they did not know the industry or the competition.

Two implications that are especially salient can be drawn from these facts.

First, entrepreneurial ventures, no matter how exciting or fast growing they may seem, must acknowledge the rules of enterprise and business "wisdom" that apply to the industry and competitive environment in which the ventures are launched. Knowledge in a specific domain is required. Second, in opportunity recognition, as with all fields of business, there is no substitute for experience. Entrepreneurs who know a business domain will have a better chance of correctly recognizing opportunities than those who have no experience in the domain.

Implication 4: "good ideas" must be formed into viable business opportunities

Many entrepreneurship scholars agree that refining business ideas and investigating their feasibility is a critical pre-launch activity. Not every "good idea" is going to result in a viable business. Timmons (1994) suggested that recognizing opportunity involves:

1   evaluating the potential opportunity itself,
2   assessing the skill set and readiness of the entrepreneurs who might pursue it, and
3   ensuring that the necessary resources are available to sustain the venture launch.

Long and McMullan (1984) argued that opportunities are formed by refining ideas using elaboration and evaluation processes aimed at overcoming major objections to the venture idea.

Entrepreneurs need to recognize that most opportunities take time to emerge. Singh (1998) found that only a small portion of entrepreneurs proceeded directly from a business insight to the launch of that insight as a viable business. Entrepreneurs who evaluate ideas more closely may launch fewer businesses than those who do not take time to evaluate, but the businesses that are launched *with* evaluation are more likely to be successful than those that are launched *without* evaluating potential problems and risks.

Implications for entrepreneurship education

Implication 1: opportunity recognition is **not** industry or business specific

The information in Table 6.2 suggests that the opportunity recognition process occurs among entrepreneurs regardless of the business or industry environment in which they are currently engaged. Entrepreneurs are continually pursuing new business opportunities. Thus, the OpR process is ongoing – over one-third of the respondents in both samples indicated that they pursued at least one business opportunity per year on average. Although some prior research suggests that most opportunities arise from prior work experience, our results indicate that this is true in only about half of all cases. Such pursuits are not always specific to the entrepreneurs' existing enterprises – nearly half of all new opportunities pursued were unrelated businesses.

This suggests that teaching opportunity recognition skills is a particularly important component of entrepreneurship education. In fact, it can be argued that OpR skills stand alone as a topic of interest for educators because they are such a pervasive aspect of what business owners do.

Implication 2: opportunity recognition is problem and/or customer specific

Table 6.3 suggests that most opportunities are recognized in connection with a specific problem or need that has been identified among customers. More than 90 percent of the entrepreneurs surveyed strongly agree with these statements. The intensity of the responses suggest that the probability of entrepreneurial success may come from commercializing a solution to a heartfelt problem rather than following the conventional wisdom of merely satisfying a need. This leads to one important conclusion for an entrepreneurship educator: to enhance the probability of success, seek to recognize solvable problems that represent commercializable opportunities.

Two other suggestions emerge from these conclusions as well. One is to use a case-based approach to teaching entrepreneurship. Because cases generally present specific situations that need to be analyzed, a case approach permits students to be specific in their approach to OpR. A second implication is that the opportunities that are central to the entrepreneurial process can be identified by maintaining a market orientation. That is, focusing on customer needs and guiding a new venture by a customer orientation is likely to enhance overall success. It is also, according to the entrepreneurs surveyed, a very strong source of new venture opportunities.

Implication 3: teaching creativity skills can enhance opportunity recognition

The entrepreneurs' perspective on creativity is particularly interesting. Table 6.3 suggests that creativity is an essential aspect of opportunity recognition – 50 percent or more of both entrepreneurial samples strongly agree that it is very important. In addition, most of the entrepreneurs consider themselves very creative. Because they are obviously quite successful, this response suggests that they owe their success, at least in part, to their creative ability.

Thus, the opportunity recognition process could be enhanced by encouraging students to be more creative and by teaching the elements of creativity. That is, entrepreneurship educators could strengthen opportunity recognition skills by giving students an ability to think creatively, to speculate on opportunities and business conditions in an "out of the box" fashion, and to learn the art of creative leadership. This could enhance their ability to see opportunities that might not be apparent to untrained entrepreneurs or to those who may not regard themselves as creative.

Implication 4: experimentation and learning are essential to opportunity recognition

Table 6.3 suggests that opportunity recognition is more than just an "Aha!" experience. Although intuition and gut feel are very important to the entrepreneurial process, sometimes opportunities become apparent only after a period of experimentation or a series of failures. Ninety-two percent of the REs and 86 percent of the HFEs agreed that identifying opportunities takes several learning steps over time, rather than being a one-time occurrence. Opportunity recognition is a process that occurs over time and should be approached accordingly.

This finding is particularly important among students who have expectations of instant success. This suggests that a classroom environment that invites experimentation would enhance understanding of the opportunity recognition process. For example, it might be effective to create an exercise in which several alternatives are regarded as "correct" but an iterative, experimental process is required to uncover all valid conclusions. Students would need to go back and re-examine their decisions and their results over and over again until they understood what the elements of success are. Such continual learning via a trial-and-error approach could be used to help students understand the dynamics of opportunity recognition.

Implication 5: networking enhances the opportunity recognition process

Among successful entrepreneurs, a network of friends and associates who bring ideas to their attention is important to OpR. Table 6.3 indicates that a majority of entrepreneurs acknowledge the importance of other people in recognizing opportunities. Interestingly, the very successful HFEs were more strongly in agreement with this statement than the REs, which suggests that relying on other people for business ideas may be one of their keys to success.

This finding suggests that entrepreneurship educators might benefit from giving students more opportunities to network with colleagues and other entrepreneurs. Such networking is often a common part of a college or university experience; this finding suggests that networking opportunities should involve more depth in terms of learning what opportunities are available in the marketplace. This could take the form of sponsoring business planning activities that result in bona fide plans actually presented to real financiers, and setting up mentoring programs and in-depth internships with firms engaged in pursuing new venture opportunities.

Conclusion

Opportunity recognition is central to entrepreneurship. In this chapter, we have outlined scholarly contributions to the study of OpR and presented empirical evidence of the importance of OpR among two groups of entrepreneurs. Numerous issues related to the OpR process have been explored in terms of their practical implications for entrepreneurs and entrepreneurship education. Finally, we have presented a comprehensive creativity-based model of opportunity recognition. Our model attempts to demonstrate how opportunity recognition is essentially a creative process. Future research is called for in order to better understand the OpR process and, with that understanding, to train and support working and prospective entrepreneurs.

References

Amabile, T.M. (1988) "A model of creativity and innovation in organizations," in Staw, B. and Cummings, L.L. (eds) *Research in Organizational Behavior*, Greenwich, CT: JAI Press.

Ardichvili, A., Cardozo, R., and Ray, S. (2003) "A theory of entrepreneurial opportunity identification and development," *Journal of Business Venturing*, 18: 105–123.

Barron, F. and Harrington, D.M. (1981) "Creativity, intelligence, and personality," *Annual Review of Psychology*, 32: 439–476.

Bhave, M.P. (1994) "A process model of entrepreneurial venture creation," *Journal of Business Venturing*, 9: 223–242.

Bygrave, W. (1997) "The entrepreneurial process," in Bygrave, W. (ed.) *The Portable MBA in Entrepreneurship*, second edn, New York, NY: John Wiley and Sons.

Bygrave, W. and Hofer, C. (1991) "Theorizing about entrepreneurship," *Entrepreneurship Theory and Practice*, 16(2): 13–22.

Christensen, P.S., Madsen, O.O., and Peterson, R. (1989) *Opportunity Identification: The Contribution of Entrepreneurship to Strategic Management*, Denmark: Aarhus University Institute of Management.

Christensen, P.S., Madsen, O.O., and Peterson, R. (1994) *Opportunity Identification: The Contribution of Entrepreneurship to Strategic Management*, Denmark: Aarhus University Institute of Management.

Christensen, P.S. and Peterson, R. (1990) "Opportunity identification: mapping the sources of new venture ideas," paper presented at the 10th annual Babson Entrepreneurship Research Conference, Denmark: Aarhus University Institute of Management.

Cooper, A.C. (1981) "Strategic management: new ventures and small business," *Long Range Planning*, 14(5): 39–45.

Csikszentmihalyi, M. (1996) *Creativity*, New York, NY: HarperCollins.

De Koning, A. (1999) "Opportunity formation from a socio-cognitive perspective," UIC/AMA research symposium on the interface of marketing and entrepreneurship. Nice, France.

Gaglio, C.M. and Katz, J. (2001) "The psychological basis of opportunity identification: entrepreneurial alertness," *Journal of Small Business Economics*, 16(2): 95–111.

Gaglio, C.M. and Taub, P. (1992) "Entrepreneurs and opportunity recognition," *Frontiers of Entrepreneurship Research*, Wellesley, MA: Babson College.

Hills, G.E. (1995) "Opportunity recognition by successful entrepreneurs: a pilot study," *Frontiers of Entrepreneurship Research*, Wellesley, MA: Babson College.

Hills, G.E. and Shrader, R.C. (1998) "Successful entrepreneurs' insights into opportunity recognition," *Frontiers of Entrepreneurship Research*, Wellesley, MA: Babson College.

Hills, G.E., Shrader, R.C., and Lumpkin, G.T. (1999) "Opportunity recognition as a creative process," *Frontiers of Entrepreneurship Research*, Wellesley, MA: Babson College.

Kaish, S. and Gilad, B. (1991) "Characteristics of opportunities search of entrepreneurs versus executives: resources, interest, and general alertness," *Journal of Business Venturing*, 6: 45–61.

Kirzner, I.M. (1979) *Perceptions, Opportunities and Profit*, Chicago, IL: University of Chicago Press.

Koller, R.H. (1988) "On the source of entrepreneurial ideas," *Frontiers of Entrepreneurship Research*, Wellesley, MA: Babson College.

Long, W. and McMullan, W.E. (1984) "Mapping the new venture opportunity identification process," *Frontiers of Entrepreneurship Research*, Wellesley, MA: Babson College.

Ronstadt, R.C. (1988) "The corridor principle," *Journal of Business Venturing*, 3(1): 31–40.

Schumpeter, J.A. (1942) *Capitalism, Socialism, and Democracy*, New York, NY: Harper and Brothers.

Senge, P. (1990) "The leader's new work," *Sloan Management Review*, 32(1): 21–28.

Shane, S. (2000) "Prior knowledge and the discovery of entrepreneurial opportunities," *Organization Science*, 11(4): 448–469.

Shane, S. and Venkataraman, S. (2000) "The promise of entrepreneurship as a field of research," *Academy of Management Review*, 25(1): 217–226.

Singh, R. (1998) *Entrepreneurial Opportunity Recognition through Social Networks*, unpublished doctoral dissertation, University of Illinois at Chicago.

Singh, R., Hills, G.E., and Lumpkin, G.T. (1999) "Examining the role of self-perceived entrepreneurial alertness to the opportunity recognition process," paper presented at the Academy of Management Annual Conference, Chicago, IL.

Stevenson, H.H. and Jarillo-Mossi, J.C. (1986) "Preserving entrepreneurship as companies grow," *Journal of Business Strategy*, 7: 10–23.

Stevenson, H.H., Roberts, M.J., and Grousbeck, H.I. (1985) *New Business Ventures and the Entrepreneur*, Homewood, IL: Irwin.

Teach, R.D., Schwartz, R.G., and Tarpley, F.A. (1989) "The recognition and exploitation of opportunity in the software industry: a study of surviving firms," *Frontiers of Entrepreneurship Research*, Wellesley, MA: Babson College.

Timmons, J.A. (1994) *New Venture Creation*, fourth edn, Homewood, IL: Richard D. Irwin.

Vesper, K. (1996) *New Venture Experience*, revised edn, Seattle, WA: Vector Books.

Chapter 7

Michael H. Morris

Syracuse University

Minet Schindehutte

Page Center for Entrepreneurship, Miami University

Raymond W. LaForge

University of Louisville

THE EMERGENCE OF ENTREPRENEURIAL MARKETING: NATURE AND MEANING

THE CONTEMPORARY BUSINESS environment can be characterized in terms of increased risk, decreased ability to forecast, fluid firm and industry boundaries, a managerial mindset that must unlearn traditional management principles, and new structural forms that not only allow for change, but also help create it (Hitt and Reed 2000). What are the implications of the new competitive landscape for marketing? Do roles and responsibilities of the marketing function change under such circumstances?

Recent years have witnessed the application of a number of adjectives to the concept of marketing, including "guerrilla," "proactive," "subversive," "expeditionary," and "radical." At the same time, marketing curricula are increasingly embracing modules or courses on creativity and innovation, and interest in the marketing/entrepreneurship interface is strong among academics. The purpose of this chapter is to systematically assess these developments, and, more specifically, to critically examine the concept of "entrepreneurial marketing" (see also Morris et al. 2002). This term will be used as an umbrella to capture a new conceptualization of marketing.

Contemporary definitions of marketing and entrepreneurship

Prevalent conceptualizations of marketing center on a set of activities that facilitate exchange relationships: "Marketing is the process of planning and executing the conception, pricing, promotion and distribution of ideas, goods and services to create exchanges that satisfy individual and organizational goals" (Bennet 1988: 2). Marketing activities are generally organized into four interrelated categories: product, price, promotion, and distribution, or the marketing mix. Virtually any controllable mechanism for facilitating transactions or creating customer value will fall into one of these categories. The challenge of strategic marketing is to blend the elements of the marketing mix in a fashion that reflects the needs of key target customer audiences, while also enabling the firm to differentiate itself from competitors on a sustainable basis. Moreover, the mix elements are adapted over time to reflect changing market dynamics as products evolve through lifecycles.

Turning to entrepreneurship, Stevenson *et al.* (1989) define it as "the process of creating value by bringing together a unique package of resources to exploit an opportunity." The process includes the set of activities necessary to identify an opportunity, define a business concept, assess needed resources, acquire those resources, and manage and harvest the venture. Entrepreneurship has three underlying dimensions: innovativeness, risk-taking, and proactiveness (Covin and Slevin 1994; Miller and Friesen 1983). Innovativeness refers to the seeking of creative, novel solutions to problems and needs. It includes the development of new products and services, as well as new processes and technologies for performing organizational functions. Risk-taking involves the willingness of managers to commit significant resources to opportunities having a reasonable chance of costly failure. The risks are calculated and manageable. Proactiveness is concerned with implementation, making events happen through whatever means are necessary. It frequently entails breaking with established ways of accomplishing a task, and implies considerable perseverance, adaptability, and a willingness to assume responsibility for failure. To the extent that an undertaking demonstrates some amount of innovativeness, risk-taking and proactiveness, it can be considered an entrepreneurial event and the person behind it an entrepreneur. Further, any number of entrepreneurial events can be produced by a person or organization in a given time period. Accordingly, entrepreneurship is a question of "degree" (how innovative, risky, and proactive are the events?) and "frequency" (how many entrepreneurial events are pursued?) (Morris 1998).

Attention to the marketing and entrepreneurship interface

An examination of the marketing–entrepreneurship interface suggests two major subject areas for investigation. The first of these can be termed the role of marketing in entrepreneurship. This aspect of the interface is concerned with the application of marketing tools, concepts, and theory in supporting new venture creation and small business growth. This area has received considerable attention over the past decade.

The second dimension of the interface can be termed the role of entrepreneurship in marketing, and is our focus here. It represents an exploration of ways in which entrepreneurial attitudes and behaviors can be applied to the development of marketing programs. An example of an issue in this area is a stream of articles exploring the relationship between the marketing orientation and the entrepreneurial orientation of a firm. Empirical work has consistently demonstrated a significant relationship between these two orientations, and between each of these orientations and company performance (e.g. Jaworski and Kohli 1993; Morris and Paul 1987; Slater and Narver 1995). One interpretation of these findings is that the two orientations might not only be related, but they may actually be part of a single, overriding organizational philosophy (Deshpande *et al.* 1993).

In general, however, the marketing discipline has largely ignored a role for entrepreneurship. Notably lacking from the definition of marketing endorsed by the American Marketing Association is any responsibility for entrepreneurial or innovative behavior. Similarly, an examination over a ten-year period of the top-ranked research questions appearing in "Research Priorities," published annually by the Marketing Science Institute, suggests that issues of innovativeness, risk-taking, and proactiveness are largely ignored. The exception is an emphasis on "successfully introducing really new products." In a related vein, Morris and Hills (1992) conducted a review of journals and leading textbooks in the field. Their content analysis revealed a striking lack of material devoted to issues of innovativeness, risk-taking, and proactive behavior. A more recent examination of books published in the past three years by the authors indicates the findings of Morris and Hills continue to apply. Historically, Alderson (1965) was one of the few scholars to stress innovation as an integral component of the marketing function. His ideas were largely ignored, and the more prevalent tendency was to separate marketing from innovation (e.g. Levitt 1962). This separation, whether implicit or explicit, has hindered the ongoing advancement of the discipline.

The trouble with marketing: prevalent criticisms

In recent years, marketing practitioners have been subject to a variety of criticisms. Examples of concerns include an overreliance on established rules of thumb, encouragement of formula-based thinking, lack of accountability (especially in a time of diminishing returns on conventional marketing expenditures), an emphasis on the so-called supporting elements of the marketing mix (e.g. promotion) over product value, a focus on the superficial and transitory whims of customers, a tendency to imitate instead of innovate, concentration on selling products instead of creating markets, and the pursuit of short-term, low-risk payoffs (Hamel and Prahalad 1992; Moorman and Rust 1999; Webster 1997). As early as 1981, Webster (p. 11) surveyed senior managers and found that marketers were perceived to be "not sufficiently innovative and entrepreneurial in their thinking and decision-making."

For their part, academics have been criticized for research that contributes little to marketing practice. As firms find themselves operating in increasingly turbulent environments, the relevancy of theoretical, conceptual, and empirical research in marketing appears less consequential and more problematic. Deshpande (1999) suggests that scholars are addressing quite mundane issues, frequently of a tactical sort, with an increasing focus on narrower and narrower definitions of problems. Srivastava *et al.* (1998) conclude that marketing theory fails to connect marketing to cross-functional business practices and to the cash flow consequences of marketing actions. As a result, some worry that the marketing discipline is being marginalized, losing control of the important research agendas, and becoming responsible only for tactical implementation of the marketing mix elements (Day and Montgomery 1999).

A number of observers have concluded that marketing must move in significant new directions. Specific calls are made for marketers to embrace a far more cross-functional, cross-border, and cross-disciplinary orientation (Deshpande 1999; Kinnear 1999). A recurrent theme concerns the need to embrace strategic relationships, alliances, and networks as opposed to simple buyer–seller exchanges. As a case in point, Achrol and Kotler (1999) claim that a knowledge-driven economy produces structural upheaval in firms, ultimately resulting in the creation of organizations that must operate within three levels of networks: internal, vertical, and intermarket. Changes in marketing's role at each level will be radical and pervasive. Other scholars have argued for a basic redefinition of the discipline. Simmonds (1986) proposes that marketers be engaged in an ongoing process not only of identifying change opportunities, but of inducing continual change in their organizations and the marketplace. The basic role of the marketer becomes "organized rational innovation." Bonoma (1986) notes that marketing is a boundary function, responsible for interacting with key components of the environment on a regular basis. As these components become more dynamic and complex, boundary functions are forced to become more flexible and opportunity-driven. Murray (1981) concluded that marketing must become the natural "home" for the entrepreneurial process in firms.

Toward entrepreneurial marketing: the emergence of alternative conceptualizations

A variety of perspectives have emerged in both the trade and academic literatures concerning a different role for marketing in firms. While others exist, six of these perspectives are summarized in Table 7.1, and discussed in this section.

Perhaps the most widely known of these efforts is the work of Levinson (1998). He introduces the term "guerrilla marketing" to refer to an approach that relies on bootstrapping, creative use of available resources, and a highly targeted mix of innovative communications techniques. Levinson's grassroots approach is more tactical than strategic, concentrates more on promotional

Table 7.1 Six perspectives on the emerging nature of marketing

Guerrilla marketing (Levinson 1998)	Radical marketing (Hill and Rifkin 1999)
<ul><li>Low-cost but effective communications.</li><li>Doing more with less.</li><li>Cooperative efforts.</li><li>Leveraging resources.</li><li>Tapping under-utilized resources.</li><li>Using alternative channels.</li><li>Using alternative media.</li><li>Networking.</li><li>Less use of money, more investment of time, energy, imagination.</li><li>Acute focus in terms of products and services.</li></ul>	<ul><li>Strong visceral ties with target audience.</li><li>Focus on growth and expansion rather than profit-taking.</li><li>Maximal exploitation of very limited marketing budget.</li><li>Small, flat marketing department.</li><li>Redefine the competitive rules; challenge the conventional wisdom of the industry.</li><li>CEO owns the marketing function.</li><li>Cautious use of marketing research.</li><li>Passion drives the firm's marketing approach.</li></ul>

Expeditionary marketing (Hamel and Prahalad 1992)	Subversive marketing (Bonoma 1986)
<ul><li>Escape tyranny of served market.</li><li>Continuous search for innovative product concepts.</li><li>Overturning price/performance assumptions.</li><li>Leading rather than following customers.</li><li>More new product innovations introduced faster and targeting an array of niches.</li><li>Tolerance of failure.</li></ul>	<ul><li>Undermining company structures to implement new marketing practices.</li><li>Individual behavior that is aggressive and action-oriented.</li><li>Working around the official budget.</li><li>Rewards and resources based on merit.</li><li>Leveraging resources from inside and outside the firm.</li><li>Use of entrepreneurial role models.</li><li>Creative use of resource slack.</li><li>Reliance on informal networks.</li><li>Inventive approaches to obtaining key data and monitoring performance.</li></ul>

Environmental marketing management (Zeithaml and Zeithaml 1984)	Proactive marketing (Davis et al. 1991)
<ul><li>Reduce dependency on key external entities.</li><li>Marketing's role is to manage and lessen environmental uncertainties.</li><li>Proactive, opportunistic management rather than a reactive and adaptive role for marketing.</li><li>Efforts to initiate change and redefine operating conditions in the firm's external environment.</li><li>Removal of constraints on marketing function and limits on organization.</li></ul>	<ul><li>Marketing's role is to effect and manage change.</li><li>Marketers strive to redefine the product and market context within which the firm operates.</li><li>An emphasis on unproven wants, new market segments, new technologies, and continuous innovation in all areas of the marketing mix.</li><li>Responsibility for ongoing identification of novel sources of customer value.</li></ul>

tools than other marketing variables, and is intended for those starting and running small businesses. A genre of similar books have appeared in recent years with such titles as *Marketing on a Shoestring* (Davidson 1994) and *Off-the-Wall Marketing Ideas* (Michaels and Karpowicz 2000). These writings are filled with creative examples of guerrilla ideas. Even so, guerrilla approaches have experienced widespread adoption by both small and larger companies (Neff and Thompson 2000). More recently, variations on the guerrilla theme termed "buzz marketing" and "viral marketing" have received significant attention from large firms, advertising agencies, and consulting houses (Gladwell 2000; Rosen 2000). Buzz and viral approaches build on innovation diffusion principles and the concept of lateral rather than vertical communication. They were employed in the successful marketing efforts of Hotmail.com, eBay.com, Vespa Scooters and the movies *The Blair Witch Project* and *A.I. Artificial Intelligence*. And yet, academic researchers have largely ignored the concept of guerrilla marketing, perhaps questioning both the intellectual substance and the potentially faddish nature of a concept rooted in popularized trade books.

Hill and Rifkin (1999) use the term "radical marketing" to describe a set of approaches that challenge the status quo. They seek to find commonalities among unconventional but highly successful marketing methods of such companies as Snap-On Tools, Harley Davidson and Providian. Examples of these commonalities include the CEO owning the marketing function, strong visceral ties with one's target audience, and the creation of a "community" of customers, a promotional mix centered around one-to-one customer communication, and rejection of the prevalent industry logic regarding salient product attributes, pricing methods, or distribution philosophy. These authors focus more on mid-sized and larger companies, initiatives that tend to be more strategic in nature, and aspects of company philosophy and orientation. They stress the roles of passion and core values in marketing efforts.

Hamel and Prahalad (1992) suggest the term "expeditionary marketing" to describe the role of marketers in creating markets ahead of competitors. In their conceptualization, marketing serves to identify unarticulated needs of customers and new potential functionalities of products, extending the firm's "opportunity horizon." They stress the need to reject prevailing industry assumptions regarding price/performance trade-offs. Further, marketers must lead customers while also managing the risks inherent in innovative activity.

In discussing "subversive marketing," Bonoma (1986) refers to the need for marketers to undermine company structure and process in order to implement innovative marketing practices. The essence of his argument is that organizations come to rely on well-tested guidelines, rules of thumb, and fixed assumptions that work well under a given set of environmental conditions. Reasonably stable conditions allow marketers to build structures that reinforce useful habits and routines, and help ensure consistency in quality, costs, and service levels. However, management tends to remain loyal to these guidelines even as fundamental changes occur in the external environment. With the onset of such change, marketing routines actually become hurdles that obstruct appropriate adaptation. Serious damage is done to the firm's competitive position unless marketers are willing to bend or break rules, work around the official budget, leverage resources from inside and outside the firm, and develop inventive approaches to obtaining otherwise unavailable key performance data.

Changing environments is a theme of Zeithaml and Zeithaml (1984), who suggest that marketing as conventionally construed is fairly deterministic. A typical organization seeks to establish customer wants, and then structures company goals and operations to provide the desired product better than competitors. In effect, marketing begins with a set of environmental constraints that are pre-defined for the company. Marketing intelligence provides inputs that allow the marketer to analyze forces in the environment and then implement changes that enable the firm to adapt to these forces. Zeithaml and Zeithaml propose that marketing theory should explicitly reject this approach and adopt a proactive, entrepreneurial orientation to the management of environmental conditions. They emphasize the need to lead customers and markets, and to redefine critical aspects of the external operating environment.

A final perspective can be found in the work of Davis *et al.* (1991) who provide empirical support for a contingency view of the role of marketing. Under placid environmental conditions, firms can concentrate on incremental improvements to their methods of satisfying existing customer needs. Alternatively, when the environment is characterized in terms of stronger interdependencies among firms, marketers must focus attention on anticipating and quickly responding to the moves of competitors. However, to the extent that environments are fairly turbulent, marketing managers must take responsibility for introducing greater levels of entrepreneurship into all aspects of the firm's marketing efforts. They must assume responsibility for redefining the product and market context within which the firm operates.

An assessment of these various perspectives suggests some commonalities, with consistent emphasis given to:

a   efficiency in marketing budgets;
b   leveraging of resources;
c   rejection of conventional approaches to marketing variables;
d   ongoing product/service innovation; and
e   leadership of customers and an ability to affect change in the environment.

Given these commonalities, it is our contention that these perspectives represent the foundation for an alternative concept of marketing.

Specifying the concept of entrepreneurial marketing

The term "entrepreneurial marketing" is proposed as an integrative concept for conceptualizing marketing in an era of information intensity and ongoing change in the environmental context within which firms operate. It can be defined as "the proactive identification and exploitation of opportunities for attracting and retaining customers through innovative approaches to risk management, resource leveraging and value creation." Entrepreneurial marketing (EM) represents an opportunistic perspective wherein the marketer is not simply responsible

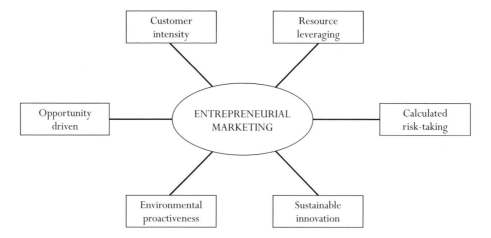

Figure 7.1 Five elements comprising the conceptualization of entrepreneurial marketing

for communication activities, but with continually discovering new sources of value for customers and new markets for the firm. Value is created through approaches to the elements of the marketing mix that challenge prevailing industry assumptions. Importantly, EM represents a different approach to envisioning the business itself, its relationship with the marketplace, and the role of the marketing function within the firm. As illustrated in Figure 7.1, EM consists of six underlying dimensions.

Customer intensity

While largely ignored in marketing theory, there is an emotional aspect to the successful market positioning of such companies as Harley Davidson, Southwest Airlines and Snap-On Tools. Southwest is a case in point. They use the concept of "spirituality" to capture profound convictions regarding the role of the employee, the nature of the customer experience, and how the two are inter-related. As Hamel and Prahalad (1994: 128) note: "Getting to the future first is more a function of resourcefulness than resources . . . Resourcefulness stems not from an elegantly structured strategic architecture, but from a deeply felt sense of purpose, a broadly shared dream, a truly seductive view of tomorrow's opportunity." We propose the term "customer intensity" to capture a sense of conviction, passion, zeal, enthusiasm, and belief in where marketing is attempting to take the firm and how it plans to get there. Beyond bringing technical competence to the marketing task, entrepreneurial marketers bring intensity; they reinforce the need for all employees to identify at fundamental levels with the firm's products and brands, and ultimately with the firm's value proposition.

Sustainable innovation

Sustained innovation involves the ability to maintain a flow of internally and externally motivated new ideas, where these ideas are translatable into new products, services, processes, technology applications, and/or markets (i.e. an "innovation factory"). A range, or continuum, of possibilities exists, from new to the world products to product improvements and new applications, to new processes. Marketing plays an integral part in sustainable innovation, with roles ranging from opportunity identification and concept generation to technical support and creative augmentation of the firm's resource base. Within marketing operations, process innovation becomes a cornerstone. Managers continually champion new approaches to segmentation, pricing, use of the brand, packaging, customer-relationship management, customer credit, logistics, customer communication, service levels, and so forth.

Opportunity driven

Firms must strike a balance in innovation activities between pioneering initiatives that lead the market and quick, creative adaptation to changes in market circumstances. Stevenson *et al.* (1989) propose a continuum of managerial approaches, ranging from a continuous emphasis on pursuing opportunity regardless of resources currently controlled (i.e. entrepreneurial behavior) to a focus on the efficient utilization of existing resources (i.e. administrative behavior). Opportunities represent unnoticed market positions that are sources of sustainable profit potential. They derive from market imperfections, where knowledge about these imperfections and how to exploit them distinguish entrepreneurial marketing. The availability of opportunities tends to correlate with rates of environmental change, indicating a need for marketers to engage in heightened levels of both active search and discovery. Further, exploitation of opportunity entails learning and ongoing adaptation by marketers before, during, and after new concept implementation.

Calculated risk-taking

Risk-taking involves a willingness to pursue opportunities having a reasonable chance of producing losses or significant performance discrepancies. The emphasis is on moderate and calculated risks. EM does not entail reckless decision-making, but rather, a reasonable awareness of the risks involved and an attempt to manage such risk factors. These risks are reflected in the various resource allocation decisions, as well as in the choice of products, services, and markets to be emphasized. Hamel and Prahalad (1991) conclude that by innovating more, with market incursions that involve exploring multiple niches, a firm actually reduces its risk profile to a more manageable level. This approach requires a systematic approach to organizational learning. Properly designed marketing intelligence systems can allow companies to quickly determine what works and what does not in a given entrepreneurial endeavor, and translate these lessons to other endeavors.

Every firm has a risk profile, although often not explicitly formulated. This risk profile evolves over time. Marketing has a responsibility for developing a keen grasp on this profile and for managing risks in a manner that reflects the profile. Risk management is accomplished with a range of devices, including intelligence-gathering efforts, test markets, working with lead customers, staged product launches, outsourcing of various activities tied to a new product, borrowing or sharing resources, and partnerships with suppliers, distributors, and competitors.

Environmental proactiveness

The entrepreneurial marketer does not take the external environment as a given, or as a set of circumstances to which the firm can only react. The environment is defined as an opportunity horizon. While acknowledging areas where the firm is more dependent on various external parties, or vulnerable to external phenomena, marketing efforts are proactively directed toward affecting change in the environment. More specifically, the marketer attempts to redefine elements of the external environment in ways that reduce uncertainty, lessen the firm's dependency and vulnerability, and/or modify the task environment in which the firm operates. In essence, the marketer enhances the firm's level of control over its destiny.

Resource leveraging

Entrepreneurial marketers are brilliant at leveraging resources. In their companies, ambition forever outpaces resources. The implication is that entrepreneurial marketers are not constrained by the resources they currently control or have at their disposal. They are able to leverage resources in a number of different ways: stretching resources much further than others have done in the past, getting uses out of resources that others are unable to realize, using other people's resources to accomplish one's own purpose, complementing one resource with another to create higher combined value, and using certain resources to obtain other resources.

Of all the leveraging approaches, perhaps the most critical one concerns the ability to use other people's resources to accomplish the marketer's purpose. Examples include bartering, borrowing, renting, leasing, sharing, recycling, contracting, and outsourcing. These efforts can be directed at other departments and units within the firm, or at suppliers, financiers, distributors, and customers, among others. They frequently entail both informal initiatives such as the exchange of favors and the use of networks, and formal initiatives, such as strategic alliances and joint ventures.

Marketers must develop a capacity for resource leveraging. The ability to recognize an under-utilized resource, to see how a resource could be used in a non-conventional way, or to convince those that control a resource to let the marketer use it, requires insight, experience, and skill. The same can be said for the ability to get team members to work extra hours, convince departments to perform activities they normally do not perform, or put together unique sets of resources that, when blended, are synergistic.

Conclusion

The six dimensions that comprise entrepreneurial marketing are not independent. Thus, risks may be mitigated through resource leveraging in the form of outsourcing, which in turn results in greater strategic flexibility. Innovation may be facilitated through resource leveraging in the form of a strategic partnership, but this might increase the firm's dependency on an outside party. In addition, not all of the dimensions need to be operating at once for entrepreneurial marketing to occur. The marketer could engage in significant innovation that redefines environmental conditions, involves high levels of customer intensity, and contains numerous risks, some of which the marketer is able to mitigate, but resources are not being leveraged. Stated differently, EM is a matter of degree, and various combinations of the underlying dimensions will result in marketing that is more, or less, entrepreneurial.

When considered collectively, these six dimensions produce a type of marketing that differs significantly from conventional marketing practice. Table 7.2 summarizes key differences. EM is fundamentally an opportunity driven and opportunity seeking way of thinking and acting. Moreover, entrepreneurial marketing differs in that it returns the discipline to its roots as creative pursuit and as art. Thus, the imagination, vision, cleverness, and originality associated with entrepreneurial behavior lie at the core of this conceptualization of marketing, and these attributes are applied to the full range of marketing activities, from market research and segmentation to the management of the marketing mix. This is not to suggest that science, established theory, systematic processes, and sophisticated insights are not vital aspects of EM. These elements must play an instrumental role if this school of marketing is to have sustainable impact.

Much work remains in the development of entrepreneurial marketing. For instance, richer insights are needed into the six dimensions of EM, including research on the interrelationships among these dimensions. Clarification of potential conflicts and their implications is important, such as the extent to which certain resource leveraging approaches make the firm more vulnerable to external forces. Obstacles to entrepreneurial marketing in organizations warrant further research, together with approaches to overcoming such obstacles. In addition, research is needed to more formally specify hypotheses regarding the linkages between antecedents (organizational and environmental) and outcomes of EM. Another issue concerns whether there are optimal levels of entrepreneurial marketing in a given firm. If so, how is such a level defined and what are the external and internal variables that determine the appropriate level of EM?

Table 7.2 Contrasting conventional marketing and entrepreneurial marketing

Conventional marketing	*Entrepreneurial marketing*
• An essentially reactive stance with respect to the external environment. • Marketing strives to follow customers. • Serving existing markets. • Focal point is efficient management of the marketing mix. • Risk is to be minimized. • Marketing as an objective, dispassionate science. • Reliance on proven formulas and established rules of thumb. • Marketing supports the innovation efforts of other functional areas of the firm, most notably R&D. • Marketing as a functional silo. • Promotion and customer communication receive the greatest amount of attention from marketers. • Scarcity mentality, zero-sum game perspective on resources. • Heavy dependency on survey research. • Marketing facilitates transactions and control.	• The firm attempts to influence or redefine aspects of the external environment. • Marketing strives to lead customers. • Creating new markets. • Focal point is new value creation for the customer through relationships, alliances, resource management approaches, and the marketing mix. • Risk is necessary and marketing's job is to manage the firm's risk profile in a calculated fashion. • While acknowledging the value of science and learning, recognition is given to the roles of passion, zeal, and commitment in successful marketing programs. • Psychology of challenging commonly-shared assumptions. • Marketing is the home of the entrepreneurial process in the organization. • Marketing as a cross-disciplinary and inter-functional pursuit. • The relative investment of resources in different areas of the marketing mix is context-specific. • Opportunity is pursued regardless of resources controlled; philosophy of resource leveraging is paramount. • Skeptical use of conventional market research; employment of alternative methods (e.g. lead user research, "backward" research). • Marketing facilitates speed, change, adaptability, agility.

References

Achrol, R.S. and Kotler, P. (1999) "Marketing in the network economy," *Journal of Marketing*, 63: 146–163.

Alderson, W. (1965) *Dynamic Marketing Behavior*, Homewood, IL: Richard D. Irwin Publishing.

Bennet, P.D. (ed.) (1988) *Dictionary of Marketing Terms*, Chicago, IL: American Marketing Association.

Bonoma, T.V. (1986) "Marketing subversives," *Harvard Business Review*, 64: 113–118.

Cornwall, J.R. and Perlman, B. (1990) *Organizational Entrepreneurship*, Homewood, IL: Irwin.

Covin, J.G. and Slevin, D.P. (1994) "Corporate entrepreneurship in high and low technology industries: a comparison of strategic variables, strategy patterns and performance in global markets," *Journal of Euro-Marketing*, 3(3): 99–127.

Davidson, J. (1994) *Marketing on a Shoestring: Low-Cost Tips for Marketing Your Products or Services*, Chapel Hill, NC: Breathing Space Institute.

Davis, D., Morris, M., and Allen, J. (1991) "Perceived environmental turbulence and its effect on selected entrepreneurship, marketing and organizational characteristics in industrial firms," *Journal of Academy of Marketing Science*, 19: 43–51.

Day, G.S. and Montgomery, D.B. (1999) "Charting new directions for marketing," *Journal of Marketing*, 63: 3–13.

Deshpande, R. (1999) "Foreseeing marketing," *Journal of Marketing*, 63: 164–167.

Deshpande, R., Farley, J., and Webster, F., Jr. (1993) "Corporate culture, customer orientation and innovativeness," *Journal of Marketing*, 57(1): 23–37.

Gladwell, M. (2000) *The Tipping Point: How Little Things Can Make a Big Difference*, New York, NY: Little, Brown and Company.

Godin, S. and Gladwell, M. (2000) *Unleasing the Ideavirus*, New York, NY: Do You Zoom.

Hamel, G. and Prahalad, C.K. (1991) "Corporate imagination and expeditionary marketing," *Harvard Business Review*, 69(4): 81–83.

Hamel, G. and Prahalad, C.K. (1994) *Competing for the Future*, Boston, MA: Harvard Business School Press.

Hill, S. and Rifkin, G. (1999) *Radical Marketing: From Harvard to Harley, Lessons From Ten that Broke the Rules and Made it Big*, New York, NY: HarperCollins.

Hitt, M.A. and Reed, T.S. (2000) "Entrepreneurship in the new competitive landscape," in Meyer, G.D. and Heppard, K.A. (eds) *Entrepreneurship as Strategy*, Thousand Oaks, CA: Sage Publications

Jaworski, B.J. and Kohli, A.K. (1993) "Marketing orientation: antecedents and consequences," *Journal of Marketing*, 57: 53–71.

Kinnear, T. (1999) "A perspective on how firms relate to their markets," *Journal of Marketing*, 63: 112–114.

Levinson, C. (1998) *Guerrilla Marketing: Secrets for Making Big Profits From Your Small Business*, Boston, MA: Houghton Mifflin Company.

Levitt, T. (1962) *Innovations In Marketing*, Boston, MA: Division of Research, Graduate School of Business Administration.

Michaels, N. and Karpowicz, D.J. (2000) *Off the Wall Marketing Ideas: Jumpstart Your Sales without Busting Your Budget*, Avon, MA: Adams Media Corporation.

Miller, D. and Friesen, P.H. (1983) "Innovation in conservative and entrepreneurial firms: two models of strategic momentum," *Strategic Management Journal*, 3: 1–25.

Moorman, C. and Rust, R.T. (1999) "The role of marketing," *Journal of Marketing*, 63: 180–197.

Morris, M.H. (1998) *Entrepreneurial Intensity*, Westport, CT: Quorum Publishing.

Morris, M.H. and Hills, G. (1992) "The role of entrepreneurship in marketing education," *Marketing Education Review*, 2: 1–10.

Morris, M.H. and Paul, G.W. (1987) "The relationship between entrepreneurship and marketing in established firms," *Journal of Business Venturing*, 2: 247–259.

Morris, M.H., Schindehutte, M., and LaForge, R. (2002) "Entrepreneurial marketing: a construct for integrating emerging entrepreneurship and marketing perspectives," *Journal of Marketing Theory and Practice*, 10(4): 1–19.

Murray, J.A. (1981) "Marketing is home for the entrepreneurial process," *Industrial Marketing Management*, 10(2): 93–99.

Neff, J. and Thompson, S. (2000) "800-pound gorilla P&G tries guerrilla marketing," *Advertising Age*, 39: 101–110.

Rosen, E. (2000) *The Anatomy of Buzz: How to Create Word of Mouth Marketing*, New York, NY: Doubleday.

Simmonds, K. (1986) "Marketing as innovation: the eighth paradigm," *The Journal of Management Studies*, 23(5): 479–500.

Slater, S.F. and Narver, J.C. (1995) "Market orientation and the learning organization," *Journal of Marketing*, 59(3): 63–74.

Srivastava, R.K., Shervani, T.A., and Fahey, L. (1998) "Market-based assets and shareholder value: a framework for analysis," *Journal of Marketing*, 62(1): 2–18.

Stevenson, H.H., Roberts, M.J., and Grousbeck, H.I. (1989) *Business Ventures and the Entrepreneur*, Homewood, IL: Irwin.

Webster, F.E. (1981) "Top management's concerns about marketing issues for the 1980s," *Journal of Marketing*, 45(3): 9–16.

Webster, F.E. (1997) "The future role of marketing in the organization," in Lehmann, D.R. and Jocz, K.E. (eds) *Reflections on the Futures of Marketing*, Cambridge, MA: Marketing Science Institute.

Zeithaml, C. and Zeithaml, V. (1984) "Environmental management: revising the marketing perspective," *Journal of Marketing*, 48: 46–53.

Chapter 8

Lynn Neeley

Northern Illinois University at DeKalb

BOOTSTRAP FINANCE

FINANCES HAVE BEEN ONE of the important aspects of starting or operating most enterprises. Many entrepreneurs have used a variety of bootstrap financing methods to satisfy their ventures' financial and resource needs without long-term commitments or external obligations. This chapter profiles a thorough listing of bootstrap finance techniques, which include social and economic transactions (Bhide 1992).

Bootstrap finance techniques

Categories of bootstrap financing include personal resources, personal short-term borrowing, funding from friends or relatives, barter, quasi-equity arrangements, cooperative assets, client-based funds, asset or cash management, leases, outsourcing, subsidies or incentives, and foundation funds. Each of these groups is described briefly.

The owner's financial and real assets

The majority of ventures that have been initiated in the United States started with the owner's financial or real assets serving as a part of the long-term and working capital of the business (Wetzel 1994: 176). Clearly, those sources of financing have exposed entrepreneurs to the potential of personal loss, but they have also allowed entrepreneurs to maintain control and ownership of their companies in return for bearing that risk. Almost any assets that can be owned and controlled by individuals have been used within this category of possible funding options. Personal savings accounts and securities, such as preferred or common stocks, corporate or municipal bonds, and certificates of deposit, have provided liquidity for ventures (Blechman and Levinson 1991: 27–28). Entrepreneurs have sold real or personal property or used their homes as the opening base of operations, while other owners have forgone personal salary or depended on income from other jobs to sustain their businesses (Winborg and Landstrom 2001: 253). These methods have focused on the actual use of personal resources or converting those assets to cash for the benefit of the venture. Entrepreneurs have also exploited their financial capacity through lending obligations (see Table 8.1).

Table 8.1 Bootstrap finance categories and techniques

Category	Techniques
Owner's resources	Savings accounts, sales of securities or property, forgone salary, salary from other job, and residence for business use.
Owner's borrowing	Installment or signature loans, lines of credit, credit cards, micro-lending programs, franchise lending, collateral loans, mortgages, home equity loans, insurance cash value, retirement account funds, on-line credit search matching services.
Relationship resources	Cash contributions, property or equipment purchases, donated labor, and below-market salary.
Barter	Service or goods trade, organized exchanges.
Quasi-equity	Partnerships, angels – individual or group – adventure capital, incubators' interest, and credit enhancements.
Cooperation resources	Equipment or facilities sharing, joint ownership, coordinated purchases, customer-sharing alliances, and franchise supported advertising and services.
Customer financing	Prepaid licenses, advance payments, customer-funded research and development, letters of credit, and "invest-omers."
Cash or asset management	Trade credit, delayed payment, deferred taxes, overdraft privileges, account transfers, skip loans, accelerated receipts, short-term investments, inventory minima, used equipment, and theft control.
Leases	Closed- and open-ended leases, sale leasebacks, and venture leasing.
Outsourcing	Professional services, temporary employees, manufacturing co-ops, and flexible networks.
Subsidies and incentives	Direct and indirect local, state or federal funds, university resources, and indirect corporate funds.
Foundation grants	Direct grants, flow-through arrangements.

The entrepreneur's personal borrowing

Personal borrowing has served as another mainstay for independent enterprises (Wetzel 1994: 186). One of the many reasons for this has been that the distinctions between personal and business assets have been vague, particularly with proprietorship or partnership as the legal form of business (Ang 1991: 6).

Installment loans, lines of credit, signature loans, and credit cards

Personal obligations made to open or sustain a business have taken the form of installment loans, personal lines of credit, signature or personal loans, and personal credit cards. Modestly sized installment loans have been extensions of personal borrowing capacity in the case of proprietorships or partnerships because the ventures have been legal extensions of the entrepreneur. Personal lines of credit have been distinct in offering enhanced convenience, flexibility, and economy (Fraser 2001: 53). Entrepreneurs have obtained personal or signature loans through many different financial institutions, although this lending vehicle has not been offered frequently in all parts of the nation (Arkebauer 1993: 148, Wasilowski 2001). In a 1997 survey, the top two methods of financing small companies were bank loans and credit cards, which were used by 38 percent and 34 percent of the respondents respectively. That was an increase from 17 percent of business owners who reported using credit cards in 1993 (Hise 1998: 1).

Micro-lending and franchise lending

Franchisers and non-profit organizations have organized micro-lending programs, which have typically granted smaller loans to serve as seed capital for start-ups (Fraser 2001: 50). Franchisers have offered small loans, unsecured cash flow loans, or loan guarantees to their prospective franchisees (Whittemore 1993: 58–59). Some micro-loan programs established through universities and governmental agencies have given borrowers training and assistance, in addition to funds for the new business (Gatewood and Hylton 1994: 246).

Collateralized loans, mortgages, and home equity loans

A person willing to surrender some personal asset in the case of default on the debt may negotiate a collateralized loan. Assets serving as collateral have included residences, other real property, automobiles, jewelry, fine art, collectibles, negotiable securities, inventories, equipment, copyrights, patents, and trademarks (Blechman and Levinson 1991: 17–28). Inventories (personal property in the case of a proprietor or partner) have been subjected to particular scrutiny because of their continually changing composition and value. Some of the funding techniques used to accommodate the nature of inventories have been warehouse receipts or liens, floating liens, field warehousing, chattel mortgages, conditional sales contracts, time-sales financing or floor planning, and public warehousing (Shulman 1994: 216–218). First or second mortgages on houses or home equity loans have also figured into the financing options for business founders (Fraser 2001: 53). Insurance companies or pension funds have occasionally provided funds to entrepreneurs through collateralized loans, but typically the portfolios of loans these institutions maintain have had a minimum loan term of five years, and have been backed by real estate (Shulman 1994: 226–227).

Insurance cash value or retirement account withdrawals

Some people have made regular payments into whole life insurance plans or made steady contributions into retirement accounts to make their personal savings habits routine. These may have been among the best choices available in a start-up situation (Van Auken and Neeley 1996: 243). Although access is relatively easy, penalties and interest charges may apply to these transactions. If the entrepreneur fails to repay the funds, the ultimate value of the policy or account may be reduced.

Online credit matching services

Web-based credit matching services, provided by firms such as American Express and First Union, have accepted applications from potential borrowers and matched them with appropriate non-bank and bank lenders for a fee. Convenience has been an advantage with this financial tool, but two points of concern have been confidentiality and the inadvertent damage to credit scores. The process may have damaged credit ratings because the same application was simultaneously "shopped" to many lenders. Repeated credit applications have been a negative in the scoring system (Fraser 1999: 133).

Relationship resources

Family members and friends have been funding sources for entrepreneurs when other lenders have been unwilling to extend credit. Friends or relatives have contributed funds by gifts of money, through direct loans, or by guaranteeing loans from institutions (Fraser 1999: 133–134). Another way families and friends have contributed has been to purchase assets in their own names for the businesses' uses, i.e. they have held title to the assets (Fenn 1999). Relatives or friends have also furnished labor and professional expertise to ventures either by donating time or by accepting below-market salaries or fees (Winborg and Landstrom 2001: 253).

Barter

Entrepreneurs have used two types of barter to sustain their ventures – direct exchange and the relatively new barter exchanges. Although barter, direct exchange, requires a one-for-one trade of assets, organized barter exchanges have offered flexibility so that searching for a coincidence of needs has not been necessary. Barter credits, earned in an exchange through any transaction, have been traded for services offered by any other member of the exchange (Szabo 1992).

Quasi-equity

Equity has indicated ownership, and many entrepreneurs have been unwilling to release this. On the other hand, quasi-equity has not been actively traded, has been held by one or a few individuals, and has not been sold with the ultimate objective of an initial public offering. Quasi-equity methods to obtain resources have included partnerships, individual or group angels, adventure capitalists, equity interests traded to incubators, and credit enhancers. Angel investors have characteristically made "informal" arrangements to infuse seed money or first-stage funding, have not financed ventures as a profession, have not been relatives, and have usually invested close to their homes (Wetzel 1994: 175–176). Angels have shown more flexibility in both the holding term and the liquidity of their investments and have occasionally pooled their resources to act as a consortium. Adventure capitalists have generally had a lower level of sophistication, used their own money exclusively, offered small amounts of funding, and have been easier to "sell" on a new business's idea (Blechman and Levinson 1991: 171–183). Credit enhancements have been a hybrid form of indebtedness that has had warrants attached so that a third party, not the lender, could buy stock at some point in the future. With this method, a third party has agreed to pledge securities to enhance the liquidity of collateral that a business owner has offered to a lender (Arkebauer 1993: 154).

Cooperative assets

Cooperation has allowed the founders of businesses to leverage their assets for more space, a wider variety of equipment, expanded capacity, greater purchasing power, better negotiated terms, and larger customer bases. Shared employees, especially administrative assistants and staff persons, have been used regularly among groups of individual service providers sharing space. These professionals have gained the added intangible benefit of a seemingly larger and more impressive firm (Starr and MacMillan 1990: 83). Other entrepreneurs have owned equipment jointly and shared space to sustain the business (Winborg and Landstrom 2001: 253). When several firms have combined smaller individual orders into a single larger order, owners have been able to meet minimum order requirements to qualify for discounts on quantity purchases, better deliveries, or better payment terms (Winborg and Landstrom 2001: 253). Businesses have also shared customers through customer-sharing alliances, in which clients have gone to entrepreneurs asking for referrals and made the ultimate choices from among their referred or secondary vendors; this is unlike an outsourcing arrangement (Tarkenton and Smith 1997: 135). Another form of cooperative assets has been the support services paid for by franchisees. The affiliated businesses have the option of pooling their purchasing, advertising, and marketing resources for greatly increased market power and visibility over what they would have had as singular business entities (Spinelli 1994: 361–367).

Customer or client financing

Customer-related sources of money have included prepaid licenses or royalties, advance payments on purchases or service contracts, client funding for research and development, letters of credit for international transactions, and "invest-omers" (Fraser 2001: 53). Although customer financing has been a source of cost-free short-term money, most forms of client funding have created an overhanging liability associated with the resources (Fraser 2001). This has clearly been the case for prepayments and advances. Customer-funded research and development contracts have been relatively common among companies in high technology or technology and research intensive industries (Freear *et al.* 1995: 396). For entrepreneurs conducting their business in foreign countries, letters of credit have been important for facilitating foreign purchases and payments (Fraser 1999: 135). "Invest-omers" have typically been large firms that provide funds to specific entrepreneurial companies with which they have formed strong economic ties (Fraser 2001).

Cash or asset management

Cash management techniques have enhanced companies' assets through delayed cash outflows, accelerated cash inflows, and enhanced asset productivity (Resnik 1988: 151).

Delayed cash outflows

Some of the more common methods to delay funds outflows have been trade credit, deferred taxes, overdraft privileges, account transfer arrangements, and skip loans. Trade credits have given approved clients interest-free financing for their purchases through the time lag between the receipt of the merchandise and the payment date specified on the billing. Payment terms to avoid fees or interest and to take advantage of any discounts have been specified in terms and conditions negotiated in advance with vendors. Delayed payments have been legitimately and legally made to governmental taxing bodies as well (Resnik 1988: 151–156). With deferred taxes, the payment date is considerably later than the date when the obligation had been recognized. Overdraft privileges and account transfers have been reliable methods for accessing very short-term money by precluding a check being drawn on an account with inadequate funds. These privileges and account transfer arrangements have resembled a permanent credit line in that funds would be drawn from another previously specified account to cover any shortage (State National Bank 1999). Entrepreneurs operating businesses with highly seasonal cash flow patterns have negotiated loans with customized payment schedules, skipped-payment loans (Arkebauer 1993: 155). In those arrangements, payments would be due when fund shortfalls were expected to end.

Accelerated cash receipts from customers

Entrepreneurs have sought to speed up the receipt of cash, and some of the more widely used techniques have been early payment discounts, late payment penalties, specified places of payment, the sale of accounts receivable, and loans against accounts receivable (Resnik 1988: 152; Szabo 1992). Collecting payments for credit sales quickly has been important, but the choice of method and deployment style of the technique has been equally important to preclude alienating customers. The devices to achieve quicker collections by giving early payment incentives have relied upon sound record keeping, clear communication regarding credit terms, careful account balance and age monitors, appropriate notices or reminders, and follow-up conversations (Resnik 1988: 152). A different approach has been to penalize late payers a small percentage of the balance and sometimes to add a monthly interest charge as a carrying fee. Factoring has been the term used for a business owner selling accounts receivable, usually at a substantial discount to access cash more quickly. Accounts receivable has been taken as collateral for loans; and when initiated, the business has often received a sharply reduced percentage of the balance for the cash settlement (Blechman and Levinson 1991: 72–76).

Enhanced asset productivity

Keeping cash in income-producing accounts or investments, minimizing any funds in inventory, buying used equipment, and controlling theft have been among the possible enhancements to asset productivity. Some assets have been more amenable than others to more effective use, but cash in non-interest-bearing or low-yielding accounts and inventories might frequently have been worked to better advantage. Changes in the commercial banking and brokerage sectors have given people many more options so that this missed earnings opportunity can be eliminated with comparatively few transactions. Minimized inventory, without poor customer service or long delivery times, has freed cash and has relied on sound record keeping, coordinating communication with customers and clients, anticipating seasonality, and monitoring the age of merchandise and supplies (Shulman 1994: 207–208). Consignment, holding goods out for sale without having title to the goods, has remained a good option for many entrepreneurs to reduce the cash invested (Goldstein 1995: 234), as have used, rather than new, equipment purchases (Winborg and Landstrom 2001: 253). Theft control has been important for virtually all entrepreneurs because theft represents 100 percent cash outflows with 0 percent cash inflows as the least damaging scenario. The more likely case is that a theft would represent more than a 100 percent "dead loss" because of the replacement cost of the asset combined with increased insurance premiums (Resnik 1988: 156–159).

Leases

Leases have given entrepreneurs a way to use equipment, vehicles, and facilities without purchasing those assets (Blechman and Levinson 1991: 13, 214–215). Many varieties of leases have been available to meet most business owners' needs, but four of the more common leases have been closed-end leases, open-end leases, sales and leasebacks, and venture leases (Shulman 1994: 228). Closed-end leases, called straight, operating or maintenance leases, have been the simplest routes to take. The lessee has paid a fixed payment over a specified period of time, and the asset has reverted to the lessor at the end of the lease term. Open-ended leases, often called capital or financial leases, have had some clear distinctions from closed-end leases. The lessee has had the responsibility for a fixed periodic payment to the lessor and has borne the expenses of ownership. Sale and leaseback agreements have been made by entrepreneurs selling equipment or real property that they owned to a leasing company, which immediately leased it back to them (Blechman and Levinson 1991: 83). These arrangements have been desirable because they have given tax or financial leverage advantages to entrepreneurs. Venture leasing, a relatively new form of lease arrangement, has had a qualifier, the enterprise having won venture capitalists' money. This form of lease financing has been acquired at comparatively high lease rates unless the entrepreneur has sweetened the deal with stock warrants (Fraser 1999).

Outsourcing

Outsourcing for professional services, temporary employees, or fabrication capabilities has allowed entrepreneurs to buy and pay on an "as-needed" basis to avoid long-term or unproductive capital commitments (Fenn 1999). Outsourcing has been the use of resources not owned or legally controlled by the company to accomplish what has been necessary. Professional services from attorneys, accountants, marketing specialists, architects, engineers, or any other "experts" have been accessed in this way, just as temporary employees of many descriptions have been (Freear et al. 1995: 397). Coordinated outsourcing has become known as a flexible network or virtual company (Helgesen 1995).

Subsidies and incentives

Governmental units, universities, and private corporations have given subsidies or incentives or made grants available to accomplish specific objectives fulfilling their missions in the larger society. This has been done through direct or indirect funding.

Direct and indirect local funding

Business owners have received supplemental payments or reimbursements from municipal or county governing bodies to reduce the costs of training or educating employees through grants, loans, and shared costs (Illinois Tax Increment Association 2001). Entrepreneurs have also benefited from lower charges for services, which include credit against an expense or a direct reduction in a charge, such as a tax bill (Illinois Tax Increment Association 2001). Municipalities have also helped with businesses' costs in the recovery of former landfills and in cleaning up property that had received hazardous discharge and by encouraging clean-up of brownfields – industrial properties that have been under-utilized or abandoned (State of New Jersey 2001). Many communities have enterprise zones or industrial corridors to provide business owners with inducements to operate in these areas (State of New Jersey 2001). City-sponsored business incubators have offered lower costs for facilities and professional services, and those with an industry segment "theme" have brought entrepreneurs in close proximity to share ideas and resources (Gatewood and Hylton 1994: 276).

Direct and indirect state support

Business owners have gained financing through direct state government support through wage subsidies and grants, although direct lending has been limited (Blechman and Levinson 1991: 115–117). A few businesses' founders have been able to negotiate bridge loans and have been relieved of responsibility for charges or levies through targeted real property tax exemptions, and sales tax exemptions (State of New Jersey 2001). Business people have also obtained indirect support through cost reductions for improvements in their work force with programs focused on hard-to-place workers and training programs (State of New Jersey 2001). Research and development tax credits from state governments have supported pure research or commercialized new knowledge, and investment tax credits have benefited targeted industrial sectors (State of New Jersey 2001). Economic development zones have also assisted businesses with tax credits, tax deferments, and other incentives. State-sponsored agencies have sometimes established business incubators, which have reduced the costs for facilities and professional services used by the tenant businesses (Gatewood and Hylton 1994: 275).

Direct and indirect federal resources

Entrepreneurs have negotiated limited direct loans and grants and some federal contracting preferences, and have accessed indirect federal resources through reduced expenses and subsidized service providers. Loan guarantee programs, offered through the Small Business Administration or Farm Credit Administration, have underwritten performance on debts negotiated with third-party lenders (Blechman and Levinson 1991: 120, 135).

Direct and indirect university resources

Some universities have established micro-lending programs to provide small loans (Wasilowski 2001). Indirect university resources have been provided through low-cost information, consultation, employees, and facilities. Student interns have expanded business owners' workforce, and university employment centers or services have matched temporary or permanent employees with ventures' positions. Colleges have also opened incubators and offered technology commercialization services, which has brought scientific discovery into the marketplace (Fenn 1999).

Indirect "big" corporate support

"Big" corporations may offer entrepreneurs many opportunities (Starr and MacMillan 1990). Large companies have sometimes abandoned product lines and clients that generated too little demand; and equipment and processes, for reasons other than poor productivity, have met the same fate (Fenn 1999). These assets have been great finds for the entrepreneur who "picked up" market niches that were too small for a large corporation (Starr and MacMillan 1990: 83–85). Large corporations have been willing to give developers access to hardware or to allow free use of equipment (Freear *et al.* 1995: 395) and have established incubators with the usual benefits, especially when the tenants were in industry segments related to the sponsor (Smilor and Gill 1986: 101).

Foundation resources

Entrepreneurs have added to their capital base through funds from foundations with overarching charitable objectives, such as economic development, medical research, and education (Gittell *et al.* 1996). Bootstrap financing has come from foundations through grants, forms of equity investments, letters of credit, donated services, and direct loans. Some foundations have funded only nonprofit organizations, and in such situations, worked through established nonprofit organizations which agreed to serve as "flow throughs" between the foundations and the entrepreneur (Blum 1995: 11–12).

References

Ang, J.S. (1991) "Small business uniqueness and the theory of financial management," *The Journal of Small Business Finance*, 1(1): 1–13.
Arkebauer, J.B. (1993) *Ultrapreneuring: Taking a Venture from Start-up to Harvest in Three Years or Less*, New York, NY: McGraw-Hill, Inc.
Bhide, A.V. (1992) "Bootstrap finance: the art of start-ups," *Harvard Business Review*, 70: 109–117.
Blechman, B. and Levinson, J. (1991) *Guerrilla Financing: Alternative Techniques to Finance Any Small Business*, Boston, MA: Houghton Mifflin Company.
Blum, L. (1995) *Free Money for Small Businesses and Entrepreneurs*, fourth edn, New York, NY: John Wiley and Sons, Inc.
Fenn, D. (1999) "Grand plans: how to start a great company for $1,000 or less," *Inc.*, 21(11): 43–48.
Fraser, J.A. (1999) "How to finance anything," *Inc.*, 21(3): 131–136.

Fraser, J.A. (2001) "Money hunt," *Inc.*, March: 49–63.

Freear, J., Sohl, J.E., and Wetzel, W.E., Jr. (1995) "Who bankrolls software entrepreneurs," in Bygrave, W.D., Bird, B.J., Birley, S. *et al.* (eds) *Frontiers of Entrepreneurship Research*, Wellesley, MA: Babson College, Center for Entrepreneurial Studies.

Gatewood, E. and Hylton, K. (1994) "External assistance for startups and small businesses," in Bygrave, W. (ed.) *The Portable MBA in Entrepreneurship*, New York, NY: John Wiley & Sons.

Gittell, R., Sohl, J., and Thompson, P. (1996) "Investing in neighborhood entrepreneurs: private foundations as community development venture capitalists," *Entrepreneurial and Small Business Finance*, 5(2): 175–191.

Goldstein, A.S. (1995) *Starting on a Shoestring: Building a Business Without a Bankroll*, third edn, New York, NY: John Wiley & Sons, Inc.

Helgesen, S. (1995) *The Web of Inclusion*, New York, NY: Currency/Doubleday.

Hise, P. (1998) "Don't start a business without one," *Inc.* Online, available at: http://www.inc.com/articles/details/printable/0,3535,CID8665_REG14,00.html (accessed February 23, 2001).

Illinois Tax Increment Association (2001) *About TIF*. Online, available at: http://www.illinois-tif.com/index.htm (accessed June 5, 2001).

Resnik, P. (1988) *The Small Business Bible: The Make-or-Break Factors for Survival and Success*, New York, NY: John Wiley & Sons, Inc.

Shulman, J. (1994) "Debt and other forms of financing," in Bygrave, W. (ed.) *The Portable MBA in Entrepreneurship*, New York, NY: John Wiley & Sons.

Smilor, R.W. and Gill, M.D., Jr. (1986) *The New Business Incubator: Linking Talent, Technology, Capital, and Know-How*, Lexington, MA: Lexington Books.

Spinelli, S. (1994) "Franchising," in Bygrave, W. (ed.) *The Portable MBA in Entrepreneurship*, New York, NY: John Wiley & Sons.

Starr, J.A. and MacMillan, I.C. (1990) "Resource cooptation via social contracting: resource acquisition strategies for new ventures," *Strategic Management Journal*, 11: 79–92.

State National Bank (2001) *Overdraft Protection*. Online, available at: http://www.state-nationalbank.com/overdraft_protection (accessed June 22, 2001).

State of New Jersey (2001) *Incentives and Resources*. Online, available at: http://www.state.nj.us/njbiz/s_incentives (accessed June 5, 2001).

Szabo, J.C. (1992) "Alternative ways to find capital," *Nation's Business*, 80(4): 33–35.

Tarkenton, F. and Smith, W. (1997) *What Losing Taught Me About Winning: The Ultimate Guide for Success in Small and Home-Based Businesses*, New York, NY: Simon & Schuster.

Van Auken, H.E. and Neeley, L. (1996) "Evidence of bootstrap financing among small start-up firms," *Entrepreneurial and Small Business Finance*, 5(3): 235–249.

Wasilowski, S. "University-based seed funds," paper presented at the Second USASBA/SBIDA Joint Annual National Conference, Orlando, FL, February 2001.

Wetzel, W.E., Jr. (1994) "Venture capital," in Bygrave, W. (ed.) *The Portable MBA in Entrepreneurship*, New York, NY: John Wiley & Sons.

Whittemore, M. (1993) "You can overcome financing hurdles," *Nation's Business*, 81(10): 57–60.

Winborg, J. and Landstrom, H. (2001) "Financial bootstrapping in small businesses: examining small business managers' resource acquisition behaviors," *Journal of Business Venturing*, 16(3): 235–254.

Chapter 9

Jianwen Liao

Northeastern Illinois University

ENTREPRENEURIAL GROWTH: PREDICTORS AND INDICATORS

Introduction

ENTREPRENEURSHIP AND SMALL BUSINESSES have been designated as the "engines of growth" because they create jobs, not only in the United States (Birch 1987) but also in developing and privatizing economies across the globe. Governments and policy-makers have become keenly aware of the economic development benefits that are derived from the establishment and growth of entrepreneurial endeavors.

In the last 20 years, the amount of literature in the growth field has increased tremendously. Organization and entrepreneurship scholars have increasingly recognized the importance of the research on new ventures (Carter *et al.* 1994; Eisenhardt and Schoonhoven 1990; Romanelli 1989). Indeed, entrepreneurial growth has been seen as a valuable outcome of administrative and technological innovation (Tushman and Anderson 1986), job creation (Birley 1986), and the competitive disciplining of industries (Scherer and Ross 1990). Growth intentions and enterprise expansion have been investigated through various conceptual approaches, from economics, organizational behavior, and strategic management, to name just a few.

However, a coherent theory of entrepreneurial growth is lacking (Ardishvili *et al.* 1998), despite the recent progress on growth studies. The field of entrepreneurial growth research has been plagued by the fact that there is no commonly accepted definition and measure of growth. For that reason, results of studies often contradict one another. Consequently, there is little cumulative research. The fact that research takes place across very diverse theoretical frameworks and that few integrative studies have been developed does not help move the field forward.

In order to explore further the subject of entrepreneurial growth, growth predictors, and growth indicators, a search of the recent growth literature was undertaken. Articles from major journals in management and entrepreneurship areas as well as research monographs were selected and reviewed. The majority of the articles come from *Journal of Business Venturing, Entrepreneurship Theory and Practice, Journal of Small Business Management, Frontiers of Entrepreneurship Research, Academy of Management Journal, Strategic Management Journal*, and *Blackwell Handbook of Entrepreneurship*. Overall, 45 articles were found and were used as a basis for determining some of the most commonly used growth indicators and growth predictors for entrepreneurial-based, high-growth firms.

This chapter is structured as follows. Attention is first devoted to a review of major publications in the area of entrepreneurial growth literature. Major theoretical frameworks are identified, and key predictors of growth are reviewed. A review of key indicators of entrepreneurial growth follows. A critical assessment of the existing studies on predictors and measures is made. The chapter concludes with suggestions for future research.

Entrepreneurial growth: predictors

What determines entrepreneurial growth? Although growth can take several forms, including organic growth and acquired growth, typically firm growth is accompanied by an increase in sales, an increase in the number of employees, and an increase in total assets. Increases in each of these indicators constitute growth, but what determines growth? Quantification and identification of these growth predictors is essential to the understanding of the growth process of a firm. Growth predictors help to explain the source of high growth and provide insight into what guides a firm to successful business expansion.

There are several streams of research in the areas of entrepreneurial growth. The first stream, the macro perspective of entrepreneurial growth, is consistent with the tenet of strategic management and organization theory, where there is considerable evidence that a firm's strategy, structure, process, environment, and the interface among these variables influence entrepreneurial growth. The second stream of research, the micro-behavioral perspective, is primarily concerned with the impact of the characteristics of individual entrepreneurs on growth. The third stream of research is related to the economic perspective of growth.

The macro-structural predictors of venture growth

Studies of the macro-structural predictors of venture growth are mainly concerned with predictors such as industry categories (Hay and Ross 1989), entry barriers (McDougall and Robinson 1988), environmental munificence and dynamism (Covin and Covin 1989), competitive strategy and structure (Covin and Slevin 1990), and the interaction between structural, cultural, and environmental factors (Fombrun and Wally 1989).

Environments

The external environment plays a central role in shaping entrepreneurs' intentions to grow and develop their enterprises. External factors such as public policy, market infrastructure, financial markets, and technological development have an impact on entrepreneurs' perceptions and actions related to small-business growth. However, with the exception of Delmar (1997), very little research has been focused on the external environment in comparison with the amount of attention devoted to entrepreneurs and other organizational-level predictors of growth. Delmar found that high-growth firms in markets with little competition tend to exhibit higher growth rates. Also, Davidsson *et al.* (2002) concluded that the industry sector does have a strong influence on growth rates of firms and that influence cannot be ignored.

Managerial practices

Successful high-growth firms exhibit strong management practices and organizational planning in order to funnel their resources and provide for expansion. Ireland *et al.* (2001) discussed the importance of organizational learning and knowledge transfer for high-wealth firms. The dissemination of knowledge is vital to entrepreneurial ventures, especially when they are moving into international markets. Chaganti *et al.* (2002) explored the importance of leadership styles and organizational philosophies for successful high-growth companies. Their research shows that a combination of consideration and initiation styles of leadership produces the best results in high-growth firms. Consideration-style management supports a high degree of concern for employees, while initiation involves the clear definition of tasks and goals in order to produce results. A balance between the two types of management styles tends to produce the best results.

Planning and control

Pearce *et al.* (1987) examined the impact of formal strategic planning activities on financial performance. Cragg and King (1988) evaluated the relationship between a wide range of planning activities in small firms and various performance measures. Boag (1987) investigated the linkages between control systems and performance in a small-business context. Duchesneau and Gartner (1990) found that emphasis upon a number of formal planning models, including assessing the market, considering a number of functional areas, and devoting more time to planning, were all related to entrepreneurial growth.

Network resources and alliances

It appears that the most frequently researched growth predictor is network resources and alliances. Network resources include human, social, cultural, and emotional capital. Personal networks are created and maintained (either formally or informally) by the entrepreneur. The accumulation of these important contacts and networks is essential as the generation of strategic alliances and formal network arrangements, such as joint ventures and licensing agreements. Ireland *et al.* (2001) identified the generation of networks as one of the six main domains that firms engage in to create and build firm wealth. The low cost of resources acquired through alliances and partnerships becomes essential to start-up and growth firms. Mitra (2002) explored the issue of growth patterns of female-run enterprises in India and found that the accumulation of resources – technical, market, and personal – was the key factor for growth and success of those firms. An empirical study by Aldrich *et al.* (1987) confirmed that networks might have an impact not only on the process of founding but also on the later practice and growth of the business. There is also a long tradition of studying the financing of new firms – a part of the entrepreneurial process that is clearly central to the assembly of resources. These studies are mainly concerned with the influence of the amount of initial capital and the sources of the capital on subsequent entrepreneurial growth (Bruno and Tyebjee 1984; Dunkelberg *et al.* 1987).

Accessibility of capital (financial, human, social, etc.)

Along with the accumulation of resources and alliances, the accessibility of capital – financial, social, and human – is critical to high-growth firms. The accumulation of capital – venture, social, human, and intellectual – is also essential to firm growth. Florin and Schulze (2002) found that the amount of social capital of a venture prior to initial public offering was positively correlated with the growth and wealth creation of the firm. Several other authors found a positive correlation between capital accumulation and firm growth, including Mitra (2002), Pena (2002), and Johannisson (2000). Evidence of the importance of venture capital is supported by several studies, including Henderson's (2002) study of rural high-growth entrepreneurial firms. These firms are able to take advantage of new rural venture capital funds and incubator networks to facilitate growth. The firms that do take advantage of these funds are often more successful with respect to growth. In a study by Rogers *et al.* (2001), firms that had access to capital acquired 55.4 percent more sales growth than those that did not receive funding.

Interactions

There is also research investigating the interaction effects of environment strategy and organizational variables. For example, Covin and Slevin (1989) found a systematic relationship between managerial orientation, strategic posture, and firm performance in different environmental contexts. In a longitudinal study of 140 independent banks, Bamford *et al.* (1996) examined the initial founding conditions and new venturing performance.

Another line of inquiry regarding entrepreneurial growth is from an organizational lifecycle perspective. It is based on the organizational stages of growth hypothesis (Greiner 1978). Studies of entrepreneurial growth in this direction often apply a lifecycle analogy to organizations that assumes firms pass through a predictable sequence of stages as their product markets enlarge. For example, Churchill and Lewis (1983) and Scott and Bruce (1987) developed five stages of small-business growth – inception, survival, growth, expansion, and maturity. The studies are concerned either with the characteristics of entrepreneurial growth in various predetermined stages of growth or with validating the stages of growth model (Hanks 1990; Smith *et al.* 1985). Because entrepreneurial growth may be neither orderly nor sequential, the studies, descriptive in nature, have limited value for generating guidelines for promoting entrepreneurial growth. One positive attribute of this approach, however, is that it recognizes entrepreneurship as a process.

The micro-behavioral predictors of venture growth

Visions must be transformed into intentions, which are the precursor of behavior. On a micro level, internal factors, such as the motivation and aspiration of the entrepreneur, are critical to an understanding of small-business growth. Behavior and attitudes are often formed by motivations that are internalized by the individual entrepreneurs. This stream of research, the micro-behavioral perspective, is primarily concerned with the impact of characteristics of individual entrepreneurs on growth, including their experience, their education, and their psychological make-up, such as a need for achievement, locus of control, risk-taking behavior, willingness to sacrifice, and motivation.

Demographics

Bailey (1986) found that a certificate of education or trade qualification was related to a higher index of growth for his sample of 67 Australian entrepreneurs. Breadth of experience, functional experience, and management experience tend to be viewed as major predictors of entrepreneurial growth (Davidsson 1991). Watson (2002) compared the performance of female-controlled and male-controlled firms in Australia. In traditional research, male-controlled firms out-performed female-controlled firms with respect to sales and profits. However, Watson compared the return on equity (ROE) and return on assets (ROA) and found that the female-controlled firms actually out-performed the male-controlled firms. Another key difference was that the female-controlled firms gained less profit and sales growth because of under-funding and lack of accessibility to capital.

The level of education of the founder and start-up team is also related to entrepreneurial growth. For example, Rogers *et al.* (2001) studied several small-growth firms in the inner city of Buffalo, NY. Their results show that level of CEO education was one of the two most important variables in explaining the differences in firm growth.

Firm age

Resources such as personal networks are important during all phases of the firm lifecycle but may be most important when the firm is youngest and ready to grow. Several studies have attempted to correlate the age of the firm, the age of the CEO, or the age of the management team with firm growth. Most of the studies have found that the younger the entrepreneur or the firm, the higher the potential for growth. For example, Davidsson *et al.* (2002) found in a study of 11,000 Swedish businesses that the age of the firm is negatively related to firm growth, meaning that younger firms tend to grow more quickly. New firms are often more dynamic and can more easily adapt to changing market conditions. An example of the ability of newer firms to adapt involves the expansion into recently opened foreign markets. Larger firms are often tied to existing markets and do not actively venture into risky foreign markets. Small, newly formed firms often must push into international competition to gain a competitive, first-mover advantage. Autio *et al.* (2000) also found that the age of high-technology firms during international market entry was negatively correlated to subsequent growth. The younger firms (at time of entry) have more of a tendency toward growth. Delmar (1997) studied 400 Swedish companies and found that younger entrepreneurs tended to achieve higher growth in their firms. Gartner and Markman (1997) found that the Top 100 firms in the Inc. 500 companies (1992–1996) tended to be "younger."

Personal attributes

The literature on the psychological characteristics of entrepreneurs demonstrates the diversity of approaches used by different researchers. Birch (1987) argued that attitudes rather than sector or location determine growth and success. Brown (1995) found that entrepreneurial orientation had a positive impact on small-firm growth. Fox (1996) pointed out that many entrepreneurs believe that growth is as much a matter of attitude as it is of economic aggregates.

In their literature review, Cooper and Gimeno-Gascon (1992) found that 31 different attributes, including willingness to sacrifice, motivation, intensity, and risk-taking behavior, have been investigated to determine their relationships to entrepreneurial growth. Overall, research findings in this direction have been extremely inconsistent and contradictory, especially the findings of studies narrowly focused on the independent effect of the psychological make-up of entrepreneurs.

One of the most interesting streams of research in the micro-entrepreneurial growth literature focuses on the question of entrepreneurs' motivation: what are the motivational factors that differentiate entrepreneurs from non-entrepreneurs? Why would an entrepreneur assume the personal, social, and financial risks associated with venture creation? Since McClelland's study (1965), many researchers have been fascinated by the elucidation of motivation factors. A host of researchers of entrepreneurship have studied motives as a distinguishing psychological characteristic of entrepreneurs. For example, on the basis of the theory of satisfaction, several scholars suggested that entrepreneurs create businesses because they want to satisfy a need for achievement. Scholars have argued that entrepreneurs expect to be recognized and appreciated when they solve a problem largely through their own efforts. Other researchers, who advocated a goal theory, contended that entrepreneurs venture into a business to pursue a long-term ambition, which may be independence, personal development, or escape. There are also researchers who subscribe to a psychoanalytic theory and argue that entrepreneurs create businesses because of their ambivalence toward authority. Entrepreneurs would like to lead rather than be led. They want to create their own space and environment.

Chaganti *et al.* (2002) studied 372 small firms in Massachusetts, New Jersey, New York, and Pennsylvania and found that a "do-it-all" CEO was the most successful in high-growth firms. A high-consideration and high-initiation leadership style yielded the best growth results. Gundry and Welsch (2002) found that the more ambitious female entrepreneurs have a better chance to generate growth and expansion in their firms. In a recent study of businesses in the People's Republic of China, Lau *et al.* (2001) found that the longer the hours that the entrepreneur worked, the higher the propensity for the firm to grow. This higher commitment tended to be found in younger entrepreneurs, who also tended to have a very high need for achievement.

There are also studies categorizing entrepreneurial motives into intrinsic "pull" factors and extrinsic "push" factors. The "pull" theories suggest that entrepreneurship is affected by the need for achievement from within (McClelland 1961), or internal locus of control, the belief that the outcome of events will be influenced by an individual's efforts (Brockhaus 1982); the practical purposiveness of the individual's actions (Bird 1989); risk-taking propensities (Slevin and Covin 1992); and the belief in the individual's capacity to perform a task (Boyd and Vozikis 1994). By contrast, the "push" theories contend that negative factors, such as conflicts at one's workplace, job loss, and limited alternative opportunities (Greenberger and Sexton 1988), resulted in some individuals being "pushed" into entrepreneurship.

The idea that the entrepreneur is somehow driven to growth by the desire to achieve complete independence and empowerment has also been researched extensively. Several studies relate small-firm growth to the desire of entrepreneurs to become independent of the "corporate" life and empower both themselves and their employees. Barringer *et al.* (1998) identified the need for employee and personal empowerment as principal management practices that high-growth firms exhibit. Davidsson (1989) found in a factor analysis that increased independence and reduction of external dependencies were two of the most important growth drivers.

Table 9.1 includes the frequency analysis of the top growth predictors cited in these selected growth articles and the corresponding percentage of articles.

As shown in Table 9.1, the most popular growth predictors found in the research articles include: Network resources/generating resources/alliances; Younger firms/CEOs/entrepreneurs; Accessibility of capital (venture, human, social, etc.); and Motivation of CEO/long hours of CEO/"Do-it-all" approach of CEO. Understanding the importance of these growth predictors is essential

Table 9.1 Frequency of growth predictors in 45 growth articles (1990–2002)

Growth predictor	Articles (%)
1 Network resources/generating resources/alliances	37
2 Younger firms/CEOs/entrepreneurs	33
3 Accessibility of capital (venture, human, social, etc.)	26
4 Motivation of CEO/long hours for CEO/"do-it-all"	26
5 Solid management practices/organization/planning	15
6 Customer and quality focus	15
7 Increased independence/empowerment	15
8 High education of CEO and management team	11
9 Low cost/differentiation strategy	11
10 Smaller firms	11
11 Growth willingness	11
12 Increased employee well-being	11
13 High-growth industry/low competition in industry	11
14 Larger firms	7
15 Need for achievement	7
16 Years of experience	7
17 Expectation of financial reward	7

to knowing what helps a firm progress through its growth processes and life-cycle.

It is also important to categorize the top 17 growth predictors into the previously mentioned three categories to see where the focus of current entrepreneurial research study falls with respect to growth predictors. The three categories, shown in Table 9.2, are: Entrepreneurs' attributes; Venture conditions (internal); and Environmental conditions (external).

Based on Table 9.2, it can be concluded that most entrepreneurial and small-firm research regarding growth is focused on the attributes of the entrepreneur/CEO and the conditions that the venture faces internally. A relatively small number of these empirical studies deal with environmental or external conditions that the firm faces when attempting to grow or expand. Environmental conditions, such as the level of competition, the maturity of the industry, and the growth rate of the industry, may be overlooked by researchers and could account for some of the conflicting results that are often found in cross-industry studies.

Table 9.2 Top growth predictors in literature study by category

Category of growth predictor	Articles (%)
1 Entrepreneur attributes	47
2 Venture conditions (internal)	47
3 Environmental conditions (external)	6

Entrepreneurial growth: indicators

Table 9.3 shows the frequency analysis of the top growth indicators used in these selected growth articles and the corresponding percentage of articles in which the specific indicator is used in the research. Note that several of the empirical research studies used multiple indicators in their studies so the percentages sum to more than 100.

The results in Table 9.3 show the top growth indicators that were discussed in the selected growth literature. The results are in very close agreement with the results published by Delmar (1997). The top-two growth indicators cited are: Number of employees/creation of jobs and Sales and revenue growth. These two indicators are by far the most popular growth indicators. In fact, the top-five indicators found in this literature search are almost identical with those listed by Delmar (1997), in which the most commonly used growth indicators include Turnover/sales (30.9 percent), Employment (29.1 percent), Multiple indicators (18.2 percent), Performance (12.7 percent), Market share (5.5 percent), and Assets (1.8 percent).

Often the choice of growth indicator (sales, number of employees, total assets, etc.) can completely alter the results of an empirical study. Researchers often disagree on the specific growth indicators to utilize in their studies, and no consensus has been reached in the research field. It appears that there is a lack of continuity and consistency in the usage of common indicators and of agreement between researchers. Also, many of the growth indicators can be defined in both absolute and relative terms that change greatly according to firm size. Delmar (1997) and Davidsson and Wiklund (2000) both discussed the topic of suitable growth indicators and their use in firm-growth studies. Sales and employment are the most commonly used indicators. Delmar (1997) suggested that subjective measures such as satisfaction or perceived market share are not reliable and recommended objective measures such as sales or employment. Growth in assets is not recommended as an indicator because it is not pertinent in the service sector, where tangible assets are often very small. Both relative and absolute measures were recommended by Delmar (1997) to help compensate for the differences in firm size. Davidsson and Wiklund (2000) reiterated several of these points and also recommended that organic growth is a more

Table 9.3 Frequency of growth indicators in 27 growth articles (1990–2002)

Growth indicator	Articles (%)
Number of employees/creation of jobs	63
Sales and revenue growth	56
Growth of net income/profits	22
Growth in assets/total assets	19
Market share	11
Return on sales (ROS)	11
Return on investment (ROI)	7
Increase in venture capital/total capital	7

relevant research study than total growth because acquired growth can cause major problems with the definition of the firm.

Discussion and conclusions

The literature review conducted here is by no means exhaustive. However, it uncovered several major limitations of current research in the area of entrepreneurial expansion. First, simple treatment of entrepreneurial growth measures seriously hampers model predictability, which contributes to conflicting results among existing studies. Consistent with the assessment of Hoy *et al.* (1992), and Baum *et al.* (2001), this review finds that most studies define entrepreneurial growth as a uni-dimensional construct operationalized by a variety of growth measures, ranging from increases in venture capital and market share to growth in sales revenue, accounting-based return on investment (ROI) and return on assets (ROA), and number of employees.

Second, one major problem with these measures is that new business ventures often do not exhibit monotonic sales growth. Single-year sales or employment growth figures may show aberrations, thus not representing the true health of the firms. Conversely, if a researcher uses growth averages, such aggregated statistics again fail to capture complex growth patterns across time and may not accurately reflect the firm's current growth. Another problem with the accounting-based measures such as ROI and ROA is that data can be heavily influenced by decisions about the owner–manager's compensation and industry margins, as well as a host of other factors. The upshot of this variety of measures is that comparison across studies is difficult. That is one of the reasons that little cumulative research has been developed in this area.

Third, most studies measure growth as the "realized" growth, which may fail to show entrepreneurial growth in resources base, technology improvement, and even market expansion. Entrepreneurial growth in those aspects would not necessarily be reflected in *current* sales or profit figures of a business venture. Whereas those measures may be "final outcomes," it is necessary to ask how the final objectives are achieved. In other words, a future perspective must be included in the measurement and a set of "implementable attributes" that are "intentions based" is called for.

In fact, researchers in the entrepreneurship area already notice that the lack of reliable, valid, and meaningful growth measures hampers researchers' efforts (Brush and Vanderwerf 1992; Chandler and Hanks 1993). Researchers criticized existing growth measures, lamenting the use of simple accounting-based measures that do not deftly fit the disjointed, discontinuous, and non-linear process of emerging businesses (Bygrave 1989). Scholars appeal for the use of concepts, measures, and methods grounded in theory and knowledge of entrepreneurial phenomena, and call for a contextual and process-oriented approach to developing measures (Low and MacMillan 1988). Researchers view the development of reliable, valid, and meaningful growth measures as imperative if our efforts to understand entrepreneurial growth are to succeed.

Fourth, research concerning entrepreneurial growth has been very frag-mented. Most studies so far have focused on the independent effect of the determinants of entrepreneurial growth, such as motivation, obstacles, and various strategies. Studies that compare and integrate both macro and micro predictors are notably absent. A mid-range theorizing approach is needed to focus on the integration of macro-level structural and micro-level motivational factors in predicting growth. For example, the infrastructure variable can be chosen because infrastructure factors can have a double effect on entrepreneurial growth. On the one hand, infrastructure conditions can have great impact on the operation of business ventures that are already in operation. Within organizational research, the environment has often been viewed as the source of resources necessary for survival and growth (Dess and Beard 1984; Pfeffer and Salancik 1978). For example, business, informational, and financial services provided by a government have been viewed as important factors in stimulating entrepreneurial growth. On the other hand, infrastructure conditions also affect new ventures' structure, processes, and strategies at the time of their founding.

Fifth, it appears that little attention has been devoted to the impact of external environment. The seminal work by Stinchcombe (1965) suggested that new firms are imprinted at the time of founding and the imprint has lasting effects on subsequent strategy, structure, and performance owing to organizational inertia (Boeker 1989; Stinchcombe 1965). This approach suggests that the ability of a new venture to grow may be affected by external contextual factors that are outside the control of the entrepreneur (Aldrich 1990). One interesting line of inquiry is to address two questions. Which is a more important predictor of entrepreneurial growth, the macro, external environmental factors or the micro internal motivation factors? This research question is consistent with the deterministic versus adaptive argument in the tradition of strategy literature. Then, to what extent are the effects of entrepreneurial motives on growth moderated by the external contextual variables? This question challenges the widely held notion of the monotonic relationship between motivation and growth. It would be interesting to investigate the interaction effect between contextual variables and intrinsic "pull" motives and extrinsic push "motives."

Sixth, despite the volume of research concerning the relationship between motivation and entrepreneurship, the question of to what extent the motivational factors determine entrepreneurial growth remains to be explored. Although a definitive link between entrepreneurial motives and growth has been established, it is not surprising that some authors have called for research on the entrepreneurial process, especially growth and expansion, and not on the psychological profile of the entrepreneur (Gartner 1988; Sandberg and Hofer 1987) or the strategic approach alone. Furthermore, previous research *implied* that pull-motivated entrepreneurs exhibit higher levels of venture growth and that this relationship may be reasonably linear. An exploratory study by Solymossy (1996) contradicted those assumptions. The limited inclusive and contradictory findings regarding the relationship between motivation and growth call for a more comprehensive examination.

References

Aldrich, H. (1990) "Using an ecological perspective to study organizational founding rates," *Entrepreneurship Theory and Practice*, 14(3): 7–24.

Aldrich, H., Rosen, B., and Woodward, W. (1987) "The impact of social networks on business foundings and profit: a longitudinal study," in Churchill, N.C., Hornaday, J.A., Kirchoff, B.A. *et al.* (eds) *Frontiers of Entrepreneurship Research*, Wellesley, MA: Babson College.

Ardishvili, A., Harmon, B., Cardozo, R., and Vadakath, S. (1998) "Metaphors for understanding the new venture growth," in Reynolds, P.D., Bygrave, W.D., Carter, N.M. *et al.* (eds) *Frontiers of Entrepreneurship Research*, Wellesley, MA: Babson College.

Autio, E., Sapienza, H.J., and Almeida, J.G. (2000) "Effects of age at entry, knowledge intensity, and imitability on international growth," *Academy of Management Journal*, 43(5): 909–924.

Bailey, J. (1986) "Learning styles of successful entrepreneurs," in Ronstadt, R., Hornaday, J.A., Peterson, R., and Vesper, K.H. (eds) *Frontiers of Entrepreneurship Research*, Wellesley, MA: Babson College.

Bamford, C.E.R., Dean, T.J., and McDougall, P.P. (1996) "Initial founding conditions and new firm performance: a longitudinal study integrating predictors from multiple perspectives," in Reynolds, P.D., Birley, S., Butler, J.E. *et al.* (eds) *Frontiers of Entrepreneurship Research*, Wellesley, MA: Babson College.

Barringer, B.R., Jones, F.F., and Lewis, P.S. (1998) "A qualitative study of the management practices of rapid-growth firms and how rapid-growth firms mitigate the managerial capacity problem," *Journal of Developmental Entrepreneurship*, 3: 32–47.

Baum, R.J., Locke, E.A., and Smith, K.G. (2001) "A multidimensional model of venture growth," *Academy of Management Journal*, 44: 292–303.

Birch, D. (1987) *Job Creation in America*, New York, NY: The Free Press.

Bird, B. (1989) "Implementing entrepreneurial ideas: the case for intentions," *Academy of Management Review*, 13: 442–454.

Birley, S. (1986) "The role of new firms: births, deaths, and job generation," *Strategic Management Journal*, 7: 361–376.

Boag, D. (1987) "Marketing control and performance in early-growth companies," *Journal of Business Venturing*, 2(4): 365–379.

Boeker, W. (1989) "Strategic change: the effects of founding and history," *Academy of Management Journal*, 32: 489–515.

Boyd, N. and Vozikis, G. (1994) "The influence of self-efficacy on the development of entrepreneurial intentions and actions," *Entrepreneurship Theory and Practice*, 18(4): 63–77.

Brockhaus, R. (1982) "Psychology of the entrepreneur," in Kent, C., Sexton, D., and Vesper, K. (eds) *Encyclopedia of Entrepreneurship*, Waco, TX: Baylor University Press.

Brown, T. (1995) "Resource orientation and growth: how the perception of resource availability affects small firm growth," abstract, unpublished Doctoral dissertation. *Entrepreneurship Theory and Practice*, 20(2): 59.

Bruno, A. and Tyebjee, T. (1984) "The entrepreneur's search for capital," in Hornaday, J.A., Tarpley, F., Jr., Timmons, J.A., and Vesper, K.H. (eds) *Frontiers of Entrepreneurship Research*, Wellesley, MA: Babson College.

Brush, C. and Vanderwerf, P. (1992) "A comparison of methods and sources for obtaining estimates of new venture performance," *Journal of Business Venturing*, 7(2): 157–170.

Bygrave, W. (1989) "The entrepreneurship paradigm (II): chaos and catastrophes among quantum jumps," *Entrepreneurship Theory and Practice*, 14(2): 7–30.

Carter, N.M., Stearns, T.M., Reynolds, P.D., and Miller, B.A. (1994) "New venture strategies: theory development with an empirical base," *Strategic Management Journal*, 15: 21–41.

Chaganti, R., Cook, R., and Smeltz, W.J. (2002) "Effects of styles, strategies, and systems on the growth of small businesses," *Journal of Developmental Entrepreneurship*, August: 175–192.

Chandler, G. and Hanks, S. (1993) "Measuring the performance of emerging businesses: a validation study," *Journal of Business Venturing*, 8(5): 391–408.

Churchill, N. and Lewis, V. (1983) "The five stages of small business growth," *Harvard Business Review*, 61(3): 30–50.

Cooper, A.C. and Gimeno-Gascon, F.J. (1992) "Entrepreneurs, process of founding, and new firm performance," in Sexton, D. and Kasarda, J. (eds) *The State of the Art in Entrepreneurship*, Boston, MA: PWS-Kent.

Covin, J.G. and Covin, T. (1989) "The effects of environmental context on the relationship between small firms' aggressiveness and performance," paper presented at the Academy of Management Meeting, Washington, DC.

Covin, J.G. and Slevin, D.P. (1989) "Strategic management of small firms in hostile and benign environments," *Strategic Management Journal*, 10: 75–87.

Covin, J.G. and Slevin, D.P. (1990) "New venture strategic posture, structure, and performance: an industry life cycle analysis," *Journal of Business Venturing*, 5: 391–412.

Cragg, P.B. and King, M. (1988) "Organizational characteristics and small firm's performance revisited," *Entrepreneurship Theory and Practice*, 13(2): 49–64.

Davidsson, P. (1989) "Entrepreneurship – and after? A study of growth willingness in small firms," *Journal of Business Venturing*, 4: 211–226.

Davidsson, P. (1991) "Continued entrepreneurship: ability, need, and opportunity as determinants of small firm growth," *Journal of Business Venturing*, 6: 405–429.

Davidsson, P., Kirchoff, B., Hatemi-J.A., and Gustavsson, H. (2002) "Empirical analysis of business growth factors using Swedish data," *Journal of Small Business Management*, 40(4): 332–349.

Davidsson, P. and Wiklund, J. (2000) "Conceptual and empirical challenges in the study of firm growth," in Sexton, D.L. and Landstrom, D.J. (eds) *Blackwell Handbook of Entrepreneurship*, London: Blackwell Publishers.

Delmar, F. (1997) "Measuring growth: methodological considerations and empirical results," in Donckels, R. and Miettinen, A. (eds) *Entrepreneurship and SME Research: On its Way to the Next Millennium*, Brookfield, VA: Aldershot Publishers.

Dess, G.G. and Beard, D.W. (1984) "Dimensions of organizational task environments," *Administrative Science Quarterly*, 29: 52–73.

Duchesneau, D.A. and Gartner, W.B. (1990) "A profile of new venture success and failure in an emerging industry," *Journal of Business Venturing*, 5(5): 297–312.

Dunkelberg, W., Cooper, A., Woo, C., and Dennis, W. (1987) "New firm growth and performance," in Churchill, N.C., Hornaday, J.A., Kirchoff, B.A. *et al.* (eds) *Frontiers of Entrepreneurship Research*, Wellesley, MA: Babson College.

Eisenhardt, K. and Schoonhoven, C. (1990) "Organizational growth: linking founding team, strategy, environment and growth among U.S. semiconductor ventures (1978–1988)," Working Paper, Department of Engineering and Engineering Management, Stanford University.

Florin, J. and Schulze, B. (2002) "Born to go public? Founder performance in new, high growth, technology ventures," Working Paper, Babson College.

Fombrun, C.J. and Wally, S. (1989) "Structuring small firms for rapid growth," *Journal of Business Venturing*, 4(2): 107–123.

Fox, J. (1996) "How Washington really could help," *Fortune*, 134(10): 92–98.

Francis, H. and Sandberg, W.R. (2000) "Friendship within entrepreneurial teams and its association with team and venture performance," *Entrepreneurship Theory and Practice*, 25(2): 5–25.

Gartner, B.W. and Markman, G. (1997) "Is growth profitable? a study of Inc. 500 fast growth companies," in Reynolds, P.D., Birley, S., Butler, J.E. *et al.* (eds) *Frontiers of Entrepreneurship Research*, Wellesley, MA: Babson College.

Gartner, W.B. (1988) "Who is an entrepreneur? is the wrong question," *American Journal of Small Business*, 12(4): 11–32.

Greenberger, D.B. and Sexton, D. (1988) "New leadership research methods for the understanding of entrepreneurs," *Journal of Small Business Management*, 26: 1–7.

Greiner, L.E. (1978) "A recent history of organizational behavior," in Kerr, S. (ed.) *Organizational Behavior*, Houston, TX: Grid.

Gundry, L.K. and Welsch, H.P. (2002) "The ambitious entrepreneur: attributes of firms exhibiting high growth strategies," *Journal of Business Venturing*, 16: 24–37.

Hanks, S.H. (1990) "The organization life cycle: integrating content and process," *Journal of Small Business Strategy*, 1(1): 1–13.

Hay, R.K. and Ross, D.L. (1989) "An assessment of success factors of non-urban start-up firms based upon financial characteristics of successful versus failed ventures," in Brockhaus, R.H., Sr., Churckhill, N.C., Katz, J.A. *et al.* (eds) *Frontiers of Entrepreneurship Research*, Wellesley, MA: Babson College.

Henderson, J. (2002) "Building the rural economy with high-growth entrepreneurs," *Economic Review – Federal Reserve Bank of Kansas City*, 87(3): 45–70.

Hoy, F., McDougall, P.P., and D'Souza, D.E. (1992) "Strategies and environments of high-growth firms," in Sexton, D.L. and Kasarda, J.D. (eds) *The State of the Art of Entrepreneurship*, Boston, MA: PWS-Kent.

Ireland, R.D., Hitt, M., Camp, M., and Sexton, D. (2001) "Integrating entrepreneurship and strategic management actions to create firm wealth," *Academy of Management Executive*, 15(1): 49–63.

Johannisson, B. (2000) "Networking and entrepreneurial growth," in Sexton, D.L. and Landstrom, H. (eds) *Blackwell Handbook of Entrepreneurship*, London: Blackwell Publishers.

Lau, C.M. and Ngo, H.-Y. (2001) "Organization development and firm performance: a comparison of multinational and local firms," *Journal of International Business Studies*, 32(1): 95–115.

Low, M. and MacMillan, I. (1988) "Entrepreneurship: past research and future challenges," *Journal of Management*, 14: 139–161.

McClelland, D. (1961) *The Achieving Society*, Princeton, NJ: Van Nostrand Publishers.

McClelland, D. (1965) "In achievement and entrepreneurship: a longitudinal study," *Journal of Personality and Social Psychology*, 1: 389–392.

McDougall, P. and Robinson, R. (1988) "New venture performance: patterns of strategic behavior in different industries," in Kirchoff, B.A., Long, W.A., McMullan, W.E., Vesper, K.H., and Wetzel, W.E., Jr. (eds) *Frontiers of Entrepreneurship Research*, Wellesley, MA: Babson College.

Mitra, R. (2002) "The growth pattern of women-run enterprises: an empirical study in India," *Journal of Developmental Entrepreneurship*, 7(2): 217–237.

Pearce, J.A., II, Freeman, E.B., and Robinson, R.B., Jr. (1987) "The tenuous link between formal strategic planning and financial performance," *Academy of Management Review*, 12(4): 658–675.

Pena, I. (2002) "Intellectual capital and business start-up success," *Journal of Intellectual Capital*, 2: 180–198.

Pfeffer, J. and Salancik, G.R. (1978) *The External Control of Organizations: A Resource Dependence Perspective*, New York, NY: Harper and Row.

Rogers, C.D., Gent, M.J., Palumbo, G.M., and Wall, R.A. (2001) "Understanding the growth and viability of inner city businesses," *Journal of Developmental Entrepreneurship*, 6(3): 237–254.

Romanelli, E. (1989) "Environments and strategies of organization start-up effects on early survival," *Administrative Science Quarterly*, 34(3): 369–387.

Sandberg, W. and Hofer, C.W. (1987) "Improving new venture performance: the role of strategy, industry structure, and the entrepreneur," *Journal of Business Venturing*, 2: 5–28.

Scherer, F.M. and Ross, D. (1990) *Industrial Market Structure and Economic Performance*, Boston, MA: Houghton Mifflin.

Scott, M. and Bruce, R. (1987) "Five stages of growth in small business," *Long Range Planning*, 20(3): 45–52.

Slevin, D.P. and Covin, J.G. (1992) "Creating and maintaining high-performance teams," in Sexton, D. and Kasarda, J. (eds) *The State of Art of Entrepreneurship*, Boston, MA: PWS-Kent.

Smith, K.G., Mitchell, T.R., and Summer, C.E. (1985) "Top level management priorities in different stages of the organizational life cycle," *Academy of Management Journal*, 28(4): 799–820.

Solymossy, E. (1996) "Motivation and success: an empirical study of push/pull paradigm," Working Paper, Western Illinois University.

Stinchcombe, A.L. (1965) "Social structure and organizations," in March, J.G. (ed.) *Handbook of Organizations*, Chicago, IL: Rand McNally.

Tushman, M.L. and Anderson, P. (1986) "Technological discontinuities and organizational environments," *Administrative Science Quarterly*, 31(3): 439–465.

Watson, J. (2002) "Comparing the performance of male- and female-controlled businesses: relating outputs to inputs," *Entrepreneurship Theory and Practice*, 26(3): 91–100.

Chapter 10

Jianwen Liao

Northeastern Illinois University

ENTREPRENEURIAL FAILURES: KEY CHALLENGES AND FUTURE DIRECTIONS

Introduction

NEW FIRMS CREATE NEW JOBS, open up chances for upward social mobility, foster economic flexibility, and contribute to competition and economic efficiency (Birch 1987). However, new firms fail at an alarming rate, and that failure is a norm, rather than the exception (Dean *et al.* 1997). Most of the entrepreneurship literature has focused on successful ventures, and little is known about why ventures fail. Even less is known about how they fail. The purpose of this chapter is to review and assess the progress to date of the research concerning entrepreneurial failure and suggest research directions. The chapter first considers the definitional issues related to business failure. The second section reviews a wide range of variables that have been employed to predict business failure. Section three examines issues related to existing research. Finally, the chapter provides an integrative model of entrepreneurial failure and also delineates future research directions. Studies reviewed in this chapter are primarily derived from publications in the mainstream management and entrepreneurship journals, with the focus on failures of start-up firms and small/medium-sized enterprises. Studies using financial ratios to predict firm failure are excluded from this review for two reasons. First, the majority of the financial ratio-based models have been tested in relatively large and well-established firms, which is beyond the scope of interest for this chapter. Second, studies based on financial ratios yield limited insights into the questions of why and how businesses fail.

Entrepreneurial failure: what is it?

The term "failure" in the *Oxford English Dictionary* is defined as "to become deficient, to be inadequate." In general, many different terminologies are related to business failure, such as firm closures, entrepreneurial exit (Gimeno *et al.* 1997), dissolution, discontinuance, insolvency, organizational mortality, bankruptcy, and organizational failures (Baum 1996). These terminologies have been used interchangeably with little distinction.

What do we really mean by entrepreneurial failure? In studies of entrepreneurship and small-business failure, researchers have mainly used four different definitions.

Discontinuance criterion

The discontinuance or exit includes every change in ownership and closures for any reason, which is referred to as discontinuance of ownership (Baum and Mezias 1992; Mitchell 1994). The problem with this definition is that not all closure is financially related. A venture closures could be a deliberate process that reflects a voluntary proactive decision to exit by entrepreneurs as part of a venture's intended exit strategy. Additionally, exit may occur for a number of other reasons.

Bankruptcy criterion

Business failure occurs when the firm is deemed to be legally bankrupt or has ceased operation with resulting losses to creditors (Perry 2002). This appears to be a very narrow definition, as it may exclude those businesses that do not declare bankruptcy yet barely break even and provide neither a reasonable income for the owner nor a fair return to the investors. This definition also excludes businesses that ceased operation with substantial losses to owners but not to creditors.

Loss-cutting criterion

Failed firms are those that are disposed of with a loss to avoid further losses (Ulmer and Nelson 1947). Not every venture that an entrepreneur would describe as "failed" necessarily ends in bankruptcy. A venture may be terminated to avoid or limit losses because deteriorating financial performance is anticipated. Firms might foresee their future fate in time and so avoid a complete loss. This closure is viewed as an intentional choice of discontinuing operation of a venture. However, many businesses that are still in operation may be regarded as failures, if they are not earning a rate of return that is commensurate with the firms' opportunity costs of capital.

Earning criterion

A firm is viewed as a failure if it is not earning an adequate return (Cochran 1981). For example, Altman (1968) defines a firm as a failure if it is earning a rate of return on invested capital which is significantly and continually below prevailing rates on similar investments.

Failure factors: what do we know?

Studies have examined entrepreneurial failure from four groups of factors – individual characteristics of the founder, resources, structural characteristics and strategies of the firm, and environmental conditions in which a firm operates – the processes leading to a firm's failure. Figure 10.1 delineates the relationships between these variables and their impact on failure. Table 10.1 provides a list of studies of entrepreneurial failure, with independent variables, dependent variables, and sample descriptions, as well as key findings.

Individual characteristics – the entrepreneurs

Most researchers in the field have learned that the founder is the key to venture survival and failure. The studies investigated the effects of the founder's education, working experience, industry-specific experience, and family (e.g. Bates 1990a, 1990b). This stream of research is mostly built on human capital theory (Becker 1975) and, in general, argues that high human capital endowment of the founder decreases the chances for entrepreneurial failure.

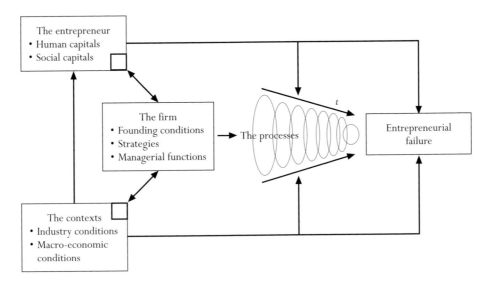

Figure 10.1 Entrepreneurial failure: an integrative model

Table 10.1 Entrepreneurial failure: a literature review

Author(s) and year	Independent variables	Dependent variables and measures	Sample descriptions	Research methods	Findings
Gimeno et al. (1997)	Work experience, formal education, similar business experience, intrinsic motivation. Control variables: size, working hours, initial capital investment, path of ownership, industry conditions.	Entrepreneurial exit (0 for continued, 1 for exit).	1,547 entrepreneurs of new businesses from National Federation of Independent Business (936 survived, 611 discontinued).	Censored regression (tobit); grouped data regression.	Entrepreneurs with more general human capital perform better but do not necessarily survive more frequently. Firms with low thresholds may choose to continue or survive despite comparatively low performance.
Ronstadt (1986)	Entrepreneurial career length, number of ventures, exit rate.		95 ex-entrepreneurs, 208 practicing entrepreneurs.	Descriptive statistics.	Entrepreneurial career length is negatively correlated to exit.
Pennings et al. (1998)	Human capital (industry and firm specific) and social capital.	Firm dissolution: the name of a firm permanently disappeared from the directories without the incidence of an acquisition or name change.	1,851 Dutch accounting firms during the period of 1880–1990.	Discrete event history analysis.	A firm's human and social capital decreases the likelihood of firm dissolution. Specificity and non-appropriatability of such capital diminished dissolutions of professional service firms.
Bruderl et al. (1992)	Years of schooling, years of working experience, industry-	Firm mortality that is measured by de-registration.	1,849 business founders in Munich and Upper Bavaria (Germany).	Event history analysis; log-logistic model.	The human capital characteristics of the founder, especially years of schooling, work experience, and

Study	Variables	Dependent variable	Sample	Method	Findings
	specific experience, self-employment experience, leadership experience, self-employed father, founding strategies, amount of capital invested, number of employees employed, competition intensity, seasonality.				industry-specific experience would increase survival chance. As would organizational characteristics, such as amount of capital invested, number of employees hired, and organizational niche strategies.
Preisendorfer and Voss (1990)	Founder's age, industry-specific experience.	Firm mortality.	78,441 small traders from firm registration and de-registration in Germany for the period of 1980–1984.	Event history analysis.	An inverted U-shaped relationship between a founder's age and firm's mortality; the relationship seems to be stronger in industries that require more industry-specific experience from the founders.
Carter et al. (1997)	Initial resources (prior start-up experience, industry experience, start-up team, number of employees), founding strategies, gender, and cross products.	Firm discontinuance.	203 retail firms.	Logistic regression analysis with variables entering as blocks.	Human capital of the founding teams, the scale of start-up business, and broad strategies significantly decrease the odds of firm discontinuance; women-owned businesses have higher odds of discontinuance; women owners were less likely to have instrumental experience from the industry and started their businesses on a smaller scale. However, resource deficiencies do not appear to affect the odds of discontinuance for women-owned businesses.

Table 10.1 continued

Author(s) and year	Independent variables	Dependent variables and measures	Sample descriptions	Research methods	Findings
Mitchell (1994)	Firm size and age, start-up firms and diversifying firms.	Rate of dissolution and bankruptcy of start-up firms and diversifying firms.	Seven American medical sector product markets established between the 1950s and 1980s.	Logistic regression analysis.	The dissolution rate declined with greater sales and age for start-up firms. Although dissolution rate also declined with greater sales for diversifying firms, the rate was not affected by business age. When age, sales, and other organizational characteristics were controlled for, there was little difference in the dissolution rate between start-up firms and diversifying firms.
Moulton et al. (1996)	Industry growth/decline rate, growth and decline in organizational debt and assets, four different patterns of failing.	Change in assets, sales, debt, and number of losing years.	73 firms that declared bankruptcy from 1980 to 1986 and 73 matching firms that did not fail during that period.	Analysis of variance, t-tests.	There were more failures in growing industries. Failing firms increase their debts more rapidly and significantly than matching firms. Firms exhibit different paths to decline.
Perry (2002)	Failed group vs. non-failed group.	Degree of business planning.	152 paired samples of failed and non-failed firms. Failed firms were selected from National Bankruptcy Bulletin (Dun and Bradstreet publication).	t-tests.	Very little formal planning goes on in U.S. small businesses; non-failed firms do more planning than failed firms did prior to failure.

Study	Variables	Dependent variable	Sample	Method	Findings
Castrogiovanni et al. (1993)	Age, size, capital intensity, business types.	Failure rate.	103 franchisers.	Analysis of covariance.	Age is positively related to franchise failure; size and capital intensity have no direct and significant impact on failure rate.
Gaskill et al. (1993)	A list of 35 causes of business failures.		130 failed businesses in retailing industry.	Factor analysis.	Four factors were uncovered, including managerial and planning function, working capital management, competitive environment, and growth/over-expansion.
Bates (1990a)	Years of education, managerial experience, small business exposure within one's family, age, year of entry into self-employment, created a firm de novo, or entered an existing business.	Exit, 1 – if the firm was still operating in late 1986; 0 – otherwise.	A random sample of business owners from the 1982 Characteristics of Business Owners.	Logit regression.	Highly educated entrepreneurs were most likely to create firms that remained in operation through 1986. Firm leverage is trivial for delineating active from discontinued businesses.
Shane and Foo (1999)	Cognitive legitimacy (age, size), social–political legitimacy (external certification), imprinting, economic variables as controls.	Failure as exit from the listing.	1,292 franchisers in the United States for the years 1979–1996.	Cox regression.	Age, size, and media certification reduced the hazard of failure. New franchisers were also imprinted by the location of their founding. Survival of new franchise systems is better explained by adding institutional explanations to economic ones.

Table 10.1 continued

Author(s) and year	Independent variables	Dependent variables and measures	Sample descriptions	Research methods	Findings
Romanelli (1989)	Industry demand, concentration ratio, market breadth, market aggressiveness.	Firm survival: survival (1); failure (0)	108 start-ups in the PC industry.	Logit regression.	Environmental conditions and founding strategies jointly affect survival. On average, specialists are more likely to survive in their early years than generalists. When industry sales are increasing, generalists have a higher survival rate than specialists. Additionally, aggressive firms fare better than efficient firms. However, the competitive conditions are unrelated to a firm's mortality rate.
Venkatraman et al. (1990)	A series of transaction sets.	Firm survival and failure.	Ten educational software start-ups.	Case study, inductive approach, a process model.	New and small firms engage in transactions with others. Owing to liability of newness and smallness, entrepreneurs often use these transactions as collateral to attract valuable customers and resources. These leveraged strategies make the set of transactions of the firm tightly coupled. When one transaction within the set fails, the set collapses, which leads to the failure of the firm.

Carter *et al.* (1997) found that experience in starting other businesses, experience working in the industry, starting a business with partners, and having employees all significantly decrease the odds of discontinuance. Their findings suggest that the human capital of the founder or founding teams and the scale of the business at start-up are equally important. Bruderl *et al.* (1992) elaborated two mechanisms by which human capital improves a firm's survival chances and decreases failure rates – higher human capital is able to recognize attractive business opportunities and also leads to higher productivity. Following Becker (1975), Bruderl *et al.* (1992) tested the impact of general human capital and specific capital on firm failure rates in a group of 1,849 German business founders. They found that general human capital such as years of schooling and years of working experience significantly decrease a firm's failure rate. In his study of small business in the construction sector in Great Britain, Hall (1994) also found that human capital was the most pivotal factor in differentiating survived from failed firms. Using a dataset of 78,441 small traders from firm registration and de-registration in Germany for the period of 1980 to 1984, Preisendorfer and Voss (1990) explored the relationship between the founder's age and firm mortality rate. They found firm mortality rate is low for middle-aged founders but high for young and older founders, suggesting an inverted U-shaped relationship between founders' age and firm mortality. By contrast, using data from the U.S. Bureau of Census, Headd (2000) found gender, race, and age play a small, if any, role in survivability. But he discovered that founders with college educations have a higher survival rate.

Resources, strategies, and other organizational attributes – the firms

Firm age and liability of newness

Organizational ecologists have elaborated on age-dependent organizational mortality in great detail (Singh *et al.* 1986). This line of research suggests that young and new organizations have a higher risk of failure than older organizations. For example, Bruderl *et al.* (1992) found that new businesses that are "followers" have a better chance of survival than those created *de novo*. Evans (1987) found that older firms in the U.S. Small Business Database are less likely to dissolve and are more likely to survive. Philips and Kirchhoff (1989) also used the U.S. Small Business Database, and found that firm survival tends to increase with enterprise age. Delacroix and Swaminathan (1991) found that older wineries were less likely to shut down. However, some studies have reported that older organizations are more likely to dissolve in service areas such as credit unions (Amburgey *et al.* 1993) and hotels (Baum and Mezias 1992).

Firm size and liability of smallness

Researchers have argued that entrepreneurial failure is also affected by the initial size, which may be measured by the amount of financial capital invested and the number of people employed at the time of founding. For example, Bruderl *et al.* (1992) found that a larger start-up size reduces a firm's mortality rate. In a similar vein, Headd (2000) found a high survival rate for firms with $50,000 or more of start-up capital and employees. A study of the winery industry by Delacroix and Swaminathan (1991) and a study of medical products by Mitchell (1994) found similar results. However, Castrogiovanni *et al.* (1993) found no support for the belief that size has an impact on failure rate.

Firm growth

Philips and Kirchhoff (1989) noted that failure rates decreased by half for firms that grew. They found that even a small amount of growth reduced the average failure rates within five years to 34 percent; and that the earlier in the life of the business that growth occurred, the lower the chance of failure.

Founding strategies

Researchers have used "generalist" (r-strategists) and "specialist" (k-strategists) strategies as the classification scheme for new ventures (Hannan and Freeman 1977). The generalists offer a wide array of products or services aiming at a broad range of customers, whereas the specialists focus on a niche market to avoid direct competition with large and more established firms. The argument is that targeting a narrow market segment and serving customers through differentiated products or services would decrease the odds for entrepreneurial failure. For example, Romanelli (1989) found that specialists fare better than generalists in most environmental conditions. Alternatively, there are researchers who argue that a generalist strategy will lead to a better chance of survival. The generalist strategy focuses on a broad range of markets and matches a broad appeal offering by competitors. For example, in their empirical study of 203 retail firms, Carter *et al.* (1997) found that broad strategies significantly affect discontinuance and are more effective than a narrow niche strategy, suggesting that new ventures must match the broad appeal offered by competitors to increase the chance of survival.

Managerial variables

In a review of small-business failure literature, Haswell and Holmes (1989) found that management incompetence and inexperience still remain the major causes of business failure. Berryman's (1981) review of literature related to business failure and bankruptcy also gives "management inefficiency" as the most commonly cited reason for failure. In their interview with ten business owners who had declared bankruptcy, Bruno *et al.* (1987) learned about three categories of causes of failure – product/market problems, financial difficulties, and managerial/key employee problems. In their analysis of 130 failed businesses in the retail industry, Gaskill *et al.* (1993) found that four factors lead to failure, namely, managerial and planning function, working capital management, competitive environment, and growth and over-expansion. In a similar vein, in their survey of failed businesses, Peterson *et al.* (1983) found that lack of management expertise and financial-related factors were mostly cited. Perry's (2002) study of a paired sample of failed and non-failed small businesses found that non-failed firms do more planning than failed firms did prior to failure.

Environmental conditions – the contexts

In the strategy area, there has been a long-standing debate about the relative importance of environmental determinism and managerial choice as explanations of organizational survival and failure (e.g. Rumelt 1991). Competitive concentration, which is measured by the percentage of sales, plant capacity, and distribution channels controlled by the largest four or eight competitors, is related to a firm's ability to acquire or increase control of available resources in the industry. Thus, increasing competitive concentration should indicate increased difficulties for young and small firms in acquiring resources and subsequently lead to high failure rates.

It is plausible that attractive industries (i.e. growing industries) should make survival easier and therefore firms in these industries should have low failure rates. Brittain and Freeman (1980) referred to these conditions as the excess-carrying capacity of an environment. The empirical study by Moulton *et al.* (1996) of 73 firms which declared bankruptcy found that more firms failed in growing industries than in declining industries. Philips and Kirchhoff (1989) found survival rates vary considerably from industry to industry, with a low of 35.3 percent in construction and a high of 46.9 percent in manufacturing. However, the authors failed to provide reasons why these discrepancies occur. Shane and Foo's (1999) study of U.S. franchisers found little support for systematic industry differences in franchisers' survival. Failure rate was no more common in new franchising areas or in more highly regulated industries. The absence of industry effects is consistent with the finding of Lafontaine and Shaw (1998) and Bruderl *et al.* (1992).

Events for failure – the processes

In their study of the failure of large corporations, Hambrick and D'Aveni (1988) found that the process of failure was a protracted downward spiral. Research by Venkatraman *et al.* (1990) shifts the focus of failure research from the question of "why" to "how" – how the process of failure unfolds. In their case studies of ten educated software start-ups, the authors found that new and small firms engage in transactions with others. Because of their liabilities of newness and smallness, entrepreneurs often use these transactions as collateral to attract valuable customers and resources. The leveraged strategy makes the set of transactions of the firm tightly coupled. When one transaction within the set fails, the set collapses, leading to the failure of the firm.

Entrepreneurial failure: how much do we know?

Definitional and measurement issues

As indicated in Table 10.1, there seems a lack of consensus by academics generally over what constitutes entrepreneurial failure. To a great extent, our understanding of entrepreneurial failure has been precluded by the lack of a generally accepted definition of such failure. Various definitions lead to various measures and sources of data collection, such as tax records (Hall 1994), state employment files (Birley 1984), telephone directories, and local chambers of commerce. For those relatively subjective measures such as earning criterion and loss-cutting criterion, it becomes more difficult to find accurate measures of failure and reliable data sources. Entrepreneurs who have failed are also reluctant to show interest in documenting their failures in detail.

Theoretical development issues

Lack of integrative models

Entrepreneurial failure is a complex and multidimensional phenomenon, and it is conceivable that the impact of one variable (e.g. founding strategy) on entrepreneurial failure may depend on another variable (e.g. competitive conditions). Therefore, theoretically, we would expect both independent effects and interaction effects among the four categories of variables – between the entrepreneur and the firm, the firm and the context, the context and the process, the entrepreneur and the process, the firm and the process, and the entrepreneur and the context. However, scant attention has been given to the interplays between variables. With the exception of Romanelli (1989), integrative models of entrepreneurial failure are notably missing.

Lack of theoretical development

The majority of empirical studies about failure prediction have produced "garbage can" models, that is, the model development has been data driven rather than theory led. Quite often, paired-sample data with failed and non-failed firms are created, followed by Logit regression analysis or descriptive statistics with t-tests. The selection of variables appears to be selected for convenience rather than with theoretical justification. Rich case analysis that documents the factors and process leading is rare. McGrath's (1999) research on option theory of entrepreneurial failure represents an initial effort in theory development.

Imbalanced research focus

Table 10.2 suggests a significant amount of attention has been given to the question of "why" – the factors from the entrepreneur, the venture, and the context affect entrepreneurial failure. By contrast, process-based research addresses the issue of "how" – the process by which failure unfolds. Process-focused research should be as important as the other research, if not more so.

Social capital as the missing piece of the puzzle

One notable omission in the research of entrepreneurial failure is the role of an entrepreneur's social capital. Social capital has traditionally been conceptualized as a set of social resources embedded in relationships (e.g. Burt 1992). Scholars have espoused a broader definition of social capital, including not only social relationships but also the norms and values associated with them (e.g. Coleman 1990). More recently, the concept of social capital has found its way into entrepreneurship research (e.g. Liao and Welsch 2003). An entrepreneur's social capital is instrumental in obtaining financial support, gaining legitimacy, and facilitating transactions. Therefore, it is conceivable that social capital could play a role in affecting a firm's failure.

Methodological issues

Studies of survived or successful ventures are much easier than studies of failed ventures. First, it is difficult to locate ventures that failed because of poor performance. Homogeneous samples are hard to come by. Second, entrepreneurs are reticent about failure. Those who do agree to participate find it difficult to identify the reasons for venture failure, especially when the failure took place in the past. Therefore, they will have a hard time understanding and articulating causations. Additionally, as attribution theory suggests, entrepreneurs are more likely to attribute failure to external causes than to internal ones.

One major caveat related to the research design of many studies reviewed is that they fail to take the temporal issue into consideration. Theoretically, there should be a time gap between predictors of venture failure and the actual failure, and data collection and modeling should reflect the time gap.

In terms of statistic modeling, entrepreneurial failure research has predominantly used two models. One model is Logit regression, a static model that examines the impact of factors on the probability of failure. This model usually applies to a research design when a combined sample of failed and non-failed firms is present. So far, researchers who have adopted this model mainly include independent effects with limited or no controlling variables. Interaction terms are rarely seen in these models. The other model is an event history analysis and hazard model – a dynamic model that is popular among population ecologists.

There is limited theoretical development in entrepreneurial failure research. Two research methods could be considered for theory-building purposes. One is case research. Researchers have noted the importance of case method in theory construction (Yin 1994), especially for an emerging area of inquiry. The other method is data mining, which is a grounded theorizing approach to build profiles of failed ventures with combinational factors from the entrepreneur, the context, the process, and the firm.

Entrepreneurial failure: where do we go from here?

Building a longitudinal database

In the United States, a significant amount of research has been based on administrative databases such as Dun and Bradstreet, and the Longitudinal Establishment Data File from the Bureau of the Census. Although the existing databases have yielded rich results, they contain measurement and sampling errors, which do not make them ideal sources for analyzing entrepreneurial failures. For example, the Dun and Bradsteet files are built on data from a credit rating service that has difficulty in keeping track of ownership changes (Kirchhoff 1994). The database does not distinguish between businesses that file bankruptcies and those that are sold by the founders for a better opportunity. As Williams (1993) pointed out, the failure rates for entrepreneurial ventures have been grossly overstated. Many closed businesses are not necessarily failed business. Lumping together different types of firm disappearances significantly can confound findings. To provide a better understanding of entrepreneurial failure, we need a database of a more homogeneous group of failed firms. Additionally, because of federal laws that prevent the releasing of any form of data that might disclose information about individual firms, firm-level micro-data is nonexistent.

The nature of the phenomenon of entrepreneurial failure calls for a longitudinal research design that traces individual firms from birth to death and then identifies the individual, organizational, and context factors that may contribute to a firm's failure. Instead of sense-making – *post hoc* realization and rationalization of why a venture fails – researchers could make ongoing observations of the entrepreneurs and the environments, as well as the firms. The Panel Study of Entrepreneurial Dynamics is just one of such research projects (Reynolds 2000). The study first identifies a group of nascent entrepreneurs and then tracks four types of them over time: those who discontinue their venture creation efforts; those who create new business ventures but still fail in the end; the general public who are not involved in any venture creation activities; and those who continue to operate and grow their businesses. Only this longitudinal study with its quasi-experimental design approach will enable us to uncover the factors that differentiate failed groups from others.

Integrative research model

Future research should focus on the interplays across different categories of variables. Specifically, the following questions may be of interest to researchers in the field of entrepreneurial failure:

1   failure $=f$(the entrepreneur $\times$ the firm). To what extent do a venture's resource endowment and founding strategy moderate the relationship between the entrepreneur's social and human capital and failure?
2   failure $=f$(the context $\times$ the firm). Does the impact of a firm's resource

endowment, and founding strategies on entrepreneurial failure vary across different industry conditions?

3   failure $= f$(the entrepreneur $\times$ the context). Given various competitive conditions, how do an entrepreneur's human and social capital affect failure?

4   failure $= f$(the entrepreneur $\times$ the process). Do entrepreneurs with different human and social capital have different processes of failure?

5   failure $= f$(the firm $\times$ the process). Do firms with different founding strategies and resource endowments exhibit different processes of failure?

6   failure $= f$(the context $\times$ the process). To what extent do industry conditions moderate the different processes leading to failure? Do we expect to see a certain failure process in certain types of industry conditions but not in others?

At the more macro level, studies can focus on the question of the extent to which a national culture affects venture failure. Culture and environment are seen as crucial to tolerance of failure. For entrepreneurs in the United States, the stigma of business failure is much smaller than in European countries, and therefore individuals are more prepared to start anew in business and ultimately develop high-growth firms. We would expect a low venture failure rate for countries with less tolerance of failure. The project of Global Entrepreneurship Monitoring (GEM) is moving in the right direction. Another issue related to the macro level analysis is that little evidence has been shown of the proportion of individuals who experience entrepreneurial failure and subsequently start new ventures.

An intentional-based failure research

This approach is somewhat consistent with the argument of entrepreneurial intentions as a central and crucial component in understanding the overall process of entrepreneurship. Entrepreneurial intentions help to establish key initial characteristics of new organizations (Bird 1988; Krueger and Carsrud 1993). Fishbein and Ajzen state succinctly that "behavior is best predicted by intentions and . . . intentions are jointly determined by the person's attitude and subjective norm concerning that behavior" (1975: 216). Individuals have different reasons and intentions when they start a business, and not everyone wants to be a lifetime entrepreneur. Therefore, a founder's intention at the start of a new venture should have an impact on its final outcome – be it a success, a closure, or a failure. Consequently, it would be fruitful to investigate how entrepreneurial intentions affect failure.

A process-based research

Most of existing studies have focused on the issue of "why" start-ups or small businesses fail. Little attention has been paid to the issue of "how" – how the process of failure unfolds. In a study of failure of large corporations, Hambrick and D'Aveni (1988) found the process of failure was a protracted downward spiral. With the exception of Venkatraman *et al.* (1990), researchers paid very little attention to the failure process of small business and start-up firms. The question of how the process of failure unfolds over time remains an under-explored area. The existing research models largely treat the venture failure process as a black box with affecting variables from individual, firm, and environmental levels. Through process-based research we can hope to develop intervening strategies to disrupt the failure process.

References

Altman, E.I. (1968) "Financial ratios, discriminant analysis and the prediction of corporate bankruptcy," *Journal of Finance*, 23: 414–429.

Amburgey, T.L., Dacin, T., and Kelly, D. (1993) "Disruptive selection and population segmentation: inter-population competition as a segregating process," in Baum, J.A.C. and Singh, J.V. (eds) *Evolutionary Dynamics of Organizations*, New York, NY: Oxford University Press.

Bates, T. (1990a) "Entrepreneurial human capital inputs and small business longevity," *Review of Economics and Statistics*, 72: 551–559.

Bates, T. (1990b) "Self-employment trends among Mexican Americans," Discussion Paper No. 90–9, Center for Economic Studies, U.S. Bureau of Census, Washington, DC.

Baum, J.A. (1996) "Organizational ecology," in Clegg, S.R., Hardy, C., and Nord, W.R. (eds) *Handbook of Organization Studies*, Thousand Oaks, CA: Sage.

Baum, J.A. and Mezias, S.J. (1992) "Localized competition and organizational failure in the Manhattan hotel industry," *Administrative Science Quarterly*, 37: 580–604.

Becker, G. (1975) *Human Capital*, second edn, Chicago, IL: University of Chicago Press.

Berryman, J. (1981) "Small business failure and bankruptcy: a survey of literature," *European Small Business Journal*, 1: 47–59.

Birch, D. (1987) *Job Creation in America*, New York, NY: Free Press.

Bird, B.J. (1988) "Implementing entrepreneurial ideas: the case for intention," *Academy of Management Review*, 13(3): 442–453.

Birley, B. (1984) "Finding new firms," *Proceedings of the Academy of Management*, 47: 64–68.

Brittain, J.W. and Freeman, J.H. (1980) "Organizational proliferation and density dependent selection," in Kimberly, J.R. and Miles, R.H. (eds) *The Organizational Life Cycle*, San Francisco, CA: Jossey-Bass.

Bruderl, J., Preisendorfer, P., and Ziegler, R. (1992) "Survival chances of newly founded business organizations," *American Sociological Review*, 57: 227–242.

Bruno, A.V., Leidecker, J.K., and Harder, J.W. (1987) "Why firms fail," *Business Horizon*, 30: 50–58.

Burt, R.S. (1992) *Structural Holes*, Cambridge, MA: Harvard Business Press.

Carter, N.M., Williams, M., and Reynolds, P. (1997) "Discontinuance among new firms in retail: influence of initial resources, strategy and gender," *Journal of Business Venturing*, 12: 125–145.

Castrogiovanni, G., Justis, R.T., and Julian, S. (1993) "Franchise failure rates: an assessment of magnitude and influence factors," *Journal of Small Business Management*, 31(2): 105–114.

Cochran, A.B. (1981) "Small business mortality rates: a review of the literature," *Journal of Small Business Management*, 19(4): 50.

Coleman, J.S. (1990) *Foundations of Social Theory*, Cambridge, MA: Harvard Business Press.

Dean, T., Turner, C.A., and Bamford, C.E. (1997) "Impediments to imitation and rate of new firm failure," *Academy of Management Proceedings*, pp. 123–132.

Delacroix, J.A. and Swaminathan, A. (1991) "Cosmetic, speculative, and adaptive change in the wine industry: a longitudinal study," *Administrative Science Quarterly*, 36: 631–661.

Evans, D.S. (1987) "The relationship between firm growth, size and age: estimates for 100 manufacturing industries," *Journal of Industrial Economics*, 35: 567–581.

Fishbein, M. and Ajzen, I. (1975) *Belief, Attitude, Intention and Behavior: An Introduction to Theory and Research*, Reading, MA: Addision-Wesley.

Gaskill, L.R., Van Auken, H.E., and Manning, R.A. (1993) "A factor analytic study of the perceived causes of small business failure," *Journal of Small Business Management*, 31(4): 18–31.

Gimeno, J., Folta, T.B., Cooper, A.C., and Woo, C.Y. (1997) "Survival of the fittest? Entrepreneurial human capital and the persistence of underperforming firms," *Administrative Science Quarterly*, 42: 750–783.

Hall, G. (1994) "Factors distinguishing survivors from failures among small firms in the UK construction sector," *Journal of Management Studies*, 10(4): 283–301.

Hambrick, D.C. and D'Aveni, R.A. (1988) "Large corporate failures as downward spirals," *Administrative Science Quarterly*, 33(1): 1–22.

Hannan, M. and Freeman, J. (1977) "The population ecology of organizations," *American Journal of Sociology*, 82: 929–964.

Haswell, S. and Holmes, S. (1989) "Estimating small business failure rate: a reappraisal," *Journal of Small Business Management*, 27(3): 68–74.

Headd, B. (2000) *Business Success: Factors Leading to Surviving and Closing Successfully*, Washington, DC: Office of Advocacy, U.S. Small Business Administration.

Kirchhoff, B.A. (1994) *Entrepreneurship and Dynamic Capitalism*, Westport, CT: Praeger.

Krueger, N. and Carsrud, A. (1993) "Entrepreneurial intentions: applying the theory of planned behavior," *Entrepreneurship & Regional Development*, 5: 315–330.

Lafontaine, F. and Shaw, K. (1998) "Franchising growth and franchiser entry and exit in the U.S. market: myth and reality," *Journal of Business Venturing*, 13: 95–112.

Liao, J. and Welsch, H. (2003) "Social capital and entrepreneurial growth aspiration: a comparison of technology and non-technology-based nascent entrepreneurs," *Journal of High Tech Management Research*, 14(1): 149–170.

McGrath, R.G. (1999) "Falling forward: real options reasoning and entrepreneurial failure," *Academy of Management Review*, 24(1): 13–30.

Mitchell, W. (1994) "The dynamics of evolving markets: the effects of business sales and age on dissolutions and divestitures," *Administrative Science Quarterly*, 39: 575–602.

Moulton, W.N., Thomas, H., and Pruett, M. (1996) "Business failure pathways: environmental stress and organizational response," *Journal of Management*, 22(4): 571–595.

Pennings, J., Lee, K., and Van Witteloostuijin, A. (1998) "Human capital, social capital and firm dissolution," *Academy of Management Journal*, 41(4): 425–440.

Perry, S.C. (2002) "A comparison of failed and non-failed small businesses in the United States: do men and women use different planning and decision making strategies?" *Journal of Developmental Entrepreneurship*, 7(4): 415–428.

Peterson, R.A., Kozmetsky, G., and Ridgway, N.M. (1983) "Perceived causes of small business failures: a research note," *American Journal of Small Business*, 8: 15–19.

Philips, B.D. and Kirchhoff, B.A. (1989) "Formation, growth and survival: small firm dynamics in the U.S. economy," *Small Business Economics*, 1: 65–74.

Preisendorfer, P. and Voss, T. (1990) "Organizational mortality of small firms: the effects of entrepreneurial age and human capital," *Organization Studies*, 11(1): 107–129.

Reynolds, P. (2000) "National panel study of U.S. business startups: background and methodology," *Databases for the Study of Entrepreneurship*, Vol. 4. Greenwich, CT: JAI Press/Elsevier.

Romanelli, E. (1989) "Environments and strategies of organization start-up: effects of early survivals," *Administrative Science Quarterly*, 34: 369–387.

Ronstadt, R. (1986) "Exit, stage left: why entrepreneurs end their entrepreneurial careers before retirement," *Journal of Business Venturing*, 1: 323–338.

Rumelt, R. (1991) "How much does industry matter?" *Strategic Management Journal*, 12: 167–185.

Shane, S. and Foo, M.D. (1999) "New firm survival: institutional explanations for new franchisor mortality," *Management Science*, 45(2): 142–159.

Singh, J.V., Tucker, D.J., and House, R. (1986) "Organizational legitimacy and the liability of newness," *Administrative Science Quarterly*, 31: 171–193.

Ulmer, K.J. and Nelson, A. (1947) "Business turnover and causes of failure," *Survey of Current Business Research:* 10–16.

Venkatraman, N., Van de Ven, A.H., Buckeye, J., and Hudson, R. (1990) "Start-up in a turbulent environment: a process model of failure among firms with high customer dependence," *Journal of Business Venturing*, 5: 277–295.

Williams, M.L. (1993) "Measuring business starts, success, and survival: some database consideration," *Journal of Business Venturing*, 8: 295–299.

Yin, R. (1994) *Case Study Research: Design and Methods*, second edn, Thousand Oak, CA: Sage Publishing.

PART THREE

Technology and entrepreneurship

Chapter 11

Rodney C. Shrader

University of Illinois at Chicago

Gerald E. Hills

University of Illinois at Chicago

G.T. Lumpkin

University of Illinois at Chicago

ELECTRONIC COMMERCE: CURRENT UNDERSTANDING AND UNANSWERED QUESTIONS

Introduction: historical perspective

THIS CHAPTER PROVIDES A detailed overview of the current e-commerce literature and points out unanswered questions that would be particularly interesting to academics and helpful to entrepreneurs wanting to engage in e-commerce.

In the latter half of the 1990s, the business press hyped electronic commerce, conducting business transactions electronically via the Internet, as the "New Economy." This hype gave birth to weekly and monthly magazines devoted exclusively to electronic commerce (e-commerce). At that time one such publication, *Business 2.0*, published issues exceeding 600 pages. Countless articles by new-found "experts" discussed how the Internet would revolutionize the way business was conducted in every industrial sector. Businesses of every type were admonished to "get wired" or risk losing their competitive advantages. Businesses were categorized as "winners" or "losers" on the basis of

Internet presence, and those who did not jump online were dismissively branded as those who "just don't get it!" (Beer and Hogan 2000).

Papers published in academic journals also hyped the impact of the Internet. They embraced and proliferated buzzwords such as e-commerce, e-business, e-enterprise, e-marketing, e-operations, e-service, e-opportunity, e-enabled, e-RandD, e-product development, e-HR, e-procurement, and e-profit (e.g. Means and Faulkner 2000). DeCovny (1998) suggested that e-commerce was becoming *essential* to business survival. Baker and Baker wrote:

> The rise of e-commerce, the World Wide Web, and the software to support the initiatives is so startling in its economic implications that it may reasonably be considered a break point in the way we do business. This "break point" is an abrupt and defining moment that obliterates standards and accepted commercial practices and replaces them with the essential business paradigm for the new era. . . . To thrive in this world, you must be online, and your online presence must be a powerful one.
>
> (2000: 87–88)

Similarly, Amar (1999) wrote:

> It can be declared with almost full certainty that the Internet will be the most important invention of the 20th century. . . . There is much to be gained by being first to venture into the new territory. . . . The biggest impact on business will be transforming business to what is classified as true competition in economic theory. . . . The Internet will generate characteristics that make business truly competitive – a large number of competitors, easy entry and exit, fewer intermediaries, less regulation, highly competitive prices, and freely available information.

Means and Faulkner (2000) suggested that the Internet would accelerate market responsiveness and drive higher levels of value creation, thereby creating an intensity of competition and increased optimization never before seen in markets.

Consultants everywhere worked feverishly to get clients online with the rationale that "you don't make money right away. But unless you grab your foothold on the Internet, *you're not going to be around in five or six years*. So it's really a land grabbing exercise" (DeCovny 1998, emphasis added). In addition, U.S. government publications argued that e-commerce would revolutionize the retail industry and world-wide trade. In 1995, U.S. President William Clinton and Vice President Albert Gore issued a paper entitled "A Framework for Global Electronic Commerce," which argued passionately that governments world-wide should aggressively support the growth of e-commerce.

During the period of hype, companies everywhere scrambled to establish an online presence. However, results of one of the few published empirical studies on e-commerce indicated that firms joined the Internet without considering its role in strategy – they perceived the Internet as a new marketplace but did not engage in cool-headed consideration of its value to the firm (McBride 1997).

This enthusiasm for a radically new, yet unproven and only vaguely under-stood, business method led to "irrational exuberance" in the stock market. Internet companies of all types issued IPOs and were capitalized at previously unheard of values. Venture capital poured into dot.coms, and millions of new websites were introduced. With a wealth of cash on hand, firms focused on technological sophistication, building brands, and gaining market share (which was often measured in terms of "eyeballs" viewing the site), with little emphasis on revenue generation or profitability. Basic laws of economics appeared to have been suspended (Reichert 2001) by those who "thought they had chopped off the invisible hand" (Benko 2000).

The irrational enthusiasm for e-commerce ended abruptly in early 2000 with what has been called the "Tech Wreck." Investors suddenly realized that dot.coms were overcapitalized and that some might never actually show profits. Stocks plummeted overnight, leading to the demise of many dot.coms. Venture capital dried up, and the pendulum appeared to have swung to the opposite extreme of an irrational aversion to anything "dot.com." Empirical studies have indicated that the majority of websites are currently used as publishing media for public relations and not for commerce (Dutta and Segev 1999; Griffith and Krampf 1998).

It appears, then, that the e-commerce pendulum has made a full swing from irrational exuberance to irrational aversion. Therefore, this is a particularly interesting time to examine the literature and take stock of what we know about e-commerce from both academic and practical perspectives.

E-commerce literature

Despite the newness of the phenomenon, the literature about e-commerce is vast, reflecting the hype of recent years. The majority of these articles appeared in specialized e-commerce journals (e.g. *Business 2.0*, *iMarketing News*) and technology journals. Within the technology literature, countless articles have discussed technical details such as software, host platforms, server capacity, fire-walls, transfer speeds, programming languages, Internet service providers (ISPs), application service providers (ASPs), and other practical issues of build-ing and hosting websites. Because the purpose of this chapter is to examine e-commerce from a managerial perspective, these technical articles are not discussed in detail. Furthermore, because the e-commerce game is now much different than it was prior to the Tech Wreck, this chapter places more emphasis on literature written after that time. The review of e-commerce liter-ature provided in this chapter is not meant to be exhaustive but is intended to represent thoroughly the general tone of the literature. Several themes within the literature include descriptive articles, tactical and strategic issues, and per-ceived differences in e-commerce. The discussion is organized around those themes.

Descriptive articles

Numerous case studies have profiled highly visible, but not necessarily "successful," e-commerce players, including Garden.com, Amazon.com, Boo.com, CDNow.com, eBay.com, Staples.com, Ikea, Jokeaday, and Priceline.com. These case studies often focused on what was new and slick (visually and technologically) about websites rather than focusing on their effectiveness or economic value. The authors described companies like Garden.com, the now defunct dot.com that was considered by many to be the "poster child" of e-commerce. Only a few articles went beyond description to discuss lessons learned from case studies (e.g. Williams and Cothrel 2000; Yoffie and Cusumano 1999).

Other descriptive articles discussed e-commerce in more general terms, such as summary statistics regarding the numbers of adults online in each major city (Lake 2000), the growth of Internet advertising revenue (Tomasula 2000), the use of permission-based e-mail (Schibsted 2000), spending among dot.coms relative to customer acquisition (Saba 2000), and the customer conversion rates of websites (Betts 2001).

Tactical issues

In addition to a sea of descriptive articles, the literature introduced numerous tactical issues specific to e-commerce. Although the articles are helpful, they fall short of offering any real strategic insight. Tactical issues addressed in the literature include stickiness (frequency and duration of website visits), focus (number of pages visited in the site during one visit), freshness (degree and frequency with which website content changed), personalization (the use of personal customer data to customize marketing pitches and website content), first purchase momentum (the number of clicks from site entry to purchase), customer acquisition costs, and ease of navigation. Other articles offered helpful advice on more general tactical issues, such as screening and selecting fulfillment partners, screening and selecting suppliers online, supply chain management, use of commerce service providers, customer segmentation and attraction, customer retention, customer service, and building trust online.

Some articles offered step-by-step advice for getting online. For example, Baker and Baker (2000) outlined six basic steps for setting up an e-commerce business:

1   develop a website;
2   take orders online;
3   add credit card capability;
4   plug-in payment transaction software;
5   worry about security; and
6   develop content.

Lord (2000) argued that, to develop an e-business strategy, firms should determine what to build and what to buy, automate non-mission-critical functions first, know customers well and take small steps, add efficiency in supply chain and customer relationship management before pursuing top-line opportunities, and, finally, move toward full-blown e-business. Ryans (1995) listed publications that can help small businesses get online. Gilbert (2001) advised second wave entrants to take their time, do their homework, leverage existing advertising, don't be wacky, and don't fret. Trout (2000) admonished newcomers to avoid common assumptions, including: "we can do that too"; "who cares if our name is strange?"; "we need a cool, creative commercial"; "let's not worry about making money and just build a brand"; "people will do everything on the Web."

Although these articles offered some helpful advice in terms of getting online and managing the website, they offered no insight into strategic issues such as whether, when, and why it makes sense to be online.

Strategic issues

Although the majority of e-commerce literature is technical, descriptive, or tactical in nature, a few books and articles provided limited strategic guidance for dot.coms. Although limited in number, these publications represent the most substantial e-commerce literature. For example, in 1998 (before the Tech Wreck!) Sterrett and Shah advocated a basic common-sense approach to establishing a presence on the Internet, starting with the question of whether it makes sense, given inherent risks and challenges. The authors suggested that e-commerce provides a major opportunity for firms that got into the market early *with a good strategy*. However, they did not provide any insight into when it makes sense to engage in e-commerce or what constitutes good strategy.

Similarly, DeCovny (1998) argued that established firms entering e-commerce should look hard at numbers and make a business case for website development in terms of cost reduction, increased customer retention, acquisition of new customers, or increased value added. He suggested that businesses should understand business rules and then put the right program together. Like Sterrett and Shah, DeCovny did not offer specific guidance on what constitutes "the right program."

Burke (1997) suggested that the greatest success stories would involve companies that are able to leverage the unique characteristics of the Internet to sell their products or services and have target customers whose profiles match those of Internet users. He described Dell as a perfect example of this strategic fit. McWilliams (2000) suggested linking online strategies to total brand strategies. Benko (2000) argued for a back-to-basics approach to adding value and niche marketing. Davis and his colleagues (2001) offered general advice they labeled strategies for the long haul: don't be a first mover – be a best mover; transform, don't conform; use the network to win partners, employees, and customers; turn customers into working assets; mission and financial design go hand-in-hand; strive to be different; show – don't tell.

Seybold (2000) believed that business-to-business exchanges should focus on specialized niches. Aufreiter *et al.* (2001) suggested that successful dot.coms get their edge not from superior business models but from superior marketing. Enders and Jelassi (2000) suggested that e-tailers have no inherent advantage over bricks and mortar retailers and what matters is the quality of strategy execution of the individual firm. Brache and Webb (2000) argued for a more strategic approach to e-commerce by pointing out eight deadly assumptions of e-business. Sawhney and Sumant (2000) suggested strategies for internationalization of e-commerce.

The articles discussed above offer helpful tips into strategic issues facing e-businesses. However, each paper only focuses on a small piece of strategy. None offers comprehensive guidance for strategy formulation or implementation.

Differences between e-business and traditional business

Although very few empirical studies of e-commerce have yet been published, numerous conceptual papers have discussed how e-commerce differs from traditional business. Post Tech Wreck hindsight has shown that some assumed differences were not so great as once thought. For example, Oliver (1999) explained that dot.coms should focus on building market share rather than profits and Allee (2000) argued that traditional return-on-investment criteria are not adequate for evaluating dot.coms. In contrast, Peter Drucker argued that dot.coms should have business plans focused on building businesses on the basis of positive cash flow and profitability (Daly 2000). Nolan (2000) argued that the end of easy money means smarter bottom lines.

In 2000, Oliver offered the seven "laws" of e-commerce strategy:

> There is no such thing as competitive advantage – success is a constantly moving target; forget secrets – everything is out in the open; space replaces place; it's the scalability, stupid; flexibility beats everything else; the only constant is chaos. Familiar business terms such as "industry analysis," "sustainable competitive advantage" and "long-term customer relationship" now seem like old-fashioned relics for a bygone age.
>
> (2000: 145–146)

Another article, by Evans (2000), further exemplifies the hyperbole surrounding e-commerce. Of traditional approaches to business strategy he wrote:

> The Internet turns all this upside down. . . . Indeed the whole idea of an Internet business having a "policy" on anything is rather quaint. The business policy school believed that all those reviews, controls, and formalities would minimize the probability of getting things wrong. But now the goal is to maximize the probability of getting things right. . . . Risk has to be embraced, not avoided; speed matters more than accuracy; innovation matters more than control. . . . In the Internet age, Father does not know best: Indeed it is quite likely that Father does not have a clue. . . . The Internet

undermines the premises of competitive analysis. . . . Definitions of the firm, industry, customers, and new entrants were given and obvious. But the Internet destroys these neat categories. . . . The New Economy liberated competencies from the core. The technologies of Silicon Valley (to take one of the purest examples) belong largely to the community, not to any individual firm.

(2000: 15)

In contrast, Michael Porter (2001) argued that Internet pioneers had errantly violated nearly every precept of good strategy. He argued that gaining competitive advantage does not require a radically new approach to business; it requires building on proven principles of effective strategy. Christenson and Tedlow (2000) suggested that, rather than a radically new way of doing business, Internet retailing simply represents a fourth major disruption in retailing. The authors argued that retailers will adjust to the disruption as they did historically to the introduction of department stores, mail order catalogs and discount department stores. Others view e-commerce as a simple variation of direct marketing (e.g. Dean 2001) and not a radically new form of business.

It has been widely argued that a primary advantage of e-commerce is disintermediation, or the removal of middlemen between the seller and customer. For example, rather than share profits with wholesalers and retailers, manufacturers could sell directly to consumers and, simultaneously, keep a greater share of profits for themselves and offer lower prices to consumers. However, Carr (2000) pointed out that instead of disintermediation, the Internet produces hypermediation, a situation in which content providers, affiliate sites, search engines, portals, Internet service providers, software makers, and others are positioned to capture most e-commerce profits.

Others have argued that a "vast sea" of information about prices, competition, and features that is readily available on the Internet helps buyers "see through" the costs of products and services, producing downward pressure on prices (Sinha 2000). However, that "vast sea" of information has proved hard to navigate in cyberspace, which quickly became extremely crowded. Locke (2001) discussed information overload on the information superhighway, Wurman (2000) noted that 60 percent to 80 percent of people searching the Web for information do not find what they are looking for, and Watson et al. (1998) discussed the difficulty of attracting customers to a site on the crowded Web.

Although many perceived differences in e-commerce have been discounted, several remain unchallenged and appear to have some merit. For example, the Internet provides an extremely efficient means of delivering products in electronic form such as music, publications, and software. However, this efficiency is tempered by the challenges of protecting intellectual property rights (Seybold 2000). The Internet also provides tremendous advantages for consumers to make reservations for transportation, hotels, and entertainment online, but this efficiency is tempered by privacy concerns (Richards 1997).

In addition to efficient delivery of some goods and services, the Internet can greatly increase the market reach of firms (Savin and Silberg 2000). In fact, the Internet provides a global storefront for any firm that is online (Cukier and

Faucon 2001; Sawhney and Sumant 2000) including young and small firms. For example, Boo.com was considered a global start-up because it started with a clear strategy for internationalization (Louis 2000). Fariselli *et al.* (1999) argued that the Internet can help small and medium-sized enterprises overcome disadvantages they face vis-à-vis large transnational corporations, and Quelch and Klein (1996) suggested that the Internet levels the playing field for smaller firms. Statistics indicate that the average U.S. website gets 30 percent of its traffic and 10 percent of its orders from non-U.S. customers. However, statistics also indicate that this international trade is concentrated in a few regions and that there are numerous logistical, legal, and cultural obstacles to internationalization. (For current statistics, see Forrester.com, CyberAtlas.com, and Headcount.com.)

The Internet provides automatic access to a tremendous amount of customer information that would be impossible to collect in any other way. Such information is often collected voluntarily through online surveys and participation in permission-based marketing. However, it can also be collected passively through analyzing cookies or through targeting online communities. This detailed information allows a level of personalization and highly targeted marketing that is impossible in other channels. Marketing efforts are further enhanced by the introduction of viral marketing, through which information is explicitly or implicitly passed from one consumer to family and friends at little cost.

Because of the ease with which changes can be made to a website, the Internet allows companies to test prices efficiently, segment customers, and adjust to changes in supply and demand. Furthermore, Dahan and Srinivasan (2000) examined how the Internet can be effectively used for product concept testing. In their study, static virtual prototypes, animated virtual prototypes, and physical products were tested. Results demonstrated that both static and animated virtual prototypes produced market shares that closely mirrored those obtained with physical products. Clearly, virtual prototypes are much less costly to test than physical prototypes.

In addition to consumer and market information, the Internet provides an efficient source of competitive intelligence and supplier contacts. At its extreme, the Internet allows for completely integrated supply-chain management. Traditional supply chains involve hand-offs, bottlenecks, and buffer stocks, creating costly inventory. Internet-based "value nets" are a practical alternative. A value net is a dynamic network of customer/supplier partnerships and information flows activated by real customer demand and capable of responding rapidly and reliably (Bovel and Martha 2000). Because of this efficiency, numerous industrial business-to-business exchanges have been established to allow unmatched cooperation among competitors (Seybold 2000).

Although much of the literature points out the potential for e-commerce to greatly improve business efficiency and effectiveness, studies also point out some startling statistics about the shortcomings of e-commerce. For example, only about 3 percent of website visitors actually buy anything (Betts 2001), and 74 percent of shopping carts are abandoned at checkout (Hughes 2001). An empirical study revealed that even the best dot.coms had major problems with fulfillment (*Electron Economy* 2000), and studies show that among U.S. dot.coms, 46 percent of all orders from outside the U.S. go unfilled because of process failures (Forrester.com). Such statistics are shocking and demonstrate the challenge dot.coms have in building consumer trust (Cheskin Research 2000).

State of the literature and future research directions

The summary provided in the preceding section clearly shows that the e-commerce literature is extremely broad and extremely shallow. The overwhelming majority of the literature is outdated hyperbole or entirely descriptive and anecdotal or focuses on specific technical details. Literature that focuses on tactics is of limited value when there is little guidance about broader strategic issues. Although some interesting conceptual papers have been published, few empirical studies have. Clearly there is tremendous opportunity for academics to make a substantial contribution to the understanding of e-commerce.

E-commerce is a relatively new and rapidly changing phenomenon. Consequently, the literature is new and underdeveloped. The literature has not yet progressed to the stage of theory-based empirical research, largely because it has been assumed that e-commerce is radically different from traditional business and, therefore, traditional theories were not thought to apply. Numerous very basic questions with extreme practical value remain to be addressed. To produce knowledge that will be useful to practitioners, scholars should focus on well-articulated questions that can be addressed in academically rigorous studies that are theoretically based. A few of the more general questions include:

- is e-commerce a radically new form of business, or does it simply represent a new marketing channel or communication medium?
- in what ways does e-commerce differ from traditional business?
- without the hype, what is the true potential of the Internet to add real value and produce wealth?
- how can traditional theories of economics and business inform our understanding of e-commerce?
- what are the lessons to be learned from the Tech Wreck?
- how can newcomers overcome the cloud of the Tech Wreck and obtain legitimacy?
- what business models are best suited for the Internet?
- which e-commerce sites are profitable and why?
- what is the optimal mix of clicks and mortar?
- how does the Internet fit with and enhance the competitive strategies of established firms?
- what are the entry barriers to e-commerce?
- how can firms overcome entry barriers to e-commerce and gain visibility online?
- how can firms differentiate themselves and erect barriers to entry of potential competitors?

- what are the best strategic approaches to expansion in e-commerce, especially global expansion?
- how do firms address order fulfillment problems, especially international fulfillment?
- how can firms best overcome problems of consumer access to "perfect" information online?
- how can firms best address problems of consumer information overload?
- how can firms build consumer trust and loyalty online?

Despite the cloud of the Tech Wreck, interest in e-commerce remains high. E-commerce still represents an extremely efficient means of conducting business. Evidence shows that some e-commerce business models are indeed profitable (Aufreiter *et al.* 2001). Many companies have large technology related sunk costs, which they are not yet ready to abandon. For entrepreneurs, the Internet still provides opportunities to start businesses at relatively low costs. There is clearly a need for thoughtful, rational guidance to e-commerce strategy.

Conclusion

This chapter has reviewed the current state of e-commerce knowledge in the practitioner and academic arenas. This review clearly demonstrates that e-commerce is a topic of tremendous importance about which we still know very little from a strategic perspective. Therefore, the literature is wide open for important contributions. Now that the pendulum has made a full swing from extreme hype and irrational exuberance about the Internet to irrational doom and gloom about it, perhaps a rational view will emerge somewhere between the two extremes. The Internet is clearly an important development that will certainly have a profound and lasting impact on the business world. However, it appears that the Internet does not herald a "New Economy." Instead, the Internet provides a new and often extremely efficient means of communicating with customers and suppliers in a way that overcomes geographic limitations and greatly broadens the market reach of firms. However, efficiency without effectiveness is not enough. The challenge at this time is to understand how businesses can use this highly efficient medium to conduct business effectively in ways that add value and thereby create wealth. The challenge is to understand circumstances in which conducing e-commerce makes sense in a way that can lead to sustained competitive advantage.

References

Allee, V. (2000) "Reconfiguring the value network," *Journal of Business Strategy*, 21(4): 36–39.

Amar, A. (1999) "E-business: selection and adaptation of products and services for the Internet commerce," *Mid-Atlantic Journal of Business*, 35(1): 5–9.

Aufreiter, N., Pierre-Yves, O., and Scott, M-K. (2001) "Marketing rules," *Harvard Business Review*, 79(2): 30–31.

Baker, S. and Baker, K. (2000) "The 7th annual software roundup: e-commerce," *Journal of Business Strategy*, 21(1): 12–17.

Beer, M. and Hogan, K. (2000) "Five get it and five don't," *Business 2.0*, June 13: 204.

Benko, C. (2000) "Dumb companies get smart," *Business 2.0*, October: 97.

Betts, M. (2001) "Turning browsers into buyers," *Sloan Management Review*, 42(2): 8–9.

Bovel, D. and Martha, J. (2000) "From supply chain to value net," *Journal of Business Strategy*, 21(4): 24–28.

Brache, A. and Webb, J. (2000) "The eight deadly assumptions of e-business," *Journal of Business Strategy*, 21(3): 13–17.

Burke, R. (1997) "Do you see what I see? The future of virtual shopping," *Journal of the Academy of Marketing Science*, 25(4): 352–360.

Carr, N. (2000) "Hypermediation: commerce as clickstream," *Harvard Business Review*, 78(1): 46–47.

Cheskin Research (2000) "Gaining on trust," *Business 2.0*, July 25: 164.

Christensen, C. and Tedlow, R. (2000) "Patterns of disruption in retailing," *Harvard Business Review*, 78(1): 42–45.

Cukier, K. and Faucon, B. (2001) "The final frontier of e-commerce," *Red Herring*, 93: 64.

Dahan, E. and Srinivasan, V. (2000) "The predictive power of Internet-based product concept testing using visual depiction and animation," *Journal of Product Innovation Management*, 17(2): 99–109.

Daly, J. (2000) "Sage advice," *Business 2.0*, August 22: 134.

Davis, J., Fox, L., and Lardner, J. (2001) "Outsmart, outgun, outlast: seven winning business strategies for the long haul," *Business 2.0*, March 20: 92.

Dean, B. (2001) "Catalogs are essential branding tools," *iMarketing News*, 3(11): 10.

DeCovny, S. (1998) "Electronic commerce comes of age," *Journal of Business Strategy*, 19(6): 38–44.

Dutta, S. and Segev, A. (1999) "Business transformation on the Internet," *European Journal of Management*, 17(5): 466–476

Electron Economy (2000) "Order disorder," *Business 2.0*, October 10: 175.

Enders, A. and Jelassi, T. (2000) "The converging business models of Internet and bricks-and-mortar retailers," *European Journal of Management*, 18(5): 542–550.

Evans, P. (2000) "Strategy: the end of the endgame?" *Journal of Business Strategy*, 21(6): 12–21.

Fariselli, P., Oughton, C., Picory, C., and Sugden, R. (1999) "Electronic commerce and the future of SME's in a global market-place: networking and public policies," *Small Business Economics*, 12(3): 261–275.

Gilbert, J. (2001) "Websites that waited and won," *Business 2.0*, April 3: 60.

Griffith, D. and Krampf, R. (1998) "An examination of the web-based strategies of the top 100 U.S. retailers," *Journal of Marketing Theory and Practice*, 6(3): 12–23.

Hughes, A. (2001) "It's time to measure success differently," *iMarketing News*, 3(11): 19.

Lake, D. (2000) "Wired in the city," *The Industry Standard*, July 10–17: 202.

Locke, C. (2001) "Irrational inquirers," *Red Herring*, March 6: 100.

Lord, C. (2000) "The practicalities of developing a successful e-business strategy," *Journal of Business Strategy*, 21(2): 40–43.

Louis, T. (2000) "What I learned at boo.com," *Business 2.0*, August 8: 238.

McBride, N. (1997) "Business use of the Internet: strategic decision or another bandwagon," *European Journal of Management*, 15(1): 58–67.

McWilliams, G. (2000) "Building stronger brand through online communities," *Sloan Management Review*, 31(3): 43–54.

Means, G. and Faulkner, M. (2000) "Strategic innovation in the new economy," *Journal of Business Strategy*, 21(3): 25–29.

Nolan, C. (2000) "Crash-test dummies," *Business 2.0*, July 11: 179.

Oliver, R. (1999) "The secret formula," *Journal of Business Strategy*, 20(4): 7–8.

Oliver, R. (2000) "The seven laws of e-commerce strategy," *Journal of Business Strategy*, 21(5): 8–10.

Porter, M. (2001) "Strategy and the Internet," *Harvard Business Review*, 79(3): 62–78.

Quelch, J. and Klein, L. (1996) "The Internet and international marketing," *Sloan Management Review*, 37(3): 60–75.

Reichert, B. (2001) "Living in the real economy: a well-known VC lays out the new rules for entrepreneurs and investors," *i-street*, 6(6): 12.

Richards, J. (1997) "Legal potholes on the information superhighway," *Journal of Public Policy and Marketing*, 16(2): 319–326.

Ryan, C. (1995) "Resources," *Journal of Small Business Management*, 33(2): 65–67.

Saba, J. (2000) "The costliest customers," *Business 2.0*, September 26: 100.

Savin, J. and Silberg, D. (2000) "There's more to e-business than point and click," *Journal of Business Strategy*, 21(5): 11–13.

Sawhney, M. and Sumant, M. (2000) "Go global," *Business 2.0*, May: 178.

Schibsted, E. (2000) "Email takes center stage," *Business 2.0*, December 26: 64.

Seybold, P. (2000) "Niches bring riches," *Business 2.0*, June 13: 135.

Sinha, I. (2000) "Cost transparency: the net's real thread to prices and brands," *Harvard Business Review*, 78(2): 43–50.

Sterrett, C. and Shah, A. (1998) "Going global on the information super highway," *SAM Advanced Management Journal*, 63(1): 43–48.

Tomasula, D. (2000) "Internet ad revenue up 63% in q3," *iMarketing News*, 2(48): 3.

Trout, J. (2000) "Gimme five blunders," *Business 2.0*, June 27: 155.

Watson, R., Akselsen, S., and Pitt, L. (1998) "Attractors: building mountains in the flat landscape of the world wide web," *California Management Review*, 40(2): 36–56.

Williams, R. and Cothrel, J. (2000) "Four smart ways to run online communities," *Sloan Management Review*, 41(4): 81–91.

Wurman, R. (2000) "Redesign the date dump," *Business 2.0*, November 28: 210.

Yoffie, D. and Cusumano, M. (1999) "Building a company on Internet time: lessons from Netscape," *California Management Review*, 41(3): 8–28.

Chapter 12

Michael Stoica

Washburn University

THE IMPACT OF MOBILE COMMERCE ON SMALL BUSINESS AND ENTREPRENEURSHIP

Technology and entrepreneurship: rationale for research

SIMILAR TO THE INTERNET SEVERAL years ago, wireless techno-logy represents an important new technology that is arousing general enthusiasm. Many assumed wireless, and therefore mobile commerce (or m-commerce), would change the economic environment to an extent that would render "old economic rules obsolete" (Porter 2001). Wireless techno-logy has recently received much attention from entrepreneurs, executives, investors, and business experts. It opens new avenues for businesses (AlterEgo 2001). Entrepreneurs will be the first to explore the opportunities offered by this new body of knowledge, as was the case with every chance and opening to "do different and better" (Bidgoli 2002).

Several issues may be of interest to entrepreneurs and managers when they are dealing with the adoption of a new technology such as wireless. *Opportunity recognition*: how can opportunities be identified in a changing environment and how can the entrepreneur take advantage of the emerging opportunity? *Timing*: is the technology mature enough to offer a significant return on investment for a company in a given industry? Are there applications that can successfully use the existent technology and enhance (change) the business model? *Trends*: what are the recent developments in the industries related to the new technology and how will they have any impact on the business world? Is the technology frag-mented? *Killer applications*: which are the foreseeable applications that will capture the market and provide significant revenue? Firms must resort to technology in order to acquire the flexibility needed to meet challenges posed by the globalization of the economy (Gagnon *et al.* 2000; Greengard 2001; Griffith 1999).

Entrepreneurs and managers play an important role in the adoption of new technology. Their personal attributes have an influence on whether new technologies, such as Internet business and wireless business (mobile commerce), are adopted by their organizations.

Roberts (1991) tried, in his more than 25 years of research, to uncover the origin of high-technology entrepreneurs. He identified several variables that could predict the entrepreneur's behavior and explain his/her propensity toward new technology. Those variables might also hold for electronic business (e-commerce and/or m-commerce) in today's economic environment. Predecessor influences for high-technology entrepreneurs detected by Roberts (1991) include: family background (parents were self-employed); age (younger when they start); patterns of work experience (especially in product/service development); long-felt desire for their own business; prior work is development (not research); and advanced education, but less than doctoral degree level.

However, entrepreneurs and entrepreneurial companies involved in technology share several transition and growth characteristics that will not help them successfully market their products/services. According again to Roberts (1991), they include a tendency not to focus on the market and a mind-set that considers technology as the firm's potential competitive advantage. Many dot.com entrepreneurs were trapped into this mode of thinking and considered that, because they were technological wizards, the technology they mastered would provide them with a sustainable competitive advantage. Many technology oriented entrepreneurs succeeded. Success characteristics for technology oriented entrepreneurial businesses cited by Roberts (1991) include: technological-based service firms outperform companies that are primarily selling their personal technical capabilities, cofounders (teams) are more likely to succeed (therefore consider partnering), and initial marketing orientation helps firms succeed.

The wireless Internet and its commercial usage, known as mobile commerce (m-commerce), represent opportunities as well as challenges for entrepreneurs. Will the findings previously presented hold for entrepreneurial companies in a mobile commerce environment developed by the use of new wireless technologies?

M-commerce: a chance to enhance the entrepreneurial endeavor

The mobile Internet is in an evolutionary phase similar to the one the traditional Web entered five or six years ago. A limited number of online services are available to users. However, the potential for the mobile Internet has already gained wide acceptance (Stern 2002). According to the market research firm Strategy Analytics, the global market for m-commerce is expected to reach $200 billion by 2004. According to Mobilocity.com, companies are beginning to consider m-commerce as a high priority because they are unwilling to make the same mistakes that led them to underestimate (or wrongly estimate) the potential of the traditional Web. Companies that view mobile devices merely as additional front-ends for the delivery of Web-based content and services will find it difficult to succeed in the new era of ubiquitous communications and commerce. On the other hand, those entrepreneurs who understand that the mobile Internet is a unique business challenge and opportunity – and embrace it as such – will build m-commerce strategies that capture market share. Offering information, services, and providing transactions via devices that allow the user full mobility are elements positioned in the core of mobile commerce (Synchrologic 2001). M-commerce represents a different business philosophy and requires different business models (Angelos *et al.* 2001). It will make the business environment more demanding on companies in an m-commerce environment (time and speed, customer location, and customer's needs and wants become critical). A huge number of business opportunities will pop up, and it is up to a new generation of entrepreneurs to take advantage and fully exploit those opportunities. The question is not whether the new technology and its mobile commerce applications should be adopted. The question is when and how to adopt m-commerce (Morace and Chrometzka 2001). What applications are already profitable for small and medium-sized businesses? How can they be successfully implemented? What is coming up in the technological pipeline? Visionary entrepreneurs, such as Bill Gates, who dreamed of having a computer on every desk, will succeed, will get rich and famous (Rupp 2003).

Characteristics of the wireless technology, according to studies developed by Durlacher, Forrester Research, Oracle, and Mobilocity are summarized in Table 12.1.

The value simplified mobile commerce value chain presented in Figure 12.1 gives an idea of the different businesses involved, as well as the multiple opportunities entrepreneurs have to start up or expand on.

Content providers and service providers, as well as content aggregators/portal providers, will receive money from consumers in return for services and content provided. Downstream, the providers will have to compensate network operators for providing the infrastructure that allows delivery of services to the end user. The role of payment service providers in distributing and clearing all financial transactions along the mobile business value chain will be crucial (Rendon 2001; Sheier 2001b).

According to Mouat (2000), mobile network operators are challenged by declining margins in their traditional business. Declining revenue per user represents a phenomenon that will force network operators to implement new services continuously to remain competitive and turn around the trend of the decreasing marginal revenue. Value-added services will become an important new source of revenue and will accelerate the rapid growth of mobile commerce. Forecasts estimate that, by 2010, mobile services will be generating about half of operators' average revenue per user. The operators' role as portal providers and content aggregators – often through alliances with content and service providers – will allow them to offer customers a new, more personalized and comprehensive range of information and services, while enabling them to differentiate themselves from the competition.

Table 12.1 Characteristics of the wireless technology

Ubiquity	Today's mobile devices fulfill the need for real-time information and communication independent of the user's location (anywhere).
Localization	Technologies like GPS (Global Positioning System), TOA (Time Of Arrival), will enable marketers and consumers to send, receive, and access information, services, and conduct transactions specific to their location. Knowing where the user is physically located at a particular moment will be of particular importance to offering relevant services.
Convenience	Users are not constrained by time and place. Devices are always at hand and are getting easier and easier to use.
Accessibility	Consumers and businesses alike are easy to access and timing and organizational responsiveness will become critical. Responsiveness relates to speed and coordination at the company level; an entrepreneurial organizational culture will become an important differential advantage for companies in the future.
Personalization	The availability of personal information (fed through the mobile phone) will move customization to a higher level.
Capacity (bandwidth)	Capacity represents an important issue today. Technology is changing rapidly and bandwidth will be accessible.
Size and form factors	The size and physical form of devices invokes a different experience from desktop PCs. Limitations due to size and portability are obvious.
Security	The use of the smart card and SSL (Secure Socket Layer) will offer a higher level of security than that available in the fixed Internet environment.

Sources: Compiled from Durlacher, Forrester Research, Oracle, Mobilocity (2001).

Payment service providers make a secure, attractively priced payment service available for mobile business and combine the skills of network operators and financial services companies. They write invoices for content, airtime, services, and goods and efficiently process even the smallest sums or micropayments (Anonymous 2003; van Haas 2001). It is very likely that both mobile operators and financial institutions will broaden their business into the field of payment service provision. Financial institutions have been quick to identify mobile business as one of their strategic lines of business and have to shape the market now to ensure their future market position. Important assets in connection with the role of mobile business payment services are the ability to process, clear, and settle larger sums of money (Blau 2001; Synchrologic 2003). Content and application providers earn their money by providing up-to-date information and services or by selling goods. The flexibility with which they are able to charge for their products via payment service providers – securely and with minimum overheads – is the key to their business success and enables them to

Technology and infrastructure vendors	Application platform	Content providers and aggregators	Mobile portal providers	Mobile network operators	Device manufacturers

Figure 12.1 The mobile commerce value chain

provide premium information and services. Content aggregators/portal providers repackage available information for distribution to wireless devices. Their added value lies in delivering content in the most appropriate package via mobile portals. Mobile portals are created by aggregating applications – calendar, e-mail, and content from different providers – in order to become the prime supplier of mobile information. Mobile portals are characterized by a higher level of personalization and localization than Internet portals. The success of mobile portals hinges upon ease of use and the ability to deliver the right information at the right time (Lowber *et al.* 2002).

The success of mobile business will hinge upon customer acceptance and a smooth interplay between all of the partners in the value network. Secure and simple forms of payment are key factors for both the customer and the partners along the value chain. Consumer acceptance of easy-to-use and convenient payment systems will be critical for mobile business. New roles and new value chains will emerge (Nelson 2001; Scheier 2001a). Partnerships along the value chain will be crucial. For success in mobile payment business, know-how and experience in these business areas are as important as the solutions themselves. Looking farther into the future, we can expect the mobile phone to develop into a personal wallet (Stoica and Stotlar 2003).

Rapidly evolving technology: technology fragmentation

The m-commerce arena is rapidly evolving, both strategically and technologically. A strong customer-focused strategy is meaningless without the ability to navigate through a range of influential external factors. Rapidly evolving technologies and business models threaten companies with obsolescence on a regular basis. In addition, the number of companies interested in exploiting this medium will provide for arduous competition, especially now that many are determined not to repeat mistakes made on the Web. Entrepreneurs should take the time to understand how these externalities can benefit or threaten their m-commerce presence (Mobilocity.com 2000). Over the next few years, mobile voice and data services will continue to be delivered over a number of network platforms (Whittingham 2000). Gradually, the market will shift from the currently used GSM, TDMA, and CDMA to various interim network technologies such as General Packet Radio Switching (GPRS) and EDGE, and then to third-generation (3G) technologies such as CDMA 2000 and W-CDMA. Aside from network issues, a variety of platforms and voice/data delivery technologies will be introduced over the coming years (Mobilocity 2000). These include Bluetooth (Desmond 2001), VoXML, WiFi

(DeSilva 2003), digital radio, and various location technologies such as Global Positioning Systems (GPS), Time of Arrival (TOA), and Cell of Origin (COO).

Reports from expert sources such as Mobilocity.com, Forrester Research, and Durlacher show the problems related to the wireless nascent technology. The multitude of device operating systems and platforms makes application development for the wireless Internet space a task hard to accomplish. This situation is in sheer contrast to the Web, which has a homogeneous operating environment. The mobile Internet lacks such a foundation. Competing operating platforms, middleware solutions, and bearer networks heavily complicate mobile application development. Efforts are under way to standardize the operating environment. WAP, a de facto standard backed by major m-business stakeholders, stands out as the most promising and has already gained firm grounding in Europe. Unfortunately, adoption of WAP in the United States has been slow. Consequently, entrepreneurs must be able to adapt to the reality of multiple competing platforms and "standards" in the near term. Aside from the complex mobile operating environment, the stark number of mobile devices further complicates the development process.

There is wide agreement that the convergence of mobile devices into a single, multi-purpose handheld appliance is not a near-term reality. Hence, entrepreneurs must address the difficult task of identifying what content and services are appropriate for specific types of mobile devices. Entrepreneurs have to develop the business plan that takes into consideration the range of options given by the multitude of tools and, to avoid losing focus, must have a clear understanding of the types of mobile devices they wish to target initially. Table 12.2 shows the present and future of mobility commerce supporting technologies. The development environment for m-commerce is more complex and will require a broader base of expertise than that for e-commerce.

Business models that can be used successfully by entrepreneurs

The mobile customer

The mobile Internet offers users the possibility of personalizing the mobile devices they own and, therefore, the option to open a direct channel to the companies that want their business. Satisfying the needs of mobile customers in a way that builds enduring relationships lies at the heart of any successful m-commerce strategy. This requires a comprehensive understanding of the mobile end-user. The three traits described by Mobilocity.net in their strategic approach to m-business (Mobilocity report 2001) represent a good starting point from which a more detailed analysis of customer needs can follow: personalization (customers viewed as individuals); dependency on location and time; and newness of mobile technology and its applications. All three are important in defining an entrepreneurial strategy; a brief description will follow.

Table 12.2 Differences between technical components in e-commerce and m-commerce

Technical components	E-commerce	M-commerce
Devices	PC	Low-end smart phones, high-end smart phones, PDAs, pagers; products within a given device category are also widely different.
Operating platforms	Windows, Unix, Linux	Linux EPOC, Palm OS, Pocket PC, proprietary platforms.
Presentation standards	HTML	HTML, WML, HDML.
Browsers	MS Explorer, Netscape	Phone.com UP.Browser, Nokia browser, MS Mobile Explorer.
Bearer networks	TCP/IP	GSM, CDMA, TDMA, CDPD, paging networks.

Source: Mobilocity.net.

Customers as individuals

Personalization, an option on the Web, is required on the mobile Internet. A mobile device is a constant personal companion, and mobile customers will personalize such devices to reflect their needs, turning to companies that treat them as individuals and avoiding those that attempt to put them into general customer segments. Mobile customers are offering companies a direct channel to themselves, and, in return, they will demand highly personalized offerings. For example, a mobile auction site may offer personalization by alerting users of the availability of items at prices in which they have previously indicated interest. Mobile customers will judge companies by the extent to which they use personalization to simplify and improve their mobile sessions. Companies that offer innovative services, but do not supply to specific tastes, will be passed over for those that can tailor services.

Time and location of the customer

Location becomes a crucial variable for the marketer. The business model by the entrepreneur has to consider the timing of the offering to meet the client's needs and wants at the different locations and moments. Customers initiate the connection and/or the transaction. They will open, by means of their mobile device, a direct channel to potential marketers. Understanding the customer's activity schedule is critical if a company is to build a meaningful mobile customer relationship. The needs of mobile customers will vary depending on where they are and when they are using these devices. Wireless services accessed during work hours will differ from services demanded during leisure time. A mobile customer may want stock positions on the way to lunch and then desire more detailed research information during the train ride home. Not only does each customer have unique needs, but also each component of the customer's mobile experience must be considered individually. For example (Mobilocity 2001), services that require instant messaging capabilities might be offered through a two-way pager, while a mobile phone would be used for voice-based or alert services.

Ease of use is a critical issue for companies in order to maintain customer loyalty. Currently, limitations imposed by mobile device form factors pose a great challenge to users. Existing experience with the Web is of little help because applications and user interfaces are entirely different. Mobile customers may be familiar with cell phones, but most have used them only for voice services and not for data manipulation. Customers will expect companies to devise creative ways to access necessary information intuitively and quickly. Frequent upgrades to existing technology will also be a source of difficulty for users. In this sense, mobile users will always be new to the mobile Internet because each purchase of a mobile device will constitute somewhat of a technological leap. Newness of the mobile technology represents a problem for the entrepreneur.

The direct-to-customer model

Currently, mobile carriers aggregate content and services from third-party partners and provide these services directly to their subscribers. As the adoption of WAP accelerates and consumers begin demanding access to m-commerce offerings independent of the wireless carrier, a model similar to that of today's Internet Service Provider (ISP) will emerge. Under this model, wireless service subscribers will have access to any mobile site. The open-access system will spur companies' development of their m-commerce presence. Companies benefiting from the current model must be prepared for the onslaught of competition that will follow from a more accessible mobile Internet. New entrants will be severely challenged by the incumbents that have already built strong customer relationships. Two business models can be envisaged: the closed model and the direct-to-customer model. In the closed model, network operators take center stage, dominating both consumers and business partners. M-businesses and m-portals are forced to reach customers through proprietary networks. In the direct-to-customer model, the competition will drive a more customer-centered model, with customers able to select personalized services from their choice of m-businesses and m-portals. Alliances across multiple service and content providers are expected. The direct-to-customer model should not prompt companies to assume that Web strategies can easily be transferred to the mobile environment. For example, users of mobile devices will generally have billing relationships with very few service providers because of the convenience the service offers. Unlike in the Web, where customers traditionally maintain multiple accounts, companies in m-commerce will be highly dependent on mobile operators and early movers that manage the billing relationships. In this sense, the direct-to-customer model will not prevent companies from creating partnership consortiums that offer the entire range of value-added consumer services.

Adaptability and the mobile operators

Until the opening of the wireless Web, the role of mobile operators will be central to m-commerce. In fact, mobile operators will continue to play a significant role even after the mobile Internet makes the transition into an open model. One reason for the power of mobile operators is their control of bandwidth distribution. For example, an auction site with high visibility on a mobile operator's customer portal may have to sign a revenue-sharing agreement in addition to a placement fee. Equally significant, operators control the billing relationship with customers.

According to Sharma (2000), today's cellular operators will have to face up to new competition from new third-generation (3G) players, from ISPs offering service over their networks, and from the new breed of mobile virtual network operators. It is clear that providing tailored, location-sensitive information services to mobile customers not only increases usage but is also central to building customer loyalty and reducing churn. Telecoms operators are traditionally obsessed with marketing a whole range of discounts and gimmicks, the sheer number and variety of which simply bewilder the customer. Instead, operators should focus on customers' needs that usually revolve around price and service. However, changing marketing strategies is just the tip of the iceberg for the existing mobile operators (Weiber and Kollman 1998). A customer-led telecoms operator will look very different from the current crop of mobile operators, who are going to have to make fundamental changes to their business infrastructure. They will not be able to treat mobile Internet as just another set of technical rollout programs; they will face a much higher degree of interaction with service partners as they gear their organizations to support a customer self-care model.

Entrepreneurial strategies

Competition

Porter's "Five-Forces Model" has been successfully used to analyze the way the Internet (including wireless) influences industry structure (Porter 2001). Companies that arrived too late to the Web party should make it a priority to tackle the m-commerce market early. Others that have always been on top of the technology curve are likely to remain there. Existing players will create wireless versions of their Web applications and leverage their overall brands. In addition, there will be no shortage of ambitious start-ups, ensuring that the m-commerce market becomes an intense battlefield. A number of corporate heavyweights, from Microsoft and Yahoo! to Delta Airlines and General Motors, have already unveiled their initial m-commerce strategies (according to Mobilocity 2001). Nonetheless, other first-movers will have the opportunity to win a substantial mind share with customers.

Pre-existing partnerships also pose a significant competitive threat to those excluded. At the center of many recent, high-profile deals are mobile operators like Sprint PCS and Vodafone Airtouch that can leverage their large, existing customer bases. Examples of such partnerships include Ameritrade and Amazon.com with Sprint PCS and E*Trade with Verizon Wireless. As the open model of the mobile Internet emerges, these partnership circles will have a pool of existing customer relationships to leverage. M-commerce entrants may find it difficult to thrive without involvement with a major player.

How can entrepreneurs build a sustainable competitive advantage? Charting a strategy

A thoroughly planned, risk-averse approach to strategy is not adequate for a nascent and evolving industry such as m-commerce. The business fundamentals in the industry will remain in constant flux as technology evolves, standards co-exist and/or converge, and different players along the value chain try different tactics to create value (Wilhelmsson 2001). As a result, there is not one specific strategy that will ensure victory (Mobilocity 2001). Mobilocity.net in its m-commerce report has identified ten guiding principles that might help entrepreneurs carve out a flexible m-commerce strategy.

Guiding principles for an M-commerce strategy (compiled from Mobilocity, Durlacher, and Forrester Research)

- Entrepreneurs should recognize mobile commerce as a unique business opportunity, dependent on time and place, not just another way to deliver the current Internet services.
- Entrepreneurs should fully understand why m-commerce is important to their organization.
- A team approach is critical: create a team dedicated to the development of a mobile strategy.
- An organization's responsiveness is essential. Speed-to-market and coordination are very important.
- Partnering is mandatory.
- Personalization of the offering: design and offer deeply personalized services.
- Ease of use is critical.
- M-commerce is technologically driven. Therefore entrepreneurs have to think strategically about the company's technology needs.
- Entrepreneurs should figure out how to leverage the company's existing Web presence. Old-fashioned Internet is not dead and should be integrated into the strategic picture.

Being a first mover in the m-commerce market confers huge advantages. Companies urgently need to launch focused m-commerce initiatives even with the realization that today's strategies are short term and will need to be iterated with the emergence of new wireless technologies. Such companies should resist the temptation simply to extend their wired Web presence to the wireless world and, instead, should pursue the opportunity with an understanding of the defining characteristics that distinguish m-commerce from e-commerce.

When and how is m-commerce adding value to the entrepreneurial business?

Applications could be envisaged along several dimensions (Muller-Veerse 2000), as discussed below.

Business life

How will business operations and communications between co-workers, customers, and suppliers change? Expenses billing, customer relation management, and procurement will all be affected.

Social life

How will the way in which individuals (consumers) communicate with each other and live out their social lives (chatting, going out) change?

Information and entertainment

How will the consumption of news and media change? Will there be access to up-to-the-minute information (e.g. stock prices and sports results), archived information, literature and visual arts, and gaming?

Personal transactions

Banking, brokering, e-tailing, and so forth will be affected. Business models such as the subscription model, the advertising model, the transaction model, and the blended model will find applications in all the domains listed.

Academic interest: programs and courses offered by universities

Are deans interested in this topic? Are entrepreneurs interested? An Internet research shows that currently more than 40 universities offer programs leading to an e-commerce and Internet degree or college certification. They include Carnegie Mellon, Emory, Loyola, North Carolina State, Northwestern, Dallas, Pennsylvania, and Washington. The number of programs exploded in the last two years. M-commerce is too new to be considered as a full program degree by a university. However, there are e-commerce programs that offer courses in new technology (Loyola University, Chicago) that include m-commerce topics. Carnegie Mellon University offers under technology electives a course on mobile e-commerce. M-commerce is popping up as an important issue in e-commerce classes and entrepreneurship courses (Stoica and Stotlar 2003).

Conclusions

Mobile commerce is not an extension of electronic commerce. It represents a different business philosophy and necessitates different business models. It will make the business environment more demanding on companies along new dimensions, such as time and speed, customer location, and his/her needs and wants. In an m-commerce environment, a huge number of business opportunities will pop up, and it is up to a new generation of entrepreneurs to take advantage and fully exploit those opportunities. A wireless presence represents an opportunity to fundamentally transform the company's customer relationships through the "always-on" approach. Wireless, and therefore m-commerce, is not about technology. It is about finding new ways to define value for customers and internal users. New creative ways of conducting business represent the appanage of entrepreneurs. Wireless Internet access devices will make it easier than ever before both for workers to gain access to vital information and perform better, and for entrepreneurs to take advantage of the multitude of opportunities that abound in all industries. However, devices differ in performance, footprint, screen format, and bandwidth capacity. The one-size-fits-all approach will not work, and entrepreneurs, when imagining and implementing business ideas or new applications, will have to navigate the technological sea to position their company for future prosperity.

The new interactive media (Internet and Wireless Web) have the potential to transform the buying and selling of products and services. This will have an impact on businesses, irrespective of size, location, and industry (Sahay et al. 1998). Therefore, there is a huge potential for business opportunities and a need for research to help guide businesses tackle the problems and issues related to the mobile economic environment. Several streams of research could be envisaged. The literature is rich in expert opinion research (M-business, Revolution, Durlacher, Forester Research, and so forth). Asking experts is the first step in conducting research in a new, emerging domain. Expert opinion data show that long-term advantages tend to go to the first successful mover (Roberts 1991; Sahay et al. 1998). The problem is particularly acute for communication technologies because of standards and network externalities. Wireless applications are expected to have high levels of diffusion. Among those that have immediate potential are banking, airline ticketing, financial services, and retailing (using

Bluetooth technology). Experts have focused on identifying the opportunities and perceived level of threat. Investigations on the timing of adoption of new technology and new applications would be the next step in this research stream. Panels of experts could be used to identify possible applications. Expert opinion was the basis for developing forecasts (Rotterdam School of Management M-conference: see Narduzzi 2001; van der Poel 2001; Winge 2001).

Another investigative avenue could be bestowed by the exploration of the status of m-commerce applications, the timing of applications adoption and identification of best practices (by state and/or by industry). Early adopter analysis can be useful (O'Keefe *et al.* 1998). The scenario development approach could be used in this area too. Trend extrapolation and scenarios for the future can be used to intuit markets when needs are uncertain and the market is evolving. However, the most robust approach will use multiple methods (Roberts 1991). Study the entrepreneurs' motivation to enter a new business environment.

Research the individual customer's needs and wants. Who expects to adopt and use wireless technology (and why)? Different approaches are visible. The scenario development approach (the Rotterdam School of Management M-conference 2001) could offer interesting insights. New developments in the marketing segmentation literature (Cadeaux 1997) concentrate on the recent trends and clusters of customers: postmodern and cultural creatives. New, emerging segments have new needs, and entrepreneurs have the curiosity and sophistication to experiment and adopt applications in cyberspace. The *European Journal of Marketing* has dedicated a whole issue to the cyberspace consumer. A notable feature of mobile commerce is that, while everyone seems to be talking about it, very few groups are actually delivering it. Over the next few years, mobile voice and data services will continue to be delivered over a number of network platforms. Gradually, the market will move to the third-generation (3G) technologies such as cdma2000 and W-CDMA. The most forward-thinking companies will appropriately update their m-commerce offerings to take advantage of the capabilities offered by more advanced network technologies. However, changes happen almost every day, new opportunities are visible, and profitability is perceptible in both the business-to-business and business-to-customer markets. Entrepreneurs with courage and vision will benefit from the mobile technology and will incorporate it in their business models.

References

AlterEgo Networks (2001) *Planning for the Adaptive Enterprise*, White Paper. Online, available at: http://www.aego.com (accessed December 17, 2001).

Angelos, P., Shaw, R., Singh, S., and Springer, I. (2001) *The Mobile Internet in 2006*, Rotterdam: Rotterdam School of Management.

Anonymous (2003) "Mobile strategies for financial services," *Synchrologic White Papers*. Online, available at: http://www.synchrologic.com (accessed April 22, 2003).

Bidgoli, H. (2002) "M-commerce and beyond: new frontiers on doing business on-line," *Proceedings of the Decision Science Institute 2002 Annual Meeting, San Diego, CA*, November 20–21, 496–501.

Blau, J. (2001) "Carriers, banks partner for payments," *M-business*, April: 36–39.

Cadeaux, J. (1997) "Counter-revolutionary forces in the information revolution. Entrepreneurial action, information intensity and market transformation," *European Journal of Marketing*, 31(11/12): 768–785.

DeSilva, E. (2003) "WiFi market is likely to boom in the next few years," *National Law Journal*, 25(69): 12–13.

Desmond, M. (2001) "Bluetooth technology: the reality factor," *M-business*, April: 56–64.

Frimmer, J. (2001) "Vendors try to build their own markets: corporate-backed venture capital helps shape the future of wireless," *M-business*, April: 86–90.

Gagnon, Y.-C., Sicotte, H., and Posada, E. (2000) "Impact of SME manager's behavior on the adoption of technology," *Entrepreneurship Theory and Practice*, 25(2): 43–59.

Greengard, S. (2001) "Mobile makes sense for fast food," *M-business*, April: 24–26.

Griffith, T. (1999) "Technology features as triggers for sensemaking," *Academy of Management Review*, 24(3): 472–488.

Lowber, P., Dulaney, K., and Hiller, K. (2002) "Mobile e-mail/pim magic quadrant: emerging choices," *Gartner Research Notes*. Online, available at: http://www.gartner.com (accessed April 22, 2003).

Mobilocity (2001) "Mobilocity.net report on m-commerce," *Mobilocity.net Home Page*. Online, available at: http://www.mobilocity.net (accessed April 22, 2003).

Morace, F. and Chrometzka, L. (2001) "The new dynamics of the wired era. Net flow and creative pollination," presentation at the *M-Conference: Seizing the Mobile Advantage*, Rotterdam School of Management, Rotterdam, Holland, January 19–20.

Mouat, W. (2000) "10 considerations in selecting a wireless strategy," Luminat Worldwide Corp. Working Paper. Online, available at: http:www.luminant.com (accessed April 22, 2003).

Muller-Veerse, F. (2000) "Mobile commerce report," Durlacher Research White Paper. Online, available at: http://www.durlacer.com (accessed April 22, 2003).

Narduzzi, E. (2001) "Is m-business the same game as the e-business?" paper presented at *M-Conference: Seizing the Mobile Advantage*, Rotterdam: January 19–20, 2001.

Nelson, E. (2001) "Wireless call-a-cab: the early mover gamble," *M-business*, April: 90–94.

O'Keefe, R., O'Connor, G., and Kung, H.-J. (1998) "Early adopters of the web as a retail medium: small company winners and losers," *European Journal of Marketing*, 32(7/8): 629–641.

Porter, M. (2001) "Strategy and Internet," *Harvard Business Review*, Reprint R0103D: 63–78.

Rendon, J. (2001) "Finland's wireless fasttrack," *M-business*, May: 46–51.

Roberts, E. (1991) *Entrepreneurs in High Technology*, Oxford: Oxford University Press.

Rupp, W. (2003) "Japanese convenience stores and e-commerce," paper presented at the Ninth International Conference on Industry, Engineering, and Management Systems, Cocoa Beach, FL, March 17–19.

Sahay, A., Gold, J., and Barwise, P. (1998) "New interactive media: experts' perceptions of opportunities and threats for existing businesses," *European Journal of Marketing*, 32(7/8): 616–628.

Scheier, R. (2001a) "Aether's big bet on m-commerce," *M-business*, April: 20–22.

Scheier, R. (2001b) "What does a mobile enterprise cost?," *M-business*, May: 32–34.

Sharma, C. (2000) "Wireless Internet applications," *Luminant Worldwide Corp. Website*. Online, available at: http://www.luminant.com (accessed March 2000).

Shih, C.-F. (1998) "Conceptualizing consumer in cyberspace," *European Journal of Marketing*, 32(7/8): 655–663.

Stern, A. (2002) "M-commerce: time for lift off?" *Distribution Management*, December 17: 10–15.

Stoica, M. and Stotlar, D. (2003) "A model for small business new technology adoption: the case of mobile commerce," paper presented at the Annual Meeting of the Federation of Business Disciplines, Houston, March 5–8.

Synchrologic (2001) *The Handheld Applications Guidebook*, Alpharetta, GA: Synchrologic.com.

Synchrologic (2003) "Mobile strategies for financial services," *Synchrologic.com Website*. Online, available at: http://www.synchrologic.com (accessed April 22, 2003).

van Haas, T. (2001) "Mobile banking and beyond," paper presented at the *M-Conference: Seizing the Mobile Advantage*, Rotterdam, January 19–20.

van der Poel, A. (2001) "Idea generation: killer ideas = killer startups?" paper presented at the *M-Conference: Seizing the Mobile Advantage*, Rotterdam, January 19–20.

Weiber, R. and Kollman, T. (1998) "Competitive advantages in virtual markets – perspective of 'information-based marketing' in cyberspace," *European Journal of Marketing*, 32(7/8): 603–615.

Whittingham, J. (2000) "Digital local storage-PVRS, home media servers, and the future of broadcasting," *Durlacher Research Reports*. Online, available at: http://www.durlacher.com (accessed April 22, 2003).

Wilhelmsson, J. (2001) "Today's competitive edge is rounded: creating successful value added services for the mobile phone," *General Mobile Commerce Forum*. Online, available at: http://www.gmcforum.com (accessed April 22, 2003).

Winge, K. (2001) "Idea generation, selection and exploitation," paper presented at the *M-Conference: Seizing the Mobile Advantage*, Rotterdam, January 19–20.

Chapter 13

Lisa K. Gundry

DePaul University

Jill Kickul

Simmons School of Management

E-COMMERCE ENTREPRENEURSHIP: EMERGING PRACTICES, KEY CHALLENGES, AND FUTURE DIRECTIONS

Introduction

MARKET NEEDS AND THE ENABLING technology required to capitalize on new opportunities has created one of the most challenging environments for entrepreneurs. In particular, e-commerce technology has forced many entrepreneurs to assess how their firms gather, synthesize, utilize, and disseminate information across customers, employees, and supplier networks. Those who are willing to experiment with new product and service offerings will be positioned to compete most effectively (Hodgetts *et al.* 1999). The extent to which entrepreneurs capitalize on the conditions presented by e-commerce and engage in experimentation and innovation is of major interest in contemporary research.

Because of the demand for innovative organizational behavior present in e-business, this is an important domain in which to study entrepreneurship. However, because it is so recent, very little is known about the role attributes or innovative activities of entrepreneurs in Internet organizations. What enables emerging organizations to achieve effective performance? What are the opportunities and constraints in operating within this environment? These and many others questions are arising as the field of Internet entrepreneurship grows and develops. The answers will inform the development of the growing research base in this area and will facilitate the subsequent comparison of key variables and relationships found in firms engaging in e-commerce with those in traditional bricks-and-mortar firms.

This chapter presents the emergent practices and processes of e-commerce entrepreneurship, explores the key challenges facing the new ventures, and offers research suggestions to guide future work in this area. The chapter draws on recent research findings and focuses on founders and organizations whose activities encompass the Internet, conducting multiple transactions on the Internet, rather than on organizations that use the Internet only for customer advertising and information-gathering purposes. It is the premise of this chapter that the first major step in developing a model of e-commerce entrepreneurship is to examine the processes and behaviors found within the ventures. The examination is conducted along several dimensions and contributes to our understanding of the nature, opportunities, challenges, and future directions of the entrepreneurial firms.

This chapter addresses the following areas of e-commerce entrepreneurship:

- what does the entrepreneurial landscape for e-commerce look like, and what are some recent trends in Internet entrepreneurship?
- what are the values and strategic orientations of Internet entrepreneurs ("netpreneurs")?
- what focus does innovation take within these firms?
- what specific human resource practices are critical to the success of these firms?

Emergent trends in e-commerce entrepreneurship

The twentieth century has been described as the "century of the entrepreneur" (Bangs and Pinson 1999). The entrepreneurial landscape continues to be transformed; as the twenty-first century unfolds, a new form of entrepreneurship is taking shape. With the rapid acceleration and availability of technology, electronic commerce is changing the nature of business.

Electronic commerce experienced dynamic and rapid growth in the late 1990s. Total world-wide Net commerce – both B2B and B2C – is expected to hit $6.8 trillion in 2004 (Forrester Research 2001). By some estimates, annual online sales will reach $200 billion by 2004 and will exceed $1 trillion a year within ten years. It is projected that, by 2003, 40 million U.S. households will shop on the Web, and revenues will approach $108 billion (Forrester Research 1999). These statistics reflect the increasing number of ventures that will be launched on the Internet.

Evident from the recent trends in e-commerce is the expression of a new set of entrepreneurial values and behaviors that are increasingly coming to characterize an emerging model of Internet entrepreneurship. In the next section, we identify from recent research some of the primary variables that shape the entrepreneurial actions in these organizations.

Netpreneurship: the key values and strategic orientations of Internet entrepreneurs

The e-commerce environment demands that netpreneurs strive for "relentless innovation," leading their firms through the continual infusion of new ideas (Cohen and Jordan 1999). A new set of core business values appears to distinguish e-commerce entrepreneurial teams from other entrepreneurial teams. These values are constant innovation, experimentation, and rapid change. Such an orientation is similar to what Miller and Blais (1992) characterize as "maverick" behaviors, with firms adopting innovative modes based on their competencies, competitive situations, or managerial preferences. The environment of e-commerce enables firms to rapidly try new approaches, quickly share successes and failures, and monitor what is new and useful (Oliva 1998). As founders of Internet ventures attempt to meet the opportunities and demands of this new economy, a set of entrepreneurial strategic orientations and behaviors will emerge that can begin to characterize the nature and process of e-commerce ventures.

Miller and Friesen (1983) first characterized the entrepreneurially oriented firm as one that innovated and fully exploited environmental opportunities while repressing environmental threats. Researchers have since identified two key dimensions that underlie an entrepreneurial strategic posture (Covin and Covin 1990) or an entrepreneurial strategy-making mode (Dess et al. 1997). The two dimensions are the competitive aggressiveness entrepreneurs display as they pursue new opportunities, innovation, and experimentation, and the proactivity that leads to their being the first mover among their competitors. An entrepreneurial strategic posture emphasizes a value for innovation. Page (1997) characterized such a posture as the identification or recognition of opportunity and its proactive pursuit. A challenge for e-commerce ventures is the entrepreneurs' ability to recognize a highly competitive environment and proactively change their strategic orientation to survive and grow (Page 1997).

Kanter (2001) has described strategy in e-commerce firms as "improvisational theater," in which the performances of many "troupes" accumulate to take the organization in a new direction entrepreneurs perceive strategy as emerging and revealed through action; the action itself shows the goal. Thus, the primary mode of strategic operation in these ventures is sense-and-respond, as opposed to the traditional make-and-sell (Bradley and Nolan 1998). This orientation enables entrepreneurs to move at Internet speed; consequently, the traditional strategic plan is one on which these entrepreneurs can no longer rely. The strategic orientation of e-commerce entrepreneurs includes behaviors such as experimentation, going to the customer, and building the customer into the venture as an "actor" (Oliver 2000). This is similar to Kanter's metaphor of strategy as improvisational theater, in which the "audience" (or customers) interact with the venture and influences its outcomes. Further, strategy tends to flow through the organization in all directions, rather than from the top down as it has conventionally moved.

Identifying and recognizing new opportunities and innovations

Kickul and Gundry (2000a) measured the relationship between the entrepreneurial posture of Internet business owners who operate within a highly uncertain environment (i.e. their rapid response to change, value for innovation, and development of inter-firm alliances) and their opportunity recognition behaviors. Further, we investigated whether this relationship influences the technological innovations implemented by Internet entrepreneurs.

Our study found that the strategic orientations of rapidly responding to change as well as placing value on innovation were linked to externally oriented opportunity search behaviors. According to Koshiur (1997), netpreneurs must be continually prepared to make changes within the infrastructure of their businesses to meet and prepare for future opportunities and technological advancements. In addition, flexibility further allows the business to be a successful player in the virtual value chain – "converting the raw information into new services and products in the information world" (Koshiur 1997: 103).

Developing relationships with other firms was also shown to be a determining factor associated with externally oriented opportunity search behaviors. A promising application for netpreneurs and their firms in electronic commerce is to use Web technology for business-to-business interactions (Choi et al. 1997; Shannon 1999). Contracting with other organizations allows the netpreneur to have a more decentralized, non-hierarchical organization that may foster the recognition and implementation of opportunities associated with new product/service ideas and solutions (Morino 1999). Moreover, having inter-firm relationships that are fluid may also be necessary for uncovering opportunities related to the marketing and distribution of information about the value of the firm's products and services.

Finally, our study also found that Internet firms engaged in opportunity search behaviors that are externally focused had implemented technological innovations dealing with new information technology, and new computer technology, as well as new methods of advertising. Our results suggest that Internet entrepreneurs tend to rely on network activity (Singh et al. 1999) to enable them to capitalize on opportunities and to reach technological innovations for their businesses and for the marketplace. Given the rapid pace of technology and business, Davis and Meyer (1998) have asserted that there is a greater need for entrepreneurs to be connected with their suppliers, customers, and business partners. This need for connectivity forces Internet-based organizations to evaluate the intangible benefits of the company's technology infrastructure and its product/service offerings. It is expected that, as more Internet businesses are established and identified, research attention will grow and focus on additional strategies and behaviors of this pioneering group.

The focus of innovative behavior in e-commerce entrepreneurship

Drucker (1998) described four areas of innovative opportunities that exist within a company or industry including unexpected occurrences, incongruities, process needs, and industry, and market changes. Even though these innovative opportunities may be present to Internet entrepreneurial teams, there may be additional areas such firms may identify for potential innovative actions. This emphasis on innovation and change will be oriented not only to the outcomes of these organizations (e.g. products, services, and new markets) but also to the structure and work arrangements of the ventures themselves. Oliva (1998) has noted that a successful Internet study needs to be designed to assess the following research questions: to what extent have these entrepreneurs been engaged in innovations? And, what is the direction (type) of these business innovations?

In another study, Kickul and Gundry (2000b) examined the type and direction of innovative actions incorporated by Internet entrepreneurs in their businesses. Six distinct innovative behaviors displayed by netpreneurs were uncovered, ranging from continuous product/service improvements to managing human resources. These innovations varied to the extent that they were considered and implemented into the operations and business of the Internet firm. Improving products/services, seeking alternative markets and opportunities, and incorporating additional marketing strategies were the critical factors associated with initiating innovation and change. According to Koshiur (1997), netpreneurs must be continually prepared to make innovations and changes within the infrastructure of their businesses to meet and prepare for future opportunities and market/industry advancements. The current electronic marketplace will require new innovative models that deal with firm organization, production, and overall market institutions (Choi *et al.* 1997; Lange 1999). Indeed, as others have suggested (Cohen and Jordan 1999; Oliva 1998), Internet firms that emphasize innovation and rapid response to change are best positioned for success in this new form of entrepreneurship.

Although our study examined the various types of innovations engaged in by Internet entrepreneurs, future researchers should investigate how these innovations are related to the firm's strategic focus and orientation. More work should test the strategic requirements for successful Internet enterprise developments that have been proposed in the literature, including: how do the strategic orientations of first-to-market, first-follower, competitive aggressiveness, and rapid response to change predict innovative behavior? Does the enactment of innovative marketing behaviors, for example, give competitive advantage to a firm? What types (direction) of innovative actions seem to matter most to a firm's ability to respond rapidly to change?

Many of the entrepreneurs in our sample reported innovative behaviors that can be characterized as growth extending, as they adapt to market conditions and negotiate a position for their ventures in the rapidly expanding e-commerce environment. Of further research interest is determining the degree to which entrepreneurs eventually increase their growth-enabling behaviors as a means to sustain performance. What role, for example, do recruiting or training play in the development of technological innovations (a growth-extending behavior)? More research is needed to ascertain the behavioral supports found in firms.

Additionally, more researchers should investigate how Internet entrepreneurs form and develop strategic relationships and alliances with other organizations. How are partnerships formed and dissolved to meet clearly defined business goals and imperatives? As discussed by Hartman *et al.* (2000), Internet firms that are able to define their core competencies and work side-by-side with complementary partners will be able to exploit many of the opportunities existing in the marketplace. Moreover, those firms that are able to continuously improve their businesses and competencies as well as their alliance structure will also have an advantage when meeting the next new opportunity (Choi *et al.* 1997; Griffith and Palmer 1999; Shannon 1999).

As more entrepreneurs enter the arena of electronic commerce, research is also needed to examine how they effectively design and integrate new business processes and practices. Although researchers have made important first steps in identifying dimensions of innovative behavior associated with and found inside Internet firms, more work should concentrate on how innovations relate to changes in organizational training and development, channel management, and client and customer relationships. These are all particularly relevant, given that the expanded description of electronic commerce includes online information technology and communication that is used to enhance customer service and support (Choi *et al.* 1997; Koshiur 1997). Keeney (1999) has outlined several areas of customers' concerns and values that can be used by an entrepreneur to design and grow Internet ventures.

In order to build and grow an entrepreneurial organization around e-commerce strategies and initiatives, an entrepreneur needs to consider several factors. Entrepreneurial firms should use the opportunities and possibilities of the Internet, Intranets and Extranets to *transform* their core e-business processes. As noted earlier, such opportunities fundamentally change the way a firm does business. Company owners should not only be very open to changing core processes but also have a vision of how such a transformation will improve their businesses. Building upon existing systems and applications, e-businesses should also build new and improved applications and systems quickly and easily, in response to the ever-changing market and customer demands. Moreover, e-commerce organizations should establish a hardware infrastructure that can grow easily with the business. They also need to understand how to manage a network computing environment and how to keep it secure. Finally, e-commerce firms need to take a strategic approach in order to leverage their knowledge and information over time. Ultimately, they should be able to capitalize on the information and experience they already have and quickly apply new intelligence and knowledge.

Emerging entrepreneurial practices and behaviors within e-commerce firms

Distinctive innovative behaviors appear to characterize the emerging group of Internet entrepreneurs when they are compared with owners of ventures not fully dedicated to electronic commerce. "What sets netpreneurs apart is not that they are different from other entrepreneurs but that they are operating in a universe of transforming change. As pioneers of the new networked society, they are both defining and learning new ways of doing business" (Morino 1999: 1). Because of the rapid acceleration of technology, it is becoming more critical that Internet entrepreneurs have the ability to respond quickly to changes by bringing revolutionary new ideas into their businesses and the electronic marketplace. In this way, they are creating new patterns of entrepreneurial behavior and performance.

Whether the managerial emphasis on innovation and change results not only in the creation of new products, services, or markets but also in the nurturing and establishment of innovative internal and external relationships is the focus of another recent study (Kickul and Gundry 2001) on the impact of top management team functional diversity and creative processes on the assessment of new e-commerce opportunities for the organization. Further, the study investigates the relationship between opportunity assessment and innovative organizational practices. These innovative practices are operationalized as external relationships (network membership with vendors, customers, and competitors), internal relationships (recruitment, retention, and rewarding of top talent in the organization), and generating new products and services.

As a first, foundational step to increasing our understanding of managerial practices in e-commerce organizations, we examined entrepreneurs' perceptions surrounding key firm behaviors that foster innovation. The emphasis of recent work by Iansiti and MacCormak (1997), Hodgetts *et al.* (1999), and Shannon (1999) has been on the significant roles of adaptation, innovation, experimentation, and change in the environments of e-commerce organizations. The necessity of realigning managerial roles and practices so that these organizations can take advantage of emerging opportunities has been proposed. Accordingly, our study attempted to measure empirically some of the managerial processes that stimulate innovation. If, as scholars have suggested, e-commerce firms must innovate to survive, we have begun to explore the prerequisites and primary influences on this critical set of actions. The results of our study yield information that will be useful in guiding future research addressing key factors present among these top management teams, including comparative studies between e-commerce and traditional, bricks-and-mortar organizations. Exploring the new managerial roles and practices, such as the development of innovative relationships with suppliers, customers, competitors, and employees of these businesses, will facilitate the construction of new models to predict success factors for managing e-commerce organizations.

A recent study by Inmomentum, Inc., an organization that researches the best practices of Internet economy businesses, reported that companies that helped their employees feel connected to their vision and values were growing at a rate of 141 percent, compared with a 10 percent growth rate for companies that did not do this well. This emphasis on the development of internal relationships in the e-commerce firm is an interesting one to watch as entrepreneurs continually search to recruit and retain top talent for their ventures. However, the reality is that, in the early part of 2001, there were more than 200 CEO searches under way in Silicon Valley. Further, 300 CEOs had been in their positions for less than one year. Developing and delivering a clear vision and connecting it to company values is a very great challenge.

Internet entrepreneurs' ability to harness the richness in breadth of perspective made available to them by functionally diverse team members is a key component of innovative actions. But a further step is needed to make the creative exploration useful in the form of actionable ideas and opportunities. Our research has shown that effective opportunity assessment has a mediating effect on the interaction of diversity and managerial creativity, facilitating the formation of external and internal organizational relationships as well as the introduction of new products and services. Thus, such an assessment enables managers to form strategic alliances necessary to achieve market growth and to develop methods to attract and retain the top talent so in demand by Internet organizations. Exploring the direction of such behavior contributes to our understanding of the changing roles, challenges, and opportunities confronting managers in e-commerce firms.

The development of innovative internal management relationships was operationalized in our (Kickul and Gundry 2001) study as finding unusual and creative ways to recruit, retain, and reward employees. These are emerging as some of the most significant entrepreneurial challenges of the information age. The predominance of knowledge workers has shifted the balance of traditional organizational resources of equipment, capital, and people. Although historically production workers have been replaced with technology, leading to strong productivity gains, the same scale of substitution is not possible in knowledge-based organizations, as pointed out by Pottruck and Pearce (2000). Those authors concluded that the most critical parts of the human resource in an organization cannot be synthesized, and those are the creative brain, imagination, and spirit that fuel the information economy. Some of the new managerial practices of the entrepreneurs in our sampled firms included unusual methods of retaining top talent in their organizations, as shown in these responses.

> We are more than an employee's paycheck. The firm is committed to the belief that it shares a large part of the responsibility for the overall well-being of a given employee, and this spiritual belief alone is what helps us keep our best employees. They see us putting their welfare at a higher priority than the numbers on the quarterly profit reports, and they wind up sticking around when the going gets rough for a while.

> Our arrangements permit a literal network of top level, talented and proven services and professionals to "morph" to suit the problematic demands of new clients. The organization is truly a team, with me as "leader" but without any hierarchical or concomitant structure. Only via affiliate resourcing can this be accomplished in the information sector where "trust is paramount" and "content is everything" in terms of both branding and perceived reliability.

Ester Dyson, one of the foremost thinkers on the implications of the Internet for business and for society as a whole has said: "The limitation on the application of technology will never be ideas or capital. It will be finding enough people who are trained and excited about taking the ideas of the technologist and making them real in the world" (Dyson 1997: 69).

We also found that entrepreneurs engaged in forming innovative external relationships with their key constituents, including suppliers, customers, and competitors. This increased connectivity may allow e-commerce organizations to become responsive and flexible in meeting each customer's particular needs and demands (Neese 2000). Contracting with other organizations also allows the e-commerce firm to have a more decentralized, non-hierarchical organization that may foster the implementation of new product/service ideas and solutions (Morino 1999). The nature of these relationships is described by the following responses of entrepreneurs in our study:

> We use what others would call competitors a lot. We have no competition, just resources we have not used yet!

> We rely upon strategic partners around the globe. They are the keys to our success.

Conclusion

The issues, challenges, and future directions presented in this chapter represent one of the first comprehensive discussions of the entrepreneurial strategies, values, and behaviors that describe the internal and external processes of emerging e-commerce firms. Although much work remains, it is our hope that future researchers will continue to examine how entrepreneurs build, realign, and grow their organizations within a marketplace that demands speed, agility, and constant innovation. Exploring these new entrepreneurial roles and practices, such as the development of innovative relationships with suppliers, customers, competitors, and employees of these businesses, will facilitate the construction of new models to predict success factors in e-commerce organizations.

References

Bangs, D.H. and Pinson, L. (1999) *The Real World Entrepreneur*, Chicago, IL: Upstart Publishing Company.

Bradley, S. and Nolan, R. (1998) *Sense and Respond: Capturing Value in the Network Era*, Boston, MA: Harvard Business School Press.

Choi, S., Stahl, D., and Whinston, A. (1997) *The Economics of Electronic Commerce*, Indianapolis, IN: Macmillan Technical Publishing.

Cohen, A. and Jordan, J.M. (1999) *Electronic Commerce: The Next Generation*, Chicago, IL: Ernst & Young Center for Business Innovation.

Covin, J.G. and Covin, T.J. (1990) "Competitive aggressiveness, environmental context and small firm performance," *Entrepreneurship: Theory and Practice*, 14(4): 35–50.

Davis, S. and Meyer, C. (1998) *Blur: The Speed of Change in the Connected Economy*, New York, NY: Warner Books.

Dess, G.G., Lumpkin, G.T., and Covin, J.G. (1997) "Entrepreneurial strategy making and firm performance: tests of contingency and configurational models," *Strategic Management Journal*, 18(9): 677–695.

Drucker, P.F. (1998) "The discipline of innovation," *Harvard Business Review*, 76(6): 149–157.

Dyson, E. (1997) *Release 2.0: A Design for Living in the Digital Age*, New York, NY: Broadway Books.

Forrester Research (1999) *E-commerce by the Numbers*. Online, available at: http://www.net-profit-center.net/bynumber.htm (accessed April 22, 2003).

Forrester Research (2001) *E-commerce by the Numbers*. Online, available at: http://www.net-profit-center.net/bynumber.htm (accessed April 22, 2003).

Griffith, D.A. and Palmer, J.W. (1999) "Leveraging the web for corporate success," *Business Horizons*, 42(1): 3–10.

Hartman, A., Sifonis, J., and Kador, J. (2000) *Net Ready: Strategies for Success in the Economy*, New York, NY: McGraw-Hill.

Hodgetts, R.M., Luthans, F., and Slocum, J.W., Jr. (1999) "Strategy and HRM initiatives for the '00s environment: redefining roles and boundaries, linking competencies and resources," *Organizational Dynamics*, 28(2): 7–21.

Iansiti, M. and MacCormack, A. (1997) "Developing product on Internet time," *Harvard Business Review*, 75(5): 108–117.

Kanter, R.M. (2001) *Evolve! Succeeding in the Digital Cultural of Tomorrow*, Boston, MA: Harvard Business School Press.

Keeney, R. (1999) "The value of Internet commerce to the customer," *Management Science*, April: 533–542.

Kickul, J. and Gundry, L.K. (2000a) "Pursuing technological innovation: the role of entrepreneurial posture in Internet firms," in *Frontiers of Entrepreneurship Research*, Wellesley, MA: Babson College.

Kickul, J. and Gundry, L.K. (2000b) "Transforming the entrepreneurial landscape: strategic innovation in Internet firms," *New England Journal of Entrepreneurship*, 3(1): 23–32.

Kickul, J. and Gundry, L.K. (2001) "Breaking through boundaries for organizational innovation: new managerial roles and practices in e-commerce firms," *Journal of Management*, 27: 347–361.

Koshiur, D. (1997) *Understanding Electronic Commerce*, Redmond, WA: Microsoft Press.

Lange, J.E. (1999) "Entrepreneurs and the Internet: the great equalizer," in Timmons, J. (ed.) *New Venture Creation*, Boston, MA: Irwin-McGraw Hill.

Miller, D. and Friesen, P.H. (1983) "Successful and unsuccessful phases of the corporate life cycle," *Organizational Studies*, 4(4): 339–356.

Miller, R. and Blais, R.A. (1992) "Configurations of innovation: predictable and maverick modes," *Technology Analysis & Strategic Management*, 4(4): 363–386.

Morino, M. (1999) "Netpreneurs: a new breed of entrepreneur," *E-Commerce*, May.

Neese, T. (2000) "Report gives new trends on e-commerce evolution, communication changes," *The Journal Record*, January 24. Online, available at: http://www.journalrecord.com (accessed April 22, 2003).

Oliva, R.A. (1998) "Match your web page to your mission," *Marketing Management*, 7(4): 38–41.

Oliver, R.W. (2000) "The seven laws of e-commerce strategy," *The Journal of Business Strategy*, 21(5): 8–10.

Page, G. (1997) "Temporal dimensions of opportunistic change in technology-based ventures," *Entrepreneurship: Theory & Practice*, 22(2): 31–52.

Pottruck, D.S. and Pearce, T. (2000) *Clicks and Mortar: Passion Driven Growth in an Internet Driven World*, San Francisco, CA: Jossey-Bass.

Shannon, J. (1999) "Net brands lead by innovation," *Marketing Week*, 22: 28.

Singh, R., Hills, G.E., Hybels, R.C., and Lumpkin, G.T. (1999) "Opportunity recognition through social network characteristics of entrepreneurs," *Frontiers of Entrepreneurship Research*, Wellesley, MA: Babson College.

PART FOUR

Social entrepreneurship

Chapter 14

Barbara A. Kuhns

DePaul University

DEVELOPING COMMUNITIES, PEOPLE, AND BUSINESSES: IN SEARCH OF A MODEL OF COMMUNITY-BASED ENTERPRISES

Introduction

COMMUNITY-BASED ENTERPRISES contribute to economic and social well-being of community members. In this chapter, eleven critical issues are inductively drawn from four categories of prior reporting and research – private initiatives, governmental programs, sustainable development projects, and roles of entrepreneurs. Identification of such critical issues presents a first step in developing a research agenda targeting community-based enterprises, an important yet sparsely documented type of social entrepreneurship. Three case studies test the applicability of the critical issues to community-based enterprises.

The defining characteristics of community-based enterprises are, first, business enterprises with a clear commercial intent and, second, support of members of a community of interest. The community might be defined geographically or geo-politically, for example, the Humboldt Park area of Chicago. The community of interest may be a social community or a community of individuals sharing a common interest or goal, such as the Delancey Street Foundation's members, who face challenges associated with having served time in prison or being homeless or addicted to drugs. Other communities share common ties of religious beliefs or membership in a church, such as Houston's Northwest Community Church.

Entrepreneurship and community development

Entrepreneurial activities contribute to community and social development, as supported by research reports in the United States and throughout the world. Research linking entrepreneurship and economic development has expanded beyond the domain of sociology, psychology, and economics, where many of the studies originated during the 1960s and 1970s (e.g. Greenfield and Strickton 1979; Hagen 1971; McClelland 1961). World-wide economic contributions of new venture formation continue to be measured annually by the Global Entrepreneurship Monitor studies (Reynolds *et al.* 2002). Social science researchers and community development experts view entrepreneurial ventures as critical ingredients for improving conditions in economically distressed areas (for example, Cornwall 1998; Lenzi 1996; Merrion 2001; Porter 1995; Steidlmeier 1993). Others, such as Venkataraman (1997), emphasize the need to consider entrepreneurship's impact on social as well as economic wealth creation. Interest by management researchers in relationships between entrepreneurship and community development is growing, as evidenced by recent articles and conference sessions (for example, Christie 2001; Dana 1995; Krueger 2000; Kuhns 2003).

Community-based enterprises fit within an inclusive definition of entrepreneurship. Bruyat and Julien (2000: 173) suggest that "entrepreneurship [research] is concerned first and foremost with a process of change, emergence and creation: creation of new value, but also, and at the same time, change and creation for the individual." Entrepreneurship as a process of change and value creation on multiple levels guides this study.

Categories of issues

Four categories are used to identify community-based enterprise research issues in this study: private initiatives, government programs, sustainable development efforts, and roles of entrepreneurs. Private initiatives provide examples of organizational strategies that blend entrepreneurship and community development, resulting in community-based enterprises. Successes and failures of government programs offer insights related to founding community-based enterprises. World-wide sustainable development efforts demonstrate methods that can be applied to diverse enterprises. Because entrepreneurs drive the formation of all types of ventures, the final category examines the roles of entrepreneurs.

Private initiatives

Mainstream national media reports have raised awareness of innovative initiatives fitting the definition of community-based enterprises. *Time* magazine (2001), under a banner proclaiming "New Agents of Change: Community Activism" portrayed individual innovators as leaders of dramatic social change, filling gaps in services to marginalized communities in the United States and elsewhere. John Stossel (2001) blasted failed governmental programs, then praised highly successful non-governmental projects that improve economies of entire communities, provide needed social support, and change lives through entrepreneurial enterprises. The *MacNeil–Lehrer News Hour* reported on the re-establishment of a plastic molding business on Chicago's southwest side, built on a former illegal waste dump (Brackett 2001). The founder, Martha Williams, promised to keep the business near the city so that community members can benefit from local job opportunities.

The private enterprises previously described were formed in response to a community need or a community crisis that was not being served by government programs. These examples lead to the first critical issue:

1   failures of government programs trigger the creation of community-based enterprises.

Governmental assistance

Community-based enterprises, by definition, are *private* initiatives of new social and economic value creation; however, the lines blur in the United States and elsewhere. Governmental and non-governmental activities overlap because of government support or financial incentives for private enterprise development in economically distressed areas. The Small Business Administration supports new ventures in economically distressed regions through many programs, including minority small business investment companies (e.g. Bates 2001). The Department of Housing and Urban Development (HUD) established urban and rural empowerment zones, enterprise communities, and renewal communities to encourage public and private partnerships to form new businesses and expand existing businesses (HUD 2001). While some federal funds create opportunities for new business, other types of federal funding perpetuate troubled bureaucracies that inadvertently hinder a community's development (Stossel 2001).

The effects of government subsidies on business start-ups has been mixed. Results of a study in Austria indicate that, in comparison with non-subsidized start-ups, the subsidized ones employed fewer individuals, but had similar growth and failure rates (Frank *et al.* 1991). Government funding appears to play complex, even conflicting, roles in the formation and growth of community-based enterprises.

United States government agencies often provide financing that leads to the formation of community-based enterprises. For example, Ambassador John Bryant, former Goodwill Ambassador to the United Nations from the United States, created Operation Hope to secure financing for minority-owned housing and business development in South Central Los Angeles (Bryant 2001). Churches establish separate corporations to tap a variety of financial assistance programs. The church-affiliated corporations build communities by developing shopping centers, business parks, and housing developments (e.g. DePriest and Jones 1997).

Multiple and diverse enterprises emerge from seed monies provided by government sources, often building on successes of the first community-based enterprise pursued by an organization. Many church-affiliated programs create diverse enterprises based in part on the types of funding available. Native American nations pursue multiple enterprises, including tourism, manufacturing, gaming, golf resorts, and housing developments. In other countries, multiple enterprise formation has also been observed in marginalized communities (e.g. Long 1979).

The preceding discussion leads to the next four critical issues:

2   government financial initiatives trigger the formation of community-based enterprises.
3   government financial support is associated with smaller community-based enterprises.
4   long-term government financial support will be associated with lower performance of community-based enterprises.
5   diverse forms of community-based enterprises emerge in economically distressed areas.

Sustainable development

In this section, sustainability is examined as it relates to the formation of community-based enterprises. The term "sustainable development" may have been formalized in 1987 in a report from the World Commission on Environment and Development, according to Raskin (2000: 67). "Sustainable entrepreneurship" was introduced at the 2000 Academy of Management Conference in a special symposium attracting presenters from leading universities around the world (Krueger 2000). Sustainable development, whether for economic or environmental purposes, has emerged as a key process for battling poverty throughout the world. Much can be learned from challenges confronted in developing economies.

Survival needs

In addressing international economic development issues, Raskin explains that the term "social sustainability" refers to "basic human needs, such as adequate food and clean drinking water" (2000: 71) and is characterized by "cooperative partnerships rather than project-oriented aid" (2000: 67). In the United States and other developed countries, social sustainability would be defined as having access to adequate housing, healthy food, and safe neighborhoods. For example, Habitat for Humanity, by building homes to be purchased at cost with low-interest loans, addresses the social sustainability issue of adequate housing. Building on this definition suggests the sixth critical issue:

6   unmet social sustainability needs will trigger community-based enterprises.

Grass-roots enterprises

Examples of community-based, sustainable organizations and enterprises are found world-wide. The Self-Employed Women's Association (SEWA), formed in 1972 in Ahmedabad, India, began as a coalition of poverty-level women. SEWA evolved into a powerful organization, initiating self-help and grass-roots business strategy that has served as a model for similar efforts in Africa, Thailand, Mexico, Poland, and the United States (Datta 2000: 55). The goal of SEWA is to increase the economic power of its members. Services include micro credit, bank lending, literacy programs, childcare co-ops, and business cooperatives (including a dairy cooperative selling to the mainstream dairy industry). Another example of a grass-roots enterprise is a seed multiplication program in Tanzania that started in 1995 as a small, informal group of farmers sharing seeds and seed multiplication techniques. This initiative has spread to 42 villages and includes training in "seed production, quality control, storage, [and] marketing " (Mwaisela 2000: 85).

Grass-roots ventures and enterprises have been important mechanisms for spreading the benefits of entrepreneurial enterprises among community members. The foregoing examples suggest the seventh critical issue:

7   successful grass-roots community-based enterprises spread to other similar communities.

Multiple outcomes

The objectives of building confidence, independence, self-sufficiency, and personal empowerment, plus individual and community responsibility, are recurring themes in sustainable entrepreneurship descriptions. The initiatives develop, then reinforce, entrepreneurial skills, as exemplified by the Songhai Environmental Rehabilitation Center in Benin on the continent of Africa. Songhai trains young farmers in sustainable farming and entrepreneurial techniques, then encourages farmers to focus on economic performance (Nzamujo 2000). The Self-Employed Women's Association (Datta 2000) also values the increased capabilities and confidence of its members. Community-based organizations in Ireland, some of which were founded in the 1960s, cross cultural and ethnic boundaries to create environments of non-dependency while battling the effects of poverty (Robson 2000). Assessing the performance of entrepreneurship in terms of social and human capital is not limited to the field of international development. Shane and Venkataraman (2000) support the notion of considering broadly defined outcomes of ventures, including outcomes for society and developing human capital.

Financial as well as non-financial performance measures should be important tools for evaluating community-based enterprises, leading to the following critical issues:

8   success/failure of community-based enterprises cannot be measured solely in terms of business outcomes but must also be evaluated in terms of human capital and social capital outcomes.

9   success should be measured in terms of the objectives of the enterprises.

Although all of the issues related to sustainable development and entrepreneurship derive from developing regions, similar mechanisms fit entrepreneurial ventures in economically distressed areas of developed nations. In fact, one could argue that economic disparity and geographic proximity to economic strength in developed nations make such efforts even more feasible considering greater access to resources and markets.

Roles of entrepreneurs

Thus far, the discussion has focused on external factors that are likely to influence community-based enterprises. However, the individual founder or owner–operator must have the capabilities to recognize opportunities and the persistence to form a business enterprise. Venkataraman (1997: 121) wrote: "Two issues are of particular interest to scholars in entrepreneurship: the sources of opportunities and the nexus of opportunity and enterprising individuals." The following sections address issues related to enterprising individuals and community-based enterprises.

Individual preparedness

To address the needs or capabilities of the individuals in forming new ventures, Lichtenstein and Lyons (2001: 5) created a formalized entrepreneurial development system (EDS) to increase "the quantity and quality of an area's entrepreneurial capital." Lichtenstein and Lyons built what they describe as an entire business community of entrepreneurs by providing assessment of entrepreneurial development levels, assistance targeted to each level, and ongoing support through networking.

The practical approach employed by Lichtenstein and Lyons targets the factors included in models of entrepreneurial intentions (e.g. Krueger et al. 2000). The entrepreneurial development system tackles social or specific desirability of entrepreneurship, improves perceived self-efficacy, and enhances or reinforces perceived desirability and feasibility. Thus, the entrepreneurial development system could theoretically be expected to affect an individual's entrepreneurial intent and propensity to act (all components of the models compared by Krueger et al.).

The entrepreneurial development system program builds individual skills and reinforces other human capital attributes, such as internal locus of control, achievement orientation, and, perhaps, autonomy. These attributes were found to be related to operational success in a study of small tourism ventures in Israel by Lerner and Haber (2000). The foregoing discussion leads to a critical issue related to the founders:

10   founders will exhibit perceived self-efficacy related to new venture creation, will value the creation of new ventures, and will have a propensity to act on the intent to form a new venture.

Collective entrepreneurship

Johannisson (1998) describes entrepreneurship as a collective process, in which individuals retain their identity but act collectively within social networks to create new ventures. Individuals are key but the whole is far greater than the sum, and social commitment balances economic commitment.

Johannisson's view suggests that the study of collective entrepreneurship requires a different level of analysis, that of the collective. Examples include industrial districts, Native American nations, business enterprise zones, and technology incubators in which the entity acts as a single unit to attract new business and employment opportunities to a region, leading to the final critical issue:

11   in collective community-based enterprises, the founding unit exhibits characteristics similar to those of individual entrepreneurs – perceived self-efficacy related to new venture creation, recognition of the value of creating new ventures, and a propensity to act.

The discussions and arguments presented reflect a review of four categories of theory and data that can be used to guide the study of community-based enterprises. Reports about private initiatives and government programs offer examples for inductively developing research propositions. Essays and studies from international sustainable development sources offer insights from field experiences in economic development programs. Theoretical arguments from the entrepreneurship field offer a basis for framing research issues and for positioning the implications of studying community-based enterprises.

Methods

Study design

This chapter builds a theoretical foundation as part of an evolving study of community-based enterprises. The initial stages of the exploratory study employ qualitative inquiry and analyses methods. Qualitative methods were chosen because of the lack of prior theoretical work and a need for a holistic perspective (Janesick 2000). A qualitative, clinical research approach "enables us to look at situations in great depth and understand some of the richness and complexity of the processes involved," Arnold Cooper said in an interview discussing entrepreneurship and wealth creation (McCarthy and Nicholls-Nixon 2001).

Case selection

Potential cases have been identified using news reports, Internet searches, and personal experiences. Each enterprise meets the following minimum criteria:

- primarily private enterprise;
- operates as part of a community;
- commercial purpose;
- benefits individuals in marginal economic areas or situations.

An initial database is being developed, currently listing more than 150 community-based enterprises and social entrepreneurship ventures or organizations. Many of the enterprises offer extensive opportunities to learn because of accessibility, a critical determinant for selecting cases (Stake 2000).

Data collection

Case data are being collected from a variety of sources to ensure comprehensive and representative pictures of identified community-based enterprises. Public records and documents constitute the main sources of data (Charmaz 2000; Hodder 2000) for the examples explored in the present phase of the study. Data collection continues as a dynamic process guided by analyses of previously collected data following methods of case development (Ryan and Bernard 2000) and grounded theory development (Charmaz 2000).

Analyses methods

Data from cases were summarized into case notes. Case notes were analyzed, making note of issues covered in the background discussion above, to track characteristics of the community-based enterprises. Tables and lists of themes and concepts were generated to facilitate comparisons of characteristics and outcomes of community-based enterprises (Ryan and Bernard 2000).

Case summaries

This section presents condensed examples of three case summaries to illustrate community-based enterprises. The selected cases are: FAME Renaissance, in South Central Los Angeles; Delancey Street Foundation, in San Francisco; and Choctaw Enterprises, in Choctaw, Mississippi.

FAME Renaissance

The FAME Renaissance enterprises (DePriest and Jones 1997; FAME 2003) include a variety of businesses, business services, and social service programs. FAME Renaissance is a California 501(C) non-profit corporation. It grew out of programs initiated by the First African Methodist Episcopal Church of Los Angeles.

The FAME Business Enterprise Center, a business incubator focusing on the entertainment industry, houses technology-intensive start-up enterprises and provides training. The FAME equity fund, started with seed money from the Wells Fargo Bank, invests in emerging, minority-owned businesses. The Business Resource Center operates a micro-lending service. The FAME Personnel Services provide staffing and placement services. Its annual Job Fair attracts more than 50 employers and several thousand applicants. Successful applicants work with Disney, DreamWorks, Warner Brothers, the Metropolitan Water District, and many smaller enterprises. The Entrepreneurial Training Program offers courses in new business start-ups, management, and networking taught by entrepreneurs and educators.

The FAME Housing Corporation constructs and manages apartment complexes for low- to moderate-income-level families and seniors. Similar enterprises operate in many major cities, including Houston, Atlanta, and New York City, often affiliated with predominantly African-American churches and dynamic church leaders (DePriest and Jones 1997).

Delancey Street Foundation

The Delancey Street Foundation operates 20 businesses through five self-sustaining residential programs serving more than 1,500 residents (Mieszkowski 1998a). The foundation, started in 1971 in San Francisco, operates a popular restaurant, a construction company, a moving company, and Christmas tree sales. In 1997 the foundation's business generated $9 million in revenues plus $3 million in private contributions (Mieszkowski 1998a). New residential programs operate in New York, North Carolina, New Mexico, and Los Angeles (Grassroots 2001).

Residents perform all the fund raising, business, training, and administrative functions. The residents are ex-convicts, recovering drug addicts, and formerly homeless people who are willing to commit at least two years to live at the foundation. Each participant teaches another, no matter how little experience he or she has upon entering the program (Mieszkowski 1998b).

Delancey Street Foundation success stories provide evidence of the effectiveness of its model. Comments posted on the University of California at Berkeley parents' association website demonstrate the success of the Delancey Street Moving Company. It is the only company repeatedly praised for excellent service among the many listed on the site (UCB Parents 2001). The restaurant receives top reviews in local papers and travel websites (Delancey Street Foundation 2003).

Choctaw Enterprises

In the late 1960s, the Choctaw Band of Mississippi experienced an unemployment rate of nearly 80 percent, even with more than 15 years of government programs attempting to alleviate regional poverty (Choctaw 2003). Today, tribal manufacturing, hospitality, retail, and international manufacturing businesses employ more than 8,000 individuals, providing employment opportunities for the entire tribal workforce. Nearly 65 percent of the workers are non-Native American.

The first business, a construction company, began in 1969. After building an industrial park and attracting an automotive wiring harness company, the development attracted a stereo speaker manufacturing company, a plastics molding manufacturer, and a greeting card manufacturing operation.

The original construction company has built residential housing and worked on a large resort complex and retail services center. Two of the companies, the wiring harness manufacturing and the plastic molding operation, have expanded to Mexico. The resort business and related retail services businesses continue to expand, serving the region's golfers and tourists (Choctaw 2003).

Analysis and results

The early stage results provide insight into the enterprises and their operations, as summarized in Table 14.1. The following discussion analyzes the three cases in terms of the 11 critical issues identified previously.

Private initiatives

Early data suggest that at least one of the community-based enterprises was established because of a failure of governmental programs. The Choctaw Enterprises were initiated following failed efforts by the Bureau of Indian Affairs to attract companies and jobs to the area (Choctaw 2003). The Delancey Street Foundation does not accept or seek any government funding or grants, but does not state that it was formed because of a failure of government programs. However, the Pacific Research Institute for Public Policy (Bragin 1998) claims that:

> the Delancey Street Foundation . . . stands as a model demonstrating the capability of indigent and unemployed peoples to bond together, step away from dependence on the aid of government welfare programs or the free hand-outs of large charities, and instead to pull themselves out of poverty and away from welfare dependence.

Government involvement

Two of the examples are clearly non-governmental; the third (Choctaw Enterprises) was formed by a local governing authority operating contrary to prior governance structures. Two of the organizations (FAME and Choctaw Enterprises) take advantage of government funding or grants, but the third (Delancey Street Foundation) operates with no government monies. Without further data, it cannot be determined whether the availability of government funding triggered the enterprises, although in the case of FAME, the availability of government financing appears to play a role in the selecting the enterprises. None of the community-based enterprises examined are small, thus it cannot be determined if smaller enterprises relate to government subsidies. All three examples have evolved into multiple, diverse businesses and have grown substantially

Table 14.1 Summary of community-based enterprise examples

CBE name (affiliation founder)	First business	Businesses	Funding	Beneficiaries
FAME (church-affiliated/church leader)	1992	Business incubator, residential housing, personnel services, business lending, charter school.	Private grants, government grants, enterprise income.	Local residents, church members.
Delancey Street (independent/individual)	1971	Restaurant, moving company, Christmas tree sales, construction, charter school.	Enterprise income, private grants.	Ex-convicts, homeless, recovering addicts.
Choctaw Enterprises (tribal nation/tribal chief)	1969	Plastics molding, automotive wiring, audio speaker components, resort development construction, senior citizens care, greeting card production, resort operations, gaming, real estate development.	Enterprise income, government grants.	8,000+ employees, tribal families, regional families, families in Mexico.

from their initial operations. Preliminary data suggest that long-term government support may not hinder the performance of community-based enterprises, contrary to some prior experiences.

Sustainable development

The enterprises clearly contribute to the social sustainability of their community members. The three enterprises fit the pattern of grass-roots formation. The enterprises have spread to other similar communities, especially the Delancey Street Foundation. FAME is also part of an expanding grass-roots effort among African-American churches. All three of the enterprises, like the entrepreneurial development system described by Lichtenstein and Lyons (2001), develop skills using various forms of member involvement, a non-financial yet critical outcome. None of the enterprises measures its success in terms of purely financial indicators. Each enterprise meets targeted needs of community members and appears successful in attaining social performance goals.

Roles of entrepreneurs

All three community-based enterprises benefit from a strong individual founder, although one of the enterprises might be considered a collective (Johannisson 1998). The characteristics of the founders suggest that each exhibits a strong sense of perceived self-efficacy, positive views toward venture formation, and a propensity to take action (Krueger *et al.* 2000). The data from Choctaw Enterprises suggest that, as a collective, it exhibits similar characteristics.

Implications for research

The results of this phase of the ongoing study suggest that similarities exist among diverse types of community-based enterprises. Triggers for the formation of the enterprises include unmet needs for social survivability within the community. Social outcomes as well as business outcomes are clearly important. The case data lend credence to the theoretically grounded critical issues, suggesting that the issues will be useful for future research leading toward the development of models and success measures of community-based enterprises. With the collection and analyses of more case data, models and hypotheses can be formed to shed light on community-based enterprises and their entrepreneurial roles in economic and social sustainability.

Implications for practitioners

A cohesive, tested model for creating successful community-based enterprises would be a useful tool for building enterprises to meet social sustainability needs within a community. This study begins to bridge the gap between theory and practice. As the study evolves, it is expected to demonstrate more similarities among community-based enterprises and to develop a testable and replicable model. Early evidence suggests that successful community-based enterprises have an entrepreneurial founder, focus on their community needs, develop entrepreneurial organizations, employ government funding without becoming dependent, and flexibly respond to changes in their external environments. Such patterns could be applied to forming new community-based enterprises.

Limitations and future directions

Although this study offers valuable insights into community-based enterprises, the limitations are clear. The limitations relate especially to the early stage of the research: the small number of cases analyzed, the need for additional field interviews and data, and a need to expand the theoretical foundations on the basis of the analyses conducted to date. Each of the limitations suggests future directions for the research.

Conclusion

In this study, the research identifies 11 theoretically based issues drawn from diverse sources including national media, public policy reports, international sustainable development reports, and entrepreneurship research. The analyses of three cases suggest that the critical issues help to reveal similarities among diverse community-based enterprises. Future research is warranted to clarify characteristics and outcome measures and to develop a replicable model of community-based enterprises.

References

Bates, T. (2001) "Financing the development of urban minority communities: lessons of history," paper presented at the Federal Reserve System's Second Community Affairs Research Conference, April 5–6, *Changing Financial Markets and Community Development*, Washington, DC.

Brackett, E. (2001) "Building a business," *MacNeil-Lehrer News Hour*. MacNeil–Lehrer Productions, Public Broadcasting System, August 30.

Bragin, M. (1998) *Moving Social Services Back to Our Communities*, San Francisco, CA: Pacific Research Institute. Online, available at: http://www.pacificresearch.org/pub/sab/health/delancey.html (accessed March 26, 2003).

Bruyat, C. and Julien, P.-A. (2000) "Defining the field of research in entrepreneurship," *Journal of Business Venturing*, 16: 165–180.

Bryant, J. (2001) *Operation Hope*, speech presented at the 2001 national conference of the United States Association of Small Business and Entrepreneurship – Small Business Institute Directors' Association. Orlando, FL.

Charmaz, K. (2000) "Grounded theory: objectivist and constructivist methods," in Denzin, N.K. and Lincoln, Y.S. (eds) *Handbook of Qualitative Research*, second edn, Thousand Oaks, CA: Sage Publications.

Choctaw Band of Mississippi (2003) *Economic Development History*, MS: Choctaw Band of Mississippi. Online, available at: http://www.choctaw.com/show.asp?durki=34 (accessed March 26, 2003).

Christie, M. (2001) "Entrepreneurship in community development caucus," paper presented at Annual Academy of Management Conference, Washington, DC.

Cornwall, J.R. (1998) "The entrepreneur as a building block for community," *Journal of Developmental Entrepreneurship*, 3(2):141–148.

Dana, L.-P. (1995) "Entrepreneurship in a remote sub-arctic community," *Entrepreneurship Theory and Practice*, 20: 57–72.

Datta, R. (2000) "On their own: development strategies of the self-employed women's association (SEWA) in India," *Development*, 43(4): 51–55.

Delancey Street Foundation (2003) "Home page," San Francisco, CA: Delancey Street Foundation. Online, available at: http://www.delanceystfndtn. citysearch.com/ (accessed March 25, 2003).

DePriest, T. and Jones, J. (1997) "Economic deliverance through the church," *Black Enterprise*, 27(7): 195–202.

FAME (2003) "FAME Renaissance," Los Angeles, CA: FAME Assistance Corporation, an affiliate of the First African Methodist Episcopal Church. Online, available at: http://www.famechurch.org/renaissance/ (accessed March 26, 2003).

Frank, H., Plaschka, G.R., and Roessl, D. (1991) "Are subsidized and non-subsidized new ventures different? An evaluation of a governmental policy," *Picolla Impresa*, 4(3): 109–121).

Grassroots (2001) "Groups that change communities: Delancey Street Foundation," USA: @grassroots.org. Online, available at: http://www.grass-roots.org/ usa/delancey.shtml (accessed March 26, 2003).

Greenfield, S.M. and Strickton, A. (1979) "Entrepreneurship and social change: toward a populational, decision-making approach," in Greenfield, S.M., Strickton, A., and Aubey, R.T. (eds) *Entrepreneurs In Cultural Context*, Albuquerque, NM: University of New Mexico Press.

Hagen, E.E. (1971) "How economic growth begins: a theory of social change," in Kilby, P. (ed.) *Entrepreneurship and Social Change*, New York, NY: Macmillan, Free Press.

Hodder, I. (2000) "The interpretation of documents and material culture," in Denzin, N.K. and Lincoln, Y.S. (eds) *Handbook of Qualitative Research*, second edn, Thousand Oaks, CA: Sage Publications.

HUD (2001) "Introduction to the RC/EZ/EC initiative," Washington, DC: U.S. Department of Housing and Urban Development. Online, available at: http://www.hud.gov/offices/cpd/ezec/about/ezecinit.cfm (accessed July 30, 2001).

Janesick, V. (2000) "The choreography of qualitative research design: minuets, improvisations, and crystallization," in Denzin, N.K. and Lincoln, Y.S. (eds) *Handbook of Qualitative Research*, second edn, Thousand Oaks, CA: Sage Publications.

Johannisson, B. (1998) "Entrepreneurship as a collective phenomenon," paper presented at RENT XII Conference, Lyon, France, November.

Krueger, N.F., Jr. (2000) "A new time and new directions for sustainable entrepreneurship: seeking and acting on 'triple bottom line' opportunities," Session 247, Academy of Management Conference, Toronto, August.

Krueger, N.F., Reilly, M.D., and Carsrud, A.L. (2000) "Competing models of entrepreneurial intentions," *Journal of Business Venturing*, 15: 411–432.

Kuhns, B.A. (2003) "Social entrepreneurship symposium," Coleman Track, United

States Association of Small Business and Entrepreneurship National Conference. Hilton Head Island, SC.

Lenzi, R.C. (1996) "The entrepreneurial community approach to community economic development," *Economic Development Review*, 14(2): 16–20.

Lerner, M. and Haber, S. (2000) "Performance factors of small tourism ventures: the interface of tourism, entrepreneurship and the environment," *Journal of Business Venturing*, 16: 77–100.

Lichtenstein, G.A. and Lyons, T.S. (2001) "The entrepreneurial development system: transforming business talent and community economies," *Economic Development Quarterly*, 15(1): 3–20.

Long, N. (1979) "Multiple enterprise in the central highlands of Peru," in Greenfield, S.M., Strickton, A., and Aubey, R.T. (eds) *Entrepreneurs in Cultural Context*, Albuquerque, NM: University of New Mexico Press.

McCarthy, A.M. and Nicholls-Nixon, C.L. (2001) "Fresh starts: Arnold Cooper on entrepreneurship and wealth creation," *Academy of Management Executive*, 15(1): 27–36.

McClelland, D. (1961) *The Achieving Society*, Princeton, NJ: Van Nostrand.

Merrion, P. (2001) "Mining new markets: urban upsides," *Crain's Chicago Business*, 24(16): 13, 16, 20.

Mieszkowski, K. (1998a) "She helps them help themselves," *Fast Company*, 15: 54.

Mieszkowski, K. (1998b) "Ex-con University," *Fast Company*, 15: 56.

Mwaisela, F.A. (2000) "WTO and sustainable seed multiplication programmes in Tanzania," *Development*, 43(2): 83–87.

Nzamujo, F. (2000) "A new approach to sustainable livelihoods: African youth and agriculture," *Development*, 42(2): 64–67.

Porter, M.E. (1995) "The competitive advantage of the inner city," *Harvard Business Review*, 73(3): 55–71.

Raskin, P.D. (2000) "Bending the curve: toward global sustainability," *Development*, 43(4): 64–74.

Reynolds, P., Bygrave, W., Autio, E. *et al.* (2002) *Global Entrepreneurship Monitor 2002 Executive Report*, Kansas City, MO: Ewing Marin Kauffman Foundation.

Ripley, A. (2001) "New agents of change: Innovators – *Time* 100: The next wave – community activism," *Time*, 157(24): 66–73.

Robson, T. (2000) "Northern Ireland: community relations and community conflict," *Development*, 43(3): 66–71.

Ryan, G.W. and Bernard, H.R. (2000) "Data management and analysis methods," in Denzin, N.K. and Lincoln, Y.S. (eds) *Handbook of Qualitative Research*, second edn, Thousand Oaks, CA: Sage Publications.

Shane, S. and Venkataraman, S. (2000) "The promise of entrepreneurship as a field of research," *Academy of Management Review*, 25(1): 217–226.

Stake, R.E. (2000) "Case studies," in Denzin, N.K. and Lincoln, Y.S. (eds) *Handbook of Qualitative Research*, second edn, Thousand Oaks, CA: Sage Publications.

Steidlmeier, P. (1993) "The business community and the poor: rethinking business strategies and social policy," *American Journal of Economics and Sociology*, 52(2): 209–221.

Stossel, J. (2001) *John Stossel Goes to Washington*. ABC Television Broadcast, January 27.

UCB Parents (2001) *UCB parents recommendations: movers*, Berkeley, CA: UC Berkeley Parents Network. Online, available at: http://parents.berkeley.edu/recommend/services/movers.html (accessed April 16, 2003).

Venkataraman, S. (1997) "The distinctive domain of entrepreneurship research," in Katz, J. (ed.) *Advances in Entrepreneurship, Firm Emergence and Growth*, Volume 3, Greenwich, CT: JAI Press.

Chapter 15

Gregory Fairchild

Darden Graduate School of Business Administration

Patricia G. Greene

Babson College

WEALTH CREATION IN DISTRESSED INNER CITIES: WHAT CAN BUSINESS SCHOOLS CONTRIBUTE?

U RBAN BUSINESS SCHOOLS ARE well positioned to facilitate wealth creation through entrepreneurship in distressed inner cities. Perhaps the obvious motivation would be to improve their surrounding communities. Less obvious are the opportunities to conduct useful research in a dynamic, readily available environment, and to provide educational experiences by means of outreach activities. Logically, scholarship should precede practical action, if business school outreach is to be most effective. Therefore, the first section of this chapter explores scholarship on inner-city entrepreneurship and the second part explores outreach activities.

A call to scholarly action

This section of the chapter provides a review of research into the nascent field of inner-city business among business researchers. First, it considers reasons for the broad interest in learning more about this field and the paradox of widespread outreach activity but relatively little published research as a consequence. This leads to the question of possible impediments to broader involvement by business school scholars. As a proposal for sparking more such involvement, it proposes categories for the existing research and recommends directions for future research efforts.

Why study inner-city businesses?

High levels of joblessness and poverty characterize America's urban, central city neighborhoods. New York City's Harlem is a prime example. In 2000, 55.8 percent of working-age Harlem residents were not in the labor force compared with 35.6 percent for the city overall, and 35.3 percent of individuals had incomes below the federally adjusted poverty level, compared with 17.6 percent overall (U.S. Department of Commerce 2000).

Inner cities are costly and inefficient to the countries in which they are located. First, they are a labor opportunity cost, as a significant component of employable labor remains unemployed. Second, they are a financial drain on the public support system of federal, state, and local governments, in both direct prescriptive costs and indirect social costs. Untold millions in prescriptive efforts have been dedicated to bringing these communities into the economic mainstream. Third, they are politically costly. The debate surrounding the problem engenders heated political discussion that devolves into argumentative, unproductive rhetoric. Too often, race baiting and political finger pointing overwhelms efforts at genuine problem-solving.

Despite their social and economic problems, inner cities represent a significant untapped business opportunity with underserved consumer markets, untapped labor pools, and overlooked locations for business development. Even though per capita income levels are low, aggregate income levels may be greater than in surrounding suburban areas (Boston Consulting Group 1998). By 1999, Harlem's zip code areas serviced a population of more than 240,000 with an annual income of more than $3.2 billion (U.S. Department of Commerce 2000). Harlem's per square mile spending is six times greater than the New York metropolitan area (Boston Consulting Group 1998). Several corporations – Nike, Tommy Hilfiger, Krispy Kreme Donuts, Walgreens, and Starbucks – have discovered the benefit of building business in overlooked inner-city markets. Sears' newest urban stores average almost triple the chain's average per store sales. Rite Aid's Harlem-based drugstore fills more prescriptions per day than any of its other stores in New York City (Fisher 1997).

Business scholarship in this field would benefit many stakeholders. Government and non-profit leaders are increasingly seeking objective, reasoned analysis of the prescriptive measures they've engaged. U.S. Federal Reserve Chairman Alan Greenspan expressed regret at the lack of empirical research on prescriptive programs:

> The relative paucity of data and research on community development programs has limited the ability to fully demonstrate their impact and credibly differentiate those that are successful from those that are ineffective. Undeniably, impressive local community development initiatives have been undertaken, and individual testimonials reveal

advances in the economic well-being of many of the beneficiaries. However, the absence of formal data collection and research for the numerous neighborhood revitalization efforts over the past several decades has resulted in a reliance on mostly anecdotal reporting at a neighborhood or individual level.

(Federal Reserve 2003)

Leaving data on the table

At a first glance, it may appear that faculty interest in the challenges of starting and running businesses in inner-city neighborhoods is virtually non-existent. However, a better analogy is adapted from the field of economics. Collectively, there is a large body of work by business school faculty that is "leaving data on the table."

Much of the activity involving schools of business and the inner city has been an outgrowth of institutional community service efforts. This is particularly the case for schools that also happen to be located in urban centers. Community-based entrepreneurship centers and small business outreach programs have comprehensive programs that encompass the three traditional arenas of faculty activity (teaching, service, and research). However, because of the time and the administrative constraints involved, there is limited research output from this activity.

Some of this limited research output results from program design. Centers that are meant to offer technical assistance to local businesses and non-profits typically lack explicit objectives that involve theory testing, experimental control, or matched-pair comparison groups. As a result, a wide range of productive activity from faculty engaged in these programs is not being captured, analyzed, and disseminated for wider use. Institutions should develop means to continue the important service work already under way, while collecting data in forms that can be utilized in academic research.

Barriers to inner-city research by business school faculty

Three barriers in particular discourage research into inner-city business. The first involves the attractiveness of sectors of explosive growth as research sites. Aldrich (1999) and Abrahamson (1996) have noted the pro-technology, pro-success, and pro-size bias in business research. Sectors experiencing explosive economic growth have often become faddishly popular research sites, only to see interest wane when rapid growth dissipates. At various times, scholars have focused increased attention on a number of "hot" areas (e.g. Silicon Valley in California, Route 128 in Massachusetts, Japan after 1980 and, recently, Internet-related businesses). These biases lead the field to concentrate less of its collective effort on areas of lagging development.

The second barrier involves the perceived social distance of inner-city businesses and their owners. Even though the physical distance to clusters of inner-city businesses may be literally a few city blocks, cultural barriers and a charged sociopolitical atmosphere can make the divide seem insurmountable. Because many business scholars are less familiar with inner-city neighborhoods and the demographic groups that populate them, few enter into uncertain territory to engage in research that is less popular in the academic mainstream. Many researchers would feel more comfortable performing cross-cultural research overseas. In practice, scholars working with inner-city businesses confirm that the challenges in building rapport and trust are not unlike those in other cross-cultural contexts. Further, prevailing stereotypes about the race and ethnicity of inner-city entrepreneurs may not hold. In a recent *Inc.* magazine ranking of leading inner-city firms, 76 percent of the CEOs reported their race as white (*Inc.* 2000). A recent analysis of a 1995 database of firm owners in Los Angeles, Detroit, Atlanta, and Boston has shown that a majority of the business owners in the central city areas were white (Fairchild and Robinson 2002).

The third barrier is the absence of archival datasets that have representative, sizable samples of inner-city businesses. Scholars prefer large-scale, quantitative samples. The absence of archival data on inner-city businesses has at least two causes. First, there is less interest in entrepreneurship in the developing context. Second, a high number of the firms located in inner cities are small, privately held firms. These two constraints have made the construction of archival datasets of inner-city businesses a significant challenge. A remedy might involve a consortium of researchers, working with intermediary government and non-profit organizations, to construct large-scale national datasets of inner-city businesses.

A brief review of existing inner-city research

Although the field of inner-city business research is in a nascent stage, there is a considerable body of research that is of relevance. In order to identify this literature, it is first necessary to define the inner city. This will allow us to categorize the related research perspectives and the influential scholars identified with each. Finally, we will be able to review existing research on inner-city business.

Definitions

The term "inner city" has many connotations and meanings. It has described geographic entities, demographic groups, and numerous categories of unproductive behavior. Neighborhoods located in the urban core, primarily composed of racial and ethnic minorities, experiencing widespread crime or high rates of illegitimate births, have all been called "inner cities." Outside of the United States, the "inner city" may refer to economically vibrant and desirable locales in a region (e.g. Paris, see Wacquant 1991). We focus on distressed inner cities, defined in spatial and economic terms, as urban neighborhoods with high levels of joblessness and poverty. It follows that any research that focuses on businesses located in high-poverty, high-unemployment neighborhoods may be relevant. For example, research on entrepreneurs who happen to belong to ethnic minorities and operate businesses in suburban neighborhoods would not be germane, but research on white entrepreneurs who operate businesses in inner-city neighborhoods would be.

This economic and social definition has the implication that an inner-city status is dynamic and not permanent. Neighborhoods that were once economically vibrant, with low unemployment levels and poverty, may become inner cities over time. Alternately, predominantly minority and immigrant neighborhoods that once exhibited inner-city conditions may become vibrant ethnic enclaves and would no longer be considered inner-city areas (Portes and Sensebrenner 1993).

Related research

As there are many terms associated with inner cities, there are also areas of related research from social science fields outside of business per se. This research can be broadly categorized into three general areas: poverty, social structure, and economic development.

Sociologists have played a significant role in research on poverty. A number of scholars have studied immigration patterns over time in urban neighborhoods. These studies of "ecological succession" have a long history and are best exemplified in the work of Wilson (1996) and Aldrich (1973, 1979). Spatial mismatch scholars, like Holzer (1991) and Vernon (1963), have charted the movement of manufacturing firms that utilize low-skill labor to suburban areas and the resulting rising unemployment of less-educated inner-city residents. The work of spatial mismatch scholars mirrors related work in the field of economics. Becker (1971) and Thurow (1969) have forwarded human capital theories that relate the high levels of poverty in inner-city neighborhoods to decreasing demand for low-skill labor.

Scholars interested in social structural explanations for inner-city conditions have focused on the social exclusion of inner-city neighborhoods. Social capital scholars, influenced by the work of Coleman (1988) and Granovetter (1985), have noted the exclusion of inner-city neighborhoods from the web of social relations that are the medium for economic change (Portes and Sensebrenner 1993; Wilson 1996).

Scholars working in the field of development economics are often interested in explaining uneven economic development within regions. Rosenstein-Rodan (1943), Nelson (1956), and Hirschman (1958) developed theories that emphasized the circular and cumulative effects of development. In their view, modernization in a country or region leads to even greater modernization, while underdevelopment leads to greater underdevelopment. They proposed that without government intervention, underdeveloped areas would remain stuck in low-level development. Collectively, their work has influenced many economists and policy-makers.

Existing work on inner cities from business scholars

In the popular press (e.g. *Time*, *Newsweek*) and business-practitioner press (e.g. *Fortune*, *Business Week*, *Wall Street Journal*) accounts of inner-city business challenge and success are increasing. At the same time, careful scholarship on inner-city business is at a nascent stage in leading academic journals. This is unsurprising, as studies show that academic scholarship tends to lag behind popular-press coverage (Abrahamson and Fairchild 1999).

The articles that have appeared in academic journals have largely been written by academic gurus, and tend to propose directions for other researchers (Kanter 1995, 1999; Porter 1995). Michael Porter's article in *Harvard Business Review* (1995) generated great interest and discussion. For instance, *The Review of Black Political Economy* (1996) devoted a special issue to responses from scholars from many disciplines to Porter's model of inner-city redevelopment. However, to date, these "call to action" articles have not produced a large body of research in business journals.

Directions for future scholarship

Much of the work has been limited by an emphasis on constraining structural forces and a de-emphasis on endogenous business development. This is an unfortunate oversight as the causes of inner-city social ills are rooted in the lack of business development. The fruits of careful study of inner-city entrepreneurship by business scholars would be beneficial to policy-makers, entrepreneurs, and potential investors.

The range of perspectives and methods that may prove fruitful in the study of inner-city businesses is as broad as the field of management research. Past studies on intra-organizational networks have found that women and minorities who make efforts to establish linkages to powerful outgroup members face social pressures from both the ingroup and the outgroups (Kanter 1977; Ibarra 1992, 1995). Network scholars might examine differences in the structure and network management strategies employed by entrepreneurs operating within the inner city and to those operating in mainstream contexts. Others may choose to examine large, archival databases of both demographic and firm-level variables to explore the influence of the hypothesized forces on business growth and decline. Proponents of organizational evolutionary theories might examine the variation, selection, and retention mechanisms that have influenced the type of businesses found in inner-city neighborhoods (e.g. check-cashing centers and pawnshops as opposed to consumer banks).

The inner city is a difficult environment for entrepreneurs, but substantial opportunities exist for those who can develop innovative strategies for exploiting market inefficiencies. Those who ignore potentially profitable opportunities in inner cities "leave money on the table." Academic institutions are leaving "data on the table." The role of scholars in influencing practical matters has a long history. Careful theorization and scholarship can do much to advance the development of endogenous, self-sustaining, wealth- and job-creating businesses in developing and developed contexts.

Student, staff, and faculty roles in the urban university

While there are opportunities for greater involvement from all business schools, business schools that are located in urban areas have unique opportunities for engaging with inner-city business. Indeed, universities have the potential to play a powerful role in urban environments, having an impact in the related arenas of both social and economic outcomes. The power is generated through the connection of the three primary functions of a university: first, the creation of new knowledge through research; second, through the dissemination of that knowledge through teaching; and third, through the application of knowledge through outreach.

This section of the chapter is divided into three. The first discusses the relationship between urban universities and the communities in which they are located. The second describes roles various individuals within an institution can play, and the third provides a case study of a comprehensive program currently underway.

Roles and capabilities within the urban university

Some urban business schools embrace urban-focused missions, whereas others view their urban location as incidental. What causes this difference, and what are the associated implications for strategy and allocation of resources? A number of factors that may influence the institutional roles and ultimate outcomes in regard to integration with the community. These include the type of university and structural issues within the university setting, internal and external resource pools, and the context of the community relationships.

Universities vary along many dimensions, particularly along their resources and strategic commitment to teaching, research, and outreach or service activities. This commitment is often formalized within the stated mission, yet can also be appreciated by examining the capabilities built within the institution that directly engage inner-city areas.

There are many opportunities throughout the university for participation in a mission of assisting local inner-city areas and a corresponding number of potential roles for each. The individuals involved may include faculty, staff, and students. Each of these independently may choose a variety of roles, based upon their position, their human capital (including education and experience), and their personal inclination. While many of the roles cross over positions, some are particular to institutional jobs and status. The following is a list of those institutional roles and the opportunities for involvement with the inner city.

Faculty

Faculty roles are directly tied to the mission of the university via the reward structures. This is a critical consideration when analyzing participation opportunities and costs. Many faculty members are committed to urban outreach programs for instrumental reasons such as making a difference to more pragmatic explanations such as testing the application of a theory. Part of the appeal for faculty involvement includes the range of possible activities.

Teachers

Faculty members, for the most part, have a required teaching load as part of their employment contract. This requirement generally relates to courses offered for credit to matriculated students. However, there are tremendous opportunities for other teaching activities. This may include continuing education classes located throughout the city. In this instance the faculty member may teach the topic to individuals similar to the matriculated students, but not for credit, or may teach the topic to a different set of students, such as high school or elementary students.

Facilitators

Faculty members, by nature of their university affiliation (and possibly also the advanced degree) may be perceived as facilitators in academic and other environments. The university setting may sometimes carry with it an objective, or safe, context that will allow a faculty member to create and to guide mechanisms for the implementation of conversations or projects.

Conveners

The safe perception of the university can also serve a more direct role as the convener for conversations or projects. In this case the faculty member may be the neutral party that brings together individuals or groups over issues of mutual interest. These issues may be internal or external to the university community.

Students

The role of students is also critical to the mission of the urban-centered university. Ideally, the students first discover how to be learners, how to engage in behaviors that allow them to develop a deep understanding of the world around them and their place in it. This is a particular role that serves them well throughout their life. However, the context of involvement in the urban mission allows them additional opportunities.

Staff

Staff members also fulfill many of the roles described for faculty and students. They may be teachers and learners, as well as facilitators. Staff members may also play the role of liaisons, linking individuals and groups inside and out of the university. Staff members, in addition to faculty and students, may have either strong or weak ties within the urban community that may assist in the identification of resources and opportunities for urban involvement or participation.

Case study: Entrepreneurial Growth Resource Center, University of Missouri–Kansas City

Figure 15.1 represents the structure of the Entrepreneurial Growth Resource Center (EGRC) of the Henry W. Bloch School of Business and Public Administration and the University of Missouri–Kansas City. The Center was created in 2000 as the umbrella organization for entrepreneurial activities, including teaching, service, and outreach. The mission of the EGRC is to integrate these three sets of activities, to have them inform each other and leverage the available resources in order to best advance each.

Every program in the EGRC includes the delineation and establishment of strategic partnerships to support the urban mission of the university. These partnerships cross boundaries of geography, academic discipline, and community organization.

Teaching

The academic offerings of the EGRC include a graduate concentration in entrepreneurship that consists of ten courses. The Faculty members serve in standard

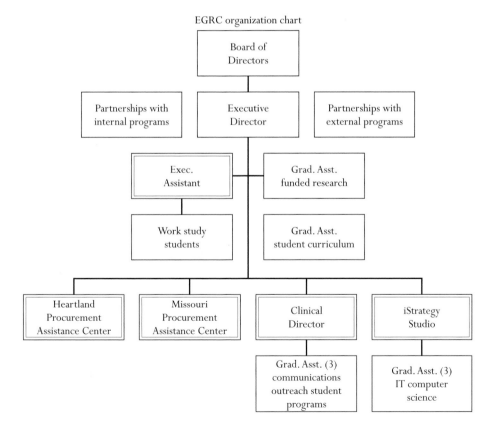

Figure 15.1 Entrepreneurial Growth Resource Center, University of Missouri–Kansas City: EGRC organization chart

roles as teachers; however, they aggressively pursue the role of learners as well, drawing new knowledge from those in the field applying existing knowledge in unique and possibly redefined ways. The selection of courses is reviewed programmatically to ensure that the information is timely, relevant, useful, and academically rigorous. All courses are based upon theory with the premise that theory is a set of statements that describes and explains or predicts the world around us. In addition, the courses are reviewed individually for another set of dimensions. Besides rigor and theory, the pedagogical approach is examined from the point of interdisciplinary and experiential opportunities. The overall curriculum provides the framework for a menu of opportunities for students and faculty to interact with the urban community.

Small Business Management Practicum (called Small Business Institute at many colleges)

Students in this course work in teams as consultants to local small-business owners. The very nature of the course extends the learner role of the student to include that of service provider, teacher, and role model. The role of the instructor encompasses teaching not only the student, but at times the community client, as well as being a direct service provider, liaison, and facilitator. In addition, the researcher role is critical, as select projects may become the basis for case development.

New Venture Creation

This course has become a feeder system into a regional business plan competition. The students again go beyond the learning role to become role models for the community. The competition focuses on both the large-scale development of opportunities but also the social responsibility of the business being created. The students interact with community members who are serving as plan screeners, team coaches, and competition judges. The community thus learns more about the possibilities of doing good while doing well.

Kauffman Entrepreneur Internship Program

In this course students are placed as interns in a variety of organizations, including both small businesses and not-for-profit entities. The students combine course work with their work activities, serving their host organization not only in a functional role, but also once again teaching, providing service, and modeling the role of an urban citizen.

Research

Many roles are also possible in research. This activity can go beyond the collection of data to inform and energize community members. One example is the connection of a National Science Foundation (NSF) grant with a local research project designed to inform public policy and guide program development. The

NSF grant, "The Impact of Race and Ethnicity on the Start-up Process," provided the resources to generate new knowledge about the prevalence rates of business start-ups by members of specific minority groups and specific challenges faced by these nascent entrepreneurs. During the same time-span, a local minority business support program funded by the city received a national grant for further program development. The new grant required that focus groups be conducted to guide the program in both content and format. The university was able to play a leadership role through administration, staff, faculty, and students in organizing and implementing the focus groups and analyzing and disseminating the findings.

Outreach

It is perhaps easiest to recognize the diversity of role opportunities in the service arena. However, universities vary greatly in the depth and breadth of their involvement, largely due to the constraints discussed above. The example here of the Entrepreneurial Growth Resource Center offers an example of functioning under a focused mission that allows for a wide range of outreach activities. All programs must pass through a service screen of two basic questions. First, is the service beneficial to our students? Programs that develop and guide students in entrepreneurial roles receive priority in the allocation of resources. Second, can we offer the program through our students? There are many outreach programs related to entrepreneurship located in urban areas. The university must decide where and how it best adds value with the application of its limited resources while recognizing that the definition of "adding value" is itself a purposeful question. Student outreach roles for the EGRC are separate from those offered through classes. Examples of outreach include:

- researchers and administrative assistants. Students helped to develop a database on more than 130 business assistance programs in the region.
- service providers. Students created a referral service based upon the database. If the requested assistance is not something the students can directly perform, the community client is referred to the most appropriate program.
- teachers. Through programs such as the Students in Free Enterprise or Junior Achievement, students serve as teachers in area high schools. These activities also place the students in positions of role models, illustrating attributes of college student and community volunteer to their eager audiences.

The EGRC case illustrates how many of the resources of a business school – research, experiential learning activities, and staffed outreach – can serve both the scholarly and citizen roles of the university. No single institution can perform all these roles with equal impact. Private institutions may enjoy less access to certain state-funded assistance programs. However, they may have other resources to offer, such as highly loyal and successful alumni willing to help their alma mater and a great cause at the same time. For example, at

Marquette University they serve as mentors, angel investors, and class visitors for executive education directed towards the inner city. The challenge we all face is to tailor these possibilities to our own institutional contexts.

References

Abrahamson, E. (1996) "Management fashion," *Academy of Management Review*, 21(1): 254–285.

Abrahamson, E. and Fairchild, G. (1999) "Management fashion: lifecycles, triggers, and collective learning processes," *Administrative Science Quarterly*, 44: 708–740.

Aldrich, H. (1973) "Employment opportunities for blacks in the black ghetto: the role of white-owned businesses," *American Journal of Sociology*, 78: 1403–1425.

Aldrich, H. (1979) "Asian shopkeepers as middleman minority: a study of small businesses in Wandsworth," in Eversley, D. and Evans, A. (eds) *Inner City Employment*, pp. 389–407.

Aldrich, H. (1999) *Organizations Evolving*, Thousand Oaks, CA: Sage.

Becker, G. (1971) *The Economics of Discrimination*, Chicago, IL: University of Chicago Press.

Boston Consulting Group in partnership with the Initiative for a Competitive Inner City (1998) *The Business Case for Pursuing Retail Opportunities in the Inner City*, The Boston Consulting Group.

Coleman, J. (1988) "Social capital in the creation of human capital," *American Journal of Sociology*, 94: S95–S120.

Fairchild, G. and Robinson, J. (2002) "Social brokerage in cities: urban entrepreneurs and the techniques they use to cross labor market social boundaries," Working Paper.

Federal Reserve (2003) "Remarks by Chairman Alan Greenspan; the Federal Reserve System's community affairs research conference, sustainable community development: what works, what doesn't, and why," Washington, DC, March 28, 2003.

Fisher, C. (1997) "City lights beckon to business," *American Demographics*, 19(10): 40–47.

Granovetter, M. (1985) "Economic action and social structure: the problem of embeddedness," *American Journal of Sociology*, 91(3): 481–510.

Hirschman, A. (1958) *The Strategy of Economic Development*, New Haven, CT: Yale University Press.

Holzer, H. (1991) "The spatial mismatch hypothesis: what has the evidence shown?" *Urban Studies*, 28: 105–122.

Ibarra, H. (1995) "Personal networks of women and minorities in management: a conceptual framework," *Academy of Management Review*, 18(1): 56–87.

Ibarra, H. (1992) "Race, opportunity, and diversity of social circles in managerial networks," *Academy of Management Journal*, 38: 673–703.

Inc. magazine (2000) "The Inner City 100: The list," *Inc.* 22(7): 129–138.

Kanter, R.M. (1977) *Men and Women of the Corporation*, New York, NY: Basic Books.

Kanter, R.M. (1995) *World Class: Thriving Locally in a Global Economy*, New York, NY: Simon and Schuster.

Kanter, R.M. (1999) "From spare change to real change: the social sector as beta site for business innovation," *Harvard Business Review*, 77(3): 122–132.

Nelson, R. (1956) "A theory of the low level equilibrium trap in underdeveloped economies," *American Economic Review*, 46: 894–908.

Porter, M. (1995) "The competitive advantage of the inner city," *Harvard Business Review*, 73(3): 55–71.

Portes, A. and Sensebrenner, J. (1993) "Embeddedness and immigration: notes on the social determinants of economic action," *American Journal of Sociology*, 98: 1320–1350.

Rosenstein-Rodan, P. (1943) "Problems of industrialization of eastern and south-eastern Europe," *Economic Journal*, 53(210/211): 202–211

Thurow, L. (1969) *Poverty and Discrimination*. Washington, DC: Brookings Institution.

U.S. Department of Commerce, Bureau of the Census (2000) Census of Population and Housing: Summary Tape File 3B. Washington, DC: U.S. Department of Commerce, Bureau of the Census.

Vernon, R. (1963) *Metropolis, 1985: An Interpretation of the Findings of the New York Metropolitan Region Study*, Garden City, NY: Anchor.

Wacquant, L. (1996) "Red belt, black belt: racial division, class inequality, and the state in the French urban periphery and the American ghetto," in Mingione E. (ed.) *Urban Poverty and the "Underclass": A Reader*, Oxford and New York: Basil Blackwell, pp. 234–274.

Wilson, W. (1996) *When Work Disappears: The World of the New Urban Poor*. New York, NY: Alfred A. Knopf.

PART FIVE

Entrepreneurship types

Chapter 16

Lisa K. Gundry

DePaul University

Miriam Ben-Yoseph

DePaul University

WOMEN ENTREPRENEURS IN THE NEW MILLENNIUM: RECENT PROGRESS AND FUTURE DIRECTIONS FOR RESEARCH, ENTREPRENEURSHIP DEVELOPMENT, AND TEACHING

Introduction: the emergence and growth of women-owned businesses as an economic force

DURING THE LAST TWO DECADES, women have entered the field of entrepreneurship in greatly increasing numbers. With the emergence and growth of their businesses, they have contributed to the global economy and to their surrounding communities. The routes women have followed to take leadership roles in business are varied; yet, more likely than not, most women business owners have overcome or worked to avoid obstacles and challenges in creating their businesses. The presence of women in the workplace driving small and entrepreneurial organizations has had a tremendous impact on employment and on business environments world-wide.

By the year 2002, women entrepreneurs had entered many industries and sectors. Many of the earlier obstacles to women's business success have been removed, yet some still remain. Many research questions have been posed, and investigators have examined the economic and social impact of women's business ownership. Further, there has been much progress in the training and development of women entrepreneurs within public policy and academic programs. Finally, scholars of entrepreneurship and small business have studied the influences of and the impact on business ownership by women. The number of research studies has grown since the 1980s, when scholars and policy-makers first cast their attention toward women entrepreneurs.

This chapter reviews recent progress in the field of women's entrepreneurship and examines the following questions

- what is the status of women entrepreneurs in 2002?
- in what economic sectors do women found their businesses?
- what are the characteristics of women entrepreneurs and their businesses?
- what are women's motivations for entrepreneurship?
- what factors influence the strategic growth of women-owned businesses?
- how can women's entrepreneurship experiences be incorporated into courses, case studies, and best practices in undergraduate and graduate programs?
- what remaining questions should be asked about women's entrepreneurship?
- what research needs to be conducted to move the field forward?

The review of the field presented in this chapter is not to be construed as an exhaustive discussion of all the work that has been done. Rather, we have selected representative publications in each of the domains mentioned to summarize the progress that has been made. From those publications we derived a set of questions that may guide future entrepreneurial development, academic research, and teaching within this area. In 1996, a comprehensive review of current research on women entrepreneurs was published by Starr and Yudkin (Wellesley College Center for Research on Women). Our attempt is not to duplicate their efforts. The focus of this chapter is on significant developments that have occurred between the mid-1990s and the start of 2002 (Gundry *et al.* 2002a, 2002b). There still remain many questions, however, and this chapter concludes with ideas and propositions to be investigated in the future.

The status of women entrepreneurs

By the end of 1999, there were 9.1 million women-owned businesses in the United States. According to the National Foundation for Women Business Owners (NFWBO), a non-profit research and leadership development foundation affiliated with the National Association of Women Business Owners, during the 12-year period from 1987 to 1999, the number of women-owned businesses increased by 103 percent nationwide, and the employment provided by these firms grew by 320 percent, while sales grew by 436 percent (NFWBO 2001a). At the end of 1999, women-owned firms represented nearly 40 percent of all firms in the United States and employed approximately 27.5 million people. In 1996, the Small Business Administration (SBA) reported that the growth in the number of women-owned businesses exceeded the national average in nearly every region of the country, with higher growth occurring in the southern states (Haynes and Helms 2000).

The NFWBO (1999) also reported that women are starting businesses at a faster rate than their male counterparts. In the United States and Canada, the number of women-owned firms has increased at about twice the national rate. The NFWBO also reported that, in 1996, 13 percent of women business owners in the United States were women of color. In total that year, there were nearly 1.1 million firms owned by minority-women employing nearly 1.7 million people and generating more than $184.2 billion in sales. Clearly, the number of women-owned businesses has grown dramatically, and, as the results of the NFWBO studies show, the economic impact of women-owned businesses is substantial (Hadary 1997).

In what economic sectors do women found their businesses?

Women entrepreneurs can be found in every sector of the economy. The top growth industries for women-owned firms between 1987 and 1999 were construction, wholesale trade, transportation/communications, agribusiness, and manufacturing (NFWBO 2001b). Traditionally, women entrepreneurs were more likely to be found in retail and service businesses, but by the end of the 1990s women were entering non-traditional business sectors in greater numbers.

For example, the NFWBO found that more Latina entrepreneurs own firms in construction, accounting, engineering, other professional services, and manufacturing than owned businesses such as hotels, restaurants, and bars (NFWBO 1998). With the rising number of women entrepreneurs starting businesses in non-traditional fields, researchers are now able to make comparisons between sectors. In this way, we can begin to determine whether differences in such areas as performance, firm structure, and strategic orientation are attributable to the sector in which the entrepreneur operates. In one study, researchers found that the level of sales and perceived performance is higher for women in non-traditional industries, although the women in traditional industries perceived higher levels of financial support (Engelbrecht et al. 1996). More research is needed on women-owned businesses in non-traditional industries, in comparison with firms in service or retail (Starr and Yudkin 1996).

What are the characteristics of women entrepreneurs and their businesses?

Women take many paths to business ownership. The broad classification of women business owners includes women who found, inherit, or acquire a business, women who start businesses with spouses or business partners and are at the forefront or behind the scenes, and women who build fast-growing firms, as well as those whose businesses are part-time or slow growing (Starr and Yudkin 1996). Early research on women entrepreneurs suggested that significant differences existed between female and male entrepreneurs. However, more recent studies have shown that there are far more similarities than differences between women and men entrepreneurs in terms of psychological and demographic characteristics (Birley 1989).

Many of the demographic predictors of entrepreneurship are identical for women and men. The dominant predictors of success for women entrepreneurs are work experience and years of self-employment (Schiller and Crewson 1997). In a cross-sectional national study of 3,000 men- and women-owned businesses, sales levels were similar for both, as was the number of years to break even (Hisrich *et al.* 1997). However, women rated economic necessity and recognition more significantly as business goals. In a recent investigation of the effect of educational level on business survival, owners who had four or more years of college and ten or more years of prior work experience were more likely to survive the first few years (Boden and Nucci 2000). Evidence also exists that women-owned businesses are more likely to remain in business than the average United States firm (NFWBO 2001a).

It has been suggested in the past that women-owned firms under-perform at the aggregate level in relation to firms owned by men. However, a recent comprehensive test of 4,200 Swedish entrepreneurs found no support for this underperformance hypothesis (Du Rietz and Henrekson 2000). The authors do state that women entrepreneurs have, on average, a weaker preference for sales growth. Does this suggest that women owners have different preferences and goals for their businesses? And, if so, does industry or strategic orientation matter? The Engelbrecht *et al.* study (1996) found that women in non-traditional industries perceived money as a preferred outcome expectation. Brush (1992) hypothesized that women view their businesses as a cooperative network of relationships rather than as a distinct profit-generating entity.

This network extends beyond the business into the entrepreneur's relationships with her family and the community. In a cross-cultural study of women entrepreneurs in the United States, Romania, and Poland, this was corroborated. Women reported that their management styles emphasized open communication and participative decision-making, and their business goals reflected a concern for the community in which the business operated (Gundry and Ben-Yoseph 1998). In the last few years, we have seen research focus move away from differentiating women from men entrepreneurs in the wake of findings that the groups are not dissimilar. Although some strides have been made in understanding how women entrepreneurs and their firms may differ from one another (e.g. consideration of industry, strategic focus, or culture), more work is needed to determine whether those characteristics influence firm outcome and survival.

Brush (1997), looking to the future, identified additional areas of opportunity for women entrepreneurs and their organizations: technology, which influences the ability of entrepreneurs to work from home and contributes to the ownership of virtual companies; women's management style, which is influencing the overall business environment; and employment policies, which contribute to the effectiveness of businesses as the workforce goes through profound changes (Brush 1997).

What are women's motivations for entrepreneurship?

The increase in the number of women entrepreneurs is, at least in part, attributable to the "glass ceiling" phenomenon that prevents women from rising above a certain organizational level (Daily *et al.* 1999). The impact of the glass ceiling on women's careers has been documented by a number of studies (U.S. Department of Labor 1995). This has led to an increasing number of women who abandon large organizations and join entrepreneurial organizations as owners or employees. According to Julie Weeks, director of research at NFWBO (1998), 44 percent of women business owners who left their former positions because of the glass ceiling believed that their contributions were not recognized, compared with 17 percent of men business owners.

Thus, starting their own businesses enables women to use, satisfy, and maintain high levels of skill, as perhaps they could not when working for a corporation (Alvarez and Meyer 1998). Women also cite layoffs, the ability to make one's own decisions, and the need for more flexible working hours to accommodate family demands as reasons for starting their own businesses. Boden (1996) and Carr (1996) found that having young children was a strong positive influence on women's self-selection of entrepreneurship. Additional motivation comes from the belief that the world can be different and that their businesses can provide a means to change things and make a difference for other women (Ben-Yoseph, Gundry and Maslyk-Musial 1994). Results from cross-cultural studies indicate that women from Eastern and Central European countries go into business ownership as a means of escaping unemployment (Ben-Yoseph and Gundry 1998; Lisowska 1998). Israeli women opt for business ownership as a way of achieving economic parity because occupational segregation and wage disparities between men and women are much greater in Israel than in the United States (Lerner *et al.* 1997). More work is needed to examine the effect of entrepreneurial motivation on sustained entrepreneurship, especially in the stages beyond start-up (Bhave 1994; Kuratko *et al.* 1997).

What factors influence the strategic growth of women-owned businesses?

Contemporary research on entrepreneurial growth strategies of women business owners has focused on the entrepreneur's willingness to grow and on strategic activities (Kim and Mauborgne 1997). For example, the presence of good working relationships with customers, financiers, and other constituents to the business has also been reported to be related to effective growth strategies (Kamau *et al.* 1999).

Research has shown that women entrepreneurs who headed high-growth-oriented businesses had a stronger commitment to the success of their businesses, a greater willingness to sacrifice on behalf of their business, earlier planning for growth, and adequate capitalization, and used a team-based form of organization design. These women reported strategic intentions emphasizing market growth and technological change (Gundry and Welsch 2001). It has been suggested in a recent study (Cliff 1998) that women entrepreneurs prefer a managed approach to business growth as opposed to following more risky growth strategies.

Since Starr and Yudkin's (1996) recommendation for more studies of the preconditions and strategies for growth of women-owned businesses, there has been some progress. However, there are still more questions. Because of strong interest in the high-growth firm within the field of entrepreneurship, this area may be a focus for more research in the future.

Teaching about women's entrepreneurship at the college and university level

Two issues are discussed here related to entrepreneurship education and women entrepreneurs in higher education. The first concerns the integration of issues related to women entrepreneurs into general entrepreneurship courses, and the second concerns courses designed to focus on women entrepreneurs (Gundry *et al.* 2002b).

With respect to the first concern, most entrepreneurship textbooks published since the mid-1990s have at least a section or a chapter devoted to women entrepreneurs (Kuratko and Welsch 1994). This suggests that some progress has been made in including the characteristics, needs, and performance outcomes of women-owned businesses in entrepreneurship curricula. However, there still exists too little representation of women in leadership roles within materials used in entrepreneurship classes. Brush (1997) found that the Harvard Business Case Catalogue featured women entrepreneurs as decision-makers (not necessarily as business founders or owners) in fewer than 10 percent of its entrepreneurial cases. While some progress has been made since 1997, there is still a need for the development and inclusion of cases and other supplementary materials that showcase the experiences of women entrepreneurs across industries, growth stages, and cultures. This would enable the entrepreneurs profiled in course materials to approximate the actual composition of entrepreneurs nationwide, perhaps even world-wide. The purpose of this is to allow our students (prospective entrepreneurs) to draw on contemporary experiences, processes, and models in forming their own entrepreneurial strategies.

With regard to the second concern, few courses at the university level focus primarily (rather than in just one or two class sessions) on women entrepreneurs. One such course, Women Entrepreneurs and Managers Across Cultures, has been offered by the authors at DePaul University. The course integrates culture, gender, and work focusing on challenges and opportunities faced by women managers and women entrepreneurs in international settings (Ben-Yoseph and Gundry 1997). Other examples include a course on Diversity Issues in Entrepreneurship at the University of St. Thomas, which focuses on women and minority entrepreneurs, and courses offered through the Center for Women Entrepreneurs at Columbia College in South Carolina, targeted specifically to the needs of women business owners (Gundry *et al.* 2002b). Of course, there may exist other courses offered at colleges and universities, but to our awareness there was no centralized source of information to guide research in this area at the time this chapter was prepared.

A study on the infrastructure of women's entrepreneurship education (Katz and Gundry 1997) revealed that colleges and universities make diverse efforts to support women's entrepreneurship, often without using the formal mechanism of a center. The Department of Management and Institute for Women's Leadership at Simmons College co-sponsors research and program conferences for women's entrepreneurship; other schools using a similar approach include Kellogg School at Northwestern University in Evanston, Illinois, Wharton School at the University of Pennsylvania, and Anderson School of Business at the University of California at Los Angeles. Women's entrepreneurship as an academic domain tends to be focused most strongly on research, less strongly on non-credit outreach programs, and least strongly on for-credit programs (Katz and Gundry 1997).

Future developments: what questions remain?

As we have seen in this chapter, since the mid-1990s new knowledge has been gained about the progress, opportunities, and challenges within women's entrepreneurship. There remain some important questions to be asked. We hope they will trigger even more questions, debate, and research that can be disseminated and integrated into entrepreneurship programs in higher education:

● is there an interactional set of entrepreneurial attitudes, motivations, and actions? Much of the research in this field examines single issues (e.g. financing barriers, growth strategies, and psychological motivations) within one cultural context. Researchers have already begun to examine the interaction between, for example, entrepreneurial roles and roles outside the business for women entrepreneurs (Gundry and Ben-Yoseph 1998; Ufuk and Ozgen 2001). Future work should expand the examination of the multiple variables that potentially influence performance in women-owned businesses.

● how are women entrepreneurs discovering business opportunities? Are there conditions that seem to make more of a difference, such as personal motivations, organizational experiences, or cultural/community influences? Studies have shown that women entrepreneurs often undertake leadership roles in volunteer organizations and are strongly motivated to engage in philanthropy (NFWBO 2000; McGeer 2001), and these experiences can lead to continued business opportunities through greater exposure within communities local and beyond.

● what is the influence of entrepreneurship on women's families and the greater communities in which they live? And, most important, how does this influence differ in various countries around the world? As early as 1990, Salganicoff noted that the boundaries between the firm and the family tend to be indistinct for women heading family businesses. Research in this area has included, and should continue to expand on, issues related to personal identity and role conflict (Salganicoff 1990), access to capital and succession planning (Harveston et al. 1996), and the effects of integration of the firm and the family on women's lives (Gundry and Ben-Yoseph 1998).

- what are the specific challenges faced by women entrepreneurs who wish to internationalize their businesses and participate in the global economy? Even though it is clear that international careers prepare both men and women for entrepreneurship in global settings, the number of women in high-level international management positions remains very low in all countries. Women entrepreneurs in transitioning economies, for example, have been found to have unique needs for a support system that can develop a set of best practices and benchmarked samples from countries with similar cultural, economic, and historical contexts (Bliss and Garratt 2001). One of the key challenges women entrepreneurs faced during the 1990s involved perceptions that they could not be taken seriously (NFWBO 1994), and that women-owned firms are less successful, less credit-worthy, and less innovative (Brush 1997). By the end of the 1990s, some researchers concluded that two hurdles remained for women entrepreneurs: correcting these perceptions and developing networks and mentors (Davis and Long 1999). Future research should examine ways in which women business owners can increase their organizationally legitimated credibility (Gundry et al. 2002a) both inside and outside women's businesses.

- since women entrepreneurs across cultures tend to link work, family, and the environment in which they conduct business, should different measures for performance or success be considered for women entrepreneurs? Future research may also help us better understand how risk-taking relates to the type of business started. Do women take fewer risks than men or are they forced to take less risk and enter traditional businesses because capital is even less available to them in non-traditional businesses (Anna et al. 2000)? How does this play out in different cultures?

In conclusion, as the field of women's entrepreneurship evolved, researchers, educators, and entrepreneurs tended to function independently of one another, each focusing on a specific aspect of interest. Even though their unique contributions are worthwhile, the field is now benefiting from the synthesis of multiple perspectives, preventing oversimplification of complex issues and the persistence of ethnocentric beliefs. Our conclusion is therefore encouraging: we have seen that with the proliferation of educational programs, research support, policy development, and an eventual increase in financial opportunities as markets and economies recover, more and more women around the world will embark on entrepreneurial paths. With continued scholarship to explore and further identify relevant and poignant questions in this area, the effects of these changes have great potential to not only change women's careers and lives, but to enhance our knowledge and understanding of entrepreneurship processes globally.

References

Alvarez, S.A. and Meyer, G.D. (1998) "Why do women become entrepreneurs?" *Frontiers of Entrepreneurship Research*, Wellesley, MA: Babson College.

Anna, A.L., Chandler, G.N., Jansen, E., and Mero, N.P. (2000) "Women business owners in traditional and non-traditional industries," *Journal of Business Venturing*, 15: 279–303.

Ben-Yoseph, M. and Gundry, L.K. (1997) "Teaching about women managers and women entrepreneurs across cultures," *Journal of Developmental Entrepreneurship*, 2(2): 147–154.

Ben-Yoseph, M. and Gundry, L.K. (1998) "The future of work: implications for women entrepreneurs in transition economies," *Kobieta I Biznes*, 3–4: 59–64.

Ben-Yoseph, M., Gundry, L.K., and Maslyk-Musial, E. (1994) "Women entrepreneurs in the United States and Poland," *Kobieta I Biznes*, 2–3: 26–29.

Bhave, M. (1994) "A process model of entrepreneurial venture creation," *Journal of Business Venturing*, 8: 223–242.

Birley, S. (1989) "Female entrepreneurs: are they really different?" *Journal of Small Business Management*, 27(1): 32–37.

Bliss, R.T. and Garratt, N.L. (2001) "Supporting women entrepreneurs in transitioning economies," *Journal of Small Business Management*, 39(4): 335–344.

Boden, R. (1996) "Gender and self-employment selection: an empirical assessment," *Journal of Socio-Economics*, 25(6): 671–682.

Boden, R. and Nucci, A. (2000) "On the survival prospects of men's and women's new business ventures," *Journal of Business Venturing*, 15(4): 347–362.

Brush, C. (1992) "Research on women business owners: past trends, a new perspective and future directions," *Entrepreneurship: Theory and Practice*, 16(4): 5–30.

Brush, C. (1997) "Women-owned businesses: obstacles and opportunities," *Journal of Developmental Entrepreneurship*, 2(1): 1–24.

Carr, D. (1996) "Two paths to self-employment? Women's and men's self-employment in the United States, 1980," *Work and Occupations*, 23(1): 26–53.

Cliff, J.E. (1998) "Does one size fit all? Exploring the relationship between attitudes towards growth, gender, and business size," *Journal of Business Venturing*, 13(6): 523–542.

Daily, C., Certo, S., and Dalton, D. (1999) "Entrepreneurial ventures as an avenue to the top? Assessing the advancement of female CEOs and directors in the *Inc.* 100," *Journal of Developmental Entrepreneurship*, 4(1): 19–34.

Davis, S.E.M. and Long, D.D. (1999) "Women entrepreneurs: what do they need?" *Business & Economic Review*, 45(4): 25–26.

Du Rietz, A. and Henrekson, M. (2000) "Testing the female underperformance hypothesis," *Small Business Economics*, 14(1): 1–10.

Engelbrecht, A., Chandler, G., and Jansen, R. (1996) "Women business owners in traditional and nontraditional industries," paper presented at the Academy of Management annual meeting, Cincinnati, OH.

Gundry, L.K. and Ben-Yoseph, M. (1998) "Women entrepreneurs in Romania, Poland, and the U.S: cultural and family influences on strategy and growth," *Family Business Review*, 7(3): 273–286.

Gundry, L.K., Ben-Yoseph, M., and Posig, M. (March 2002a) "Contemporary perspectives on women's entrepreneurship: a review and strategic recommendations," *Journal of Enterprising Culture*, 10(1): 67–86.

Gundry, L.K., Ben-Yoseph, M., and Posig, M. (2002b) "The status of women's entrepreneurship: pathways to future entrepreneurship development and education," *New England Journal of Entrepreneurship*, 5(1): 39–50.

Gundry, L.K. and Welsch, H.P. (1994) "Differences in familial influence among women-owned businesses," *Family Business Review*, 7(3): 273–286.

Gundry, L.K. and Welsch, H.P. (2001) "The ambitious entrepreneur: high-growth strategies of women-owned enterprises," *Journal of Business Venturing*, 16(5): 453–470.

Hadary, S. (1997) "Women-owned businesses: a powerful and growing economic force," *Business Credit*, 99(4): 71–72.

Harveston, P.D., Lyden, J.A., and Davis, P.S. (1996) "Toward a succession paradigm: a comparison of male- and female-led family businesses," paper presented at the annual meeting of the Academy of Management, Cincinnati, OH.

Haynes, P.J. and Helms, M. (2000) "When bank loans launch new ventures: a profile of the growing female entrepreneur segment," *Bank Marketing*, 32(5): 28–34.

Hisrich, R., Brush, C., Good, D., and DeSouza, G. (1997) "Performance in entrepreneurial ventures. Does gender matter?" *Frontiers of Entrepreneurship Research*, Wellesley, MA: Babson College.

Kamau, D.G., McLean, G.N., and Ardishvili, A. (1999) "Perceptions of business growth by women entrepreneurs," *Frontiers of Entrepreneurship Research*, Wellesley, MA: Babson College.

Katz, J.A. and Gundry, L.K. (1997) "The infrastructure of entrepreneurship education: implications for women's entrepreneurship," report prepared for the Committee of 200.

Kim, W.C. and Mauborgne, R. (1997) "Value innovation: the strategic logic of high growth," *Harvard Business Review*, 75(1): 102–112.

Kuratko, D.F., Hornsby, J.S., and Naffziger, D.W. (1997) "An examination of owner's goals in sustaining entrepreneurship," *Journal of Small Business Management*, 35(1): 24–33.

Kuratko, D.F. and Welsch, H.P. (1994) *Entrepreneurial Strategies: Text and Cases*, Fort Worth, TX: Harcourt Brace.

Lerner, M., Brush, C., and Hisrich, R. (1997) "Israeli women entrepreneurs: an examination of factors affecting performance," *Journal of Business Venturing*, 12(4): 315–339.

Lisowska, E. (1998) "Entrepreneurship as a response to female unemployment and discrimination against women in the workplace," *Kobieta I Biznes*, 3–4: 54–58.

McGeer, B. (2001) "Bank programs target women biz owners," *American Banker*, 166(87): 8–10.

National Foundation for Women Business Owners (1994) *Credibility, Creativity and Independence: The Greatest Challenges and Biggest Rewards of Business Ownership Among Women*. Washington, DC: National Foundation for Women Business Owners.

National Foundation for Women Business Owners (1998) *Women Business Owners of Color: Challenges and Accomplishments*, Washington, DC: National Foundation for Women Business Owners.

National Foundation for Women Business Owners (1999) *Characteristics of Women Entrepreneurs Worldwide Are Revealed*, Washington, DC: National Foundation for Women Business Owners.

National Foundation for Women Business Owners (2000) *Survey Finds Business Owners are Philanthropic Leaders*, Washington, DC: National Foundation for Women Business Owners.

National Foundation for Women Business Owners (NFWBO) (2001a) *Key Facts*, Washington, DC: National Foundation for Women Business Owners.

National Foundation for Women Business Owners (2001b) *Entrepreneurial Vision in Action: Exploring Growth Among Women- and Men-Owned Firms*, Washington, DC: National Foundation for Women Business Owners.

Salganicoff, M. (1990) "Women in family business: challenges and opportunities," *Family Business Review*, 2: 125–137.

Schiller, B.R. and Crewson, P. (1997) "Entrepreneurial origins: a longitudinal inquiry," *Economic Inquiry*, 35(3): 523–531.

Starr, J. and Yudkin, M. (1996) *Women Entrepreneurs: A Review of Current Research*, Wellesley, MA: Center for Research on Women.

Ufuk, H. and Ozgen, O. (2001) "Interaction between the business and family lives of women entrepreneurs in Turkey," *Journal of Business Ethics*, 31(2): 95–106.

U.S. Department of Labor (1995) "Good for business: making full use of the nation's human capital," Glass Ceiling Commission, March.

Chapter 17

Steve Taplin

Taplin Enterprises, LLC

SERIAL ENTREPRENEURSHIP: AN IN-DEPTH LOOK AT THE PHENOMENON OF HABITUAL ENTREPRENEURS

Introduction

A FREQUENTLY RECURRING THEME in entrepreneurship research has been the existence of two main types of entrepreneurs: the "crafts-man" and the "opportunist." The "craftsman" is motivated by a desire for auto-nomy, while the "opportunist" is motivated by a desire for financial gain and the opportunity to build a successful organization (Wright *et al.* 1997a). Serial entrepreneurs are a unique subset of entrepreneurs who, depending on their type, can fall into both categories. Serial entrepreneurs are defined in this chapter as entrepreneurs who sell their original businesses but at a later date, inherit, establish, and/or purchase other businesses (Westhead and Wright 1998b). This special breed of business people enjoys the challenge of constantly starting new ventures. Many entrepreneurs have thrived in this environment, taken advantage of the increasingly favorable tax climate, and made millions.

The research on entrepreneurship in general has received much scrutiny over the last few decades. To date, not much progress has been made. Little is known about serial entrepreneurs even though researchers agree that there are many benefits that can be gained and lessons learned from studying and under-standing this special breed of entrepreneur. This chapter pulls together the existing research on the phenomenon of serial entrepreneurship, identifies the major gaps in the literature, and attempts to provide an overview and analysis of the topic.

Defining serial entrepreneurship

Habitual (serial) entrepreneurs have existed since the dawn of industrialization (Scranton 1993). In 1991, Starr and Bygrave pointed out that there did not seem to be a generally accepted definition of serial entrepreneurship. This is still the case. The most common definition suggests that serial entrepreneurs are those entrepreneurs who have sold or closed their original businesses but at a later date have inherited, established, and/or purchased other businesses (Westhead and Wright 1998b). Or, stated differently, they own one business after another but effectively own only one business at a time (Hall 1995). Serial entrepreneurs typically desire to exit from an initial venture when entrepreneurial opportunities are perceived to have been exhausted. Once they leave the firm, they search for new possibilities with a new venture (Wright *et al.* 1997a). Serial entrepreneurs are known to start several firms, some of which are successful and others are not.

Many researchers have used different terms and definitions to describe the different types of entrepreneurs. Figure 17.1 shows an overview of the various types of entrepreneurs: nascent, novice, habitual, serial, and portfolio.

The following section provides definitions for the various types of entrepreneurs that are shown in Figure 17.1. Some of the categories have multiple definitions because of the terminology used by multiple entrepreneurship researchers.

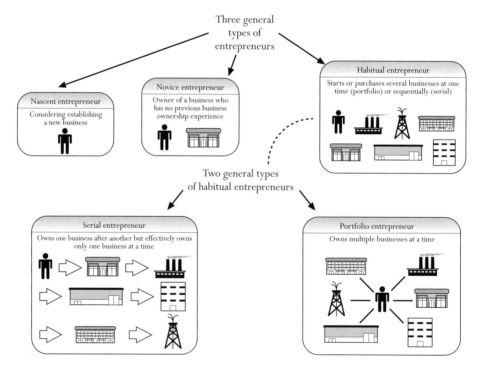

Figure 17.1 Overview of the types of entrepreneurs

Nascent entrepreneurs

Individuals who are considering the establishment of a new business (Ucbasaran *et al.* 2001).

Novice entrepreneurs

Also referred to as beginner, first time, or rookie entrepreneurs. These individuals currently own one business and have no prior business ownership experience as a founder, an inheritor, or a purchaser (Westhead and Wright 1998a).

Habitual entrepreneurs

Also referred to as business generators and experienced founders. These are individuals who have established, inherited, and/or purchased more than one business (Westhead and Wright 1998a). Stated differently, they start or purchase several businesses at one time or sequentially and are identified on the basis of two dimensions: whether a new or existing business is involved and whether the entrepreneurial act is sequential (serial) or concurrent (portfolio) (Ucbasaran *et al.* 2000).

Serial entrepreneurs (subset of "habitual entrepreneurs")

Also referred to as venture repeaters and opportunist entrepreneurs. These are individuals who have sold or closed their original businesses but at a later date have inherited, established, and/or purchased other businesses (Westhead and Wright 1998b). Or, as defined by Hall (1995), they are individuals who own one business after another but effectively own only one business at a time.

Portfolio entrepreneurs (subset of "habitual entrepreneurs")

Also referred to as multiple (business) entrepreneurs and parallel entrepreneurs. These are individuals who have established more than one business but still own the most recent businesses established prior to the start-up of their current, new, and/or independent ventures (Kolvereid and Bullvag 1993). Or, as stated by Westhead and Wright (1998b), they are individuals who have retained their original businesses but at a later date have inherited, established, and/or purchased other businesses (Westhead and Wright 1998b).

Types of serial entrepreneurs

Are there different types of serial entrepreneurs? Wright *et al.* (1997a) published an article in the *British Journal of Management* titled, "Serial entrepreneurs" that suggested that indeed various types do exist. Wright *et al.* (1997a) believed that serial entrepreneurial behavior falls into two broad groups: venture repeaters and opportunist serial venturers. They define these groups as follows:

1   venture repeaters are entrepreneurs who undertake a second venture primarily for defensive reasons. This group tends to be reactive, effectively undertaking a second venture because there were few obvious alternatives. They tend to have subsequent ventures in the same sector or even in the same firm, often as a reflection of loyalty to that firm.
2   opportunist serial venturers are entrepreneurs who aim to achieve rapid growth of their ventures. This group has common features in that capital gain and the challenge of developing a business are frequently important factors. They are generally proactive between first and second ventures in searching for a suitable opportunity.

Are there any other forms of serial entrepreneurs? In 2003, Diana Hicks introduced the term "serial innovators" to describe small firms that are extremely innovative and continually successful at attaining patents. Hicks' report explains that small firms are younger than large firms, but are not considered new start-ups. She claimed that they are distinguished from other innovative small firms by their innovative success and persistence, and from large patenting firms by their concentration on high-quality and leading-edge technical change that builds on a broad array of outside knowledge. The open question remains: are "serial innovator" firms typically started by serial entrepreneurs?

Backgrounds of serial entrepreneurs

Much evidence suggests that characteristics and motivations differ between the various types of entrepreneurs.

Characteristics

Numerous researchers have tried to collect data that suggests common characteristics of serial entrepreneurs. Cowe cited that serial entrepreneurs tend to be starters, people who are extremely good in the early stages of a business, but less so at the maintenance work: "They are brilliant at leading from the front and not so good at being in the background making sure the machinery works (1988: 86)." He also noted that they are typically the leaders of a team and very good at transmitting the vision.

Birley and Westhead (1993) suggested that serial entrepreneurs are typically younger than other entrepreneurs when they start their first business and are more likely to have gained university level degrees. They are typically younger than their counterparts, more likely to be continuing a tradition, more likely to have emphasized following role models, and more likely to have used personal savings at the launch of their businesses.

Westhead and Wright (1998a) suggested that serial entrepreneurs are most likely to be concerned with accumulating wealth and gaining recognition for their entrepreneurial activities. Serial entrepreneurs are significantly more likely than novice founders to have worked in small firms with fewer than 100 employees prior to the start-up of their venture.

Some of the common characteristics that many of the previously cited researchers have suggested are that serial entrepreneurs have a strong will to win, a love of responsibility, a need to be in control, and excellent leadership skills, are hard workers, often have a background in a volatile industry, and have had early success and a strong track record.

Motivations

All of the different types of entrepreneurs tend to have unique motivations for their chosen activities. Serial entrepreneurs tend to have stronger preferences for innovation, greater propensity for risk-taking, and a higher need for achievement than do novice (or first-time) entrepreneurs (Carland *et al.* 2000). Serial entrepreneurs are sometimes, but not always, motivated by money. Westhead and Wright (1998a) found that the motivations cited by serial entrepreneurs were not the same as those cited by portfolio entrepreneurs. Wright *et al.* (1997a) have suggested that the motivations of habitual (serial) entrepreneurs for owning businesses change over time, with monetary gain becoming less important in subsequent ventures and some owners of second businesses generally desire less risky ventures. The authors also pointed out that habitual entrepreneurs are highly achievement motivated, innovative, and risk-takers.

Motivations for a first venture

A common reason for a first venture is the frustration resulting from working in large, bureaucratic, and political organizations. Ucbasaran *et al.* (2000) also found that financial motivations were a strong factor for entrepreneurs in their first ventures and that risk limitation became more important in subsequent ventures. The authors also found that common motivations for the second start-up were the desire to continue the challenge of owning a successful business, the desire to work closer to family, and the desire to benefit from tax breaks.

Birley and Westhead (1993) stated that the serial entrepreneurs started their first ventures because of a propensity to stress self-achievement, job satisfaction, and personal independence. They also stated that they have a need for approval, personal development, increased wealth, tax reductions, and to follow their role models.

Westhead and Wright (1998a) found that serial entrepreneurs emphasized the need for independence and personal development. After founding a business, an entrepreneur may be less willing to undertake riskier ventures and may reduce the percentage of personal wealth that he/she is willing to commit to a new venture (Westhead and Wright 1998b).

Motivations for second (or subsequent) ventures

Some serial entrepreneurs go directly to their next ventures and some take an indirect path via periods of employment, extended vacations, and other projects. They may start a new venture or explore purchasing an existing business. Westhead and Wright (1998a) suggested that serial entrepreneurs may purchase rather than establish their subsequent ventures in order to achieve ownership of larger businesses. The authors also suggested that there may or may not be a reduction in the emphasis on financial returns in the subsequent ventures and that personal motivations and resources influenced the search process. More than 90 percent of rural and urban serial entrepreneurs reported that they wanted their subsequent businesses to grow in both revenue and employment (Westhead and Wright 1998b). Wright *et al.* (1997a) suggest that serial entrepreneurs tend to be motivated by independence, the desire to run their own company, and wealth creation for their first ventures. For their second ventures, the key motivational factors tend to be the desire to build up a successful business (or turn around a non-successful one), limit their financial risk, and face the challenge of continuing to succeed in their entrepreneurial activities. Table 17.1 provides a summary of the key motivational factors for first and second ventures.

How many serial entrepreneurs have founded successful companies?

Some research suggests that serial entrepreneurs own a very large number (more than one-third) of new firms in many countries (Birley and Westhead 1993; Kolvereid and Bullvag 1993). Wassadorp (2001) suggests that 41 percent of high-growth companies in Europe's 500 List have been founded by serial entrepreneurs. He also found that 81 percent of the CEOs of Americas Inc. 500 list of high-growth companies started their businesses with a plan to go public or sell out to another company after some time, which suggests serial entrepreneurial behavior. Westhead and Wright (1998a) cited research that 51 percent of entrepreneurs in Southern California in 1991 had contributed to the initiation of two or more ventures. However, the data did not suggest whether this was serial or portfolio behavior. Finally, Birley and Westhead (1993) reviewed studies that focused upon new firm founders in the United Kingdom and noted that 12 percent to 36 percent of new businesses were founded by habitual entrepreneurs. However, once again this data did not break down habitual entrepreneurs into serial and portfolio behavior.

Table 17.1 Motivational factors

Motivational factors for first venture
Noticed opportunity to develop a business
Enjoyed exercising management control and getting people to do things
Wealth creation
Strong desire to work on their own
Did not want to retire
Needed to retain job
Always wanted to run own company
Family
Desire to avoid working for large companies
Wanted to have something to hand down to others

Motivational factors for second venture
Desire to build up businesses and add managerial skills
Money not as important, believed they could control their personal financial risk more effectively
Personal commitment became important
Money prime motivation
Ability to limit financial risk by building up a new business in a familiar sector
Wanted to repair and rebuild a company rather than just make money
Desire to continue to build something successful
Enjoys the challenge of helping companies grow, develop to their full potential, and succeed

Source: This table is based on the research by Wright *et al.* (1997a).

How serial entrepreneurs find and put deals together

Why, when, and how certain individuals exploit opportunities appears to be a function of both the opportunity and the nature of the individual (Shane and Venkataraman 2000). Opportunity recognition is a key trait that serial entrepreneurs tend to do extremely well. They are generally more "fine tuned" to identify opportunities than inexperienced entrepreneurs. Venkataraman (1997) highlighted three key reasons for certain individuals recognizing opportunities while others do not: knowledge and information differences, cognitive differences, and behavioral differences. This would suggest that serial entrepreneurs know how and where to obtain useful information, how to interpret and analyze this information to make sound business decisions, and when and how to act appropriately.

Business start-up process

Do serial entrepreneurs prepare business plans? How do their start-up activities differ from those of novice and portfolio entrepreneurs? Alsos and Kolvereid (1998) show a comparison of how novice, serial, and parallel (portfolio) entrepreneurs have handled and prepared for their businesses in the initial stages of the new venture process. Their research suggests that serial founders are typically more likely to prepare a business plan and be devoted full time to their businesses. This research also suggests that they are least likely to apply for bank funding and to apply for any licenses or patents. This implies that serial entrepreneurs are forward thinking, aggressive with their ventures, and willing to put all their time and money in them to help ensure their success.

How do serial entrepreneurs get projects?

There is always a possibility of an entrepreneur being in the right place at the right time. Ucbasaran *et al.* (2001) stated that evidence relating to the search behavior of habitual (serial) entrepreneurs is limited. Low and MacMillan (1998) suggested that networks are an important aspect of the context and process of entrepreneurship. The authors pointed out that serial entrepreneurs may be less likely to engage in proactive search strategies because they can draw upon experiences that worked well in the past and tap into the information and contacts (i.e. their networks) for potential opportunities. Kirzner (1973) suggested that the serial entrepreneurs identify opportunities by being alert to and noticing opportunities that the market presents. Wright *et al.* (1998) suggested that habitual (serial) entrepreneurs are more likely to be proactive in initiating subsequent ventures. Table 17.2 provides a summary of the research by Ucbasaran *et al.* (2000) on the search strategies used by serial entrepreneurs during their first and second ventures.

The data from Table 17.2 suggest many unique search strategies tend to exist for their first ventures; however, the data suggest that for their second ventures, the deals tended to come to them, suggesting reactive as opposed to proactive search strategies. There tends to be conflicting research in this area as the various researches cited above have found very different results.

Business partners

Are serial entrepreneurs "lone rangers" or do they tend to find partners to assist in their ventures? Ucbasaran *et al.* (2001) believe that research on entrepreneurial

Table 17.2 Search strategies

Search strategies for first venture
Used industry-specific experience to set up in the same sector
Desire to be close to home
Searched for deals via the corporate departments of accountancy firms
Searched for venture capitalists who had deals that had gone wrong
Employed in family business

Search strategies for second venture
Searched for opportunities that would not interest large multinational companies
Approached with deal
Came about suddenly when exiting from the first venture

Source: This table is based on the research by Ucbasaran *et al.* (2000).

teams has been neglected. Kamm and Shuman (1990) reviewed several studies and notes that 50 percent of businesses were started by entrepreneurial teams. The performance research by Ucbasaran *et al.* (2000) suggests that serial entrepreneurs are more likely than other entrepreneurs to use teams to acquire expertise and resources. Cooper *et al.* (1994) reinforced this position and stated that the presence of partners can reduce some of the liabilities associated with smaller new businesses. Serial entrepreneurs tend to realize that having business partners can provide many advantages, including more diversified skills and a larger business network, and are seen as more credible by external investors.

Financing

How do serial entrepreneurs obtain financing for their ventures? Do they use their own money, financing from banks or venture capitalists, or other means? Westhead and Wright (1998b) suggested that serial founders generally use more sources of financing than other types of entrepreneurs. These various types of financing include personal savings, credit cards, family, friends, venture capital, and various types of bank loans.

Financing for their first venture

Westhead and Wright (1998b) found that 72 percent of serial founders in urban areas used start-up capital from personal savings and/or their family and friends for the launch of their first ventures. The authors also found that more than 49 percent of serial entrepreneurs in rural areas had used start-up capital funding from banks and financial institutions for the launch of their businesses.

Financing for their subsequent ventures

It is often assumed that serial founders may be able to use some of the proceeds from the sale of the businesses they earlier owned for financing subsequent ventures. During their second venture, serial entrepreneurs often obtain financing (sometimes for the first time) from venture capitalists or financial institutions in order to ensure further business development (Westhead and Wright 1998b).

Surprisingly, few serial entrepreneurs remain loyal to banks that they have used in the past for their personal accounts and previous ventures. This behavior suggests that serial entrepreneurs do not predict long-term relationships.

There do not seem to be many parallels across the various studies. The method of financing used by each serial entrepreneur tends to be different, as it is determined by their backgrounds, personal financial situations, networks, tendencies toward risk, and other personal preferences. The research in this area is very limited and should be a focus for serial entrepreneurial researchers in the future.

Assets and liabilities associated with prior business ownership experience

Going through the business start-up phase successfully or unsuccessfully provides serial entrepreneurs with a unique set of skills, resources, and capabilities that provides significant benefits (and some disadvantages) for a new venture process.

Assets

The main assets of serial entrepreneurs are their ability to build on their expertise in running an independent business, to identify networks appropriate to a particular situation, and to adapt their expertise to new circumstances and their reputations as successful entrepreneurs (Wright *et al.* 1997b). They are also typically more successful at obtaining financing (credibility with financiers). Their experience brings benefits in terms of contacts, knowledge of the new venture process, and knowledge about obtaining finance.

Liabilities

Starr and Bygrave (1991) have suggested that prior business ownership experience may bring a variety of liabilities and that the performance of a subsequent venture may be less successful than that of the first. They found that some experienced entrepreneurs have decreased motivation and lack of flexibility. Westhead and Wright (1998b) suggested that there is a danger that serial entrepreneurs will either attempt to repeat successful actions under changed conditions or simply continue to repeat unsuccessful actions.

As part of their research, Ucbasaran *et al.* (2000) interviewed serial entrepreneurs, asking them how they would describe their assets and liabilities for their subsequent business ventures. The results of these interviews suggest that serial entrepreneurs believe their experience in general provides them with great assets. Surprisingly, the serial entrepreneurs surveyed did not believe that they had any liabilities, which differ from the results of the research by Starr and Bygrave (1991) and Westhead and Wright (1998b). The latter authors' findings suggest that serial entrepreneurs do believe that their previous entrepreneurial experience has been a liability to them at times. The number one reason was that they believed that they could repeat their previous successes in a similar fashion for subsequent ventures, which was not always possible because of different market conditions and variables.

Reasons that serial entrepreneurs exit ventures

It is generally believed that serial entrepreneurs leave ventures by their own choice and are not forced out of the ventures because of poor performance; or, stated differently, they have successfully exited the venture. Dyer (1994), however, argues that it is widely believed that an entrepreneur starts another business only when the first one fails. All entrepreneurs need to determine at some point in the venture process if they will continue in their current venture, engage in subsequent ventures (portfolio behavior), or exit completely from the current venture and move on to the next venture (serial behavior). Whether entrepreneurs exit from a business is dependent on their threshold of performance (Ucbasaran *et al.* 2000).

The desire to exit from an initial venture when the entrepreneurial activities are perceived to have been exhausted seems to be common to serial entrepreneurs. They tend to be more intrigued by the dynamic business start-up process and find it very undesirable to manage an ongoing business for the long term. A common phrase for this type of behavior is the "Grasshopper" versus the "Butterfly." Serial entrepreneurs would be considered the "Grasshoppers" because they "hop" from one venture to another. Portfolio entrepreneurs would be the "Butterflies" because they "expand their wings" (i.e. take on additional businesses). Many of the research studies performed on this topic do not take into consideration why the serial entrepreneurs left their previous ventures. In addition, no research is available that provides any insight as to why serial entrepreneurs buy and sell the same business over and over. This may have significant impact on the results of a survey and is an area where future research should be conducted. Motivations for both serial and non-serial entrepreneurs continue to elude us because there are so many with such complex patterns.

Conclusion

Do we have a comprehensive set of studies on serial entrepreneurship? As mentioned throughout this chapter, very few empirical studies have been conducted and there is virtually no theoretical development concerning serial entrepreneurship. To date, there is not even a generally accepted definition of serial entrepreneurs. Entrepreneurial researchers need to agree to a common terminology, which would lead to more accurate research in the future. Some of the key gaps missing in the current literature on serial entrepreneurship include:

- time sequences between ventures of serial entrepreneurs. Are actions taking place for their new ventures performed randomly, sequentially, or individually driven? Is there a transition period between serial entrepreneurial behaviors that may fall into the category of portfolio entrepreneurs?
- opportunity recognition methods used by serial entrepreneurs. Do the methods used differ on the first ventures versus their tenth one? Does this process get faster and easier as the serial entrepreneur gets more experienced? What happens with the variations of opportunity recognition as the number of start-ups increase? Do the follow-up opportunities come out of networks, angels, or sophisticated investors as the serial entrepreneur gets towards their tenth deal? Are later ventures done on the golf course as opposed to earlier ventures coming out of the newspaper?
- variations in financing across serial entrepreneurs. It is commonly known

that only 1 percent of start-ups are funded by venture capitalists. Are more venture capital deals done in later company start-ups than earlier ones? Are serial entrepreneurs using their second mortgage for both their first, second, and third ventures? What about their seventh or eighth? Is there a maturation process that takes place on the financing techniques as the number of start-ups increase?

● motivations for serial entrepreneurs in later ventures. What are the motivations for their second venture? Will what motivates a serial entrepreneur today necessarily motivate them tomorrow? Does a strong achievement motive exist for all ventures?

It is important that all of these factors are understood so that the behavior can be replicated.

Figure 17.2 provides a suggested model for framing future research. This model breaks down serial entrepreneurship into two areas.

1   Predictors of serial entrepreneurial behavior.
   a Are individuals with a certain background, age, or location more prone toward serial behavior?
   b Does any specific type of prior work experience trigger serial behavior?
   c Are there specific attitudes that constitute serial behavior?
   d What are the real reasons serial entrepreneurs start up businesses?
   e Do serial entrepreneurs start up more businesses during economic downturns, when there are higher levels of unemployment?
   f Are certain industries more prone to serial behavior?
2   Specific traits, processes, and/or procedures that serial entrepreneurs follow.
   a Where do serial entrepreneurs get their opportunity recognition skills and methods?
   b How do serial entrepreneurs' variations in financing differ as they get more experienced?
   c What are the methods and techniques that serial entrepreneurs use to go through the entire business cycle process?
   d How many businesses will a serial entrepreneur own throughout their career? When do they decide to retire?

Trends such as changes in demography, individualization, and information technology are creating more opportunities for innovative entrepreneurship. In a challenging economy, the risks of entrepreneurship will probably increase. Incentives to reward entrepreneurial behavior should be encouraged. Focusing the research on these suggested areas will help to create a more specific and clearer framework for serial entrepreneurial behavior so that others can learn and benefit from the great accomplishments of this subset of entrepreneurs.

This chapter has pointed out many other key areas that need to be explored further in order to gain further understanding of what constitutes serial entrepreneurial behavior. Once this is understood, public policy can be implemented to train entrepreneurs to be more successful, which would have an extremely positive effect on the economy as a whole.

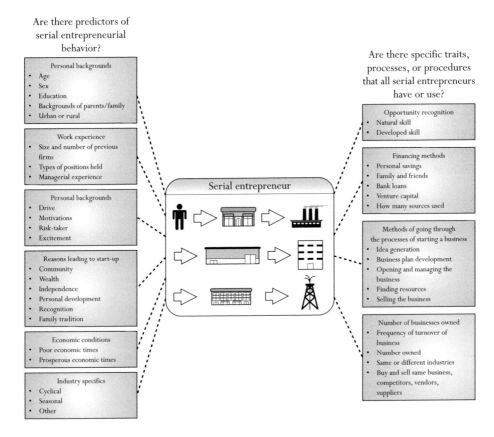

Are there predictors of serial entrepreneurial behavior?

Personal backgrounds
- Age
- Sex
- Education
- Backgrounds of parents/family
- Urban or rural

Work experience
- Size and number of previous firms
- Types of positions held
- Managerial experience

Personal backgrounds
- Drive
- Motivations
- Risk-taker
- Excitement

Reasons leading to start-up
- Community
- Wealth
- Independence
- Personal development
- Recognition
- Family tradition

Economic conditions
- Poor economic times
- Prosperous economic times

Industry specifics
- Cyclical
- Seasonal
- Other

Are there specific traits, processes, or procedures that all serial entrepreneurs have or use?

Serial entrepreneur

Opportunity recognition
- Natural skill
- Developed skill

Financing methods
- Personal savings
- Family and friends
- Bank loans
- Venture capital
- How many sources used

Methods of going through the processes of starting a business
- Idea generation
- Business plan development
- Opening and managing the business
- Finding resources
- Selling the business

Number of businesses owned
- Frequency of turnover of business
- Number owned
- Same or different industries
- Buy and sell same business, competitors, vendors, suppliers

Figure 17.2 Suggested model for framing serial entrepreneurial research

References

Alsos, G.A. and Kolvereid, L. (1998) "The business gestation process of novice, serial, and parallel business founders," *Entrepreneurship Theory and Practice*, 22(4): 101–114.

Birley, S. and Westhead, P. (1993) "A comparison of new businesses established by 'novice' and 'habitual' founders in Great Britain," *International Small Business Journal*, 12(1): 38–60.

Carland, J.C., Carland, J.W., and Stewart, W. (2000) "The indefatigable entrepreneur: a study of the dispositions of multiple venture founders," *Association for Small Business and Entrepreneurship Website*. Online, available at: www.sbaer.uca.edu/research/2000/asbe/00asbe168.htm (accessed April 22, 2003).

Cooper, A.C., Gimeno-Gascon, F.J., and Woo, C.Y. (1994) "Initial human and financial capital predictors of new venture performance," *Journal of Business Venturing*, 9: 371–395.

Cowe, R. (1998) "Serial entrepreneurs," *Management Today*, September 3: 90.

Dyer, W.G., Jr. (1994) "Toward a theory of entrepreneurial careers," *Entrepreneurship: Theory and Practice*, 23: 85–102.

Hall, P. (1995) "Habitual owners of small businesses," *Small Firms Partnership for Growth*, London: Paul Chapman, pp. 217–230.

Hicks, D. (2003) "Small serial innovators: the small firm contribution to technical change," Working Paper, Office of Advocacy – Small Business Administration.

Kamm, J.B. and Shuman, J.C. (1990) "Entrepreneurial teams in new venture creation," *Entrepreneurship: Theory and Practice*, 14: 7–24.

Kirzner, I.M. (1973) *Competition and Entrepreneurship*, Chicago, IL: University of Chicago Press.

Kolvereid, L. and Bullvag, E. (1993) *Novice Versus Experienced Founders: An Exploratory Investigation*, Amsterdam: Elsevier Sciences.

Low, M.B. and MacMillan, I.C. (1998) "Entrepreneurship: past research and future challenges," *Journal of Management*, 35: 139–161.

Scranton, P. (1993) "Build a firm, start another: the Bromleys and family firm entrepreneurship in the Philadelphia region," *Business History*, 35(4): 115–151.

Shane, S. and Venkataraman, S. (2000) "The promise of entrepreneurship as a field of research," *Academy of Management Review*, 25: 217–226.

Starr, J. and Bygrave, W. (1991) "The assets and liabilities of prior startup experience: an exploratory study of multiple venture entrepreneurs," *Frontiers of Entrepreneurship Research*, 21(3): 227.

Ucbasaran, D., Howorth, C., and Westhead, P. (2000) "Habitual entrepreneurs: human capital, opportunity search, and learning," Babson Entrepreneurship Conference.

Ucbasaran, D., Westhead, P., and Wright, M. (2001) *The Focus of Entrepreneurial Research: Contextual and Process Issues*, Nottingham, England: Institute for Enterprise and Innovation, Nottingham University Business School.

Venkataraman, S. (1997) "The distinctive domain of entrepreneurship research," in Katz, J.A. (ed.) *Advances in Entrepreneurship: Firm Emergence and Growth*, vol. 3, Connecticut: JAI Press, pp. 139–202.

Wassadorp, P. (2001) "Serial entrepreneurship in the 21st century," paper presented for Concerted Actions Forum on Entrepreneurship, Vaxjo, Sweden, March 19–20.

Westhead, P. and Wright, M. (1998a) "Novice, portfolio and serial founders in rural and urban areas," *Entrepreneurship: Theory and Practice*, 22: 63–100.

Westhead, P. and Wright, M. (1998b) "Contributions of novice, portfolio and serial founders located in rural and urban areas," *Regional Studies*, 33(2): 157–173.

Wright, M., Robbie, K., and Ennew, C. (1997a) "Serial entrepreneurs," *British Journal of Management*, 8: 251–268.

Wright, M., Robbie, K., and Ennew, C. (1997b) "Venture capitalists and serial entrepreneurs," *Journal of Business Venturing*, 12: 227–249.

Wright, M., Westhead, P., and Sohl, J. (1998) "Habitual entrepreneurs and angel investors," *Entrepreneurship: Theory and Practice*, 22(4): 5–21.

Chapter 18

Eugene Fregetto[1]

University of Illinois at Chicago

IMMIGRANT AND ETHNIC ENTREPRENEURSHIP: A U.S. PERSPECTIVE

Introduction

THIS CHAPTER REVIEWS THE literature about the immigrant and individuals from ethnic-minority backgrounds who seek self-employment over employment in order to attain economic security as permanent residents in the United States or to return to their native countries with increased wealth.

Light (1988–1989), a leading researcher, asks whether immigrant entrepreneurship is still a phenomenon of immense importance as it was historically for major cities. To partially answer his question, he notes that the rate of self-employment among immigrants is generally higher than the rate among native-born citizens, and immigrants tend to utilize entrepreneurship in identifiable industries and localities. There is an emerging consensus among social scientists that ethnic entrepreneurship is a critical element in the current restructuring of Western industrial economies (Waldinger and Aldrich 1990). With the broadening and deepening integration of emerging economies in the global network, high-skilled immigrant entrepreneurs from Third World countries may become much more prominent in the near future.

Another aspect is that immigrant and ethnic-minority entrepreneurs may have linkages with their native countries. What import and export trade do they foster with their home countries? Are they only self-help firms, or are they becoming interlinked with the global economy? Do ethnic-minority entrepreneurs make a local economy in the host country more export-driven? Considering the likelihood that many ethnic-minority entrepreneurs tend toward

informal or even underground enterprises, how can we really count their contribution to the U.S. economy and the economies of their countries of origin?
These are a few of the many questions that still have to be answered.

What do we know about the ethnic entrepreneur? We know that ethnic
entrepreneurs are concentrated in certain areas, certain markets, and certain
industries, and we know that the ethnic entrepreneur's propensity to own a
firm varies by national origin. We know ethnic-minorities comprise about 11
percent of the U.S. population, and we know that all large metropolitan areas in
the U.S.A. have a proliferation of ethnic-owned businesses. What we do not
have is a single explanation for this phenomenon, although several explanations
seem feasible: discrimination in the employment market, market demand for
ethnic goods, home country's limited employment and self-employment
opportunities, ethnic-minority entrepreneurs are successful because they have
community information networks, sources of credit within their communities, a
built-in customer base for their goods and services, and an excess supply of
cheap co-ethnic labor. Ethnic-minority entrepreneurs come from the "middleman minority" that was historically most active in trading and helped to support
and perpetuate business success.

How are immigrant entrepreneurs different? Research shows that immigrant entrepreneurs from less developed countries are different from the
indigenous population (Kloosterman and Rath 2001). They are more dependent
on a limited set of opportunities because they can only take advantage of segments that require a small outlay of capital, low levels of education, or specific
skills. Some immigrants, therefore, stretch the conventional meaning of entrepreneurship. For instance, low-skilled day-laborers from Latin America, so-
called "survivalist entrepreneurs" because of their lack of documents or
proficiency in English, face significant barriers in the regular labor market. By
becoming self-employed, they are able to circumvent those barriers. Conversely, in the U.S.A., the number of very highly skilled immigrant entrepreneurs from emerging economies is rapidly growing. Software specialists
from China and India have become very important entrepreneurs in Silicon
Valley.

Immigrant, ethnic, and minority entrepreneurship

What is meant by "ethnic"? Is it in the background of the entrepreneur? In the
products sold or delivered? In the perception of doing business? Is it a combination of these? In many instances, there is a gradual shift away from the stereo-
typical ethnic-minority-run corner shop toward more diversified sectors, such
as computers, global trade, leisure and recreation management, estate agencies,
and cultural enterprises. The new generations of migrant and ethnic-minority
entrepreneurs, especially young men and women, are moving in that direction
(Freitas 2003).

At first glance it seems that studies of immigrant-, ethnic-, and minority-
owned businesses should all be the same. Are not all immigrants a minority?
Yes. Are not all immigrants ethnic? Yes, but the term "ethnic" includes more

than immigrants. From a federal perspective, the three groups are treated differently. Minority businesses are provided with preferential treatment in the competition for government contracts. Immigrants are controlled by federal immigration laws; and a majority of "ethnics" are citizens of this country and part of our American fabric that we commonly identify as "the melting pot." The three are certainly interrelated but are treated separately in research and policy.

How does immigrant and ethnic entrepreneurship differ? In some works, the distinction between the immigrant and the ethnic entrepreneur is not always apparent. Some authors use the terms "immigrant entrepreneur" and "ethnic entrepreneur" interchangeably, but most authors tend to use the terms to identify two mutually exclusive groups. For instance, Light (1972) proposed to use "immigrant entrepreneur" to distinguish between the first-generation immigrant entrepreneur and the second-generation ethnic entrepreneur. Chaganti and Greene (2002) define "ethnic entrepreneur" as a function of the strength of an individual's identification with an ethnic enclave regardless of generation.

A second confusion is the use of surnames to identify ethnicity. Researchers have used ethnic surnames regardless of immigration status to measure immigrant and ethnic entrepreneurs. To complicate the definition further, Fairlie (1996) has identified the sojourner entrepreneur as an immigrant who comes to this country to accumulate wealth rapidly and then return to his or her native country. Therefore, such a person is not an immigrant seeking permanent residency.

Finally, researchers use the term "minority entrepreneur" for an aggregation of all immigrant entrepreneurs as well as indigenous ethnic entrepreneurs. The issue of African–American entrepreneurs is being treated separately and in-depth by two authors because African–Americans have been exposed to a long history of more intense and enduring discrimination than other ethnic groups.

Literature

The literature on the immigrant and ethnic entrepreneur shows three parallel research efforts: immigrant and ethnic entrepreneurs, African–American entrepreneurs, and minority entrepreneurs.

The current research on immigrant and ethnic entrepreneurs started in the early 1970s with the publication of Ivan Light's book, *Ethnic Enterprise in America* in 1972, and Edna Bonacich's article, "A theory of middleman minorities," in *American Sociological Review* in 1973. Two other notable publications followed: Light's *Ethnic Enterprise in America: Business and Welfare Among Chinese, Japanese, and Blacks* in 1972 and John Modell's *The Economics and Politics of Racial Accommodations: The Japanese of Los Angeles, 1900–1942* in 1977. During the same time period, Howard Aldrich published related articles in the *Urban Affairs Quarterly* and presented articles at annual meetings of the American Sociological Association. Those researchers of the 1970s were joined by Waldinger in the 1980s. These five researchers were also co-authors of several articles during the 1990s.

The research on African–American entrepreneurs started decades earlier, but this stream of research was based on individual case studies and therefore lacked a theoretical framework. Early researchers who wrote about the African–American business experience include W.E.B. DuBois in 1898, with the publication of *The Negro in Business*; Jesse B. Blayton (1936), "The Negro in banking"; William Kenneth Boyd (1927), *The Story of Durham: City of the New South*; Colonel Clarence Douglas (1921), *The History of Tulsa, Oklahoma*, Vol. 1; Walter L. Fleming (1927), *The Freedman's Saving Bank: A Chapter in the Economic History of the Negro Race*; Abram Harris (1936), *The Negro As Capitalist*; Arnett Lindsay (1929), *The Negro in Banking*; Henry M. Minton (1913), "Early history of Negroes in business in Philadelphia"; Harry Pace (1927), "The business of banking among Negroes"; and Booker T. Washington (1911), "Durham North Carolina: a city of Negro enterprises."

Two present-day researchers have added to our understanding of the African–American entrepreneurial experience by explaining it within a theoretical framework: Robert W. Fairlie (1996) and John Sibley Butler (1991). Both authors have revisited the prevailing paradigms about entrepreneurship and ethnic entrepreneurship to help us understand the significant contributions of the entrepreneurial spirit in African–Americans, which remained buried under the more dominant social and historical events of our country. The authors suggest that the entrepreneurs from different ethnic groups have reacted differently owing to explicit and implicit forms of discrimination.

The primary questions addressed by scholars concern the varying levels of business involvement and success of different ethnic and immigrant groups (Teixeira 2001): what are the determinants and implications of the ethnic enterprise (Waldinger and Aldrich 1990; Barrett *et al.* 1996; Light and Gold 2000)? Why do certain immigrant groups concentrate in entrepreneurship? What factors facilitate or prevent the entrepreneurial phenomenon from occurring within particular ethnic groups? Why do some groups do better than other ethnic groups? What are the proportional effects of the discrepancies between wealth and civil liberties in the native and foreign countries? Is the growth of ethnic entrepreneurship driven by the growth of entrepreneurial opportunities, or are entrepreneurial opportunities driven by the immigration of entrepreneurially inclined individuals (Light 1988–1989)?

Leading explanations

A fundamental belief about ethnic entrepreneurship is that the new ethnic business begins by serving other members of that ethnic community, and that business growth is facilitated by the tendency of ethnic groups to live geographically concentrated in ethnic enclaves (Galbraith and Stiles 1999). After achieving success in serving their ethnic enclave, the entrepreneurs expand their businesses to non-ethnic markets.

Although this explanation is valid in some cases, it does not provide a sufficient explanation for immigrant ethnic entrepreneurs. In the literature, researchers have used three basic explanations: sociological, economic, and immigration policy.

Sociological explanations

Disadvantage theory: displacement, human capital, and blocked mobility

Displacement theory argues that the disadvantages of poverty, unemployment, and racial discrimination cause immigrants and ethnics to seek self-employment because a wage or salary job is not open to them or advancement is blocked by a "glass ceiling."

Lack of human capital prevents immigrants and ethnics from obtaining wage or salary jobs because they are not fluent in English and their experience, skills, and education are not completely transferable to the U.S. labor market. Therefore, self-employment is the only choice.

Blocked mobility occurs because ethnics have limited knowledge of the language and culture of the majority and discrimination leads some ethnic minorities to seek self-employment rather than employment.

Ethnic resource theory (or cultural theory)

Immigrants and ethnics have a preference for entrepreneurial, self-employment opportunities rather than being driven to them as an only alternative. Ethnic groups have resources that facilitate entrepreneurial behavior and benefit the ethnic self-employed (Fairlie 1996). Light argues that equally disadvantaged ethnics can have different rates of self-employment because of differences in ethnic resources (Light 1972; Waldinger and Aldrich 1990).

Ethnic enclaves

The ethnic enclave acts as the greenhouse for the development of budding capitalists (CEIP 1997), providing critical community support for the start-up business during uncertain times. It is rare that an entire family network from the native country is transplanted. Therefore, the missing familial connections increase the need to cultivate the non-family links for social and economic support. Light (1972) describes the "immigrant brotherhood," and Lovell-Troy's (1980) work found evidence of a broad clan structure that extended beyond the nuclear family. Zhou (1992) discusses two entrepreneurship-promoting attributes of the ethnic enclave:

- enforceable trust. The communities are both business and social and provide efficient mechanisms for enforcing fairness and contractual honesty
- bounded solidarity. Immigrants manifest a tendency to affiliate with others of their own ethnicity or national origin, creating a community of buyers, sellers, laborers, employers, and financiers, as well as tightly meshed networks of information.

Theory of middleman minorities. Some ethnics who cluster in certain commercial occupations and supply an abundance of entrepreneurial talent to some areas are generally considered economically unpromising, such as inner-city grocery services.

Immigrant entrepreneurs as sojourners. Some immigrants come to this country to accumulate wealth quickly so that they can return to their native countries. Therefore, they avoid occupations that require extensive training or education and instead seek wealth in small business trade and commerce. Light (1979) suggested that the Chinese in the nineteenth century are good examples of sojourners. However, Waldinger and Aldrich (1990) suggested an alternate explanation, that sojourners would choose the less risky wage or salary job over opening a small business.

Economic theories

The economic explanations provide insights into the variation in self-employment across ethnic groups as a function of skill, capital, and motivation. Aronson (1991) has a good review of economic literature on self-employment.

- *Risk aversion.* The immigrant has a choice between wage or salary employment and self-employment; and his or her decision is determined by which is less risky.
- *Liquidity.* The assumption is that the greater the wealth the higher the likelihood that the immigrant will seek self-employment.
- *Utility.* The immigrant seeks the better of the two choices on the basis of his or her ability and aspirations.
- *Niche economic and market conditions.* Ethnic entrepreneurs may provide goods and services that serve the unique needs of co-ethnics and enter businesses with low barriers to entry (Waldinger and Aldrich 1990).
- *Abandoned markets.* Business sectors are abandoned by the majority culture and left open to "middleman" minorities (Bonacich 1973) and other ethnic entrepreneurs (Waldinger and Aldrich 1990).
- *Regional and sub-regional economics within the country's overall gross domestic product.* Small businesses form within the ethnic group, initially grow by trading with other ethnic groups, and, then, after attaining a critical mass, become viable businesses by expanding into high-volume trade with the general population.
- *Equal expansion hypothesis.* When opportunities exist in the market, all ethnic groups do not share equally. Light (1988–1989) suggests that ethnic groups are endowed differently; market opportunities never increase evenly; ethnic groups do not share a common definition of what constitutes a market opportunity; and they have different "mean opportunity costs of entrepreneurship." The same sources of information that lock certain ethnics into a certain industry lock other ethnics out of that same industry; ethno-religious groups also serve as a community standard for acceptable and unacceptable market opportunities.

Immigration policy

The Immigration Act of 1990 limits immigration and sets the preference categories used to select immigrants that may have a direct impact on immigrant and ethnic entrepreneurships (U.S. Immigration and Naturalization Service 2001):

- the U.S.A. has a flexible annual cap on immigration of 675,000, or approximately 0.25 percent of the current population, involving three categories: employment-based immigrants make up approximately 21 percent of allowable immigrants; family-sponsored, approximately 71 percent; and diversity program selections, approximately 8 percent.
- the current policy places a strong emphasis on high-skilled immigrants and allows a lower proportion of unskilled workers.
- the program is designed to ensure that "the admission of aliens to work in this country on a permanent or temporary basis will not adversely affect the job opportunities, wages and working conditions of U.S. workers."

Light and Bonacich (1988) were the first to explore the importance of U.S. immigration policy and its ultimate responsibility for the degrees of immigrant and ethnic entrepreneurships. Immigrant entrepreneurship will vary as U.S. immigration policy changes due to levels of war and peace, international trade and tariffs, unemployment and welfare, world capital markets, and now terrorism.

Model development

Self-employment is anything but self-evident (Light and Rosenstein 1995). This holds true for indigenous aspiring entrepreneurs and, arguably, even more so for immigrants from less-developed countries who have moved to advanced economies (Kloosterman and Rath 2001). Several models have been developed to help explain the phenomenon of immigrant and ethnic entrepreneurships. This section summarizes those models and provides a brief explanation. Variable definitions and measures are especially difficult for all models.

Model 1: neo-classical model

Entrepreneurship is rational within the traditional neo-classical model (Kloosterman and Rath 2001).

- Opportunities for business occur, and entrepreneurs seize them because committing resources to set-up shop is more rewarding than any alternative use for their resources.
- Opportunity structure is completely transparent and is assumed to be economically rational with profit-seeking actors.

- Opportunities can be pursued by easily transferring resources from one economic activity to another with no obstacles from closed shops, cartels, rules and regulations, branding, or marketing to hamper the new entrepreneur.
- Opportunities will eventually disappear when the markets clear and blissful equilibrium returns once more.

Model 2: simple linear model

Immigrant and ethnic entrepreneurships can be explained as a linear regression relationship by using the attributes as the independent variables and ethnic start-up as the dependent variable.

Model 3: structural versus cultural factors

This model suggests that there are two fundamental explanations for ethnic entrepreneurship. Structural and cultural factors explain the differences in business involvement and the rate of success among ethnic and immigrants groups.

Structural factors such as the blocked mobility thesis or disadvantage theory point to racial discrimination and cultural barriers as structural forces that block the advancement of ethnic minorities in mainstream economic markets, forcing them to channel themselves into entrepreneurship as their principal means for economic prosperity. In this view, entrepreneurship is not seen as a sign of success but as an alternative to underemployment and low wages and becomes a sign of the ethnic group's disadvantage and social position in society (Bonacich and Modell 1980; Li 1992, 1997; Reitz 1980, 1990; Waldinger 1986).

Cultural factors suggest that immigrant and ethnic entrepreneurs seek entrepreneurship because of unique cultural characteristics that promote entrepreneurial success as an attribute of their ethnic group. This thesis holds that certain traditional values and cultural backgrounds serve to explain both the rates of entrepreneurship for immigrant and non-immigrants, as the blocked mobility thesis does, and the differences in entrepreneurship between ethnic and minority groups (Light 1972; Li 1992, 1997; Light and Bonacich 1988; Light and Rosenstein 1995a; Waldinger 1986).

Model 4: ethnic markets versus mainstream markets

This model presumes that there are two basic markets for ethnic entrepreneurs

Figure 18.1 An illustration of the basic linear regression relationship

– ethnic markets and mainstream markets – and proposes that the ethnic entrepreneur begins with a business in the ethnic community.

For the ethnic market, promotion will only be through ethnic sources, ethnic media, ethnic community, and ethnic information networks. The reasons to stay with the ethnic market is the sharing of background, language, and consumption patterns, such as homeland products, rituals, holidays, and celebrations.

In order to grow and expand into the mainstream market, ethnic entrepreneurs must have the desire for integration and/or assimilation into the larger mainstream market, including a more developed perception of risk based on the native culture and the support and encouragement of their ethnic community, for example, encouragement by co-ethnics or by social embeddedness characteristics.

Model 5: interactive model

The interactive model of ethnic business development says that there is not a single characteristic that is responsible for the entrepreneurial success of an ethnic group but the success is related to a complex interaction between two dimensions: opportunity structures and group characteristics (Waldinger and Aldrich 1990). The interactive model brings together four factors (Figure 18.2):

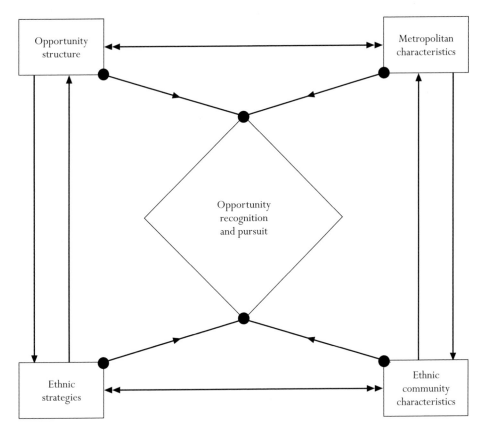

Figure 18.2 Interactive model of ethnic business development

1   the characteristics of the ethnic community, especially those characteristics that contribute to immigrants' entrepreneurial success;
2   opportunity structure, including market conditions and blocked mobility;
3   business strategies that come from the interaction between the ethnic group and the opportunity structures; and
4   characteristics of the metropolitan area.

Waldinger *et al.* (1990: 22) also provide a model to explain ethnic strategies when the strategies emerge from the interaction of four factors (shown in Figure 18.3) as ethnic entrepreneurs use the available resources to carve out their own niches.

Model 6: mixed embeddedness: opportunity structure and market

Mixed embeddedness is used by several researchers in order to identify the matching process between entrepreneur and potential opportunity that takes place within social networks and socio-economic and politico-institutional environments (Kloosterman and Van der Leun 1999).

This model maintains that markets are not metaphysical phenomena that transcend mere social realities and are the same everywhere at any time. Quite the reverse: markets, and therefore opportunity structures, are thoroughly social phenomena and thus embedded in wider social contexts that may differ according to time and place (Scott 1998; Storper 1997).[2] Consequently, opportunity structure is seen to consist of market conditions in ethnic markets, non-ethnic markets, and open markets accessible for newcomers to start a business with growth potential. Opportunities should be analyzed at all three levels: national (e.g. national boundaries still matter in many respects), regional/urban (e.g. the global city is becoming part of the global mosaic), and local or neighborhood (e.g. natural or captive markets and mixed embeddedness) because

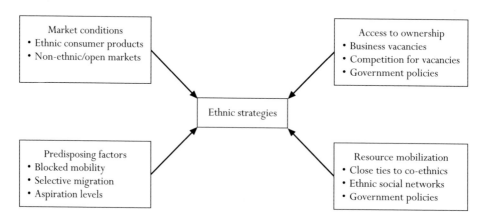

Figure 18.3 Sources of ethnic strategies

different factors at each level shape the opportunity structure (Kloosterman and Rath 2001). The three assumptions of the mixed embeddedness models are:

1   opportunities have to be accessible to aspiring entrepreneurs and not blocked by very high minimum efficiencies of scale or industry rules or government regulations;
2   an opportunity must be perceived as one for starting a business that will provide sufficient income; and
3   entrepreneurs must be able to seize opportunities in a palpable way, i.e. by actually starting their own businesses, as shown in the following model of ethnic entrepreneur's innovative behavior (Kloosterman and Rath 2001).

Hypotheses

The following hypotheses are not intended to be mutually exclusive. Instead, the list includes various hypotheses discussed or tested by researchers in the field.

Horatio alger hypothesis. Immigrants are naturally entrepreneurial owing to the challenge of beginning life in a new country. Enterprises owned and operated by immigrants are one of the primary routes for the immigrant's economic success and eventual social integration in the host society.

Family business. "The family business literature may provide a conceptual framework through which the relationship of entrepreneurs with their ethnic communities may be understood" (Dyer and Ross 1997). Dyer and Ross suggest the following hypothesis: ". . . the interest is not in the role of the family or ethnic group in creating entrepreneurs, but in the processes by which the sense of obligation to a family or ethnic group shapes the beliefs and activities of the business person" (Dyer and Ross 1997: 16).

Ethnic subculture (social capital). An ethnic subculture has modes of expression – body language, spoken language, and cultural knowledge – that permit better and more rapid communication, making it easy for co-ethnics to work together and negotiate business deals with one another. Co-ethnics use cultural insights to support one another (Dyer and Ross 1997).

Immigrants' dominant entrepreneurial attributes. Many authors expressed the opinion that immigrants possess a dominant attribute that simulates their entrepreneurial aspirations and success. Even though these authors consider many other factors in their writings, they still express the belief in the correlation between one or two dominant attributes and the immigrants' entrepreneurial success. They were more independent, sacrificing close extended family ties in their homelands for the opportunities in America. Such social independence is a common entrepreneurial characteristic (Gannon 1979: 367); those who decided to immigrate were already risk-takers, often trading off job security for economic potential, just like entrepreneurs (Gannon 1979; Helweg and Helweg 1990), i.e. "a lifeboat rather than a ladder (CEIP 1997)"; the sojourner mentality, a belief that temporary sacrifices in a foreign country will lead to riches the immigrants can take with them when they return to their homeland, makes some immigrants work harder than normal (Light and Bonacich 1988); the decision to emigrate to a foreign country can stem from a strong desire to get ahead and more tolerance for uncertainty and risk than others in their own country have (Rosentraub and Taebel 1980); the lifestyle of many immigrants has led to success. Although financially secure, the immigrant professionals had no one to go home to, so they worked long hours at their jobs to relieve the loneliness (Helweg and Helweg 1990: 158).

Zero-sum competition thesis. Failure or success of immigrants, economically or socially, is a function of whether they are perceived negatively by individuals who identify with the receiving society (Esses *et al.* 2001). This hypothesized relationship may explain why we may admire immigrant entrepreneurs for their rags-to-riches success but may target them with envy and hostility. The perception of an immigrant is explained by the zero-sum competition thesis. Esses *et al.* (2001) provide insights regarding the perceived competition for resources that determines negative attitudes toward immigrants. Their article does not specifically mention the ethnic entrepreneur but does identify an underlying principle that affects immigration policy and, in term, affects the ebb and flow of immigrants. The authors explain how the chronic belief in zero-sum relations among groups is a major factor in the prevailing negative attitude toward immigrants and immigration policy, i.e. more for immigrants means less for non-immigrants.

Topics that need to be covered

Dual nationality

Dual nationality is a growing issue not yet discussed in the immigrant and ethnic entrepreneurship literature. Dual nationality represents the growing complexity in a world that increasingly comes to resemble a global village, and can affect patriotic loyalty. Dual citizenship can make it easier for holders to work, travel, and own property abroad and make unrestricted investment back home. Some researchers estimate that as many as 25 million U.S. residents can hold dual citizenship. In 1967, the U.S. Supreme Court affirmed the right to dual citizenship, but the argument continues: "no man can serve two masters" versus "a child has two parents and can love both mother and father."

Women ethnic entrepreneurs

Unfortunately, the literature about ethnic entrepreneurship includes very little concerning the self-employment initiatives of ethnic women. Demographic analysis shows that ethnic women represent a very small percentage of the self-employed. Yet we know that often the skills of a married ethnic woman are the basis for an ethnic business that is built in cooperation with her husband.

True Native American Indian entrepreneurs

They start the fewest businesses (see Garsombke and Garsombke 1998). There is still a need for a researcher to discover the uniqueness of the Native American ethnic entrepreneurship background: "Most information available regarding Native American businesses has been compiled by the U.S. Bureau of Indian Affairs and has focused on tribal business such as natural resource development enterprises, production of Native American tourist products and gambling casinos" (USASBE 1998).

The illegal immigrant

No in-depth discussion of the impact of illegal immigrants is formally included in any model. We know the illegal immigrant is here, but we seem to imply that they are included in the aggregate, meaning what is true for the legal immigrant will also be true for the illegal immigrant.

According to the present INS Commissioner, James Ziglar, there are an estimated seven million illegal immigrants in the U.S.A. (Ziglar 2002). Seven million illegal immigrants as a proportion of the total U.S. population is either a significant or relatively small number, depending on your perspective. However, seven million as a percentage of the population under study, immigrant and ethnic entrepreneurs, is very significant.

Notes

1 The author wishes to acknowledge Elif Izberk-Bilgin, UIC Ph.D. student, for her assistance in this research project.
2 Kloosterman and Rath (2001) refer to these two sources. (Note: the immigrant entrepreneurs and their social embeddedness are well covered by Granovetter 1985, 1990, 1995; Portes and Sesenbrenner 1993; Waldinger 1996.)

References

Aronson, R.L. (1991) *Self-Employment: A Labor Market Perspective*, Ithaca, NY: ILR Press.
Barrett, G.A., Jones, T.P., and McEvoy, D. (1996) "Ethnic minority business: theoretical discourse in Britain and North America," *Urban Studies*, 33: 783–809.
Bates, T. (1994) "An analysis of Korean immigrant-owned small business startups with comparisons to African–American and non-minority-owned firms," *Urban Affairs Quarterly*, 30(2): 227–248.
Blayton, J.B. (1936) "The negro in banking," *Bankers Magazine*, 133: 511–514.
Bonacich, E. (1973) "A theory of middleman minorities," *American Sociological Review*, 38: 583–594.
Bonacich, E. and Modell, J. (1980) *The Economic Basis of Ethnic Solidarity in the Japanese American Community*, Berkeley, CA: University of California Press.

Boyd, W.K. (1927) *The Story of Durham: City of the New South*, Durham, NC: Duke University Press.

Butler, J.S. (1991) *Entrepreneurship and Self-Help Among Black Americans: A Reconsideration of Race and Economics*, Albany, NY: State University of New York Press.

Carnegie Endowment for International Peace (CEIP) (1997) "Immigrant entrepreneurs," *Research Perspectives on Migration*, 1(2). Online, available at: http://www.ceip.org/programs/migrat/migrpm.htm (accessed September 25, 2003).

Chaganti, R. and Greene, P.G. (2002) "Who are ethnic entrepreneurs? A study of entrepreneurs' ethnic involvement and business characteristics," *Journal of Small Business Management*, 40(2): 126–143.

Davis, J. and Tagiuri, R. (1989) "The advantages and disadvantages of the family business," reprinted in Ibrahim, A.B. and Ellis, W. (1994) *Family Business Management*, Dubuque, IA: Kendall/Hunt Publishing Co.

Douglas, Colonel C.B. (1921) *The History of Tulsa, Oklahoma*, Vol. 1, Chicago, IL: S.J. Clarke Publishing Company.

DuBois, W.E.B. (1898) *The Negro in Business*, Atlanta, GA: Atlanta University Press.

Dyer, L. and Ross, C. (1997) *The Entrepreneur in the Community*. Online, available at: http://www.sbaer.uca.edu/Research/1997/ICSB/97ics068.htm (accessed April 23, 2003).

Esses, V.M., Dovidio, J.F., Jackson, L.M., and Armstrong, T.L. (2001) "The immigration dilemma: the role of perceived group competition, ethnic prejudice, and national identity," *Journal of Social Issues*, 57(3): 389–412.

Fairlie, R.W. (1996) *Ethnic and Racial Entrepreneurship: A Study of Historical and Contemporary Differences*, New York, NY: Garland Publishing.

Fleming, W.L. (1927) *The Freedman's Savings Bank: A Chapter in The Economic History of The Negro Race*, Chapel Hill, NC: University of North Carolina Press.

Freitas, M.J. (2003) *The LIA Report*. Online, available at: www.lia-partnership.org/en/liareport/foreword-06.htm (accessed April 23, 2003).

Galbraith, C.S. and Stiles, C.H. (1999) *Ethnic Enclaves and Inter-Enclave Trade: Ethnic Group Characteristics and Between Group Interactions*, Babson Park, MA: Babson College

Gannon, M.J. (1979) *Organizational Behavior: A Managerial and Organizational Perspective*, Boston, MA: Little, Brown and Co.

Garsombke, D.J. and Garsombke, T.W. (1998) *Non-Traditional vs. Traditional Entrepreneurs: Emergence of A Native American Comparative Profile of Characteristics and Barriers*. Proceedings from the USASBE National Conference in Clearwater, Florida, January 15–18.

Granovetter, M. (1985) "Economic action and social structure: the problem of embeddedness, *American Journal of Sociology*, 91(3): 481–510.

Granovetter, M. (1990) "The old and the new economic sociology: a history and an agenda," in Friedland, R. and Robertson, A.F. (eds) *Beyond the Marketplace: Rethinking Economy and Society*, New York, NY: Aldine de Gruyter, pp. 89–112.

Granovetter, M. (1995) "The economic sociology of firms and entrepreneurs," in Portes, A. (ed.) *The Economic Sociology of Immigration: Essays on Networks, Ethnicity and Entrepreneurship*, New York, NY: The Russell Sage Foundation, pp. 128–165.

Harris, A.L. (1936) *The Negro as Capitalist: A Study of Banking and Business Among Negro Americans*, Philadelphia, PA: American Academy of Political and Social Science.

Helweg, A.W. and Helweg, U.M. (1990) *An Immigrant Success Story: East Indians in America*, Philadelphia, PA: University of Pennsylvania Press.

Kloosterman, R. and Rath, J. (2001) "Immigrant entrepreneurs in advanced economies: mixed embeddedness further explored," *Journal of Ethnic and Migration Studies*, 27(2): 189–201.

Kloosterman, R.C. and Rath, J. (eds) (2001) *Venturing Abroad: A Comparative Study of Immigrant Entrepreneurs in Advanced Economies*, Oxford: Berg.

Kloosterman, R.C. and van der Leun, J. (1999) "Just for starters: commercial gentrification by immigrant entrepreneurs in Amsterdam and Rotterdam neighborhoods," *Housing Studies*, 14(5): 659–676.

Li, P.S. (1992) "Ethnic enterprise in transition: Chinese business in Richmond, B.C., 1980–1990," *Canadian Ethnic Studies*, 24: 120–138.

Li, P.S. (1997) "Self-employment among visible minority immigrants, white immigrants, and native-born persons in secondary and tertiary industries of Canada," *Canadian Journal of Regional Science*, 20: 103–117.

Light, I. (1972) *Ethnic Enterprise in America: Business and Welfare Among Chinese, Japanese, and Blacks*, Berkeley, CA: University of California Press.

Light, I. (1979) "Disadvantaged minorities in self-employment," in Petersen, W. (ed.) *The Background to Ethnic Conflict*, Leiden: E.J. Brill.

Light, I. (1988–1989) "Local economy and ethnic entrepreneurs," *ISSR Working Papers in the Social Sciences*, 4(13). Online, available at: http://www.sscnet.ucla.edu/issr/paper/papissr.html (accessed September 25, 2003).

Light, I. and Bonacich, E. (1988) *Immigrant Entrepreneurs: Koreans in Los Angeles*, Berkeley, CA: University of California Press.

Light, I. and Gold, S.J. (2000) *Ethnic Economies*, New York, NY: Academic Press.

Light, I. and Rosenstein, C. (1995) *Race, Ethnicity, and Entrepreneurship in Urban America*, New York, NY: Aldine de Gruyter.

Lindsay, A.G. (1929) "The negro in banking," *Journal of Negro History*, April: 156–201.

Lovell-Troy, L. (1980) "Clan structure and economic activity: the case of Greeks in small business enterprise," in Cummings, S. (ed.) *Self-Help in Urban America*, Port Washington, NY: Kennikat Press.

Minton, H.M. (1913) *Early History of Negroes in Business in Philadelphia*, read before the American Historical Society, March 1913.

Modell, J. (1977) *The Economics and Politics of Racial Accommodations: The Japanese in Los Angeles, 1900–1942*, Urbana, IL: University of Illinois Press.

Pace, H.H. (1927) "The business of banking among negroes," *Crisis*, February.

Portes, A. and Sensenbrenner, J. (1993) "Embeddedness and immigration. Notes on the social determinants of economic action," *American Journal of Sociology*, 98(6): 1320–1350.

Reitz, J.G. (1980) *The Survival of Ethnic Groups*, Toronto: McGraw-Hill Ryerson.

Reitz, J.G. (1990) "Ethnic concentration in labour markets and their implications for ethnic inequality," in Breton, R., Isajiw, W., Kalback, W.E., and Reitz, J.G. (eds) *Ethnic Identity and Equality: Varieties of Experience in a Canadian City*, Toronto: Thompson Educational Publishing.

Rosentraub, M. and Taebel, D. (1980) "Jewish enterprise in transition," in Cummings, S. (ed.) *Self-help in Urban America*, New York, NY: Kennikat Press Corp.

Scott, A.J. (1988) *Regions and the World Economy: The Coming Shape of Global Production, Competition, and Political Order*. Oxford: Oxford University Press.

Storper, M. (1997) *The Regional World: Territorial Development in a Global Economy*, London and New York, NY: Guilford Press.

Teixeira, C. (2001) "Community resources and opportunities in ethnic economies: a case study of Portuguese and black entrepreneurs in Toronto," *Urban Studies*, 38(11): 2055.

U.S. Immigration and Naturalization Service (2001) *Immigration Act of 1990*. Online, available at: http://www.bcis.gov/lpBin/lpext.dll/inserts/publaw/publaw-1?f=templates&fn=document-frame.htm#publaw-begin (accessed September 25, 2003).

Waldinger, R. (1986) *Through the Eye of the Needle: Immigrants and Enterprise in New York's Garment Trades*, New York, NY: New York University Press.

Waldinger, R. (1996) *Still the Promised City? African–Americans and New Immigrants in Postindustrial New York*, Cambridge, MA: Harvard University Press.

Waldinger, R. and Aldrich, H. (1990) "Trends in ethnic business in the United States," in Waldinger, R., Aldrich, H., and Ward, R. (eds) *Ethnic Entrepreneurs: Immigrant Business in Industrial Societies*, Newbury Park, CA: Sage Publications.

Waldinger, R., Aldrich, H., and Ward, R. (eds) (1990) *Ethnic Entrepreneurs: Immigrant Business in Industrial Societies*, Newbury Park, CA: Sage Publications.

Washington, B.T. (1911) "Durham North Carolina: a city of negro enterprises," *Independent*, 70: 642–651.

Zhou, M. (1992) *Chinatown: The Socio-economic Potential of an Urban Enclave*, Philadelphia, PA: Temple University Press.

Ziglar, J. (2002) U.S. Immigration Policy in an Era of Greater Security Concerns. Luncheon address to the National Press Club, March 19, Washington, DC.

PART SIX

Entrepreneurship education

Chapter 19

Patrick Sandercock

Harris Bank

INNOVATIONS IN ENTREPRENEURSHIP EDUCATION: STRATEGY AND TACTICS FOR JOINING THE RANKS OF INNOVATIVE ENTREPRENEURSHIP PROGRAMS IN HIGHER EDUCATION

ENTREPRENEURSHIP EDUCATION TODAY is like a child who has suddenly grown up. The discipline has achieved newfound respect and is enjoying growing demand. Higher education has seen a growing need to help facilitate entrepreneurial success and closer ties between schools and the start-up and small business communities have been the result. As the University of Louisiana at Monroe pondered creating an entrepreneurship major, researchers discovered considerable demand for entrepreneurship education among both business and non-business students, as well as a strong desire by local business for graduates with entrepreneurship training (Dunn and Short 2001). While conceding the study addressed a specific region, the authors noted their findings indicate that latent demand may exist in other areas in which university entrepreneurship programs are not currently available.

However, even with an overwhelming need for entrepreneurship education, how might a college or university go about developing a program that will offer the most value to students, the university, and the community? In the mid-1990s, a major California university set out to become a regional leader for innovative entrepreneurship education and "a model for college-wide entrepreneurial activity." A paper presented at the Internationalizing Entrepreneurship

Education and Training Conference in Arnhem, Netherlands, described the 16 specific steps this California school was using as an "action plan" to accomplish this lofty goal (Welsch 1996: 32).

This chapter broadens those institution-specific steps by offering six "themes" that any school can embrace in designing its strategy for entrepreneurship program development, then provides numerous examples of how colleges and universities are currently addressing each of these themes in a variety of innovative ways. Of course there are numerous other innovative examples that could not be related in this chapter. Table 19.1 (pp. 273–276) lists the initiatives described in this chapter as well as several others. Many of these initiatives were submitted as grant applications to the Coleman Foundation, an active supporter of innovation in entrepreneurship education through its Entrepreneurship Awareness and Education Grant Initiative. Other examples of innovative practices are drawn from higher education journals, popular press, and university websites.

All the institutions noted (and many others that could not be included) should be commended for the significant work they are doing to further a discipline that is continuously developing. Schools are encouraged to ponder their own progress in terms of the six themes described herein, borrow from the examples provided, tailor them where appropriate and, in whatever way possible, report outcomes for the benefit of all. Drawing an analogy to the programming world, consider this chapter an "open-source development" model for improving entrepreneurship as a discipline.

Influential parties – internal and external

Capitalizing on the impact of centers, advisory boards, practitioners (entrepreneurs and investors), faculty, and students.

The success of any venture, project, or other endeavor depends upon the persons involved and an entrepreneurship program is no different. Important internal "influencers" include, among others, an advisory board, entrepreneurship center directors and key staff, university faculty, and students. External influencers include entrepreneurs and small-business owners, investors, and related service providers (especially alumni in those fields). An initial step in planning an innovative entrepreneurship program is to build a well-connected advisory board with expertise in venture creation, growth management, innovation, curriculum and outreach program development, and financing. Advisory board members are an important link to the business community and provide a wealth of diverse perspectives, contacts, ideas, and opportunities for students. In effect, advisory board members are transitioned from "external" influencers to important "internal" influencers. For greatest impact, assistance should be tailored to the developmental stages of the entrepreneurship program. For example, curriculum input, outreach, and fund-raising efforts are stressed for early stage programs while innovative offerings, enhancing visibility, and deepening connections with the business community are stressed as the program matures (Upton 1997: 33).

Table 19.1 Summary of innovative entrepreneurship practices

Sub-theme	Description	College/university program
Influential parties		
Entrepreneurship center	Gigot Center-sponsored Northeast Neighborhood Community Learning Center supporting business incubation through micro-lending and student-provided education	Notre Dame University (IN)
	Maintains both engineering and business entrepreneurship centers	*Stanford University (CA)
	● Entrepreneurial Law Center supporting research and education;	*University of Colorado at Boulder (College of Law)
	● Provides services to entrepreneurs, venture capitalists, and the lawyers	
	Interactive, statewide collaboration on course curricula	*Kennesaw State University (GA)
	Partnership with investment firm streamlining access to equity; students screen business plans	*National Consortium of Entrepreneurship Centers
Faculty education	Three-day clinic	*Miami University (OH)
	Just-in-time consultation for engineering faculty	*Georgia Institute for Technology
	Volunteer business forum	*College of Charleston (SC)
Student interaction	Entrepreneurship residence hall	*University of Maryland
	Students write/publish for *Entrepreneurial Review* (similar to law reviews)	Babson College (MA)
Local business owners/ entrepreneurs	Enhancing the entrepreneur experience	*Black Hills University (SD)
	Business owners included in course and student evaluations	University of Arkansas
	Students research local medical center and aerospace center technologies	*Rice University (TX)
Funding assistance for entrepreneurship outreach	Alumni housing assistance	*Baylor University (TX)
	Program-sponsored supplemental internship pay	*Stanford University (CA)
	Partial tuition reimbursement	*Brigham Young University (UT)
Investor's view	"Assessing Creative Business Concepts" course	*Miami University (OH)
Interdisciplinary programs and recognition		
Technical disciplines	Integrated Science, Business and Technology (ISBT) degree program	*La Salle University (PA)
	Engineering course in patenting and licencing processes	*Rensselaer Polytechnic Institute (MA)
	Physics entrepreneurship master's program	

Table 19.1 continued

Sub-theme	Description	College/university program
Entrepreneurship across the campus	Entrepreneurship course for first-year engineering students Commercialization class with an invention as a prerequisite	*Case Western Reserve (OH) *Clarkson University (Rome, NY) *University of Massachusetts at Amherst
	Entrepreneurship Center for Music Center for Entertainment Industry Entrepreneurship Education Entrepreneurship course for film and television and fine arts majors Digital Center for Arts – student-run Web development to teach/interest children in art	*University of Colorado at Boulder *Belmont University (TN) *Chapman University (CA) Fairfield University (MA)
	Entrepreneurship center to serve (in part) art and horticultural science majors Degree programs in School of Design	*Berry College (GA) *Mount Ida College (MA)
Applying other disciplines to study of entrepreneurship	"The Psychology of Entrepreneurship" course	*William and Mary College (VA)
	Ryan Center for Creativity (with course offering in Creativity in Business)	*DePaul University (Chicago, IL)
Celebrating entrepreneurship	"Month of the Entrepreneur"	*Kennesaw State University (GA)
	Founder's Day and Academy of Distinguished Entrepreneurs	*Babson College (MA)
Specialized entrepreneurial offerings Accelerated offerings/programs	Immersion summer program Entrepreneurship Intensity Track (EIT) Mayfield Fellows Program "Inheriting a company" Comprehensive business plan by third (of nine) terms	*University of Victoria (Canada) *Babson College (MA) *Stanford University (CA) *University of Tennessee *CESA (Columbia)
Local community benefit	Certificate courses in Federal Government Contracting Center for Urban Business Two-day "Gathering" for Family business seminar Mother and Daughter Entrepreneurs in Teams (MADE-IT)	*Bowie State University (MD) *University of Illinois at Chicago Stetson University (FL) *Ball State University (IN)

Healthcare-related programs	Entrepreneurship courses with medical, nursing, and allied health focus	*Rush Presbyterian St. Luke's Medical Center (IL)
	Entrepreneurship course with focus on chiropractic practice	New York Chiropractic College (NY)
	Program leverages Internet to support disabled entrepreneurs	Regent University (VA)
Social entrepreneurship	Program pairs minority entrepreneurs with seasoned business owners	Canisius College (NY)/UTEP
	Internships at entrepreneurial not-for-profit organizations	*St. Edward's University (TX)
	Summer internships in developing nations	*Brigham Young University (UT)
	Student assistance visits to benefit entrepreneurs in South Africa	*Miami University (OH)
	Social entrepreneurship course studies both for-profit and non-profit organizations	Babson College (MA)
Leveraging local technology centers	Cooperative program involving four universities and local high-technology firms	*Council for Entrepreneurial Development (NC)
	Technology Access Program – Lockheed Martin Vought Systems Corp. and NASA incubator program	*Norfolk State University (VA)
	Department of Energy's Oak Ridge National Laboratory (ORNL) NASA Commercialization Center	*University of Tennessee, Knoxville
		*California State Polytechnic, Pomona

Entrepreneurship skill development

Business plan evaluation	"Hatchery" program	*Washington University, St. Louis (MO)
Internships	Internship experience prior to entrepreneurship coursework	*State University of New York at Buffalo
Resources	Entrepreneurial Resource Laboratory	*Miami University (Ohio)
Website design	Students design websites for small businesses and entrepreneurs	*Drake University (IA)
Financial consulting	Financial Management Mentors Program	*California Polytechnic University, Pomona
Internship placement	Matching Project Office	*University of Calgary (Canada)
Professional services support	Entrepreneurial Legal Assistance Program	*Albany Law School (NY)

Table 19.1 continued

Sub-theme	Description	College/university program
Real-life entrepreneurial opportunities		
Starting "live" businesses	Venture Initiation course	*Baylor University (TX)
	Seed capital provided to student teams	*Babson College (MA)
	For Business S.A.K.E. (Students Acquiring Knowledge through Entrepreneurship)	University of Arkansas
	"Business Ventures" – acquires businesses that students then manage	Benedictine College (KS)
	Public interest (self-sufficient) law firm	*University of California at Los Angeles
Acting as the investor	Student-run private equity funds	*Oklahoma State University
	MBA program evaluates commercialization opportunities for university's research	*Pennsylvania State University
Technology implementation		
Distance learning	Comprehensive modular MBA program	*Cranfield (UK)
	Online case method	*University of Massachusetts, Amherst
	EPSCoR Program – six statewide student teams collaborate with local entrepreneurs via interactive audio–video and the Internet	*Dakota State University (SD)
	Web-based software for contracts (used as course supplements)	Columbia University (NYC)
	Family business distance learning course	*Oregon State University
	30-minute television program produced by business school	*University of Montreal (Canada)
Case study development	SmartStart 2000 interactive video conference addressing legal issues	*Albany Law School (NY)
	Regional-based case study development	*University of Colorado

Note
*Program discussed in text.

Entrepreneurship centers, a prominent way programs expand their offerings, are venturing beyond the domain of the business college. Stanford University maintains entrepreneurship centers in schools of both engineering and business. The University of Colorado at Boulder's Entrepreneurial Law Center publishes an online journal, coordinates internships, and sponsors networking events and annual conferences to support research and education for entrepreneurs, venture capitalists, and the lawyers that serve the start-up community. Entrepreneurship centers are also actively teaming up to increase their impact. Kennesaw State University in Georgia initiated a statewide cooperative network to share syllabi and course content and create a statewide bulletin board for entrepreneurship education. Equally ambitious, the National Consortium of Entrepreneurship Centers, a 60-member organization, formed a partnership with BeaconVentureCapital.com to streamline the process for getting equity investment to entrepreneurs in locations under-served by private equity markets. Students evaluate business plans and refer screened plans to the Maryland investment firm (Collier 2000).

University faculty are critical influencers and, as entrepreneurship quickly gains credibility, schools find it imperative to better support faculty. Miami University (Ohio) offers a three-day clinic designed to assist new faculty who will teach entrepreneurship experientially through cases, business plans, small business consulting projects, entrepreneur visits, student interviews of entrepreneurs, entrepreneurial audits, and marketing inventions (Morris 2000). The Georgia Institute for Technology offers an entrepreneurship course for engineering faculty that is taught in a modular format with "just-in-time" consultation by the management faculty, entrepreneurs, and entrepreneur service providers. Direct participation in the business community is another tactic for building faculty expertise. The College of Charleston operates a Volunteer Business Forum, consisting of faculty and business community volunteers who provide assistance to local entrepreneurs in marketing, accounting, product development, patent acquisition, and other areas (Vesper and Gartner 1999: 38).

Students themselves are an invaluable source of internal influence and several innovative programs have designed ways for students to share their depth and variety of perspectives. The University of Maryland dedicated a residence hall for use by 60 students with entrepreneurial interests. The hall is equipped with offices, meeting rooms, and state-of-the-art equipment. Maryland's Business and Engineering Colleges are collaborating on the project, which brings students with business, engineering, computer science, life science, and liberal arts backgrounds together in a living, studying, and working environment of group projects. Students compete to be a part of the program, which includes four courses (leading to a minor in entrepreneurship) and mentor assistance.

An entrepreneurship program must also seek external influences to build a strong and innovative offering. Local entrepreneurs play an important role by providing a "window" to experience through job shadowing; mentoring; attending business meetings, social functions, business lunches and dinners, seminars, and conferences; conducting hands-on projects and community service projects/

events; and making entrepreneur visits to campus athletic or cultural activities (Miami University 2001). Black Hills University in Spearfish, South Dakota, brings a handful of local business owners into weekly class sessions to share their real-life perspective on class examples and problems. In exchange, students provide confidential written and oral reports that analyze the business owners' financial/accounting, marketing, expansion feasibility, and general management. Rice University offers engineering and science students a series of team-taught sequential courses facilitated by faculty, entrepreneurs, and entrepreneurial service providers. An in-depth feasibility study based on a technological innovation leverages advancements at the university medical center and the NASA Johnson Space Center.

When early stage or small companies are unable to financially sponsor students, programs are finding creative ways to finance student opportunities. Baylor University coordinates with alumni to provide housing for interns (Anonymous 1996b); Stanford University supplements intern pay (Vesper and Gartner 1999: 146); and Brigham Young University partially reimburses tuition for successfully completing summer internships (Vesper and Gartner 1999: 22).

Entrepreneurship programs, in their focus on the entrepreneur's perspective, often overlook the important viewpoint of the investor. To broaden students' views, Miami University (Ohio) and a venture capital firm team-teach a course in which students apply an investor's perspective as they critique business models and plans (Morris 2000).

Interdisciplinary programs and recognition

Spreading the seeds of entrepreneurship education across the campus, and publicizing significant accomplishments of students, faculty, and alumni.

Ambitious entrepreneurship programs of all sizes are sharing the techniques and mindset of entrepreneurs with disciplines across the campus. Programs are accomplishing this goal through new degree programs, entrepreneurship minors, and new course development.

Technical disciplines – engineering and applied science in particular – are complemented by an entrepreneurial mindset. La Salle University offers a degree in Integrated Science, Business and Technology (ISBT), which includes an undergraduate year-long course called "Entrepreneurship and High Tech Business." The ISBT program is an interdisciplinary major that blends science, business, and technology and analyzes the process of taking an opportunity (in biotechnology, information, and knowledge management, or energy and natural resources) from conceptual stage to commercialization. Rensselaer Polytechnic Institute offers engineering students a year-long course on intellectual property protection that combines business, law, and technology in a discussion of the patenting and licensing processes. Case Western Reserve University is going to great lengths to develop its graduate students' skills in commercialization. The university is piloting a two-year master's program in physics entrepreneurship that concludes with a science-based thesis involving an entrepreneurial project.

An ongoing seminar program engages students with scientists, technologists, and entrepreneurs who are developing (or have developed) technology ventures. Clarkson University offers an existing entrepreneurship course to first-year engineering students with the goal of encouraging entrepreneurial thought earlier in an engineering student's curriculum.

While some programs have pinpoint focus on specific disciplines, others take a broad approach to technology commercialization. The University of Massachusetts at Amherst developed a course for student inventors from any of 20 scientific and technical departments throughout the university. The only course prerequisites are to have developed an existing invention and the desire to commercialize it.

In addition to technical programs, innovative schools are introducing entrepreneurship to liberal and fine arts colleges, and performing arts, in particular. The University of Colorado at Boulder (College of Music) established an Entrepreneurship Center for Music that is publishing case studies of successful entrepreneurs in music. Belmont University in Tennessee runs a Center for Entertainment Industry Entrepreneurship Education that provides entrepreneurial educational opportunities to the Nashville entertainment industry. A survey of 447 entertainment industry executives verified the importance of marketing and entrepreneurial knowledge in the development of successful music and entertainment industry careers. Chapman University is also targeting the entertainment field by offering an Introduction to Entrepreneurship course to film and television and fine arts majors.

Berry College in Georgia is expanding coursework and establishing an entrepreneurship center that will serve art and horticultural science majors. These disciplines have historically produced a number of small business ventures in the regional area. Mount Ida College (in partnership with Babson College) extended its foundation of entrepreneurial studies to its Chamberlayne School of Design. Mount Ida maintains a "Loan Fund" to help establish student-initiated small businesses on campus.

In addition to bringing the discipline of entrepreneurship to other colleges, several programs are applying other disciplines to the study of entrepreneurship. The College of William and Mary developed a course called the "Psychology of Entrepreneurship," which includes an analysis of the psychological and personal factors that contribute to entrepreneurial success (Schaver 2000). Creativity is serious business for DePaul University's Ryan Center for Creativity, which includes a course offering "Creativity in Business," that applies pattern-breaking exercises and visits to the art museum as strategies to overcome business challenges (DePaul University 2001).

Many schools are making the effort to celebrate the successes of their growing entrepreneurial community. Campus-wide events recognize the hard work of students, faculty, and alumni and enhance the credibility of entrepreneurship programs that are relatively new to many campuses. Kennesaw State University celebrates April as the Month of the Entrepreneur while Babson College's annual Founder's Day celebrates the pioneers in the field through induction into the school's Academy of Distinguished Entrepreneurs (Babson College 2001).

Specialized entrepreneurial offerings

Specializing to meet individual, local, and regional needs and leveraging partnership opportunities with federal and corporate commercialization efforts.

Because entrepreneurship can be so individual, many programs discover the need for "accelerated" offerings to recruit and encourage students who have strong entrepreneurial aspirations and/or well-developed plans. Several schools are experimenting with programs that provide intensive education and practical experience for such students. A program at the University of Victoria in Canada (McKenzie 2000) includes a full immersion summer program followed by an eight-month cooperative education work term. Similarly, Babson College's "advanced track" Entrepreneurship Intensity Track (EIT) endorses the idea that entrepreneurship education must be individually tailored by providing a year of focused study for students prepared to launch a business (Warshaw 2000: 53–54). Students complete a summer internship at a start-up, followed by four modules that address business plan development and include initial meetings with investors. The final module focuses on obtaining first-round financing and managing growth. Over nine months, the Stanford University's Mayfield Fellows Program (Byers 2000) explores both theoretical and practical perspectives of growing emerging technology companies. Mayfield fellows are a select group of undergraduate seniors who take a class in the spring, intern with a start-up company over the summer, then return for another quarter of course-work on the way to a master's degree in engineering. The goal is to teach students "soft skills," including the ability to negotiate and to synthesize tangible and intangible data.

Although most schools have students prepare a business plan as a final exercise (or in their final courses), students at a Columbian business school called CESA (Colegio de Estudios Superiores de Administracion) must begin a business plan as soon as they start the accelerated program (Benson 1996: 28). CESA requires students to have developed a complete plan that includes detailed financials by the third of their nine terms. First-year MBA students at the University of Tennessee "inherit" the same company and are given some 300 pages of background information on the business (Anonymous 1993). Related exercises incorporate techniques and analytical tools to make sense of the "inherited business" – often in response to desperate pleas from students. Tennessee finds this "just-in-time" learning much more effective than delivering course material primarily through lectures.

Several schools have designed programs that meet the needs of their local community. Bowie State University, located near Washington, DC, created a two-day certificate course that uses Web-based training and practical exercises to teach small-business owners the nuances of federal acquisition and contracting procedures. The University of Illinois at Chicago (UIC) created the Center for Urban Business and runs programs in cooperation with local urban and business community organizations. Students work directly with African–American- and Hispanic-owned businesses located in west-side Chicago neighborhoods (Upton 1997: 150). With an eye to supporting local women entrepreneurs, Ball

State University developed a program called "Mother and Daughter Entrepreneurs in Teams" (MADE-IT), which helps seventh-grade girls launch businesses with their mothers and put profits toward future college education (Ball State University 2001).

Healthcare-related programs provide entrepreneurship education for those who will start (or take over) practices and businesses of their own. Rush Presbyterian St. Luke's Medical Center developed the Center for Health Care Entrepreneurship to support healthcare professionals interested in innovative practice management and the improvement of healthcare delivery.

To address an often-overlooked sector, St. Edward's University in Texas recruits students for internships in innovative non-profit organizations. Interns gain experience from positions of responsibility and have a positive impact on entrepreneurial non-profits and their client base. The school may expand the model to include internship teams – for example a natural science major and a business major jointly developing a marketing plan for an environmentally-focused client.

Some entrepreneurship programs are creating an impact across national borders. Brigham Young University sponsors summer internships to assist entrepreneurs in developing nations (Vesper and Gartner 1999: 22) while Miami University (Ohio) takes students to South Africa each summer to consult entrepreneurs in townships and squatter camps (Miami University 2001).

Schools located near technology centers can create mutually beneficial relationships that leverage multiple institutions. In North Carolina's "Research Triangle," the Council for Entrepreneurial Development leverages academia and high-tech firms in developing symposia, internship, mentoring, education, and networking opportunities for students at Duke University, the University of North Carolina at Chapel Hill, North Carolina Central University, and Meredith College. In Virginia, Norfolk State University partners with Lockheed Martin Vought Systems Corporation and NASA to commercialize aerospace technology, biotechnology, and new materials (Vesper and Gartner 1999: 114). The University of Tennessee, Knoxville, operates a "Techno-preneurial Leadership Center (TLC)" in partnership with the Department of Energy's Oak Ridge National Laboratory (ORNL). The Center supports students as they license and commercialize ORNL's portfolio of more than 1,000 patents. Leveraging its experience working with the nearby NASA Commercialization Center, California State Polytechnic University, Pomona, is designing an online certificate program in technology commercialization. This program is to grow to three courses that focus on technology assessment, market assessment, and communications with investors, supply chain, media, and end-users. After first testing on the university's incubator tenants, the courses are to be made available for other incubators, entrepreneurs, students, and others interested in commercializing technology.

Entrepreneurship skill development

Creatively designing competitions, internships, and consulting opportunities that allow students to apply entrepreneurial skills.

Business plan competitions are a way to infuse some competitive fire into an inherently safe environment, and innovation is reaching even this "mainstream" tool of entrepreneurship education. Several universities offer local entrepreneurs the opportunity to have their businesses "evaluated" by students and/or faculty at little or negligible cost. However, Washington University's (St. Louis) entrepreneurship program goes further in operating a "hatchery" that benefits students, entrepreneurs, and investors. Students write a business plan for an outside entrepreneur, or for their own idea, and collectively present the plan to a panel of potential investors. Students receive course credit and up to $500 per person depending upon their input. Outside entrepreneurs pay a fee of $2,500 and receive a business plan and exposure to potential investors. Investors see pre-screened ideas carefully analyzed by a team of business school students. This program is structured to provide the necessary incentives to attract quality, well-developed ideas and motivate students and entrepreneurs to work together successfully.

Most programs place interns with start-up firms after the student has taken some entrepreneurship courses. Reversing this model, State University of New York at Buffalo places interns with entrepreneurial companies prior to coursework. After gaining experience, the students begin classroom instruction.

Miami University created an Entrepreneurial Resource Laboratory (Morris 2000), or ERL, to house a number of experiential programs including an "idea lab," a small business hatchery for student-initiated businesses, an entrepreneurial mentors' program, and an outreach program for women entrepreneurs. Other examples of low-risk experiential learning include student-designed websites for small businesses (Drake University) and a Financial Management Mentors program (California State Polytechnic University, Pomona) that supervises and certifies students who provide financial decision-making assistance to small businesses at no charge.

The University of Calgary in Canada integrates project work into the curriculum through a Project Office (Chrisman 1997) that painstakingly assesses company needs and matches students at the appropriate point in their curriculum. Approximately 100 projects are completed each year in areas such as opportunity analysis, market research, market or product feasibility, product design, and business and financial planning.

Albany Law School in New York operates an Entrepreneurial Legal Assistance Program that educates law students on the needs of entrepreneurs while providing actual legal assistance to practicing entrepreneurs and small-business owners (technology firms in particular). Law students attend to the legal needs of local early-stage firms under the guidance of a local volunteer attorney, including incorporation documents, real property contracts and leases, employment issues, financing arrangements, licencing arrangements, and other needs. Students gain practical experience while clients conserve precious cash. The volunteer attorneys give back to their community and expand their prospective client list, as these early-stage firms grow to become successful, paying clients.

Real-life entrepreneurial opportunities

Creating first-hand experience of the risks and rewards of venture creation and venture investing.

Programs have understood for years that education in entrepreneurship – perhaps more than other business disciplines – requires practical application. Beyond more traditional efforts such as internships, schools are developing innovative ways to ensure that students "stretch" their entrepreneurial muscles and become aware of the true risk–reward nature of entrepreneurship. Baylor University's Venture Initiation course requires students to form teams and start actual businesses (Anonymous 1996: 16). Students prepare a mini-business plan, then operate their firms throughout the semester. A final business plan analyzes how actual operations compared to original plans. Similarly, Babson College's Freshman Management Experience (FME) divides its class into teams. Each team develops a business plan and is provided with up to $3,000 in seed capital to start a business. Coursework guides students in planning, launching, and managing their for-profit venture. The teams liquidate the businesses at the end of the school year and fund a charitable project with the proceeds (Babson College 2001).

Innovative schools in other programs also encourage their students to experience entrepreneurship personally in order to serve other entrepreneurs and their local community. The University of California at Los Angeles (UCLA) supports law students that operate a public interest (and financially self-sufficient) firm for course credit. Students develop skills needed to establish their own public interest practices. Recent law school graduates provide continuity and polish their own skills overseeing operations at the firm for periods of six months to two years.

As noted earlier, innovative programs ensure students understand the investor's point of view as well as the entrepreneur's. Oklahoma State University does this particularly well by placing 10 to 20 students in operation of a $1.5 million private equity investment fund. The highly selective program teaches private equity investing and business development process through both classroom instruction and actual operation of the fund, and also provides assistance to the local start-up community. Along similar lines, the MBA program at Pennsylvania State University (Vesper and Gartner 1999: 122) screens the university's research developments for commercialization effort, highlighting the school's advancements in research while imparting critical analysis skills to business students.

Technology implementation

Leveraging technology that enhances entrepreneurial education.

Advancements in Internet technology have profoundly impacted how colleges and universities communicate with their students and communities. Distance learning, online collaboration, and self-paced, computer-based courses are re-inventing how education is delivered, managed, and "consumed."

Online and other distance-learning methods attract busy individuals who wish to pursue studies without putting professional aspirations or familial responsibilities "on pause." In the United Kingdom, Cranfield offers a particularly innovative "modular MBA" that, over two years, combines eight intensive two-week classroom sessions with in-company work experience and remote learning (Cranfield University 2001). Each student is provided with a laptop, collaborative software, and electronic "case packs." Students work in five- or six-person teams that represent a diverse mix of functional, business, and international experience.

The real-time interactivity afforded by the Internet can relate educational themes to ongoing business events. The University of Massachusetts at Amherst is developing an entrepreneurship course that incorporates the online case (OLC) method. The goal is to encourage greater use of online cases that will network universities around the nation with real-time entrepreneurial events at high-growth start-up firms. Dakota State University is connecting its six statewide campuses (Dakota State University 1998). Business and technology student teams at each campus work with local entrepreneurs to identify a business model and produce, research, and develop a business and technology plan. The South Dakota National Science Foundation provides funding for a team leader to help facilitate the process. Interactive audio-video and the Internet connect the widespread group for team meetings as well as courses on legal issues, raising capital, and budgeting. Oregon State University (OSU) created the first course on family business management in the country to be distance delivered. Leveraging an existing course, OSU is now using satellite technology and the Internet to connect to other major universities in the state. The long-run objective is to provide family business education to any young person who seeks such an entrepreneurial learning experience.

Many programs are bringing more relevant content (i.e. case studies) to the classroom via "old" methods of media, especially video. The University of Montreal Business School airs a weekly 30-minute television program that features a short documentary on two different entrepreneurs along with expert commentary (Vesper and Gartner 1999: 74). Film segments are used in the classroom. Albany Law School is educating entrepreneurs, business owners, and students across New York State about pertinent legal issues via live interactive video conferencing. Ten annual seminars discuss the various legal and funding issues of entrepreneurs. Discussion panels include entrepreneurs, attorneys, investors (debt and equity), and other professionals.

To put a more familiar face on the entrepreneurial activity, the University of Colorado at Boulder and Purdue University launched separate, but similar, initiatives to develop regional-specific case studies. Accompanying videos featuring regional firms describe start-up and small business management issues in a more familiar framework.

In applying all these themes to your entrepreneurship program, you should ask the following questions:

1   Who are, and should be, our entrepreneurship program's internal and external influencers? What is our plan for engaging and getting commitment from those who we would like involved?

2   What is our program doing to expose entrepreneurship to other parts of our institution? How can we provide more opportunities across the campus?

3   What are our local community's areas of strength (and need) to which we can apply an entrepreneurial perspective? How can we broaden our students' opportunities for entrepreneurial and small-business experience by leveraging local institutions and our wider network?

4   What are the skills that our program believes are most important for entrepreneurial success and how are we developing these skills in students? What are some additional ways we can reinforce development of these skills?

5   How does our program provide first-hand experience of entrepreneurial risk and reward? How might this experience be provided for our students?

6   How does our program leverage technology to improve delivery of innovative education? Are there ways we might better incorporate new developments in this expanding discipline of entrepreneurship?

More information on any of the grant submissions described herein can be obtained by contacting the Coleman Foundation:

The Coleman Foundation, Inc.
575 W. Madison Street
Suite 4605
Chicago, IL 60661

Phone: 312.902.7120
Email: coleman@colemanfoundation.org

References

Anonymous (1993) "A taste of entrepreneurship: Tennessee tries 'JIT learning'," *Industry Week*, 242(19): 14–15.

Anonymous (1996a) "Innovative curriculum award goes to family business & entrepreneurship," *Baylor Business Review*, 14(1): 16.

Anonymous (1996b) "Hankamer seeks competitive edge with internship programs," *Baylor Business Review*, 14(2): 9.

Babson College (2001) "Babson FME," Wellesley, MA: Babson College. Online, available at: http://www.babson.edu/entrep/fme (accessed January 21, 2001).

Ball State University (2001) "Entrepreneurship home page," Muncie, IN: Ball State University. Online, available at: http://www.bsu.edu/business/entre/pages/page2.htm (accessed February 10, 2001).

Benson, D. (1996) "Colombia's school for business revolutionaries," *Fast Company*, 4: 28.

Byers, T. (2000) Unpublished presentation to the AACSB Program, "Innovations in Entrepreneurship Curriculum."

Chrisman, J.J. (1997) "Program evaluation and the venture development program at the University of Calgary: a research note," *Entrepreneurship: Theory & Practice*, 22(1): 59–73.

Collier, J.G. (2000) "University of South Carolina joins national entrepreneurship partnership," Columbia, South Carolina: KRTBN Knight-Ridder Tribune Business News. Online, available at: http://www.nationalconsortium.org/newsmedia.html (accessed February 4, 2001).

Cranfield University (2001) "Cranfield Modular MBA," Bedfordshire, UK: Cranfield University. Online, available at: http://www.som.cranfield. ac.uk/som/ (accessed June 14, 2001).

Dakota State University (1998) "Technology innovation and entrepreneurship grant submission #117–198," Hadley, MA: The National Collegiate Inventors and Innovators Alliance (NCIIA). Online, available at: http://www.nciia.org/faculty/cp.html (accessed May 24, 2001).

DePaul University (2001) "Ryan Center," Chicago, IL: DePaul University, Department of Management. Online, available at: http://www.depaul. edu/~lgundry (accessed May 2, 2001).

Dunn, P., and Short, L. (2001) "An entrepreneurship major?" Conway, AR: The Small Business Advancement National Center at the University of Central Arkansas. Online, available at: http://www.sbaer.uca.edu/ Newsletter/issues/4301.htm (accessed June 14, 2001).

McKenzie, B. (2000) "Innovations in entrepreneurship curriculum," unpublished presentation to the AACSB Program

Miami University (2001) "Miami University MBA," Athens, OH: Miami University. Online, available at: http://www.sba.muohio.edu/PageCenter. htm (accessed February 5, 2001).

Morris, M. (2000) "Innovations in entrepreneurship curriculum," unpublished presentation to the AACSB Program.

Schaver, K. (2000) "Innovations in Entrepreneurship Curriculum," unpublished presentation to the AACSB Program.

Upton, N. (1997) "Successful experiences of entrepreneurship center directors," *Baylor University Center for Entrepreneurial Leadership*. Center for Entrepreneurial Leadership, Inc. Waco: Baylor University.

Vesper, K.H. and Gartner, W.B. (1999) *University Entrepreneurship Programs – 1999*, Los Angeles, CA: Marshall School of Business at the University of Southern California.

Warshaw, M. (2000) "Top gun for start-ups," *INC*. 14: 53–54.

Welsch, H.P. (1996) "Entrepreneurship education innovations: curriculum and community strategies," unpublished presentation to the *Internationalizing Entrepreneurship Education and Training Conference* (Int Ent 96).

Chapter 20

Gerald E. Hills

University of Illinois at Chicago

ENTREPRENEURSHIP EDUCATION: MARKET SEGMENTATION AND LEARNER NEEDS

ENTREPRENEURSHIP AS A SUBJECT is blossoming like the spring-time flower with new layers of unfolding detail. The entrepreneurship layers include new knowledge never before revealed and new entrepreneurship learner segments with layers of unique needs. The beauty of entrepreneurship, as in the beauty of the flower, is in the minute elements that are juxtapositioned into an impressive, larger whole. There are many different types and forms of entrepreneurship and this complexity is beginning to be reflected in entrepreneurship education programming. Although other disciplines, such as management and marketing, historically began in universities with one course offering, they have evolved into the teaching of numerous courses on subtopics within their conceptual and definitional domains. This blossoming of course offerings was made possible by the generation of new knowledge combined with conceptual and theoretical development of the management and marketing disciplines. Scholars delineated several historical "schools of marketing thought" including, today, managerial marketing and, more recently, even a proposed "entrepreneurial marketing" school, described earlier in this book.

Similarly, entrepreneurship, despite its short life as a new discipline, has already evolved from its earliest focus on an "entrepreneur personality characteristics school of thought" to a more holistic, resource view of entrepreneurship, modeled as a process. Just as historically occurred in marketing, the entrepreneurship field is blossoming into a variety of important subjects. There is increased specialization of researchers and teachers so as to develop more compelling scientific explanations of entrepreneurship processes and their outcomes. And market forces are playing an important role by influencing this blossoming, due to entrepreneurship learners with heterogeneous needs demanding more specialized and homogeneous subtopic offerings that better meet their needs. As the entrepreneurship discipline flowers, and indeed completely earns the term "discipline," it will increasingly serve new clientele with a wider array of learning needs. This chapter addresses this evolution, which has already begun, and positions this change in the context of market segmentation concepts.

A market-driven model: entrepreneurship education

Process models of entrepreneurship education have been advanced, including Mitra and Matlay's (2000) stakeholder model, Welsch's (1993) input–output perspective, and Monroy's (1993) super imposition of the input–process–output model with a client-based contingency perspective. A market-oriented model is shown in Figure 20.1 and is proposed as a means for developing effective entrepreneurship educational programming (Hills and Miles 2000; Hills and Morris 1995; Romaguera et al. 1997). The focus here, however, is only on the component of identifying target entrepreneurship learners. Numerous potential learner market segments exist for entrepreneurship education, and for universities, considerable flexibility exists for prioritizing participant groups. The use of explicit strategic thought processes often leads to programming that better achieves educational objectives. For example, developing and teaching one entrepreneurship course to non-business students in each of six non-business colleges might have a greater impact than offering six different entrepreneurship courses only to business students. Or, alternatively, targeting Ph.D. students, the entrepreneurship educators of the future, in all of the functional business areas could better leverage the impact on future generations of students.

It is proposed that, as educators, we need to develop a fuller understanding of a variety of prospective entrepreneurship learners and cluster them into subgroups by common entrepreneurship education needs and interests. This then provides a foundation for developing customized programs to serve these differing needs. Welsch (1996), for example, noted the growing differentiation of entrepreneurship as a subject and discussed industry segments (i.e. music and chiropractic), specialized audiences (i.e. minority and children), and disciplinary groups (i.e. information systems and creativity). Ghosh and Block (1993–1994) discuss different entrepreneurship education audiences and suggest three bases for segmentation: career objective, stage of the entrepreneurial process, and the existing knowledge and skills of the individual. Pichler and Frohlich (1995) derived two entrepreneurial types – pioneer and organizer – and cited related educational implications.

Various learner segments require different educational objectives (Hills 1988). For Ph.D. candidates, teaching objectives encompass building an awareness of the entrepreneurship literature, setting appropriate research priorities, and learning potential methodologies for the conduct of research. For existing business owners, teaching objectives build on a conceptual entrepreneurship foundation, but with immediate action implications. Growing attention has

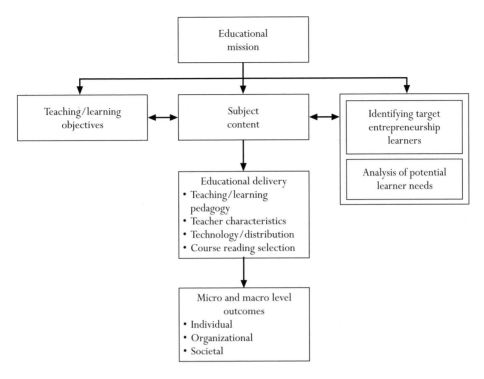

Figure 20.1 Entrepreneurship education: a decision process model

been devoted to setting educational objectives in terms of capacities, competencies, and/or skills. Gibb (1998) for example, proposes several broad entrepreneurship capacities as well as specific skills such as intuitive decision-making; creative problem solving; managing interdependency on a "know-who" basis; ability to conclude deals; strategic thinking; project management; time management; persuasion; selling; negotiating; and motivating people by example. Regarding entrepreneurial *marketing* competencies, it has been proposed that competencies include judgment, experience, knowledge, communication, as well as vision, motivation, and planning (Carson *et al.* 1995).

Mass markets to segmentation

The conceptual foundation for responding to the heterogeneous needs among various entrepreneurship learners is found in the marketing literature. These tools are used by business executives and marketing managers who decide how to best tailor their products and services and other marketing strategy elements to match the needs of potential customer segments. The better the match, the better the sales volume and, typically, the profit level. This chapter advances the thesis that, through marketing segmentation, universities and other organizations can deliver educational products and services to better match the needs of entrepreneurship learners.

A mass marketing strategy involves targeting all of the potential learners in this product market, using the same marketing elements, including the particular educational program/service, to appeal to their needs and wants. There is little or no effort to recognize differences among learners/customers. Mass marketing is often more appropriate in new markets relative to mature markets because, initially, there are few competitors and buyers who have had experience with the "product" and they have not developed differences in their needs and wants. Cell phone marketing, for example, was generic at first within a large defined market, but then became more targeted with numerous calling plans and services to better match different customer needs. Similarly, we are witnessing increased differentiation of entrepreneurship education programming to respond to learners who are becoming more informed buyers and who are becoming more precise in defining their specific learning needs. In contrast, mass marketing, fully implemented, would have entrepreneurship educators offer the same programs, courses, or modules, delivered in the same way at the same price and with the same promotional program. Mass marketing is less complicated but also often less effective. At the other extreme, facilitated by new technology, "mass customization" strategies may be developed, the opposite of mass marketing. Customization of the educational product or service for each customer in the broader market takes place. This is segmentation at its fullest, calling for a one-on-one educational program for each entrepreneurship learner.

Grouping potential learners into market segments or market niches is usually more cost-effective, however. Segmentation concepts call for grouping learners who would be more responsive to one "marketing mix" than another. For entrepreneurship educators, the marketing mix is comprised of not only an educational course or program, but also any other elements that could increase demand, such as location/delivery, price, and promotion. Indeed, if learners in one group (e.g. MBA students) are not more responsive to a particular marketing mix than another (e.g. art students), then effective segments have not been formed.

Entrepreneurship segmentation requirements

Grouping learners into segments is only meaningful when certain segmentation requirements are met. First, the differences in preferred entrepreneurship programs, and related marketing, must in fact exist. That is, customer responses to the marketing mix must vary across market groupings. Marketing an entrepreneurship education program specifically designed for women, for example, may yield a greater sales response among women than among men, two potential market segments. The response elasticity is the ratio of the percentage change in market response to the percentage change in marketing program expenditure. If women entrepreneurs are not more responsive to differentiated programs, promotion, time of day offered, and/or pricing, then a mass marketing strategy would be more effective. In fact, there would need to be high enough elasticity and response to more than offset the additional costs of designing and managing a more specialized program as compared to a generic, mass marketing approach.

Second, for there to be a viable market segment, learner preferences must be identifiable and must match with a learner group which can be described. Because of different potential customer/learner preferences and responsiveness, a segmentation strategy may seem to be in order. But what bases are called for? What subgroups are identifiable? In the example just noted, gender is a readily identifiable demographic basis for creating market segments. Potential learners/customers who already own and operate a business are also readily identifiable. But nascent entrepreneurs who have not yet started a business, but are engaging in activities to that end, are difficult to readily identify. To be a viable market segment, they must be identifiable, even if through self-selection.

A third requirement for a market segment is that they are "reachable" with a marketing program. Not only must the educational program be a good match with the segment group, but the promotion and distribution should be a good fit as well. Are there cost-effective newspaper advertising or mailing lists available that efficiently reach potential entrepreneurship program participants? Also, can the program be located in a convenient place for the segment, such as in a high-technology corridor? Are they sufficiently clustered geographically to make program participation possible? Or would online learning be required, and if so, would the design and offering be financially viable?

Fourth, there must be sufficient potential demand to justify a segmentation strategy. The high-technology entrepreneurs just noted may exist in a smaller city, for example, but in too few numbers for a program to make or exceed financial break-even. More of a mass marketing strategy may be required and, if competitors' offerings are limited, demand may be sufficient with less differentiation.

Finally, the segmentation literature also cites the need for demand to be sufficiently stable over a period of time to justify a given strategy. Although the fundamental need and demand for entrepreneurship education programming will always exist, the level and type of demand varies over time. Economic cycles, for example, change the learner demand from solving business growth problems to coping with recession. And specialized programs that have targeted, for example, Internet entrepreneurs, have experienced volatile demand. Although predicting demand stability is difficult, it is important to address this before making major investments to pursue new entrepreneurship learner segments.

Developing learner segmentation strategy

The concept of segmentation is simple and largely intuitive. Yet it is helpful to approach the task systematically, while weighing experience and intuitive insights. If the mission of a college entrepreneurship center, or an entrepreneur designing and selling educational programs, is to fulfill a mission of providing high-quality programs to increase the success of participants then initially, and periodically thereafter, a creative planning exercise is valuable. In this exercise, it is assumed that no entrepreneurship programs are currently offered for the purposes of analysis.

First, potential segmentation bases are identified and at least two approaches are used: aggregating and disaggregating. The most common approach used by entrepreneurship educators is disaggregating, where one or more learner/customer characteristics is used to "break off" a subgroup of the larger mass market. Examples already cited include women, high-technology, and nascent entrepreneurs. Based on experience in the entrepreneurship education marketplace, educators typically select one or more markets to target. It is instructive, however, to periodically start anew and consider the numerous possibilities, in light of the five segmentation requirements discussed. Many of these possibilities are shown in Figure 20.2, based on geography, demographics, company size, psychographics, a entrepreneur's personal/business goals, stage of the lifecycle, industries, types of opportunities, benefits sought, learning styles, delivery preferences, behavioral intentions, and behaviors (Hills and Barnaby 1977; Hills and Welsch 1986). Fundamental to weighing the viability of a market segment is to consider barriers to launching a business for each group. Vesalainen and Pihkala (2000), for example, measure the relative strength of different barriers such as lack of resources, lack of social support, economic risks and, of most relevance to entrepreneurship education, lack of skills. They observe that the potential for ameliorating these barriers through education vary greatly, with skills being the most amenable to educational efforts.

Second, an aggregating approach to segmentation may be taken, where each potential learner's basis for selecting one program over another is identified and then summed by group. For example, if a leading need of many individual entrepreneurs is to learn how to cope with rapid growth, and if a sufficient number exists using this aggregating approach, this may be an excellent basis for segmenting the entrepreneurship education market. A segmentation basis would ideally be a direct measure of response elasticities to entire marketing offers. Sufficient measures for this have not been developed, however, so segmentation bases used are typically characteristics of potential buyers/learners that are, at best, proxy measures of response elasticities (Cravens et al. 1987). The process for identifying segmentation bases often begins with a focus on buyer/learner characteristics, then proceeds to learner preferences and perceptions, and concludes with purchase behavior. A combination of segmentation bases is used to define a market segment, rarely using only one characteristic (Bearden et al. 2001). In Figure 20.2, for example, a potential combined market segment may be nascent women entrepreneurs within a 50-mile radius who want to generate a second family income.

Once alternative market segments/niches have been identified, a greater qualitative and quantitative understanding of the potential target market is developed. In some depth, for example, what educational programs do potential customers perceive to be of the greatest benefit to them, when also considering pricing, program location, and other marketing factors? An in-depth learner profile provides a foundation for subsequent programmatic decisions. Although the normative judgments of professional educators regarding the needs and programming for potential learners are important, these should be compared to the perceptions of potential participants for a particular program. For a given educational organization, their mission and past experience, and

Geographic area	**Stage of entrepreneur/business lifecycle**
Demographics	Pre-start-up decision entrepreneurs
Gender: women	Nascent/intention entrepreneurs
Age: youth/young age	Start-up entrepreneurs
Minorities	Early growth: consolidation
Delivery preferences	Growth entrepreneurs
Classroom, on-line, interactive	Corporate entrepreneurs
Personal/business goals	Cashed out entrepreneurs
Independence	Serial entrepreneurs
Family business	**Benefits sought/problem solving**
Wealth oriented	**Learning styles**
• modest	**Behavioral intentions**
• high	**Behavior**
Income oriented	• Previous entrepreneurship
Industries	• Education program participation
Technology	Previous loyalty to XYZ
Music	University programs
Medical services	**Company size**
Other	**Psychographics**
Types of opportunities	Activities, interests, attitudes, beliefs, opinions

Figure 20.2 Segmentation bases for entrepreneurship education market

strengths and weaknesses, inevitably become part of the program design/market segmentation decision-making. The evaluation of a potential learner segment includes forecasting potential demand, assessing competition, and weighing the different costs of targeting alternative segments. In geographic areas that have long been served by entrepreneurship education programs, the better opportunities may be in narrower segments not well served by other programs. Or, if a program is new, such as how to use relationship marketing in start-up firms, a larger segment may still be available.

An entrepreneurship education organization may decide to focus on only one learner/market segment or serve more than one and, if so, offer totally differentiated educational and marketing programs for each, or only partially differentiated programs. Two programs, for example, may have the same session content topics but, through the development of a strategic plan by each entrepreneur who participates, customize the application of concepts for each type of business represented.

Although this chapter is focused on better serving entrepreneurship learners through market segmentation strategies, competitive forces are often important as well. Market or competitive positioning is the reverse of the market segmentation coin. Segmentation strategy determines which entrepreneurship learners/customers to target, and market positioning involves selecting a marketing mix (educational program, site, price, etc.), which matches the perceived needs of the target learners *better than competitors*. The relative market positions are defined by the relative perceptions of potential educational program participants. For example, two virtually identical programs could be perceived by potential learners as positioned very differently if one is offered by a small, private sector business and another by a major university. Positioning is in reference to competition. Positioning strategy not only requires an understanding of organizations' learner markets, but also how competitor programs are relatively seen in the eyes of potential participants.

In Figure 20.3, for example, two perceptual dimensions are shown – entrepreneurship education program content, from nascent entrepreneur program content to content for those who have developed mature businesses (the business lifecycle); and the degree of conceptual/theoretical orientation to programs with immediate practicality. Market research, combined with the experience of entrepreneurship educators, can be used to determine how many potential education customers exist at different positions within this map. Segment I, for example, as indicated by the circle in Figure 20.3, contains a large number of potential education customers who prefer nascent or very early stage entrepreneurship education content and also prefer a very practical program. Segment VI, in contrast, could be a small segment of Ph.D. candidates with a high theoretical preference with greater focus on the earlier stages of the business lifecycle. Segment V could be family business owners with mature firms who prefer practical content. Segment II could be undergraduate and MBA university students who are nascent/early stage oriented and are willing to study conceptual content. Segment IV could be comprised of existing business owners who demand practical content. Segment III could include those engaged in corporate venturing, attempting to revitalize mature corporations.

Each of these market segments would ideally be identified using surveys of expert educators' opinion, from long-time "students" of the needs of different types of potential and existing entrepreneurs, and/or from large sample surveys of this large market of entrepreneurship learners in which the more important segmentation bases dimensions are identified and the respondents are aggregated into segments based on their positioning. This exercise in cognitive mapping would determine market segments using a grass-roots, aggregation approach. By using different combinations of important education program dimensions (Figure 20.2), additional insights are gained into the market and regarding the better ways to subgroup this heterogeneous mass into more homogeneous market segments. Just as the automobile market is segmented by the automakers based on dimensions such as prestige/status, degree of sporty style, price and quality, from Hyundai to Lexus, the entrepreneurship education market needs to be better "analyzed" (which literally means "to break down") and better understood.

After the market segments are identified, based on the preferences of entrepreneurship learners, as in Figure 20.3, then specific, existing education programs can be positioned within this broader map and the strategic implications drawn. For example, as shown in Figure 20.3, relative to the ideal Segments IV and V, Entrepreneurship Education Program (EEP-A) is shown. This program, as perceived by participants, may be positioned "between the cracks," in providing program content to serve both established and more mature firms, but not fully serving either segment. Segment IV may contain firms (and content) that are still seeking high growth, whereas Segment V may provide content to refound floundering mature firms. EEP-B, in contrast, is solidly within Segment IV. EEP-A could either move to better compete with EEP-B, or evaluate the

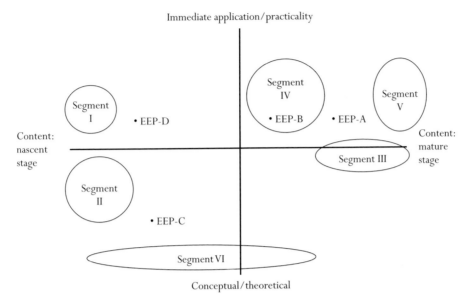

Figure 20.3 Entrepreneurship learner/customer perception maps for entrepreneurship education programs

merits of moving into Segment V where no competition exists. EEP-C, a prestigious university serving MBA students, is perceived by participants to be providing somewhat later-stage firm content and more theoretical content than Segment II prefers. To capture a large market share, at least using these two dimensions, the university would need to reposition itself in the eyes of potential customers. EEP-D, the training arm of a community organization shown in Figure 20.3, is providing practical content that does not focus solely on the needs of nascent entrepreneurs. A modest repositioning, as perceived by participants, is seemingly in order.

To conclude, developing perceptual maps of ideal educational program attributes and the relative positioning of existing programs can lend important insights as well as actionable implications. Unfortunately, there has been little, if any, published research focused specifically on the market segmentation of entrepreneurship learners. It is instead assumed, although from valuable experience, how the broader market should be divided. Despite the value of these assumptions, more empirical evidence should be brought to bear on better understanding the bases for and the needs of various market segments.

A research agenda

Much is to be learned about which segments are the better bases for differentiating entrepreneurship education. Research is needed to more fully understand the different needs and perceptions within each market segment. Certain of these segments, and related research propositions, are shown in Table 20.1.

Table 20.1 Research opportunities at the entrepreneurship/segmentation interface

---

Segmentation effectiveness

P1 Effectively defining market segments for entrepreneurship education requires de-massification using segmentation bases.

P2 Use of market segmentation evaluation criteria will improve decision-making regarding target market selection.

P3 There will be improved entrepreneurship educational outcomes if more homogeneous learner segments are defined and served.

P4 Segmentation methods and related market positioning concepts will improve educational outcomes and competitive success.

P5 Entrepreneurship education segmentation bases can be rank-ordered with respect to their size and appropriateness.

Nascent entrepreneurs' segment

P6 Different learning strategies and styles are used by successful and less successful nascent entrepreneurs (Levitt and March 1988; Moorman and Miner 1988).

P7 Different pedagogical approaches to entrepreneurship education are required for nascent entrepreneurs than later-stage entrepreneurs (Reynolds 2001).

P8 Different learning strategies are required to support different stages of entrepreneur and organization development (Honig 2001).

Gender segmentation

P9 Traditional family role definitions combined with the time demands of business ownership compete with available time for entrepreneurship education.

P10 Female entrepreneurs are more receptive to new learning than men (Lerner and Almor 2002).

P11 Female entrepreneurs prefer female (over male) teachers (Gateway 2002).

P12 Online learning (vs. in person) is less appealing to female (vs. male) entrepreneurs (Gateway 2002).

P13 Women and men entrepreneurs have different learning styles (Gateway 2002).

P14 Women entrepreneurs tend to be more market responsive to gender-based marketing/promotion.

P15 Where gender-related barriers to entrepreneurial success exist (e.g. market network access, capital), education should encompass effective strategies.

P16 Entrepreneurship education for women (vs. men) should be customized to reflect more participatory decision-making, higher commitment to people, more resistance to growth (and a hierarchy), and more sharing of control (Bird and Brush 2002).

Cross-cultural market segments

P17 Entrepreneurship education design and marketing must adapt to cultural differences to be effective (Morrison 1998).

P18 Effective entrepreneurship education in emerging economies requires differentiation in recognition of the values and attitudes toward private enterprise.

Entrepreneur failures market

P19 Entrepreneurship education programming targeted to failing entrepreneurs would ameliorate the probability of failure and the related economic and psychological consequences (Gupta 1998).

P20 High societal costs are associated with not offering entrepreneurship failure education.

Age segments

P21 The development of values and attitudes toward enterprise, independence, and rewards is more important for effectively serving K-12 students than for university or later stage students.

P22   Effectively serving different age entrepreneurs and potential entrepreneurs requires different pedagogical approaches.

Franchising segment

P23   Franchisee entrepreneurship education effectiveness is dependent not only on franchisors, but also on the franchisees, suppliers and customers (Castrogiovanni and Justis 2002; Hoe and Watts 2000).

P24   Market segments with different franchise/entrepreneurship needs include prospective single-unit franchisees, prospective multi-unit franchisees, business owners seeking to become franchisors, and professional service providers with franchisee/franchisor clientele (Hoy 2002).

P25   Those with less entrepreneurship education and less business experience will be more successful as franchisees than as independent business owners (Hoy 2002).

P26   Franchisors are more successful if they deliver entrepreneurship education to franchisees rather than use management education for "employees" (Hoy 2002).

P27   Important learning needs of franchisors include understanding financing requirements associated with company outlets vs. franchisee outlets: and appropriate market entry strategies for international expansion (Hoy 2002).

Family business segment

P28   Effective entrepreneurship education must be targeted based on the different roles of the key family business members (Kaplan *et al.* 2000).

P29   Effective entrepreneurship education content for family businesses must recognize the legitimate role of personal and family goals and variables, in addition to business goals (Birley 2002).

P30   The teaching of strategic management in the family business must incorporate the central role of the founder and/or family leaders on the firm's strategic values, goals, and behavior (Kelly *et al.* 2000).

P31   Entrepreneurship education delivery that simultaneously involves key family business members, not only the CEO, will be more effective.

P32   Effective entrepreneurship education for family businesses must incorporate psychological and sociological dimensions (Brockhaus 1994).

Learning style segments

P33   Learning style preferences of potential and existing entrepreneurs are different than for other individuals, creating bases for market segmentation (Dornberg and Winters 1993–1994; Sexton and Bowman 1986).

P34   Entrepreneurship education will be more effective if delivery is based on the knowledge of learning style preferences of entrepreneur segments (Kolb 1984).

P35   Nascent entrepreneurs tend to have "diverger" learning styles, a market segment.

P36   Different stages of the entrepreneurship process, and related learner groups at each stage, reflect a different mix of learning style preferences (Ulrich and Reinhart 1998).

P37   Entrepreneurship education will be more successful if instructors create learning environments to match the different learning styles.

Conclusion

Entrepreneurship education programs are multiplying in quantity around the globe. There is an opportunity to multiply the quality as well. Quality is in the eye of the beholder, so to increase quality we must ask, "Who is the beholder?" In this chapter it is argued that there are many beholders – relatively homogeneous subgroups, or market segments, of entrepreneurship learners – relative, that is to the heterogeneous mass market. The quality of entrepreneurship education depends in no small part on improved definition of target market segments and new knowledge to better customize and deliver educational programs.

References

Bearden, W.O., Ingram, T.N., and LaForge, R.W. (2001) *Marketing: Principles and Perspectives*, third edn, Chicago, IL: Richard D. Irwin.
Bird, B. and Brush, C. (2002) "A gendered perspective on organization creation," *Entrepreneurship Theory and Practice*, 26(3): 50.
Birley, S. (2002) "Attitudes of owner–managers' children towards family and business issues," *Entrepreneurship Theory and Practice*, 26(3): 5.
Brockhaus, R.H. (1994) "Entrepreneurship and family business research: comparisons, critique and lessons," *Entrepreneurship Theory and Practice*, 19(1): 35.
Carson, D., Cromie, S., McGowan, P., and Hill, J. (1995) *Marketing and Entrepreneurship in SMEs*, London: Prentice Hall International.
Castrogiovanni, G. and Justis, R. (2002) "Strategic and contextual influences on firm growth: an empirical study of franchisers," *Journal of Small Business Management*, 40(2): 98–108.
Cravens, D.W., Woodruff, R.B., and Hills, G.E. (1987) *Marketing Management*, Chicago, IL: Richard D. Irwin.
Dornberg, S. and Winters, L. (1993–1994) "Learning styles and needs of the adult learner," in Hoy, F., Monroy, T., and Reichart, J. (eds) *The Art and Science of Entrepreneurship*, Berea, OH: The Project for Excellence in Entrepreneurship Education.
Gateway Entrepreneurship Research Conference (2002) Discussion, St. Louis University, April.
Ghosh, V. and Block, Z. (1993–1994) "Audiences for entrepreneurship education: characteristics and needs," in Hay, F., Monroy, T. and Reichert, J. (eds) *The Art and Science of Entrepreneurship*, Berea, OH: The Project for Excellence in Entrepreneurship Education.
Gibb, A. (1998) "Entrepreneurial core capacities, competitiveness and management development in the 21st century," in Klandt, H. (ed.) *IntEnt 1998: Internationalizing Entrepreneurship Education and Training*, Cologne, Germany: Josef Eul Verlag.
Gupta, A. (1998) "Coping with failure: religious and spiritual support for entrepreneurs," in Klandt, H. (ed.) *IntEnt 1998: Internationalizing Entrepreneurship Education and Training*, Cologne, Germany: Josef Eul Verlag.
Hills, G.E. (1988) "Variations in university entrepreneurship education: an empirical study of an evolving field," *Journal of Business Venturing*, 3(1): 109–122.
Hills, G.E. and Barnaby, D.J. (1977) "Future entrepreneurs from the business schools: innovation is not dead," *Proceedings of the International Council for Small Business*, George Washington University: ICSB.

Hills, G.E. and Miles, M.P. (2000) "Entrepreneurship education: a marketing perspective," in Rushing, F.W. (ed.) *The Visible Hand: The Challenge to Private Enterprise in the 21st Century*, Atlanta, GA: Georgia State University.

Hills, G.E. and Morris, M. (1995) "Entrepreneurship programming and customer focus: a process approach," in Monroy, T., Reichert, J., and Hoy, F. (eds) *The Art and Science of Entrepreneurship Education: Volume III*, Berea, OH: The Project for Excellence in Entrepreneurship Education.

Hills, G.E. and Welsch, H. (1986) "Entrepreneurship behavioral intentions and student independence: characteristics and experiences," in Ronstadt, R., Hornaday, J.A., Peterson, R., and Vespers, K.H. (eds) *Frontiers of Entrepreneurship Research*, Wellesley, MA: Babson College.

Hoe, C.H. and Watts, G. (2000) "Learning from franchising: the personal development of Malaysian franchisees," *Intent 2000: Internationalizing Entrepreneurship Education and Training*, Cologne, Germany: Josef Eul Verlag.

Honig, B. (2001) "Learning strategies and resources for entrepreneurs and intrapreneurs," *Entrepreneurship Theory and Practice*, 26(1): 21–36.

Hoy, F. (2002) University of Texas at El Paso. Propositions were provided to the author by this expert in the franchising academic field (Personal communication).

Kaplan, T.E., George, G. and Rimler, G. (2000) "University-sponsored family business programs: program characteristics, perceived quality and member satisfaction," *Entrepreneurship Theory and Practice*, 24(3): 66.

Kelly, L.M., Athanassiou, N., and Crittenden, W. (2000) "Founder centrality and strategic behavior in the family-owned firm," *Entrepreneurship Theory and Practice*, 25(2): 27.

Kolb, D. (1984) *Experimental Learning*, Englewood Cliffs, NJ: Prentice Hall.

Lerner, M. and Almor, T. (2002) "Relationships among strategic capabilities and the performance of women-owned small ventures," *Journal of Small Business Management*, 40(2): 109.

Levitt, B. and March, J. (1988) "Organizational learning," *Annual Review of Sociology*, 14: 319–340.

Mitra, J. and Matley, H. (2000) "Entrepreneurship and learning: a stakeholder model of entrepreneurship research, education and training," in Klandt, H. (ed.) *IntEnt 2000: Internationalizing Entrepreneurship Education and Training*, Cologne, Germany: Josef Eul Verlag.

Monroy, T. (1993) "Epilogue – towards a descriptive national model of entrepreneurship education," in Hoy, F., Monroy, T.G., and Reichert, J. (eds) *The Art and Science of Entrepreneurship Education*, Berea, OH: The Project of Excellence in Entrepreneurship Education.

Moorman, C. and Miner, A. (1988) "Organizational improvisation and organizational memory," *Academy of Management Review*, 23(4): 698–723.

Morrison, A. (1998) "Entrepreneurship and culture specificity," in Klandt, H. (ed.) *IntEnt 1998: Internationalizing Entrepreneurship Education and Training*, Cologne, Germany: Josef Eul Verlag.

Pichler, J.H. and Frohlich, E. (1995) "Entrepreneurial 'types' for the larger market," in Klandt, H. (ed.) *IntEnt95: Internationalizing Entrepreneurship Education and Training*, Cologne, Germany: Josef Eul Verlag.

Reynolds, P. (2001) Presentation on the Panel Study of Entrepreneurial Dynamics, Kauffman Foundation, Kansas City.

Romaguera, J.M., Fernandez, L., Gonzalez, C. *et al.* (1997) "Entrepreneurship curriculum development in Puerto Rico: a test of the hills' model," in Monroy, T., Reichert, J., Hoy, F., and Williams, K. (eds) *The Art & Science of Entrepreneurship*

Education: Volume IV, Akron, OH: The Project of Excellence in Entrepreneurship Education.

Sexton, D.L. and Bowman, N.B. (1986) "Evaluation of an innovative approach to teaching entrepreneurship courses," in Roberts, G. (ed.) *Proceedings: Venturing into Entrepreneurship and Small Business*, Saint Louis, MO: International Council for Small Business.

Ulrich, T.A. and Reinhardt, W.J. (1998) "Entrepreneurship as a learning process," in Klandt, H. (ed.) *IntEnt98: Internationalizing Entrepreneurship Education and Training*, Cologne, Germany: Josef Eul Verlag.

Vesalainen, J. and Pihkala, T. (2000) "Barriers to entrepreneurship: educational opportunities," in Klandt, H. (ed.) *IntEnt 2000: Internationalizing Entrepreneurship Education and Training*, Cologne, Germany: Josef Eul Verlag.

Welsch, H. (1993) "The infrastructure of entrepreneurship education," in Hoy, F., Monroy, T.G., and Reichert, J. (eds) *The Art and Science of Entrepreneurship Education*, Berea, OH: The Project of Excellence in Entrepreneurship Education.

Welsch, H. (1996) "Entrepreneurship education innovation: curriculum and community strategies," in Klandt, H. (ed.) *IntEnt96: Internationalizing Entrepreneurship Education and Training*, Cologne, Germany: Josef Eul Verlag.

Index

Abbott, Wallace C. 36
Abernathy, W.J. 7
Aboud, J. 46
Abrahamson, E. 213, 216
Achrol, R.S. 94
Ajzen, I. 147
Akselsen, S. 159
Albright, W.F. 45
Alderson, W. 93
Aldrich, Howard 4, 5, 59, 61, 120, 127, 213, 215, 253, 255, 256, 257, 258, 261
Allee, V. 158
Allen, J. 95, 97
Allen, Paul 20, 36
Almeida, J.G. 122
Alsos, G.A. 245
AlterEgo 165
Altman, E.I. 135
Altman, J. 39
Alvarez, S.A. 231
Amabile, T.M. 79
Amar, A. 154
Amburgey, T.L. 141
American Assembly of Collegiate Schools of Business (AACSB) 25
American Franchisee Association 63
American Marketing Association 93
Anderson, P. 117
Ang, J.S. 107
Angelos, P. 167
Anna, A.L. 234
Ansoff, H.I. 6

Ardichvili, A. 74, 117, 231
Arkebauer, J.B. 107, 109, 111
Armstrong, A. 5
Armstrong, T.L. 264
Arnold, R. 29
Aronson, R.L. 258
Astrachan, J. 62, 63
Athanassiou, N. 297
Aufreiter, N. 157, 162
Austin Model 49–53
Autio, A. 38, 39, 122, 196
Azriel, J.A. 34

Babson Research Conference 5, 48
Bailey, J. 121
Baker, K. 154, 156
Baker, S. 154, 156
Bamford, C.E.R. 120, 133
Bangs, D.H. 182
Barnaby, D.J. 292
Barrett, G.A. 256
Barringer, B.R. 123
Barron, F. 85
Barwise, G. 176
Bates, T. 135, 139, 197
Baum, J.A. 134, 141
Baum, R.J. 126
Baumol, William 31, 32, 46, 47
Beard, D.W. 127
Bearden, W.O. 292
Becker, G. 135, 141, 215
Beer, M. 153

Beinhacker, S. 65
Bell, Alexander Graham 29
Benko, C. 155, 157
Bennet, P.D. 92
Benson, D. 280
Ben-Yoseph, M. 230, 231, 233, 234
Bernard, H.R. 202
Berryman, J. 142
Betts, M. 156, 160
Bezos, Jeff 5
Bhave, M.P. 74, 75, 77, 80, 231
Bhide, A.V. 8, 48–9, 105
Bidgoli, H. 165
Birch, D.L. 3, 31, 33, 48, 117, 122, 133
Bird, B. 62, 63, 123, 147, 296
Birley, B. 144
Birley, S. 117, 230, 242–3, 244
Bittle, M. 59
Black, Fisher 7
Blais, R.A. 183
Blau, J. 168
Blayton, Jesse B. 256
Blechman, B. 106, 107, 109, 111, 113
Block, C. 288
Blum, L. 114
Boag, D. 119
Boden, R. 230, 231
Boeker, W. 127
Bonacich, Edna 255, 258, 259, 260, 264
Bonoma, T.V. 59, 94, 95, 96
Bootstrap finance techniques: asset or cash
    management 110–11; barter 108–9;
    categories of 106; client-based funds 110;
    cooperative assets 109–10; foundation
    resources 114; leases 112; outsourcing
    112; personal borrowing 107–8;
    personal resources 105–6; quasi-entity
    arrangements 109; relationship
    resources 108; subsidies and incentives
    112–14
Boschee, J. 65
Boston Consulting Group 212
Bovel, D. 160
Bowman, N.B. 297
Boyd, N. 123
Boyd, William Kenneth 256
Brache, A. 158
Brackett, E. 197
Bradley, S. 183

Bragin, M. 204
Brandenburger, A. 8
Brazeal, D.V. 34
Brittain, J.W. 143
Brockhaus, R.H. 123, 297
Brown, T. 122
Bruce, R. 121
Bruderl, J. 136, 141, 142, 143
Bruno, A.V. 120, 142
Brush, C. 126, 230, 231, 232, 234, 296
Bruyat, C. 196
Bryant, J. 197
Buchanan, J.M. 32
Buckeye, J. 140, 148
Bullvag, B. 241, 244
Burke, R. 157
Burt, R.S. 145
Business-general knowledge 19
Butler, J.S. 45, 46, 256
Buttner, E.H. 38
Byers, T. 280
Bygrave, W.D. 30, 32, 38, 39, 73, 75, 126,
    196, 240, 248

Cadeaux, J. 177
Camp, M. 119, 120
Cantillion, Richard 7, 29, 30, 32
Cardozo, A. 74
Cardozo, R. 117
Carland, J.C. 243
Carland, J.W. 243
Carnegie, Andrew 29
Carnegie Endowment for International Peace
    (CEIP) 257, 263
Carr, D. 231
Carr, N. 159
Carson, D. 289
Carsrud, A.L. 147, 198, 200, 206
Carter, N.M. 117, 137, 141, 142
Casson, M. 32
Castrogiovanni, G. 139, 142, 297
Certo, S. 231
Chaganti, R. 119, 123, 255
Chandler, A.D., Jr. 7
Chandler, G. 121, 229, 234
Charmaz, K. 202
Choctaw Enterprises 203, 204
Choi, S. 184, 185, 186
Chrisman, J.J. 282

Christensen, C. 7
Christensen, P.S. 74, 75, 77, 84
Christenson, C. 159
Christie, M. 196
Chrometzka, L. 167
Churchill, N. 121
Clark, John Bates 30
Clark, Kim 7, 9
Cliff, J.E. 232
Clinton, William 154
Cochran, A.B. 135
Cohen, A. 183, 185
Cole, A. 3
Coleman Foundation 272, 285
Coleman, J.S. 145, 215
Colleran, K. 34
Collier, J.G. 277
Collins, O. 5
Community-based Enterprise Research
    Issues: analysis and results of research
    204–7; case summaries 202–4;
    governmental assistance 197–8; methods
    of research 201–2; private initiatives
    196–7; roles of entrepreneurs 200–1;
    sustainable development 198–200
Community-based Enterprises 195
Cook, R. 119, 123
Cooper, A.C. 5, 18, 26, 74, 120, 122, 134,
    136, 247
Cooper, W.W. 50
Cornwall, J.R. 196
Cothrel, J. 156
Covin, J.G. 92, 118, 120, 123, 183
Covin, T. 118, 183
Cowe, R. 242
Cox, Larry 38, 39
Cragg, P.B. 119
Cravens, D.W. 292
Crewson, P. 230
Critical mass 67–8
Crittenden, W. 297
Cromie, S. 289
Csikszentmihalyi, M. 75, 76, 79, 80
Cukier, K. 159
Cusumano, M. 156

D'Aveni, R.A. 143, 148
D'Souza, D.E. 126
Dacin, T. 141

Dahan, E. 160
Daily, C. 231
Dalton, D. 231
Daly, J. 158
Dana, L.P. 196
Darwall, C. 4
Darwin, Charles 59
Datta, R. 199
Davidson, J. 96
Davidsson, P. 36, 119, 121, 122, 123, 125
Davis, D. 95, 97
Davis, J. 157
Davis, P.S. 234
Davis, S. 184
Davis, S.E.M. 234
Day, G.S. 94
De Koning, A. 78, 79
Dean, B. 159
Dean, T.J. 120, 133
DeCovny, S. 154, 157
Delacroix, J.A. 141
Delancy Street Foundation 203
Delmar, F. 119, 122, 125
Dennis, W. 120
DePriest, T. 197, 202, 203
Deshpande, R. 93, 94
DeSilva, E. 170
Desmond, M. 169
DeSouza, G. 230
Dess, G.G. 127, 183
Di Pierro, A. 32
Dicke, T.S. 63
Direct Selling Association 66
Dornberg, S. 297
Douglas, Clarence 256
Dovidio, J.F. 264
Drucker, P.F. 3, 33, 34, 47, 185
Du Rietz, A. 230
DuBois, W.E.B. 256
Duchesneau, D.A. 119
Duffy, S.G. 39
Dulaney, K. 169
Dunkelberg, W. 5, 120
Dunn, P. 271
Dutta, S. 155
Dyer, D. 7
Dyer, L. 263
Dyer, W.G., Jr. 248
Dyson, Ester 189

Eastman, George 36
Eccles, R. 8
e-commerce: entrepreneurial practices and behaviors within firms 186–9; identifying innovations in 184; innovative entrepreneurial behavior in 185–6; trends of entrepreneurship in 182–3
e-commerce literature: descriptive articles 156; differences between e-business and traditional business 158–61; state of and future directions 161–2; strategic issues 157–8; tactical issues 156–7
Edison, Thomas 29
Eisenhardt, K. 117
Ellis, W.H. 33
Ely, R.T. 31
Enders, A. 158
Engelberger, Joseph 36
Engelbrecht, A. 229
Entrepreneur(s): evolving of 36–7; minorities 37–9; risk taking 7; strategic orientations and values of with the internet 183–4; types of 240–1; women 37–9
Entrepreneurial branches: corporate entrepreneurship 63–4, 68 entrepreneurship in the arts 64–5; family business 62–3; franchising 63; network marketing 66–7; social entrepreneurship 65; strategic collaboration 66; taxonomy for 60–1; trajectory of 59
Entrepreneurial failure: characteristics of firms 141–3; environmental conditions 143; definitional and measurement issues 144; definitions of 134–5; factors of 135–44; integrated model of 135; literature of 136–40; methodological issues 145; process of 143; solutions to future research of 146–8; theoretical development issues 144–5
Entrepreneurial Growth Indicators 125–6: frequency of 125
Entrepreneurial Growth Predictors: frequency of 124; in literature study of 124; macro-structural 118–21; micro-behavioral 121–4
Entrepreneurial Growth Resource Center, University of Missouri–Kansas City: case study regarding entrepreneurial education in urban universities 219–22; see also

Inner-city Business Research; organizational chart of 219
Entrepreneurial Marketing: as opposed to conventional marketing 102; emergence of 94–7; marketing–entrepreneurship interface 92–3; specifying the concept of 97–101
Entrepreneurial Organizations: as opposed to administratively driven organizations 6–8
Entrepreneurship Education: entrepreneurship skill development 281–2; interdisciplinary programs and recognition 278–9; Models 288–9; parties of influence 272, 277–8; real-life opportunities 283; specialized entrepreneurial offerings 280–1; summary of innovative entrepreneurship practices 273; technology implementation 283–5
Entrepreneurship Field: structure of 57–8
Entrepreneurship Segmentation Requirements 290–1
Entrepreneurship: in business schools 47–9; and community development 196; definition of 92; evolution of 44–6; future of 9–10; patterns and the future of 37–9; process definition of 6; risks of 11; taxonomies of 59–67; in various disciplines 35
Entrepreneurship in the academic world: approaches to teaching 20–1; balance of research 21–3; content in 18–19; endowments for 23–4; legitimacy of 15–16; need for innovation in 24–6; paradigms 18; targeting curriculum for 16–18
Esses, V.M. 264
Ethnic Entrepreneurship 254–5; economic theories of 258; hypothesis of 263–4; literature regarding 255–6; models explaining 259–63; sociological explanations for entrepreneurial trends 256–8; topics not yet covered 264–5
Evans, D.S. 141
Evans, P. 158
Ezzedeen, S. 39

Fahley, L. 94
Fairchild, G. 214, 216
Fairlie, R. 34, 256, 257
Fariselli, P. 160

Faucon, B. 159
Faulkner, M. 154
Federal Reserve 202–3
Fenn, D. 108, 114
Fernandez, L. 288
Fishbein, M. 147
Fisher, C. 212
Florin, J. 120
Folta, T.B. 134, 136
Fombrun, C.J. 119
Foo, M.D. 139, 143
Forrester Research 182
Fox, J. 122
Fox, L. 157
Francis, H. 127
Frank, H. 197
Fraser, J.A. 107, 108, 110
Freear, J. 110, 114
Freeman, E.B. 119
Freeman, J.H. 142, 143
Freitas, M.J. 254
Friesen, P.H. 92, 183
Frohlich, E. 288

Gaglio, C.M. 77, 78, 79, 80
Gagnon, Y.-C. 166
Galbraith, C.S. 256
Galbraith, J.K. 32
Gannon, M.J. 263
Garratt, N.L. 234
Garsombke, D.J. 265
Garsombke, T.W. 265
Gartner, W.B. 3, 119, 122, 127, 277, 278,
    281, 283, 284
Gaskill, L.R. 139, 142
Gates, Bill 5, 20, 36
Gatewood, E. 113
Geffen, David 64
Gent, M.J. 120, 121
Ghosh, V. 288
Ghoshal, S. 7
Gibb, A. 33, 289
Gibson, David 50–1
Gilad, B. 74, 77, 821
Gilbert, J. 157
Gill, M.D., Jr. 114
Gillis, M. 34
Gimeno, J. 134, 136
Gimeno-Gascon, F.J. 122, 247

Ginsberg, S. 34
Gladwell, M. 96
Global Entrepreneurship Monitor (GEM) 34,
    36, 37, 38
Go, F. 59
Gold, J. 176
Gold, S.J. 256
Goldstein, A.S. 111
Gompers, P. 3, 7, 8
Good, D. 230
Gore, Albert 154
Granovetter, M. 4, 215
Grassroots 203
Greenburger, D.B. 123
Greene, P. 45, 46, 255
Greenfield, S.M. 196
Greengard, S. 166
Greenspan, Alan 212
Greiner, L.E. 121
Griffith, D.A. 155, 186
Griffith, T. 166
Grossman, S.J. 7
Grousbeck, H.I. 74, 92, 99
Gulick, L. 8
Gumpert, D.E. 3
Gundry, L.K. 123, 184, 185, 187, 188, 228,
    230, 231, 232, 233, 234
Gupta, A. 296

Habbershon, T. 63
Haber, S. 200
Hadary, S. 229
Hagel, J. 5
Hagen, E.E. 196
Hall, G. 141, 144
Hall, P. 240, 241
Hambrick, D.C. 143, 148
Hamel, G. 93, 95, 96, 99
Hanks, S.H. 121
Hannan, M. 142
Harder, J.W. 142
Harmon, B. 117
Harrington, D.M. 85
Harris, Adam 256
Hart, O.D. 7
Hartl, R. 66
Hartman, A. 186
Harvard Business Review 216
Harveston, P.D. 234

Haswell, S. 142
Hay, M.G. 38, 39
Hay, R.K. 118
Hayes, R.H. 7
Haynes, P.J. 229
Headd, B. 141, 142
Helgesen, S. 112
Helms, M. 229
Helweg, A.W. 264
Henderson, J. 120
Henkerson, M. 230
Hess, R.H. 31
Hicks, Diana 242
Higgins, B.H. 31, 32
Hileman, A.E. 39
Hill, J. 289
Hill, S. 95, 96
Hiller, K. 169
Hills, G.E. 74, 75, 77, 79, 80, 93, 184, 288, 292
Hirschman, A. 215
Hise, P. 107
Hisrich, R. 230
History of Entrepreneurship: behaviorist intervention in 32; economics of 30–4; emergence throughout 28–30; national entrepreneurial propensity 32–4; philosophy of 30–4; Phoenicia, beginnings 27–8
Hitt, M. 119, 120
Hitt, M.A. 91
Hoad, W. 23
Hodder, I. 202
Hodgetts, R.M. 181, 187
Hoe, C.H. 297
Hofer, C.W. 30, 32, 73, 127
Hogan, K. 153
Holmes, S. 142
Holzer, H. 215
Honig, B. 296
Hornaday, J.A. 46
Hornsby, J.S. 231, 232
Hoselitz, B.F. 32
House, R. 141
Howe, Elias 36
Hoy, F. 126, 296, 297
Hudson, R. 140, 148
Hughes, A. 160
Hunt, K.N. 63

Hybels, R.C. 184
Hylton, K. 113

Iansiti, M. 187
Ibarra, H. 216
Immigrant Entrepreneurship 254–5: hypothesis of 263–4; literature regarding 255–6; models explaining 259–63; topics not yet covered 264–5
Immigration Policy 259; see also Ethnic Entrepreneurship
Inc. 214
Ingram, T.N. 292
Inner-city Business Research: barriers to 213–14; directions for future research of 216; existing research 214–15; reasons for 212–13
International Association of Institutional Venturing (IAIVI) 64
Ireland, R.D. 119, 120
Izberk-Bilgin, Elif 265

Jackson, L.M. 264
Janesick, V. 201
Jansen, E. 234
Jansen, R. 229
Jarillo-Mossi, J.C. 3, 5, 74
Jaworski, B.J. 93
Jelassi, T. 158
Jensen, M. 7, 8
Johannisson, B. 120, 201, 206
Johnson, H.T. 6
Jones, F.F. 123
Jones, J. 197, 202, 203
Jones, T.P. 256
Jordan, J.M. 183, 185
Julian, S. 139, 142
Julien, P.-A. 33, 196
Justis, R.T. 139, 142, 297

Kador, J. 186
Kafka, P. 64
Kaish, S. 74, 77, 84
Kamau, D.G. 231
Kamm, J.B. 247
Kanter, R.M. 183, 216
Kaplan, R. 6
Kaplan, T.E. 297
Karlenzig, W. 66

Karpowicz, D.J. 96
Katz, J.A. 55, 78, 79, 233
Katzenberg, Jeffrey 64
Keeny, R. 186
Kelly, D. 141
Kelly, L.M. 297
Kickul, J. 64, 65, 184, 185, 187, 188
Kihlstrom, R.E. 32
Kilby, P. 33
Kim, W.C. 231
King, M. 119
Kinnear, T. 94
Kirchoff, B.A. 34, 47, 141, 142, 143, 146
Kirzner, I.M. 32, 34, 76, 246
Kjeilen, T. 28
Klees, E. 36
Klein, L. 160
Kloosterman, R.C. 254, 259, 262, 263
Knight, F.H. 32
Kohli, A.K. 93
Kolb, D. 297
Koller, R.H. 76
Kollman, T. 173
Kolveried, L. 241, 244, 245
Koshiur, D. 184, 185, 186
Kostecka, A. 63
Kotler, P. 94
Kozmetsky, G. 50, 143
Krampf, R. 155
Krueger, N.F. 147, 198, 200, 206
Krueger, N.F., Jr. 196
Kuhn, T. 61
Kuhns, B.A. 34, 196
Kung, H.-J. 177
Kuratko, D.F. 64, 231, 232

Laffont, J.-J. 32
Lafontaine, F. 143
LaForge, R.W. 292
Lake, D. 156
Landstrom, H. 106, 108, 109, 111
Lange, J.E. 185
Lardner, J. 157
Larson, A. 7
Lau, C.M. 123
Lavoie, D. 38
Law, John 29
Lawrence, P. 8
Learned, E. 6

Lee, K. 136
Leibenstein, H. 31, 32, 34, 36
Leidecker, J.K. 142
Lenzi, R.C. 196
Lerner, J. 3, 7, 8
Lerner, M. 200, 231
Levinson, C. 94, 95
Levinson, J. 106, 107, 109, 111, 113
Levitt, B. 296
Levitt, T. 93
Lewis, D. 45, 49–50
Lewis, P.S. 121, 123
Lewis, V. 121
Li, P.S. 260
Liao, J. 145
Lichtenstein, G.A. 200, 206
Light, Ivan 253, 255, 257, 259, 260, 264
Linde, L. 4
Lindsay, Arnett 256
Lisowska, E. 231
Locke, C. 159
Locke, E.A. 126
Lodge, G. 7
Long, D.D. 234
Long, N. 198
Long, W. 29, 32, 33, 74, 75, 76, 79, 86
Lorange, P.M. 7
Lord, C. 156
Lorne, J. 59
Lorsch, J. 8
Louis, T. 160
Lovell-Troy 257
Low, M.B. 126, 246
Lowber, P. 169
Lucaccini, L. 62
Luckenbill, D. 44
Lumpkin, G.T. 77, 80, 183, 184
Luthans, F. 181, 187
Lyden, J.A. 234
Lyons, T.S. 200, 206

McBride, M. 154
McCarthy, A.M. 201
McClelland, D. 33, 122, 123, 196
MacCormak, A. 187
McDougall, P.P. 118, 120
McEvoy, D. 256
McGeer, B. 233
McGowan, P. 289

McGrath, R.G. 144
McGuire, J.W. 33
McKenzie, B. 280
McKibben, L. 5
McLean, G.N. 231
MacMillan, I.C. 109, 114, 146, 246
McMullan, W.E. 74, 75, 76, 79, 86
McWilliams, G. 157
Macy, Rowl & Hussey 36
Madsen, O.O. 84
Management: through networks 8
Manning, R.A. 139, 142
March, J. 296
Marchesnay 33
Marketing Science Institute 93
Marketing: criticisms of 93–4; definition of
    92; perspectives on the emerging nature of
    95; to prospective entrepreneurship
    students 289–90
Markman, G. 122
Martha, J. 160
Martinez, M. 59
Maslyk-Musial, E. 231
Massarksky, C. 65
Matley, H. 288
Mauborgne, R. 231
Means, G. 154
Meckling, W. 8
Mero, N.P. 234
Merrion, P. 196
Meyer, C. 184
Meyer, G.D. 231
Mezias, S.J. 134, 141
Michael, S.C. 63
Michaels, N. 96
Mieszkowski, K. 203
Miles, M.P. 288
Mill, Stuart 29, 31
Miller, B.A. 117
Miller, D. 92, 183
Millman, A. 39
Mills, D. 5
Milne, D. 59
Miner, A. 296
Minority Entrepreneurship 254–5; literature
    regarding 255–6
Minton, Henry M. 256
Mitchell, T.R. 121, 126
Mitchell, W. 134, 138

Mitra, J. 288
Mitra, R. 120
Mobile Commerce (m-commerce):
    adaptability and mobile operators 173;
    applications of 175–6; business models of
    170–3; characteristics of 168; and
    e-commerce, differences between 171;
    entrepreneurial strategies in 173–5;
    evolving technology of 169–70; trends in
    166–9
Mobilocity.com 169, 170, 174
Modell, John 255, 260
Monroy, T. 288
Montgomery, D.B. 94
Moore, D. 5, 23, 38
Moore, K. 44, 45, 49–50
Moorman, C. 93, 296
Morace, F. 167
Morino, M. 184, 187, 189
Morris, M. 64, 91, 92, 93, 95, 97, 277, 278,
    282, 288
Mouat, W. 167
Moulton, W.N. 138, 143
Muller-Veerse, F. 175
Muoio, A. 37
Murray, J.A. 94
Muscat, E. 62
Mwaisela, F.A. 199

Naffziger, D.W. 231, 232
Nalebuff, B.J. 8
Narduzzi, E. 177
Narver, J.C. 93
National Federation for Women Business
    Owners 228–9, 230, 233
Neely, L. 108
Neese, T. 189
Neff, J. 96
Nelson, A. 134
Nelson, E. 169
Nelson, R. 215
New Industial State, The 32
Newcomb, P. 64
Newman, P.C. 33
Ngo, H.-Y. 123
Nicholls-Nixon, C.L. 201
Niebuhr, H.R. 59
Nixdorff, J.L. 39
Nohria, N. 8

Nolan, C. 158
Nolan, R. 183
Nucci, A. 230
Nzamujo, F. 199

O'Connor, G. 177
O'Keefe, R. 177
Oliva, R.A. 183, 185
Oliver, R.W. 158, 183
Opportunity Recognition: comprehensive
    model of 74–80; definition of 73–4;
    implications for entrepreneurship
    education 86–8; literature, highlights of
    76–8; practical implications of 84–6;
    researching behaviors of 80–4
Opportunity-specific knowledge 19
Oughton, C. 160
Oxenfeldt, A.R. 31
Ozgen, O. 233

Pace, Harry 256
Page, G. 183
Palmer, J.W. 186
Palumbo, G.M. 120, 121
Paris 214
Patrick, J. 66
Paul, G.W. 93
Pavlov, V. 29
Pearce, J.A. 119
Pearce, T. 188
Pena, I. 120
Pennings, J. 136
Penrose, E.T. 32
Perkins, D.H. 34
Perry, S.C. 134, 138, 143
Peterson, R.A. 84, 143
Pfeffer, J. 127
Philips, B.D. 141, 142, 143
Phillips, F. 50
Pichler, J.H. 288
Picory, C. 160
Pierre-Yves, O. 157, 162
Pihkala, T. 292
Pinson, L. 182
Pistrui, D. 62, 63
Pitt, L. 159
Plaschka, G.R. 62, 197
Pleitner, H. 66
Porter, L. 5

Porter, M.E. 6, 7, 159, 165, 173, 196, 216
Porter, W.A. 51
Portes, A. 215
Posada, E. 166
Pottruck, D.S. 188
Praag, C.M. 36
Prahalad, C.K. 93, 95, 96, 99
Prasad, A. 4
Pratt, J. 7
Preisendorfer, P. 136, 137, 141, 142, 143
Pruett, M. 138, 143

Quelch, J. 160

Raiffa, Howard, 7
Raskin, P.D. 198
Rath, J. 254, 259, 263
Ray, S. 74
Reed, T.S. 91
Reich, R.B. 34
Reichert, B. 155
Reilly, M.D. 198, 200, 206
Reinhart, W.J. 297
Reitz, J.G. 260
Rendon, J. 167
Resnik, P. 110, 111
Review of Black Political Economy, The 216
Reynolds, P.D. 38, 39, 117, 137, 141, 142,
    146, 196, 296
Ricardo, David 29
Richards, J. 159
Ridgway, N.M. 143
Ritkin, G. 95, 96
Ritchie, J. 33
Robb, A. 34
Robbie, K. 246
Roberts, E. 166, 176
Roberts, M.J. 4, 74, 92, 99
Robinson, J. 214
Robinson, R. 118
Robinson, RB., Jr. 119
Robson, T. 199
Rockefeller, John D. 29
Roemer, M. 34
Roessl, D. 197
Rogers, C.D. 120, 121
Romaguera, J.M. 288
Romanelli, E. 117, 140, 142, 144
Ronstadt, R.C. 85, 136

Rosen, E. 96
Rosenstein, C. 259, 260
Rosenstein-Rodan, P. 215
Rosentraub, M. 264
Rosko, P. 23
Ross, C. 263
Ross, D.L. 117, 118
Rotterdam School of Management
    M-conference 2001 177
Rumelt, R. 6, 143
Rupp, W. 167
Rust, R.T. 93
Ryan, C. 157
Ryan, G.W. 202

Saba, J. 156
Sahay, A. 176
Sahlman, W. 7, 11
Salamon, L. 65
Salancik, G.R. 127
Salganicoff, M. 234
Salter, M. 7
Sandberg, W.R. 34, 127
Sapienza, H.J. 122
Savin, J. 159
Sawhney, M. 158, 160
Saxenian, Annalee 50
Say, Jean-Baptiste 30, 32
Schaver, K. 279
Scheier, R. 167, 169
Scherer, F.M. 117
Schermerhorn, J. 66
Schibested, E. 156
Schiller, B.R. 230
Schinderhutte, M. 64
Schlaifer, Robert 7
Schloss, H.H. 31, 32
Scholes, Myron 7
Schoonhoven, C. 117
Schulze, B. 120
Schumpeter, J.A. 3, 5, 29, 30, 31, 32, 33,
    47, 74, 79
Schwartz, R.G. 76, 84
Scott, A.J. 262
Scott, M.K. 121, 157, 162
Scott-Morton, M.S. 7
Scranton, P. 240
Segev, A. 155
Segmentation Strategy 291–5;

entrepreneurship learner/customer
    perception maps for entrepreneurship
    education programs 295; research
    opportunities 295–7; segmentation bases
    for entrepreneurship education market 293
Self-Employed Women's Association (SEWA)
    199
Senge, P. 85
Sensebrenner, J. 215
Serial Entrepreneurial Research Model 251
Serial Entrepreneurs 239–40: characteristics
    of 242–3; creating businesses 245–8; lack
    in literature regarding 249–50;
    motivational factors of 245; motivations of
    243–4; reasons for exiting ventures 248–9;
    search strategies for ventures 246; types of
    242
Sexton, D.L. 48, 119, 120, 123, 297
Seybold, P. 157, 159, 160
Shah, A. 157
Shane, S.A. 3, 73, 75, 139, 143
Shannon, J. 184, 186, 187
Sharing: value of 8
Sharma, C. 173
Shaw, K. 143
Shaw, R. 167
Shervani, T.A. 94
Short, L. 271
Shrader, R.C. 77, 80
Shulman, J. 107, 108, 111
Shuman, J.C. 247
Siccotte, H. 166
Sifonis, J. 186
Silberg, D. 159
Simmel, Georg 45, 46
Simmonds, K. 94
Singer, Isaac 36
Singh, J.V. 141
Singh, R. 78, 79, 86, 184
Singh, S. 167
Sinha, I. 159
Slater, S.F. 93
Slevin, D.P. 92, 119, 120, 123
Slocum, J.W., Jr. 181, 187
Smeltz, W.J. 119, 123
Smilor, R.W. 34, 48, 114
Smith, Adam 29, 51
Smith, K.G. 121, 126
Smith, W. 109

Snodgrass, D.R. 34
Societal Change: hypothesis of 4; internet and 5
Sokolowski, S.W. 65
Solymossy, E. 127
Sombart, Werner 46
Spencer, R. 46
Spielberg, Steven 64
Spinelli, S. 110
Springer, I. 167
Srinivasan, B. 160
Srivastava, R.K. 94
Stahl, D. 184, 185, 186
Stake, R.E. 202
Stalk, G. 7
Starr, J.A. 109, 114, 229, 230, 232, 240, 248
Stearns, T.M. 117
Steidlmeier, P. 196
Stern, A. 166
Sterrett, C. 157
Stevenson, H.H. 3, 5, 6, 8, 11, 74, 92, 99
Stewart, W. 243
Stiles, C.H. 256
Stinchcombe, A.L. 127
Stoica, M. 169
Storper, M. 262
Stossel, John 197
Stotlar, D. 169, 176
Strickton, A. 196
Sugden, R. 160
Sumant, M. 158, 160
Summer, C.E. 121, 126'
Swaminathan, A. 141, 142
Swartz, E. 38, 39
Swedberg, Richard 46, 47, 48
Synchrologic 168
Szabo, J.C. 111

Taebel, D. 264
Tarkenton, F. 109
Tarpley, F.A. 76, 84
Taub, P. 77, 79, 80
Teach, R.D. 76, 84
Technology: impact on business 9
Tedlow, R. 159
Teixeira, C. 256
Thomas, H. 138, 143
Thomas, P. 56
Thompson, S. 96

Thore, S. 50
Thorton, P. 3
Timmons, J.A. 86
Tomasula, D. 156
Toulouse, J.M. 33
Trout, J. 157
Trutko, I. 63
Tucker, D.J. 141
Turner, C.A. 133
Tushman, M.L. 117
Tybjee, T. 120

UCB Parents 203
Ucbasaran, D. 241, 243, 246, 247, 248, 249
Ufuk, H. 233
Ulmer, K.J. 134
Ulrich, T.A. 297
United States Association of Small Business and Entrepreneurship (USASBE) 15, 23, 64, 265
Upton, N. 277, 280
Urban Universities: roles of faculty and students in 217–18
Urwick, L. 8

Vadakth, S. 117
Van Auken, H.E. 108, 139, 142
Van de Ven, A.H. 140, 148
Van der Poel, A. 177
Van Haas, T. 168
Van Ophem, H. 36
Van Witteloostuijin, A. 136
Vanderwerf, P. 126
Venkataraman, S. 73, 75, 196, 199, 200, 245
Venkatraman, N. 140, 148
Venture-general knowledge 19
Venture-specific knowledge 20
Vérin, H. 29
Vernon, R. 215
Vesalainen, J. 292
Vesper, K.H. 19, 33, 48, 80, 85, 277, 278, 281, 283, 284
Voss, T. 137, 141
Vozikis, G. 123

Wacquant, L. 214
Waldinger, R. 5, 253, 255, 256, 258, 260, 261, 262

Walker, Francis 30
Wall, R.A. 120, 121
Wally, S. 119
Walton, R.E. 5–6
Warshaw, M. 280
Washington, Booker T. 256
Wasilowski, S. 107, 113
Wassadorp, P. 244
Watson, J. 121
Watson, R. 159
Watts, G. 297
Webb, J. 158
Weber, A. 5
Weber, Max 33, 46
Webster, F.E. 93
Weiber, R. 173
Welsch, H.P. 34, 62, 64, 65, 66, 123, 145, 232, 272, 288
Westhead, P. 239, 240, 241, 242–3, 244, 247
Wetzel, W.E., Jr. 105, 107, 109
Wheelwright, S.C. 7
Whinston, A. 184, 185, 186
Whitman, Meg 5
Whittemore, M. 107
Whittingham, J. 169
Whyte, William H. 32
Wiedenmayer, G. 5
Wiklund, J. 36, 125
Wilhelmsson, J. 174
Wilken, P.H. 34

Williams, M. 137, 141, 142, 146
Williams, R. 156
Williamson, O. 4, 8
Wilson, W. 215
Winborg, J. 106, 108, 109, 111
Winge, K. 177
Winslow, E.K. 39
Winters, L. 297
Wolf, K. 45
Women Entrepreneurs: characteristics of 229–32; dominant economic sectors for 229; future developments with 233–5; status of 228–9; university-level teaching regarding 232–43
Woo, C.Y. 120, 134, 136, 247
Woodruff, R.B. 292
Wright, M. 239, 240, 241, 242, 243, 244, 246, 247
Wurman, R. 159

Yin, R. 145
Yoffie, D. 156
Yudkin, M. 229, 230, 232

Zeckhauser, R. 7
Zeithaml, C. 95, 97
Zeithaml, V. 95, 97
Zhou, M. 257
Ziegler, R. 136, 141, 142, 143
Ziglar, James 265

£15.99

ORTHODOX
AND
COMPLEMENTARY
MEDICINE